GRAPHIC BORDERS

WORLD COMICS AND GRAPHIC NONFICTION SERIES

Frederick Luis Aldama and Christopher González, Editors

World Comics and Graphic Nonfiction series includes monographs and edited volumes that focus on the analysis and interpretation of comic books and graphic nonfiction from around the world. The books published in the series will bring analytical approaches from such fields as literature, art history, cultural studies, communication studies, media studies, and film studies, among others, to help define the comic book studies field at a time of great vitality and growth.

GRAPHIC BORDERS

Latino Comic Books Past, Present, and Future

EDITED BY FREDERICK LUIS ALDAMA
AND CHRISTOPHER GONZÁLEZ

UNIVERSITY OF TEXAS PRESS *Austin*

Requests for permission to reproduce material from this work should be sent to:
Permissions
   University of Texas Press
   P.O. Box 7819
   Austin, TX 78713-7819
   www.utexas.edu/index.php/rp-form

♾ The paper used in this book meets the minimum requirements of
ANSI/NISO Z39.48-1992 (R1997) (Permanence of Paper).

LIBRARY OF CONGRESS CATALOGING-IN-PUBLICATION DATA

Graphic borders : Latino comic books past, present, and future / edited by
Frederick Luis Aldama and Christopher González. — First edition.
   pages cm. — (The world comics and graphic nonfiction series)
   Includes bibliographical references and index.
   ISBN 978-1-4773-0914-8 (cloth : alk. paper)
   ISBN 978-1-4773-0915-5 (pbk. : alk. paper)
   ISBN 978-1-4773-0917-9 (library e-book)
   ISBN 978-1-4773-0916-2 (non-library e-book)
1. Comic books, strips, etc.—Latin America—Criticism and interpretation. 2. Latin
America—History—Comic books, strips, etc. 3. Comic books, strips, etc.—Social
aspects—Latin America. 4. Popular culture—Latin America. I. Aldama, Frederick
Luis, 1969– editor. II. González, Christopher, editor.
   PN6790.L29G73 2016
   741.5918—dc23   2015033633

doi: 10.7560/309148

FOR OUR MAGICALLY MISCHIEVOUS *NIÑAS*, WHOSE JOYFUL CREATIVITY TAKES US *UP, UP, AND AWAY!*

CONTENTS

TAKING BACK CONTROL OF OUR STORY SPACE:
A FOREWORD

FRANK ESPINOSA

"HE WHO CONTROLS THE SPICE, controls the Universe"—so says Baron Harkonnen in Frank Herbert's revolutionary science fiction classic *Dune*. These words set the stage for the epic struggles and the motivations that will shift the galactic power and bring the Fremen to their destiny.

These are our lives, and these our stories. Let us shape them both with our wills. Let us write them all down, explore our culture with drawings, and fill these modern caves with our lovely handprints. We will play these stories in our music and sing it with our songs. This is our spice.

To take back control of our own stories is to destroy all forms of helotry. From the smallest fairy tales, told to our children, to the largest of our epics that sing to the future.

And this is where *Graphic Borders* comes in. Within these pages you will find the tales of one after another of Latino creators. You will learn who they are, and you will investigate what is behind the strokes of brush and flourishes of pen. With every page turned, the bounteous symbols of our great Latino visual literature become known to you.

So delicate is this new Latino symbolization that much of it is unknown, even, dare I say, to some of the very artists who write, draw, and create our new stories. As artists, we work so hard and fast that it is impossible to see one's work in all its facets at once. Aldama and González's book acts like a mirror. It does the job of reflecting our work. It gives us a new dimension to work toward.

As we all know, magic mirrors are important in many stories, from Narcissus's, to Snow White's, to Alice in Wonderland's. Sometimes those mirrors show the future; other times they become in themselves a doorway to a different world. This is what Aldama and González have so masterly crafted— a book that lets us see ourselves. This is a book that peels back the layers so we can understand, experience illumination—so that we can have reflection.

With *Graphic Borders* you walk into new fissures—new territories of meaning. *Graphic Borders* helps us to experience Latino comic symbology in an entirely new way. As a people constantly faced with borders, Latinos have learned to sleuth out gaps—dangerous passages that can and do lead to the newly imagined. Aldama and González invite you into the gaps, those liminal spaces whereby you will travel straight into a Latino visual and mental superbarrio. Aldama and González are the Trainmen in what can be seen as the Latino iteration of *The Matrix*'s Mobil Ave—a smuggling portal for exile programs to enter the main source. They are the guides who transport us to and through a new superbarrio that is being created with words and brushstrokes.

We all work from our own personal understanding of things. Each of us brings together, during the act of creation, colors, sights, sounds, tastes, language, and experiences from many different influences in our lives. We become a channel to our past and future. As creators, we then mix up this creative soup with our brushes, sharpen our pencils with it, or remix our paints with this Latino combination of emotion, memory, and familiarity of culture.

This book is a reflection of exceptionally brave Latino artists, writers, and storytellers who are clearing a rich and complexly layered space within a world that often excludes us—that even desperately seeks to pave over us. Sadly, many artists who work extremely hard are sometimes forgotten. We all exist in a persnickety modern world. The flavor of the month changes as easily as Flash and Superman change their costumes. This book, with its resplendent thought pieces and interview, make sure we are not forgotten. It's the respirator that keeps me and my comic book creations pumping with life. In this twenty-first-century Archimedes mirror, we Latino creators are reflected back much stronger than ever. What a blessing that is.

Whoever controls the stories controls the borderland space of *el Super Barrio*. Enjoy, reflect, create . . . *cuidate*.

GRAPHIC BORDERS

LATINO COMIC BOOKS PAST, PRESENT, AND FUTURE — A PRIMER

FREDERICK LUIS ALDAMA AND CHRISTOPHER GONZÁLEZ

COMIC BOOKS AND GRAPHIC nonfiction by and about Latinos constitute a swiftly growing area of production and study. The comic book medium has steadily gained greater credence in academia, and Latino comics are certainly no exception. As Latino creators and consumers continue to explore varied forms of narrative expression, we are currently witnessing a fast-proliferating expansion of Latino fiction and nonfiction narratives through highly diverse graphic media: from fictional newspaper comic books and strips to sprawling, decades-long graphic autobiographies, and visual histories. Latinos are producing visual–verbal narratives as diverse in form and content as reflected in the massively burgeoning production of Latino culture today.

Latino creators have come into their own as comic book storytellers. The medium increasingly has attracted Latino creators since the 1980s, building into the critical mass we see today. The comic book storytelling medium is especially attractive to Latino makers of narrative fiction and nonfiction. It offers all variety of tensions and harmonies between its visual and verbal ingredients. It costs little to make. It offers the possibility of a grassroots-style distribution—through social media and word of mouth, for instance. It appeals to an assortment of readers: young and old, Latino and otherwise, females and males. Its consumption can take place in on-the-fly short bursts and in prolonged reading sessions.

Today, Latino comic book authors create stories that run the gamut of all genres. We have those such as Frank Espinosa (*Rocketo*) and Los Bros Hernandez (*Citizen Rex*), who zip readers into the future with their sci-fi epic-dimensioned storyworlds. We have those who choose noir as their storytelling envelope, such as Rafael Navarro (*Sonambulo*) and Gilbert Hernandez (standalones like *Julio's Day*). We have those who write youth-oriented, coming-of-age (and coming out) stories, such as Ivan Velez Jr.'s *Tales of the Closet*, Graciela Rodriguez's *Lunatic Fringe* (2010), and Liz Mayorga's *Outgrowing Plastic*

Dolls. We have those who choose the life-education journey (or *Bildung*) story, such as Rhode Montijo (*Pablo's Inferno* and *Tartamudo*) and Wilfred Santiago (*In My Darkest Hour*). Then there are those who choose the superheroic mode, such as Fernando Rodriguez (*Aztec of the City*), Richard Dominguez (*El Gato Negro*), Laura Molina (*Cihualyaomiquiz, the Jaguar*), Carlos Saldaña (*Burrito*), Anthony Oropeza (*Amigoman*), Rafael Navarro (*Sonambulo*), Javier Hernandez (*El Muerto*), Anthony Aguilar and Luke Lizalde (*El Verde*), Christian Ramirez (*Americana*), and Joe Quesada (*Santerians*), among many others. We have those working in the horror mode, such as Crystal Gonzalez's *In the Dark* and Liz Mayorga's *Monstrous Love Stories*. We also have those who choose the fictional mode of the grotesque, such as Erik Rodriguez (*Hispanic Batman*); the satiric and parodic, such as Ilan Stavans and Robert Weil (*Mr. Spic Goes to Washington*); and the erotic, such as Gilbert Hernandez (*Birdland*). We also have comics aimed at the younger set, such as by Eric Gonzalez and Erich Haeger (*Rosita y Conchita*), Gilbert Hernandez (*The Adventures of Venus*), and Ray Mendivil and Neil Segura (*Forever Freshman*).

We have Latino creators who choose the non-fictional graphic mode, such as Inverna Lockpez's *Cuba: My Revolution* (2010) and Ilan Stavans's *El Iluminado* (2012). We also have those who choose the biographical form, such as Wilfred Santiago (his masterful *21: The Story of Roberto Clemente*); those who choose the historical form, such as Ilan Stavans (writer) and Lalo Alcaraz (artist) in the making of *Latino U.S.A.: A Cartoon History*; and authors like Daniel Parada who choose to give a graphic narrative form to pre-Columbian history in *Zotz: Serpent and Shield*.

We offer a sampling of the range of Latino comic book genres and stories:

SCIENCE FICTION

Los Bros Hernandez, as Jaime, Gilbert, and Mario Hernandez are collectively known, have been working in and out of this genre since the early 1980s, when they first published *Love & Rockets*—each element of the title identifying its inclusion of romance melodrama and futuristic travel to and from other planets. While this series increasingly subordinated the sci-fi element in the storytelling to the tellurian drama, Los Bros often returned to it in their own and others' series. In 1984 they tried their hand at writing and drawing Dean Motter and Paul Rivoche's *Mister X*, but creative differences in vision between the producers and Los Bros (they brought too much "barrio feel," apparently) led to an unhappy end. (See the interview with Gilbert Hernandez in *Your Brain on Latino Comics*.) In 2009 Mario and Gilbert Hernandez teamed up to create the six-issue series *Citizen Rex*—a series that was collected and published in book form by Dark Horse Comics in 2011. In the preface Mario (writer) makes explicit that this is science fiction but also a critical commentary on our present-day society separated by the class divide of the Haves and the exploited and oppressed Have-nots. Gilbert's characteristic thick black/white line style, minimal cross-hatching, and heavy use of a contrastive black and white give substantive dimension to the city of Neutropolis and its denizens. The story is largely filtered through the point of view of the alternative news reporter (blogger) and historiographer, Sergio "Bloggo" Bauntin. This subversive, counterintelligence character, along with the cybernetic Citizen Rex, galvanizes resistance—human and robot alike—to corporate capitalist and underworld bosses and their goons: the gasmask- and hazmat-suit-wearing Truth Takers who patrol the streets for resistance and who *disappear* defiant citizens.

There is also the triple-Eisner-Award-nominated *Rocketo* by Frank Espinosa. Set in another New World, the earth 2000 years in the future, it follows the story of Rocketo Garrison: born on Kova, one of the few fragments of earth left after an apocalypse, he comes into his own as a Mapper, one of a select few who have a memory of place and therefore know how to navigate the planet. Along the way we meet a variety of new hybrid species: Dogmen, like Spiro, and Fishmen, among many others. While Rocketo can be read as Latino—Kova as an allegorical stand-in for Cuba, and Rocketo's experiences are largely those of the outsider trying to come to terms with those of different cultures—Espinosa's influences are planetary. He draws inspiration from his own biographical experience as a Latino (as a kid in 1970, he and his family left Cuba for Washington Heights) but also that of *Flash Gordon* and *Buck Rogers* as well as *Heart of Darkness*, German Expressionist and Japanese art, and much more. Indeed, *Rocketo* includes enough signposts within the story for us to superimpose it over yesteryear's colonization of the Americas (New World), but of course with a crucial twist. This is the story of a Mapper superhero from Kova (Cuba) who vanquishes colonizing foes to protect a harmonious and humane world filled with possibility.

EROTICA AND OTHER NOIRISH SHADES

While not exactly prevalent, there are Latino comic book creators who make stories that we might identify as erotica. In creating *Birdland*, Gilbert Hernandez comments in an interview: "I wanted to create an action comic that wasn't superheroes, an action comic that was just sex and no violence. It was as wild as I could make it at the time, holding little back in terms of sex and making sure not to have any cruelty or violence" (*Your Brain on Latino Comics*

179). Indeed, *Birdland* is more than just a story aimed at sexually arousing its audience. It functions as a parodic demystifier of social and sexual conventions. With Hernandez's implicit reference to Roger Vadim's film *Barbarella* (1968) as well as with his setting the story in the future, Hernandez pokes fun at institutions such as the family, work—even psychoanalysis. Male and female characters such as Mark, his "wife" Fritz, BangBang, Inez, Beta, La Valga, and Simon have same-sex sex, straight sex, and group sex—which even includes polymorphously perverse aliens. Gilbert uses code-switching strategically, too, between English, Latin, and Spanish, to destabilize hierarchies of language that hold that Latin is highbrow and intellectual and Spanish is lowbrow and tellurian.

Rafael Navarro's *Sonambulo* follows the sleuthing adventures of *luchador*-mask-wearing Latino detective Sonambulo. He has been walking in the land of the dead (Mictlan) for decades before returning to the land of the living (Los Angeles), where he solves crimes during his sleepless nights wandering the city. Gilbert Hernandez's recent streak of stand-alone graphic novels—*Chance in Hell* (2007), *Speak of the Devil* (2008), *The Troublemakers* (2009), and *Maria M.* (2014)—also takes us back to the origins of comics in the pulps of the 1930s and 1940s and their inclusion of crime noir stories. These works resonate with the noir of Jim Thompson, David Goodis, James Cain, and Elmore Leonard. They remind us of the two-way flow between comics and pulps. (Recall that the progenitor of superhero comics, Jack Kirby, moonlighted in the early 1940s as an artist for pulps published within Martin Goodman's publication empire.) Not surprisingly, Navarro and Gilbert Hernandez are drawn to the noir genre. In *Speak of the Devil* Gilbert establishes at the outset that the protagonist Val and her pals live in a topsy-turvy world. In this world, as the character Paul remarks, a "guy gets twenty-five to thirty years for drug possession" and "another guy goes in for rape and manslaughter, but gets out after doing just nine years." Val's friend Zed simply announces: "The world's going to hell." We come to understand better Val's out-of-the-blue murderous rages as the result of living in a world where nothing makes sense and its youth have given up imagining a future—and doing what it takes to realize this future. As Ralph Rodriguez writes in *Brown Gumshoes*, the hardboiled form and its alienated other is a subjectivity that "resonates especially well with Chicana/os, who though subjects of the nation are often represented as alien to it" (6). Gilbert Hernandez and Navarro choose to envelop their stories in the noir fictional mode—a mode with a social-Darwinist, behaviorist, fatalistic worldview—as a way to comment on a world ripped apart at the seams and where characters are fated to live a life in a world that offers no real options.

SATIRES AND SUPERHEROES

Steve Ross's *Chesty Sanchez* and Erik Rodriguez's *Hispanic Batman* operate within the grotesque mode of storytelling. Elsewhere Aldama defines this as the author's aesthetic aim to present characters, behavior (relations among characters), settings (space and time), and circumstances (physical and social) in a manner that is simultaneously congruent with the aims of realism and that breaks with such aims. It is the breakdown of social rules. It is the breakdown of laws of nature. Steve Ross's protagonist Chesty Sanchez is a Latina superhero who topples corporate villains who profit from biochemical weapon sales and the like; her sidekick is Torpedo, whose deadly weapon is his *pedos*, or farts. And Erik Rodriguez's Batman is bisexual, lives in South Central Gotham, and speaks with highly stylized and self-conscious sprinkles of "jess" and "joo," "papi," and other exaggerated Spanglish phrases. When he discovers his sidekick (and lover) Roberto is reading porno magazines, he tells him: "I'm going to ha-ride jorr hide, Roberto!" (16). Nothing is off limits in this comic, including a sexed-up Condoleezza Rice costumed as Cat Woman. At one point she thinks to herself: "Damn, this Batman guy has got a cut gut" (11). The comic ends with Batman's giving the 1970s television show actor Erik Estrada a big "smooch" and Batman's telling him: "How about joo just shut up, Ponch, and take jer medicine, joo big ol' tough-talking chopper-ha-ridin' beetch!" (50).

We mentioned above the many comics that feature Latino superheroes. Richard Dominguez's El Gato Negro fights drug cartels along the US–Mexico border. Rafael Navarro's Sonambulo sojourns in the land of the dead (Mictlan), giving him the power of sleeplessness that allows him to solve crimes and vanquish foes when others are in deep REM. And there are many others. Of late, too, we see comic book/film crossovers. For instance, in 2010 film director Robert Rodriguez (with Aaron Kaufman and Stuart Sayger) introduced the comic book superhero vigilante Machete, in conjunction with his film *Machete*. The comic book is a prequel of sorts to the film, telling the story of Daniel "Machete" Lopes before he throws in his Mexican Federal badge. More Batman vigilante than Superman hero, in the comic book Machete brings justice for the unconscionable slaying of a woman from the nearby town, Netzahualcoyotl. After slicing in half the head of a villain, Machete states: "I tried to do the right thing. But they pissed off the wrong Mexican this time!" (Rodriguez 2010). In a single-focused analysis of Javier Hernandez's *El Muerto*, David William Foster analyzes how this superhero makes visible the process of recovering lost or submerged pre-Columbian cultural roots. He interprets the superhero as a Chicano living in the "de-natured" environment of Whittier, California. His transformation into an Aztec zombie superhero during the Day of the Dead celebration connects his identity to a primeval world before the Spanish conquest and US Anglo colonization. (See his essay "Latino Comics: Javier Hernandez's *El Muerto* as an Allegory of Chicano Identity.")

STORIES OF THE SELF

Latino author–artists are also drawn to the bildungsroman, allowing them to explore a wide range of early experiences inflected by race, culture, sexuality, class, and gender. Ivan Velez Jr. employs the coming-of-age form in his *Tales of the Closet Vol. 1* (2005) to texture a rich variety of multiracial gay and lesbian teenager coming-out stories. Not only do these characters feel alienated from the adult world as teens with their own sets of issues, but they feel doubly and triply alienated as racially and sexually marginalized. While Velez presents a certain affirmation of gay teen coalition-building, as Tony, Imelda, and a handful of other characters discover their common closeted experiences, the inclusion of a tragic gay-bashing scene near the story's end recalls the murder of Matthew Shepard in 1995 and acts as brutal reminder of the suffering experienced by gay and lesbian youth of color living in a homophobic and racist society. A decidedly more upbeat coming-of-age story is Gilbert Hernandez's *The Adventures of Venus*, which Derek Parker Royal identifies as being an episodic adventure story that appeals to both young and older readers (its surrealistic ingredients). Royal considers how Hernandez filled his book with metafictional moments and narrative experimentation, as with the appearance of the Blooter Baby and the Blooter Baby hunter. And *Marble Season* is a clear nod to the influence of Charles Schulz's *Peanuts* and *Archie* comics on Gilbert Hernandez's work, as it revels and luxuriates in the ache of discovery and receding innocence of preadolescent youth. Just as with his Palomar stories, Hernandez creates a complex cast that supplies boundless energy to the episodic stories that revolve primarily around Huey and his little brother Chavo. The dominance of the visual narrator amplifies the emotional components of the stories of children within sight of the adult world.

Latino creators also work in the autobiographical genre, where there is a greater expectation on the part of readers that the story will correspond in some way to the life of the author–artist. Of course author–artists play with this expectation. In *Rabbi Harvey Meets Ilan Stavans*, Ilan Stavans (writer) and Steve Sheinkin (artist) do something interesting. Stavans meets and converses with the Wild West cowboy-hat-wearing Harvey Rabbi (who has his own run of graphic novels created by Steve Sheinkin); as Ilan shows Harvey around Mexico City, they talk over issues of identity and the Jewish history in Mexico, ending up at a Jewish enclave in *el centro histórico* where Ilan's parents and grandparents lived. In his discussion of self-identity and belonging, he explains of the Spanish language, "It's my true home. Or one of my homes" (Stavans 3). And when Ilan self-identifies as Jewish Mexican and Latino, he remarks, "I feel more comfortable saying I'm a Spanish speaker than that I'm Mexican. [. . .] I feel like an accidental Mexican" (Stavans and Sheinkin, *Rabbi Harvey* 3).

We also think of *Cuba: My Revolution*, wherein Inverna Lockpez (author) and Dean Haspiel (artist) create a character named Sonya who acts as a stand-in for Lockpez's own experiences and biographical story. Brown and gray lines with sepia wash and splashes of red, together with regular and irregular panel layouts (the use of triangle panels, too), effectively convey the story of one's disillusionment with the Castro regime. It opens with a full-page splash depicting a bourgeois household and the identification of this as Havana, Cuba. December 31, 1958. 10:00 PM. "I'm Sonya. I'm 17 years old. I support Fidel Castro, who is still in the mountains but is said to be marching on Havana soon. I live with my mother and stepfather. I have dreams of becoming an artist, a painter—but my mother wants me to be a doctor, like my father" (1). The comic book ends in 1966 with a close-up of Sonya's face with tears running down her cheeks and with sunglasses with only one lens; she is seated in a prop plane as she leaves Cuba: "Welcome to America. Welcome to freedom" (Lockpez 2010). There is also Robert Renteria's (with Corey Michael Balke) and Shane Clester's (artist) *Mi Barrio* (2011), which tells of Renteria's rags-to-riches story. Renteria includes a short introduction that tells the reader: "Estoy dedicando este libro de cómicas a todos los niños del mundo que están enfrentando cualquier tipo de adversidad. No importa de dónde vengas, los secretos para éxito son trabajo duro, determinacíon y educación" (Renteria 2011) (I am dedicating this comic book to all the children around the world who face any kind of adversity. Regardless of where you come from, the secrets to success are hard work, determination, and education). This is an up-from-bootstraps morality tale—steer clear of corporeal desire and violence, live a pure life, and work hard, and you will make it.

Several Latino creators choose to tell stories that one way or another also adhere to historical and social facts, but as experienced by individual people. For instance, in Wilfred Santiago's 200-page masterful *21: The Story of Roberto Clemente* (2011), we learn of the life of MVP baseball player Roberto Clemente. While González will go into more detail in his chapter herein, we want to mention briefly how Santiago chooses to tell this story as an extended flashback. It begins with a series of panels set in 1972 when Clemente hit his three thousandth home run, then takes us back to his early life in Puerto Rico followed by his life of dislocation in the United States. It ends in 1972 with his smashing the world record and also his death—a plane crash while on a mission to get medical supplies to earthquake-ravaged Nicaragua. Santiago's careful use of panel layout, point of view, and close-ups and long shots not only gives the story rhythm and energy, but conveys the loneliness felt by Clemente as a Latino in the United States and as one of the first to break the Brown color line in the national baseball leagues, following in the footsteps of Jackie Robinson.

And there are creators who choose the shorter, comic book vignette form. For instance, in Gilbert Hernandez's "I'm Proud to Be an American" and Roberta Gregory's "California Girl" (both collected in Pete Friedrich's *Roadstrips: A Graphic Journey across America*), the authors choose to relate moments of their coming into a racial consciousness as children. And there are those who use the vignette form to intermix autobiographical epiphany with historical epoch. We think of Mario Hernandez along with others collected in *The Comic Book Guide to the Mission: A Cartoon Tour through San Francisco's Mission* (Hernandez, "Mission Statements"). In Hernandez's three-page comic vignette titled "Mission Statements" he depicts himself visually as a younger Mario living in the mission in the late 1980s. Mario the narrator looks back and tells us: "Fresh from the 'burbs of So-Cal, I was determined to not overly react to my new neighborhood adventures . . ." (53). While the verbal narration is quite staid, the visuals are full of motion, capturing the zaniness of the place, creating a nice tension between the mature voice of Mario and the younger, more adventurous Mario. In a stretch panel near the end, the double voice is given visual texture with the depiction of the young Mario to the left (thin and with hair) and to the right an older Mario (large and bald) sitting at the same table eating different ethnic foods of the Mission. The narrator exclaims: "Morphing from this, to . . . this!" (55).

HISTORICAL AND MYTHOLOGICAL NARRATIVES

Several Latino creators want to right the wrongs of either erased or incorrectly represented Latino history. Some go as far back as pre-Columbian history. In *Pablo's Inferno* (2004) Rhode Montijo creates a narrative that asks readers/ viewers to align themselves with the innocent child protagonist, Pablo, and to learn through his eyes and ears of the evils of the Euro-Spanish genocide and conquest of the Americas. The story offers a perspective of the conquest from not a Spanish conquistador, but rather the myth-inspired character Quetzal.
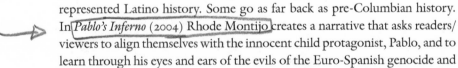

Playing Virgil to Pablo's Dante, he informs Pablo, "Most of the knowledge we have of the Aztecs was learned from books of those who came to conquer us" (Montijo 86). Andrea M. Guadiana's bilingual flipbook, *Azteca: The Story of a Jaguar Warrior* (1992), is more tied to the historical archive, giving less play to the visual and more to the textual, to teach its readers details of Aztec mythological gods such as Catlike, historical figures like Hernán Cortés, and early chronicles of the conquest by the likes of Bernal Díaz del Castillo and Miguel León-Portilla. Still other Latino comic book creators choose to set the books straight by recounting a more contemporary history. In *Latino U.S.A.* (2000) both Ilan Stavans (writer) and Lalo Alcaraz (artist) self-consciously insert themselves into the making of Latino history—a history that begins in 1492 and is filled with oppression and exploitation. A schoolteacher standing at a chalkboard gives conventional and Anglo-American-biased history lessons that are refuted and undermined in a trickster-like manner by Ilan and Alcaraz. Notably, too, in *Once@9:53am* (2011) Ilan Stavans (writer and editor) and Marcelo Brodsky (artist) use the *fotonovela* comic book format to recount and make vital today the terrorist attack that took place July 18, 1994, in a Jewish neighborhood in Buenos Aires that killed 85 people.

Of course, the weighty presence of Latino comics today did not appear without struggle or ex nihilo. Those first out of the gates in the 1980s and early 1990s, like Los Bros Hernandez, Richard Dominguez, Ivan Velez, Laura Molina, Carlos Saldaña, and Rafael Navarro, struggled long and hard to get their work into the hands of readers. (Gus Arriola's nationally syndicated *comic strip* "Gordo" appeared in the early 1940s, and William de la Torre's "Pedrito" appeared in the *New Yorker* in the late 1940s and early 1950s.) With few exceptions, they still hold other jobs to make ends meet. These first-wave creators opened doors and role-modeled possibilities for a second-wave, younger generation of Latino comic book storytellers such as Montijo, Santiago, Rodriguez, and Anthony Oropeza, among others.

THE REPRESENTATIONAL MAP has become more inclusive for other reasons, too. Along with the individual and collective struggles of Latino creators, there has been a massive demographic shift in the late twentieth and early twenty-first centuries. Latinos today have become the largest minority population in the United States. One in six people in the United States is now Latino/a. Second only to Mexico City, Los Angeles has the largest Latino population. This ethnographic reality puts marketing pressure on media behemoths to represent Latinos/as.

We see this trend in the mainstream comic book world. Today, Marvel and DC (including its Vertigo imprint) have a fuller array of fleshed out, single-issue Latino characters. This is surely the result of Latinos Joe Quesada and Axel Alonso at the helm as editors-in-chief and creative directors as well as the demographic pull of Latinos wanting to see ourselves *as superheroes* in the comic book universe.

In the Marvel and DC universes there are over fifty Latino superheroes (and supervillains) that first began to appear after WWII. And while DC and Marvel certainly produced some whoppers, several of the most engaging superheroes created to date have been Latino: Hector Ayala as White Tiger (and later his niece, Angela del Toro), the Hispanophone Caribbean-born and raised Bane, the mestizo Maya Lopez as Echo, and the Blatino Miles Morales as Spider-Man (formerly of Marvel's Ultimate Comics and today *the* Spider-Man in Marvel's main continuity, 616 Universe). And, since George Pérez first broke into the Marvel creative scene in the 1970s, Latino writers, drawers, colorists, and inkers have been a significant presence in the building of the mainstream comic book world. One such writer and artist, Joe Quesada, ran Marvel for over a decade as its editor-in-chief (2000–2011) only to hand the baton over to another Latino, Axel Alonso, an editor at DC from 1994–2000 who then moved to a senior editor spot at Marvel before taking over as the most recent editor-in-chief.

The presence of Latinos in comics and in the making of comics can be accounted for because of our increased presence in the United States as creators and consumers of comics. We have not only become increasingly more an urban-dwelling population with a growing range in tastes for all cultural products, comic books included. We have also become more and more a population with the time to make and read and enjoy comics. The alienation and anonymity associated with urban life that was especially prevalent among the older generation has begun to transform into a sense of cultural renewal for a newer generation of Latinos not working in the factories or agricultural fields.

We see the pattern of the increased number of Latino superheroes with greater complexity from the 1970s through to today. Just to mention a few, in the 1970s with George Pérez's (artist) and Bill Mantlo's (writer) Nuyorican White Tiger we witnessed the birth of a Latino superhero richly characterized in both story and drawing. In 1981 Marvel introduced the Latina superhero Bonita Juarez as Firebird, with great depth of character. In the twenty-first century we see DC and Marvel daring to give some of their A-list stalwarts makeovers as Latinos. Orson Scott Card's *Ultimate Iron Man Vol. 1* (October 11, 2006) introduces us to the mixed Anglo/Latino Antonio "Tony" Stark as a biogenetic genius. DC re-inhabited the Blue Beetle as the Latino Jaime Reyes. Keith Giffen (writer) and Cully Hamner (artist) anchor him firmly within a loving, working-class family, his mom (nurse), father (mechanic), and sister Milagro living in El Paso. They also create stories that interface directly with the day-to-day existence of Jaime and those living along the US–Mexico border. And, Miles Morales as the Blatino Spider-Man has replaced Peter Parker in Marvel's comic book universe. Morales is firmly situated within a loving African American (father) and Latina (mother) family who become integral parts of his total education as he moves from teenagehood to adulthood. As Adilifu Nama states in "Staking Out a *Blatino* Borderlands," "not only is Spider-Man arguably Marvel Comic's most signature character across the Marvel superhero universe and an iconic superhero in American pop culture but he is also black and Puerto Rican, a source of debate and popular discourse concerning race in America" (131). Nama analyzes how Morales expresses and affirms the atypical hybrid mixture of Latino and black biological ancestry and culture, clearing the way for a remapping of aesthetic boundaries traditionally based on segregating black from Latino identity and experience.

LATINO COMICS' SCHOLARLY RENAISSANCE

This edited volume on Latino comics presents an array of historical (styles, genres, representations), formal (aesthetic devices and structures), and cognitive approaches to the study of comics and graphic narratives by and about Latinos. The volume does not exist in a vacuum, of course. Academic conferences and journals have published special issues on US ethnic comic books that include important work on Latino comic book creators. In 2009 Aldama published *Your Brain on Latino Comics*, which aimed to (1) archive the history of comics by and about Latinos/as, (2) offer a theory for their analysis, and (3) put on the map the actual voices of the many practicing Latino creators today by conducting and then including interviews.

This same year Héctor Fernández L'Hoeste and Juan Poblete published the edited collection *Redrawing the Nation: National Identity in Latin/o American Comics.* While more centrally focused on comics south of the border, the essays collected by L'Hoeste and Poblete aim to deepen an understanding of comics within both national and historical contexts. For these scholars, the "urbanization" of populations in the Americas has led to the rise of a great diversity of popular cultural tastes, including one for comic books, that at once speaks to a specifically, say, Brazilian or Mexican or US Latino experience as well as to shared experiences of marginality. The increased production and consumption of comics in the Americas presents, the editors write, "a challenge to homogenous national imaginaries in Latin/o America" (15). At the same time, the essays highlight crucial differences between comics north and south of the US–Mexico border. The biggest difference is that generally speaking those south of the border tend to focus more on issues of class than race or ethnicity; those north of the border tend to focus more on issues of race and ethnicity. In "The Bros. Hernandez: A Latin Presence in Alternative U.S. Comics" (one of the two essays that focus on US Latino comics), Ana Merino shows clearly how Los Bros Hernandez foreground issues such as "migratory conflicts, and violent, racist hostility" (256).

In 2010 Aldama published the volume *Multicultural Comics: From Zap to Blue Beetle*, which widened its focus to include theory, interpretation, analyses, and archival resources of comics by and about Asian Americans (Filipino inclusive), African Americans, Native Americans, postcolonial subcontinental Indians—and Latinos/as. Three of the thirteen essays focus on comics by and about Latinos/as. For instance, in "'Authentic' Latinas/os and Queer Characters in Alternative and Mainstream Comics" (2010) Jonathan Risner considers different expressions of *latinidad* in a range of comics: Los Bros Hernandez's Las Locas, who employ the bricolage Chicano aesthetic sensibility known as Rasquachismo—the aesthetic of the street and have-nots that recycles any and all manner of objects, styles, and techniques to convey a message of resistance through irony and humor; DC's new Blue Beetle series, whereby the design of Jaime Reyes's Blue Beetle mask is styled after that of a *luchador* (a professional Mexican wrestler who wears a mask) and the scarab on his spine inspired by Mexican film director Guillermo del Toro's film *Cronos*; and DC's creation of the ex-lover of Batwoman as the lesbian Latina Renee Montoya. Risner also comments on, for instance, uses of English/Spanish code-switching as well as setting. Blue Beetle's El Paso location, for instance, "gives the reader a window into a border milieu" (50). He also identifies how a comic book like Blue Beetle brings to the foreground "generational and assimilation issues within some Latina/o families, nativism among US citizens, the trafficking of immigrants, and the militarization and politics of the El Paso–Ciudad Juárez border" (51). In "Chronology, Country, and Consciousness in Wilfred Santiago's *In My Darkest Hour*" Nick Hetrick determines how the temporal ordering and visual art of the story show how Santiago blurs the boundary between his Puerto Rican character Omar's interiority (private) and the post-9/11 American psyche (public). Santiago's atypical use of exterior narrating devices makes physically present this blurring of the boundary between the private and public, the real and unreal, in a post-9/11 American consciousness. On one occasion, Hetrick writes,

> instead of fronting ethnicity as a central thematic concern, Santiago's bold aesthetic experimentation emphasizes the relationship between form and content, specifically with respect to the representation of consciousness. Ulti-

Wilfred Santiago

mately, this experimentation gives rise to the novel's chief concern: to call relations between real and unreal significantly into question. (189)

There is scholarship, too, that attends to complex configurations of the author–artist identity and the making of the comic book. This could be a focus on how non-Latino comic book creators render Latinos or how Latino creators choose to portray non-Latino identities and experiences. In *Your Brain on Latino Comics* Aldama discusses, for instance, how Roberta Gregory self-identifies as a Latina but chooses to create not only a white character, but a white bigoted character with her *Bitchy Bitch* comic books. Aldama also explores how Filipino creators, the Luna Brothers, create an engaging and empowered Latina superhero character in their comic book, *Ultra*. Others, such as Patrick L. Hamilton, choose to explore how non-Latinos create Latino characters, but to dismal effect. In "Lost in Translation: Jessica Abel's *La Perdida*, the Bildungsroman, and 'That "Mexican" Feel,'" Hamilton, for instance, is critical of Abel's objectification of Mexicans and caricaturing of *mexicanidad*. For Hamilton, her protagonist, Carla, does not transform or grow in her Mexico City journey but rather "persists in her naïveté and ignorance" (121), and therefore Abel fails to deliver a complex critique of her internalized racism.

And in 2013 Christopher González and Derek Parker Royal edited a special issue of the journal *ImageText* on the works of Gilbert and Jaime Hernandez, marking the first time an entire issue of a journal was devoted to the comics of Los Bros Hernandez. The essays underscore the high level of sophistication and creative design characteristic of Los Bros' comics and show how form and content can coalesce in a comic book author's will to style. For instance, Christopher Pizzino, using trauma theory, postulates the violence in Hernandez's "Palomar" stories through "autoclastic icons, or self-breaking images," an aesthetic approach, Pizzino argues, "specific to comics produced in the US (and in some cases the UK) after the purge, and . . . best understood as a response to the oppressive conditions it ushered in for comics as a medium and for comics makers." Jesse Molesworth considers the infusion of a variety of media as it manifests in Gilbert Hernandez's "Human Diastrophism," noting that "like *Tom Jones* and *Joseph Andrews*, Hernandez's work is also an artistic manifesto, a similarly grand statement about the creative and moral capacity of comics." With respect to the rise of media and the process of remediation in Hernandez's comics, Molesworth argues, "Palomar itself also experiences a version of the diastrophism experienced by most of its principal inhabitants— a diastrophism in which once-cherished values find themselves menaced and ultimately overturned by the incursion of Western forms of media." Thus,

Hernandez adopts, appropriates, and, frankly, claims all manner of existing media and infuses his own storyworld with them on his own terms. F. Vance Neill, building on the work of rhetorical narrative theorists such as Wayne C. Booth and James Phelan, sees Gilbert Hernandez as a rhetor who makes a "dramatistic argument" via his comics. It is the rhetorical qualities of Hernandez's work that add an insightful depth to the message he communicates, Neill maintains. Hernandez's

> argument is dramatistic rather than essayistic, but that condition does not obliterate the fact that he, or at least his *ethos*, argued. In this sense, he is a rhetor instead of being a storyteller. The substance of his argument and his means of argument reflects the bicultural perspective of his implied author.

Jennifer Glaser maintains that "Gilbert Hernandez's work is transnational in character and spirit," but also that "the comics medium itself is often a fundamentally transnational enterprise." Glaser highlights how Hernandez uses the comic book medium itself as a means of exploring the transnational imagination as well as borderlands space. González uses Jaime Hernandez's "Vida Loca: The Death of Speedy Ortiz" as a case study for a deeper understanding of how spatiality works in comics as well as how space informs the thematic content in the rise and fall of Speedy Ortiz. As González insists, "In spite of this emphasis of turf, tags, and territory in 'The Death of Speedy,' that is, the narrative contributions of infringed territory or claims to ownership, spatial elements both at the level of form and the level of reading all work together to strengthen the emotional transaction between reader and text."

These critical assessments reveal that there are different formulations on how to approach Latino comics. There are different statements about what comics (Latino, multi-ethnic, and otherwise) may or may not do. Overall, there is the sense that comic books are a particularly good medium to overturn denigrating stereotypes. We consider it important to keep in mind the material constraints and issues involved in the production and consumption of comics by and about Latinos. For instance, comic book author Richard Dominguez chose not to have his comics distributed by Diamond. While the comics get into more hands, the distributor takes all the return, leaving little to nothing for Dominguez to use to produce new comics. Others, like Ivan Velez, have worked for Marvel and DC, discovering a straightjacket on their creativity; when he was in charge of writing *Ghost Rider*, Velez tried unsuccessfully to give him a Latino background; even though the DC-backed Milestone comics (African American operated) was hugely successful and made a profit, it pulled the plug, killing the successful 36-issue run of Ivan Velez's and Criss-cross's *Blood Syndicate* series. (See *Your Brain on Latino Comics*.)

Simply put, the mainstream DC and Marvel publishers are not interested in innovation—unless it sells. For as long as the innovative comic sells, there is money backing its production and distribution. (Of course, this innovative product becomes quickly formulaic when produced in a factory-belt style.) When it stops selling, resources are cut. Not surprisingly, those like Velez and most other Latino creators choose not to have their creativity and storytelling art constrained in such a way, choosing the independent route instead. We see Latino creators either self-publishing or publishing with independents such as Seattle's Fantagraphics Books, Montreal's Drawn & Quarterly, Berkeley's Image Comics—and occasionally, as with Gilbert Hernandez, with the more open-minded DC imprint, Vertigo.

We should be mindful of this contest between creative freedom and publishing constraints, especially for those who are trying to break molds and innovate in the comic book medium. For working Latino creators, maintaining control over their product is essential. The cost of making comics is much less than, say, other visually driven storytelling media such as film and television. Aside from the necessary storytelling verbal and visual skills, all that Latino comic creators require are pencils, paper, and a drafting table; all they require for distribution is the web. Not surprisingly, Latinos with limited means and who want to maintain total control over their artistic product turn to the visual-verbal format of comics.

We consider it important that we consider not only the material contexts that shape the making and consumption of Latino comic books but also how the specific formal features, structures, and devices operate in the comics and how they generate meaning and feeling. Whether of the superheroic or telluric variety, comic books by and about Latinos demand a great concentration of visual and verbal narrative devices and design to hit their mark and realize their intended effect on the reader/viewer—and usually with as few means and as quickly as possible.

The choice of greater or lesser degrees of the visual or the verbal present in any given comic book is the choice of the author. Mostly, however, when too much text fills the space of the panel, the comic book begins to read less like a comic book; the author–artist is not taking full advantage of the storytelling medium as both a visual and verbal experience. Latino creators know well that there should be a balance and rhythmic variation between the visual and the verbal elements. They do not overcrowd their pages with text and art. Many, like Frank Espinosa, will draw a figure or scene, and then erase unnecessary lines, leaving it to the viewer to fill in the blank spaces. There is also a clear sense of the author–artist's willful use of space design whereby we jump from one panel to the next in ways that create movement between the panels—we mentally fill in the gutters with movement—and that can give significance to any given panel; the choice of panel distribution not only creates a certain rhythm to the flow of the story, but it generates a semantic significance and energetic charge. We see this most effectively when an author like Espinosa chooses to slice up a panel in unconventional ways to give it a kinetic force.

While Latino comic book creators make the choice to use such devices, one might further speculate that they function as *space-clearing devices* to open the reader's eyes to different ways of being in the world—ways typified by the respective Latino (Chicano, Dominican, Puerto Rican, Cuban) experience. With such an economy of means in creating setting and character as well as speeding up and slowing down the tempo of the telling (flashbacks/flashfor-wards, elisions, and panel layouts), Latino comic creators create stories that present a rich array of worldviews and moral options and dilemmas.

Along with this willful use of technique and storytelling comes a respon-sibility to subject matter. There is a distinction that makes a crucial difference between comic book author–artists who particularize Latino experience in places *in* time with a clear will to style and those who abstract character ex-perience in places *out of* time. A theory of comics by and about Latinos would do well, therefore, to attend to the formal features involved in the writing and drawing of the story (its universal infrastructure) and how they work to par-ticularize features contained in the subject matter (themes, places, and time). Attention to the formal features can offer insight into just how a Latino comic book author–artist opens the reader's eyes to social, political injustice and outright racism. Attention to the particularized texturing of theme, place, and time often reveals just how a given Latino creator infuses his or her respective story with a cultural and historical specificity. Laura Molina clearly situates her comic book *The Jaguar* in a 1990s Los Angeles—a time when Governor Wilson passed repressive laws such as Prop 187 that made it illegal for un-documented people ("illegal aliens") to go to school and receive medical care. This impacts directly her Chicana superhero, Linda Rivera as The Jaguar, and her Chicano community. In Wilfred Santiago's *In My Darkest Hour*, Omar Guerrero experiences the events of 9/11 deeply as a Puerto Rican who faces racism at every turn living in Chicago, spiraling into unforeseen depths of depression.

The respective comic book creators' choice of time and place typically iden-tifies cultural heritage. This is where we see inter-Latino differences come into play and where we identify and experience the distinctive features of each within a trans-Latino expressive milieu. So we have Santiago, whose Omar is clearly Nuyorican—his phenotype and dark kinky hair—but he is also simply Nuyorican. He doesn't think about it too much . . . and then we have Molina . . . Each is clearly different, not just in gender focus but also in terms of Latino ethnic experience, which is, after all, a *varied* ethnic experience. One is that of a Puerto Rican in and around 9/11 in New York (Santiago) and the other of a Chicana living in 1980s LA (Molina). At the same time that there are clear differences (regional, ethnic), there are also commonalities. Both characters experience racism and feelings of *disenfranchisement* as Latinos/as.

Importantly, too, Latino comic book creators are very aware of the interplay of the visual and verbal elements and how this moves the story forward. A comic book that is dominated by the visual or conversely by the verbal falls short; dynamic comic book storytelling involves the organic integration of both. Elsewhere Aldama considers, for instance, how Espinosa uses text sparingly to guide our gap-filling of his very abstract and expressionist visuals and the pleasure that ensues. While he pushes the envelope—and he can given that he publishes with the independent Image Comics press—he doesn't push us so far that we no longer move between the verbal and the visual. They continue to work together to guide our gap-filling activity in our formation of a total visual–verbal gestalt. This activity is crucial to reading, understanding, and enjoying comics.

As we discuss in our various works on Latino comics, the process of writing and drawing implies myriad choices (one word instead of another, one image instead of another, one or another style of lettering, etc.) on the part of Latino author–artists; in thinking in images they are constantly deciding which gaps to leave and which gaps to fill in; they are deciding which gaps *we* will fill and how *we* will be guided to fill them. In many ways, Latino creators craft visual–verbal stories that not only engage their readers/viewers but also expand in new and novel ways the perceptual, emotive, and cognitive capacities of their readers/viewers.

TO THE ESSAYS

The thirteen essays and one interview collected in this volume remind us how resplendent and richly various today's comics are by and about Latinos; they make clear that the culture, history, and experiences of Latinos are varied. They remind us that comics can be just as powerful and sophisticated a storytelling form as the next. They remind us, too, that comics by and about Latinos are made and consumed in time (history) and space (geographic region).

We divide the collection into five main sections. Essays in the first section, *Alternativas*, focus on comics created by Latinos that push at the boundaries of generic convention. Patrick L. Hamilton's essay, "Out of Sequence: Time and Meaning in Los Bros Hernandez," opens this section. His nuanced analysis of temporal play in Jaime Hernandez's earliest stories from *Love & Rockets* and of Gilbert Hernandez's *Heartbreak Soup* lead him to decisively declare the need for a more comprehensive theory of comics. That sequentiality is the sine qua non of comics, for McCloud (and his followers) fails to provide an adequate theory of the complex way Los Bros and other *alternativa* comic book author–artists tell stories. In the spirit also of building a total system for understanding how Latino *alternativa* comics work, in "Recreative Graphic Novel Acts in Gilbert Hernandez's Twenty-First-Century Neo-Noirs" Frederick Luis Aldama considers how Gilbert Hernandez's "stand-alones" at once create a near-hermetically sealed intertextual *total* storyworld and a palimpsestic overlay with a long tradition of pulp storytelling. Aldama considers, too, how the careful orchestration of geometric shape and plot device allows readers to insert themselves emotionally and cognitively into the comic book storyworlds. To wrap up this section on Los Bros, Christopher González takes us on a journey in an interview with Gilbert and Jaime. In "Three Decades with Gilbert and Jaime Hernandez: An Odyssey by Interview" we learn of their long history of fine-tuning their storytelling craft that includes detailed meditations on their the process of realizing storytelling art through careful use of word and image, unexpected career turns, their outrageous adventures with other genres (erotica, for instance), and storytelling in other formats as well as creation of characters and audience response over three decades.

In the second section, *Cuerpo* Comics, we include essays that focus on Latino comic book author–artists who choose to complicate issues of race and gender through their careful reconfigurations of the body—or *cuerpo*. Christopher González's essay, "Biographic Challenges: Wilfred Santiago's *21: The Story of Roberto Clemente*," examines the biographical form of comics, or "biographic," and how it enables the dynamic malleability of Clemente's body. Together with an array of affordances granted by the comic book medium itself, Santiago challenges readers to imagine Clemente as something more than a baseball statistic. Ellen M. Gil-Gómez's essay, "Wrestling with Comic Genres and Genders: *Luchadores* as Signifiers in *Sonambulo* and *Locas*," follows. Gil-Gómez analyzes just how Rafael Navarro and Jaime Hernandez use the figure of the *luchadore* and *luchadora* to disrupt traditional comic genre forms. She also carefully considers how in this bending of generic convention Navarro reifies and Hernandez liberates male and female gender-role expectations.

The third section, Tortilla Strips, continues to consider visual–verbal stories created by Latinos, but in the format of the comic strip. In the first essay that makes up this section, "Latino Identity and the Market: Making Sense of Cantú and Castellanos's *Baldo*," Hectór Fernández L'Hoeste reveals how *Baldo* at once reflects a complex Latino experience *and* draws attention to ways that we have to reimagine being Latino in the world. Castellano and Cantú's use of self-reflexive storytelling devices draws critical attention to how the media packages *latinidad* and also how the Latino experience resists any type of essentialist reductionism. In this same spirit of mapping out a new moment in Latino sociocultural history, in "The Archeology of the Post-social in the Comics of Lalo Alcaraz: *La Cucaracha* and *Migra Mouse: Political Cartoons on Immigration*" Juan Poblete analyzes how Alcaraz's strips reveal how Latinos (and especially the Latino immigrant) have come to exist in a perpetual state of anxiety as a result of living in a post-industrial capitalist, global neoliberal post-social moment. In a careful analysis of Alcaraz's work, however, Poblete demonstrates that Latinos refuse to accept a victim state, instead clearing "a place for themselves in the national space" that allows us to laugh at others *and* ourselves. We end this section with Ilan Stavans's autobiographical meditation, "My Debt to Rius," on the work of Eduardo del Río García— a.k.a. Rius—best known for his *Los Supermachos* and *Los agachados*. As Alcaraz, Cantú, and Castellanos have all admitted, Rius has been a huge influence on Latino comic book and comic strip artists. Not only do we learn of Rius's influence on Stavans as a teen then as an adult, but also how the satiric spirit of Rius informed Stavans's (and Alcaraz's) own, *Latino U.S.A.: A Cartoon History* (2000) and *A Most Imperfect Union: A Contrarian History of the United States* (2014). Rius inspired Stavans's irreverent, anti-establishment approach in both—and the importance of the need to tell the story history's underdogs.

In the fourth section, "A Bird, a Plane . . . Straight and Queer Super-Lats," we include scholarship that focuses on the creation of Latino superheroes in mainstream comics. Mauricio Espinoza's essay, "The Alien Is Here to Stay: Otherness, Anti-Assimilation, and Empowerment in Latino/a Superhero Comics," opens this section, analyzing how the alien-ness (monsterness) that characterizes Marvel's Spider-Girl and Ultimate Spider-Man as well as DC's Blue Beetle becomes an effective way for "performing and commenting on many of the realities and challenges facing Latino/a communities." Indeed, for Espinoza it is paradoxically their alien-ness that allows these superheroes to resist assimilation into an oppressive, othering mainstream culture. In "Anya Sofía (Araña) Corazón: The Inner Webbings and Mexi-Ricanization of Spider-Girl," Isabel Millán focuses on Spider-Girl, but in all her teen and young adult developmental phases. From the young Anya Corazón to the old Spider-Girl and in the various comic book storyworlds that she inhabits,

Millán demonstrates how the nuances and complexities of her identity reflect shifts in sociopolitical contexts. Moreover, she analyzes just how the creators of her character use her marginality as a Latina (Puerto Rican and Mexican) to destabilize fixed notions of what it means to be Latina. Richard T. Rodríguez's "Revealing Secret Identities: Gay Latino Superheroes and the Necessity of Disclosure" brings this section to a close. Rodríguez punctuates his excavation of a genealogy of gay Latino superheroes (one that precedes the appearance of Anglos such as Northstar [Alpha Flight] in 1992) with a careful analysis of the construction and reception of such characters as Gregorio de la Vega (aka Extraño), Living Lightning, Hero Cruz, and the more recent Miguel José Barragán (aka Bunker). Moreover, such gay Latino superheroes open the possibility for readers to identify with and possibly even to defend Latino queer politics.

The final section of the collection, "Multiverses, Admixtures, and More," brings together essays that identify the complex ways that Latino superheroes are created and consumed within larger popular cultural trends. In "Everybody Wants to Rule the Multiverse: Latino Spider-Men in Marvel's Media Empire," Kathryn M. Frank looks closely at those Latino superheroes that have headlined their own titles. She considers not just Jaime Reyes as the Blue Beetle and Anya Corazón as Spider-Girl, but also the different multiverse incarnations of Spider-Man: the half-Irish, half-Mexican Miguel O'Hara (*Spider-Man 2099*) and the Afro-Latino or Blatino Miles Morales (*Ultimate Comics: Spider-Man*). Frank argues that while the multiverse conceit allows for racial transformations of seminal superhero figures (without therefore alienating readers of their flagship titles), it also leads to their sporadic appearance and next-to-none crossover to other comics-derived media formats. Adilifu Nama and Maya Haddad focus on the significance of Marvel's creating a Blatino superhero that brings to the fore a history of racial and ethnic fears, fantasies, and politics. In "Mapping the *Blatino* Badlands and Borderlands of American Pop Culture" they consider how synergistic cultural and racial construction of Miles Morales as a Blatino Spider-Man redraws racial and cultural maps, reflecting "an expansive pan-racial borderland" that make up the Americas. Wrapping up this section, we include Brian Montes's "The Paradox of Miles Morales: Social Gatekeeping and the Browning of America's Spider-Man," a further exploration of the cultural and political significance of the creation and consumption of Miles Morales as a Blatino Spider-Man. Montes's use of borderland theory and policy-making contexts (Arizona's Senate Bill 1070) provide the basis for an analysis that reveals how Morales's racial border-crossing fortifies a Eurocentric status quo. While at first blush the comic seems radical in its racial characterization, in the end it evinces a politics of multiculturalism whereby racial mixture or a post-race United States hides the fact of continued racial exclusion and access to the spaces of political power and national identity.

As will be seen in the essays and interview that follow, comics by and about Latinos go everywhere and anywhere. The Latino comic book authors–artists can choose to include cultural references or not. They can choose to include Spanish along with English, or not. They can choose to include identifiable Latino characters, or they may also choose to create non-ethnic-identifiable characters. There is no limit to how Latinos can be represented and imagined in the world of comics.

PART I

ALTERNATIVAS

ONE

OUT OF SEQUENCE: TIME AND MEANING IN LOS BROS HERNANDEZ

PATRICK L. HAMILTON

THE PRAISE FOR THE COMICS work of Jaime and Gilbert Hernandez—collectively, with occasional contributor Mario Hernandez, known as Los Bros Hernandez—has been near universal in stressing how their work expands the possibilities within comic narratives. As Derek Parker Royal describes, from its inception in 1981, the brothers' series *Love & Rockets* has "exemplified what alternative comics, and comic books in general, could actually achieve."[1] Charles Hatfield similarly lauds the brothers' work as having "fused underground and mainstream traditions, in the process reaching new audiences for whom such distinctions were moot." In particular, Hatfield credits the series for "revitalizing long-form comics with new themes, new types of characters, and fresh approaches to narrative technique."[2] Jaime and Gilbert have likewise been celebrated individually for their unique contributions to comics. Regarding Jaime, Todd Hignite writes how his work "has altered the trajectory of the comics medium and expanded the popular and critical understanding of its possibilities";[3] similarly, Frederick Aldama explains how Gilbert's use of the "romantic-tragicomic" genre "innovates this genre by altering its conventions, infusing the story with a good dose of self-reflexivity to reform the conventions of the romantic tragicomedy [. . .]."[4] As well, this volume's introduction celebrates the generic diversity of Los Bros' work, as they—collectively and individually—create comics from sci-fi to noir, and youth-oriented to the erotic. From audience to characters to genres and more, the comics penned by Los Bros Hernandez have been regularly celebrated for how they expand all aspects of comic narrative.

Standing in contrast to Los Bros, however, is the constricted nature of how such narratives have been routinely understood to function. In his 2009 article "Narrative in Comics," Henry John Pratt notes how "[n]early all prominent commentators on comics assert that narrativity is one of the defining characteristics of the medium."[5] Also prominent in many such commentators' work is the concept of sequence as essential to those narratives. Will Eisner initiated this status by designating comics a "sequential art,"[6] an idea that was unpacked and expanded by Scott McCloud in *Understanding Comics*. Here, McCloud defines comics as "juxtaposed pictorial and other images in deliberate sequence intended to convey information and/or to produce an aesthetic response in the viewer,"[7] providing a (if not the) basic definition for comics. Echoing Eisner and McCloud are other prior and subsequent scholars. Greg Hayman, in collaboration with the aforementioned Pratt, casts comics as "juxtaposed pictures that comprise a narrative."[8] Robert C. Harvey similarly describes comics as "a narrative told by a sequence of pictures,"[9] as does David Carrier in labeling them "a narrative sequence with speech balloons."[10] Aaron Meskin likewise accepts, and sums up, sequence as a "core idea" that "is central to almost all accounts of comics."[11] The net effect of such analyses has been to establish sequence as a sine qua non of comics that has shaped the understanding of how narrative unfolds within the medium. (Notably, I focus on those critics especially influenced by Eisner and McCloud, and less on Thierry Groensteen, whose formulations I consider to be the opposite of McCloud's.)

That understanding, however, has also been limited by the preeminence given to sequence within comic narrative. In particular, it has led to fairly narrow constructions of how both time and meaning exist within and are communicated on the comic page. Understandings of time in comics, for example, have suffered from a conflation of "sequences": the literal series of panels on a page, the order in which the comic reader encounters those panels/ images, and the temporal relationship between those panels/images.[12] Too, the generation of meaning within comics has been tied to sequence and, to the neglect of the comic image, located within the "gutter" or the space between panels. Within the pages of *Love & Rockets*, however, both Jaime and Gilbert Hernandez challenge these constrictions sequence has imposed upon critical understandings of comic narratives.

TIME IN JAIME HERNANDEZ'S "MECHANICS": SEQUENCE AND SIMULTANEITY

In his chapter on "Temporalities" in *Story Logic*, David Herman called for the exploration of "how narratives [. . .] call into question the processing strategies that predispose recipients to read stories in sequential ways—indeed, to read narrative as the preeminent way of conceptualizing sequence itself."[13] What becomes clear from Eisner, McCloud, and other comic scholars is that understandings of narrative in comics have suffered from a preeminence of sequence. The result has been a conflation and blurring of different "kinds" of sequence at work on the comics page. There is, as Harvey and Hayman and Pratt identify, the literal sequence of panels appearing and arranged on a page and within a text. This notion of sequence also characterizes how the comic reader encounters the images: sequentially, moving from panel to panel. Other descriptions, though, conflate the sequential arrangement of the images and the sequential nature of reading comics—going from panel to panel, page to page—with the temporal relationship between those panels.

The best demonstration of this conflation comes in McCloud's fourth chapter, "Time Frames," and its discussion of temporality in comics. In four panels, McCloud makes clear how the chronology of reading determines what he describes as the temporality of the comic page. "In comics, as in film, television and 'real life,' it is always now."// "This panel and this panel alone represents the present."// "Any panel before this—that last one, for instance—represents the past."// "Likewise, all panels still to come—this next panel, for instance, represent the future."[14] Here, McCloud defines each individual panel as its own present that, when linked with other panels, creates a linear chronology of past, present, and future. However, this chronology is not defined by what each panel contains; it is defined, rather, by the comics-reading experience. For the reader, each panel encountered is the "present" panel, the one presently being read, and, consequently, those before it are those the reader encountered in the past, and, those to come, will encounter in the future. But McCloud equates this sequential nature of reading comics to the temporality within comics. He is not saying that, for the reader, each individual comic panel is a present that links with the others into a linear, chronological sequence of reading. He is saying that each individual panel, by its nature (even as he ignores its unique "nature," i.e., what it represents), is a present and links into a linear sequence, making temporality in comics inherently sequential and linear by default.

This assumed sequentiality and linearity thus permeate much of how McCloud and, as a result of McCloud's influence, others understand temporal progression in comics. In his third chapter, McCloud classifies six types of panel-to-panel transitions in comics: "moment-to-moment," "action-to-action," "subject-to-subject," "scene-to-scene," "aspect-to-aspect," and "non-sequitur."[15] With the exception of the broad non sequitur category, the remaining five are rigidly linear and, furthermore, homogenous. Each is a move from one representation—a moment, an action, a subject, a scene, an aspect—to another of the same kind. Besides again mirroring the panel-to-panel comic-reading experience, these categories are rigid in their homogeneity. Why, for example, cannot a scene transition to a moment or an aspect, or a subject to an action? McCloud's taxonomy appears to leave such possibilities out, thus proving quite restrictive.[16]

Linearity and sequence underpin other treatments of temporal progression in comics, even those that acknowledge something beyond sequence and chronology in what comic panels indicate. Johanna Drucker, for example, makes an equation similar to McCloud's when she states (in reference to George Herriman's *Krazy Kat*) that "the framing of one vignette within another so that the difference between one view, one moment, one event, or another can be understood temporally certainly is at once extradiegetic (merely discursive, chunking the units) and narrative (structuring the chronological sequence of events)."[17] Here again, the reader's move from one view/moment/event—and thus panel—to another structures the comic narrative. As well, Eric Rabkin, who outright declares that "the idea of sequence alone is inadequate to explore the subtlety of graphic narrative,"[18] talks most centrally about manipulations of duration in comics. He writes, "Time in graphic narratives, then, is controlled, among other ways, by the degree of information density and representational immediacy in each frame,"[19] but in explaining how the frame/panel's content density can speed up or slow down the reading experience, Rabkin again predicates temporality upon the reader's linear and sequential reading experience, even as he at least takes somewhat into account the images themselves.[20]

What needs to be teased out further than these conceptions, however, is the difference between how the panels are arranged and encountered in a literal sequence on the physical comic page and the temporal relationships that inhere between those panels as a result of how they—and their contents—are arranged. In the latter, sequence is conceived of at the level of a comic's discourse, its way or form of expression—in other words, "the sequence within which events are presented to the reader."[21] However, depending on what the individual comic panels represent, and the order in which their contents appear, the temporal relationships can transcend linear sequentiality. It is this sequence—the sequence of (re)presentation and what those images indicate as to time—that remains underexamined and undertheorized within the study of comics.

Jaime Hernandez's earliest stories in the first volume of *Love & Rockets* aptly demonstrate this point that there are other temporal relationships, other forms of how time exists between panels, than are dreamt of in McCloud's and others' "philosophies." Furthermore, the consequence of so imposing sequence and linearity on the temporal progression within comics has been to obscure nonlinear, nonsequential temporal relationships that inhere within the comic page as indicated by the panels themselves. Examples of one such effect—simultaneity—appear throughout Jaime's "Mechanics" story line. This plot, from the first volume of *Love & Rockets*, featured Maggie, one of his two main female protagonists known as "La Locas" (the other being Hopey). In this story, Maggie travels to a jungle in the country of Zhato as part of a team of "pro-solar mechanics" to repair a crashed ship, *The Saturn Stiletto*. The pages often juxtapose text that is the content of Maggie's various letters home to Hopey with individual panels depicting some of those narrated experiences, as well as more traditionally laid out comic panels.

Both kinds of layouts contribute to Hernandez's creation of simultaneity between panels, beginning with his traditional panel-to-panel layouts. For example, in part 2 of "Mechanics," Hernandez juxtaposes two traditional panels representing distinct events. In the first, Maggie and her recently arrived friend Penny Century graffiti the side of a dinosaur. Maggie hunches over, laughing, while Penny finishes their tag. The next panel depicts Hopey back home as she eats popcorn while looking over the shoulder of a man reading the newspaper. The headline—"IT'S WAR"—followed by "Zhato be Mad," informs the reader of the political situation in Zhato, which is ruled by Sancho San Jo.[22] Thus, the effect of the second panel is to reveal the political situation developing around—and thus simultaneous with—Maggie and the others in the jungle. Although the reader reads from the first panel to the second, that is not the relationship between the events they represent. To put it another way, the events in the first panel—Maggie and Penny's graffiti—do not necessarily take place prior to the events of the second, Hopey's eavesdropping, even though they are read in that order and thus sequentially. Particularly as the second communicates information about the political situation surrounding the two women, there is a greater effect of simultaneity between their contents than linear/sequential progression. Jaime uses the second panel to inform the reader about what is occurring around, and thus at the same time as, the first. And this temporal knowledge comes precisely because of how these panels and what they represent appear on the page. Though they proceed and follow one after the other, the story they tell, the narrative, is not progressing sequentially and linearly. Thus, Hernandez here requires a distinction to be drawn between the discourse of "Mechanics," the way these panels are arranged on the page and what that arrangement indicates as to time, and the sequence in which they appear and are read on the physical page itself. To put it another way, there is an important difference between the sequence of these two panels, and what that sequence indicates as far as time.

A trio of similarly arranged panels achieves the same effect in the sixth and concluding chapter of "Mechanics" (see figure 1.1). In the first panel, Rand

Race, the famous pro solar mechanic, talks with a prison guard, after having been imprisoned for beating up another man, Pedero, whom he (mistakenly) thought assaulted Maggie.[23] In the second, Duke and Yaxley—also members of Maggie's team—make plans to free Rand while worrying about what Sancho San Jo may do next. The third panel confirms Duke's concern, as a San Cho lieutenant communicates his leader's plan to begin bombing the site of *The Saturn Stiletto*.[24] As with the previous pair of panels, the events within these three do not necessarily follow one from the other. Temporally, it is not as if Rand's conversation happens, then Duke and Yaxley's, and then the lieutenant's orders occur. Rather, the effect is more akin to these events taking place simultaneously: Rand speaks with the guard, while Duke and Yaxley are planning his escape, while San Cho's orders are being executed. Similarly, though each in the sequence builds thematically from another—Rand's desire to escape feeds into the planned escape, and Duke and Yaxley's concerns find their apotheosis in the final panel—their temporal logic appears more simultaneous than sequential.

Such effects of simultaneity also occur in Jaime's juxtapositions of Maggie's letters and adjacent images. Part 3 of the story opens with another of Maggie's letters, within which two panels are similarly juxtaposed (see figure 1.2). In the first panel, surrounded on both sides by text from Maggie's letter, Maggie leans back in her chair, while a fully shadowed figure (revealed to be the aforementioned Pedero at a time before his perceived assault) peeps in on her through a window; when she realizes his presence, Maggie concludes the letter. Following all this is a panel depicting a politician declaring the need

1.1. Jaime Hernandez. *Maggie the Mechanic: A Love and Rockets Book*. Seattle, WA: Fantagraphics Books, 2007. 63, panels 1–3.

1.2. Jaime Hernandez. *Maggie the Mechanic: A Love and Rockets Book*. Seattle, WA:
Fantagraphics Books, 2007. 43, panels 5–6.

to invade Zhato and remove San Jo from power.[25] Again, Jaime effectively
communicates the worsening political situation occurring at the same time as
what the previous panel depicted regarding Maggie. A similar pairing occurs
in the fourth part of "Mechanics," where in the first panel Maggie describes
her nightmares about *The Saturn Stiletto*, suffered as a result of an illness,
while, in the second, a trio of planes approach Zymbodia, the second radioing,
"Squad leader to Sadie one, two, three, and four! Next stop: Zhato!"[26] As in
his more traditional layouts, Jaime, in these, conveys a sense of simultaneity
between characters, events, and actions that contrasts, and thus challenges,
presumptions of sequence and linearity between comic panels. And this challenge emanates from how he arranges these panels and their contents, so that,
while appearing and encountered sequentially and linearly, they also work to
indicate a nonsequential and nonlinear simultaneity when we consider how
their arrangement functions at the level of the comic and its discourse.

GENERATING STORY AND MEANING IN THE PANELS
OF GILBERT HERNANDEZ'S *HEARTBREAK SOUP*

As with temporality, the generation of meaning within comics has been both
tied to sequence and located in the reader, an emphasis emanating again from
McCloud's work. In McCloud's discussion of gutters—the empty space between panels on a comic page—and closure—which he defines as "the phenomenon of observing the parts but perceiving the whole"[27]—McCloud
again gives primacy to sequence and reader. As he explains, "[D]espite its
unceremonious title, the gutter plays host to much of the magic and mys-

tery that are at the very heart of comics. Here in the limbo of the gutter, the human imagination takes two separate images and transforms them into a single idea."[28] According to this explanation, the "ideas" of comics—their stories and their meaning(s)—exist at the intersection of the reader's active imagination and the interstitial space of the gutter. However, the comic panels themselves are seemingly secondary and passive in this process.

Such passivity appears even more explicitly in others' assessments of comic narrative. For example, Eric Berlatsky notes, in his application of comics to literary framing, that "'[g]utters' are the spaces between comic book panels [. . .] in which [. . .] the reader puts the juxtaposed pictures together and generates meaning." He goes on to more succinctly declare, "It is thus in the gutter that meaning is created [. . .]."[29] Berlatsky grants the reader the power to "put" the pictures together to create meaning; however, doing so neglects how a comic's creator or creators might have put the panels together in significant or meaningful ways. Similarly, though Pratt does acknowledge how "without pictures, there are no comics," the functions he assigns to those "pictures" are prescriptively narrow. Specifically, he designates them as possessing what he tellingly terms "straightforward narrative functions": establishing setting and spatial relationships within the diegetic space of the narrative; providing "narrative information"—mood, emotion, drama—through design, inking, and color; and conveying characters' emotional or other mental states.[30] After having assigned these informational and objective functions to individual panels, Pratt moves on to what he explicitly terms "a much more complicated issue," how the reader actively constructs a narrative and, implicitly, its meaning from the sequence of these, again, passive panels.[31] Again, the reader functions as the active and generative force of narrative in comics. Throughout these discussions, individual comic panels play little to no role in either the generation of a comic narrative or its meaning. These functions instead are the reserve of the gutter between panels and the interaction of this empty space with the reader's own mind.

However, as the stories by Gilbert Hernandez collected as *Heartbreak Soup* demonstrate, narrative and meaning do not exist only between panels, but also within them. Similarly, those panels do not play an at best passive role in relation to the reader's mind and the generation of narrative. In fact, the techniques, such as juxtaposition, and operations, such as closure, that McCloud conceives of as working between panels function within Hernandez's panels to convey ideas and meanings. His comic text, then, is not one upon which the reader solely acts. In *Living to Tell about It*, James Phelan describes the way in which readers and narrative texts interact more dynamically:

Texts are designed by authors in order to affect readers in particular ways, [and] those designs are conveyed through the language, technique, structures, forms, and dialogic relations of texts as well as the genres and conventions readers use to understand them, and [. . .] reader responses are a function, guide, and text of how designs are created through textual and intertextual phenomena.[32]

This dynamic process—where text affects reader and reader affects text—has not been fully captured in previous discussions of comics, which appear to have focused solely on its latter portion. Various panels from Gilbert Hernandez's work, though, ably demonstrate the ways in which individual panels on the comic page can, for lack of a better term, "mean" on their own and outside of the sequence in which they exist.

Heartbreak Soup comprises the first half of Gilbert Hernandez's stories set in the fictional village of Palomar, which appeared in the first volume of *Love & Rockets*. The first story, "Chelo's Burden,"[33] begins with the figure of Chelo—originally the town bather and midwife, and later the town sheriff—and the stories of the children she helped deliver. Several of these panels, via their unique juxtapositions of caption and image, achieve various narrative effects. Much of "Chelo's Burden"—11 of its 21 total panels—focuses on three characters: best friends Manuel and Soledad, who, the narration notes, were "born almost simultaneously,"[34] and Pipo, whom the doctor dropped on her head immediately following her birth. Pipo's father "would beat [the doctor] to death with a live ocelot" and go to jail, but "Pipo grew up to be a lovely girl with no apparent sign of damage."[35] The narrative also reveals how Soledad "deflowered her [Pipo] seven days after her thirteenth birthday" and the two began a brief, clandestine affair.[36]

The panel that follows this revelation (see figure 1.3) achieves an effect of comic understatement. The two-paragraph caption reads as follows:

The affair did not last long as Pipo quickly tired of Soledad's oppressive libido. She sought refuge behind her mother's skirts.

Soledad respected Pipo's decision to part ways and backed off, perhaps influenced by Pipo's mother as well. . . .[37]

To the right of this caption is a single image: in the foreground appears a bemused Pipo and her diminutive friend Carmen laughing beside a large tree; in the background and to the left, a braceleted hand extends from a doorway, its

1.3. Gilbert Hernandez. *Heartbreak Soup: A Love and Rockets Book*. Seattle, WA: Fantagraphics Books, 2007. 11, panel 2.

throwing motion indicated by various speed lines moving from left to right. In the far right background, several pots and pans appear at the end of these speed lines and, most importantly, above the head of a fast-fleeing Soledad, his arms and right leg outstretched before him to indicate the furiousness of his flight. The way in which this image undercuts or belies statements in the caption is the means by which the effect of understatement occurs. What the caption described as Soledad having "backed off" is in the image depicted as him running as fast as he can to avoid being pummeled by cookware. Similarly, the influence of Pipo's mother characterized as possible in the caption is presented as much more direct and forceful in the image. Thus, the juxtaposition of the image with the caption in this panel reveals the latter to be a humorous and comic example of understatement.

Another panel from "Chelo's Burden" (see figure 1.4) creates an effect of foreshadowing as a result of its juxtaposition of caption and image. The story's third panel introduces us to another denizen of Palomar, Jesús Angel:

Jesús Angel took two days to remove himself from his weary mother Rita. Witnesses of the birth agreed it looked like Jesús might stay inside his mother forever, but the moment after Chelo suggested a caesarean section, out he came as if he had heard her and understood that he was already making things difficult for everybody.[38]

Accompanying this caption in the panel is an image of the adult Jesús standing a little left of center and in profile with his face turned toward the reader. However, the real significance lies in his surroundings: the cracked walls, chains, dark spatters, and black bars convey the fact that Jesús will later end up

JESÚS ANGEL TOOK TWO DAYS TO REMOVE HIMSELF FROM HIS WEARY MOTHER RITA. WITNESSES OF THE BIRTH AGREED IT LOOKED LIKE JESÚS MIGHT STAY INSIDE HIS MOTHER FOREVER, BUT THE MOMENT AFTER CHELO SUGGESTED A CAESAREAN SECTION, OUT HE CAME AS IF HE HAD HEARD HER AND UNDERSTOOD THAT HE WAS ALREADY MAKING THINGS DIFFICULT FOR EVERYBODY.

1.4. Gilbert Hernandez. *Heartbreak Soup: A Love and Rockets Book*. Seattle, WA: Fantagraphics Books, 2007. 6, panel 3.

in prison, again understated in the caption as his "making things difficult for everybody." This panel also foreshadows the events of "The Laughing Sun," the eighth story in *Heartbreak Soup*, in which Jesús flees the town following a fight with his wife, Laura, in which he wrecked their house and bruised both Laura and their infant child before fleeing, actions that put him in that jail. Another story in the collection, "Holidays in the Sun," portrays some of Jesús's experiences in jail, and thus it may be foreshadowed in this panel as well. As with the previous panel, this one achieves its effects solely through its juxtaposition of caption and image, separate from the sequence of panels within the narrative of "Chelo's Burden."

In addition to effects such as foreshadowing and understatement, Hernandez likewise juxtaposes other elements within panels to construct and communicate meaning. One such panel (see figure 1.5) comes from the second part of "An American in Palomar," a two-issue story line originally published in *Love & Rockets* (Vol. 1, nos. 13–14). In this story line, American photojournalist Howard Miller sojourns in Palomar, hoping to photograph its presumed poverty and squalor and thus achieve fame. Miller's intentions, however, have been frustrated by two of Palomar's denizens. The first is Luba, the town's current bather and proprietor of its movie theater, after he insulted her with his efforts to photograph what he presumed was her family's squalor, earning him a kick in the shins and cursing out.[39] The second is Tonantzin, whom Miller seduced through a (false) promise to bring her to Hollywood. After ending their relationship (which happens subsequent to figure 1.5), Miller again finds himself physically assaulted, this time by a group of young men in retaliation for Tonantzin's heartbreak.

Within this particular panel, which occurs chronologically after Miller's

1.5. Gilbert Hernandez. *Heartbreak Soup: A Love and Rockets Book*. Seattle, WA: Fantagraphics Books, 2007. 186, panel 5.

final interaction with Luba and just prior to his breakup with Tonantzin, Hernandez juxtaposes a variety of elements in meaningful ways. Most striking is the contrast between Miller's thought balloons and the images presented in the panel's foreground. Miller's thoughts lament the naiveté and impoverishment in which he assumes the citizens of Palomar languish. As he muses to himself, "[. . .] being stuck forever in a place like this would impoverish anybody's life. Sad. . . ."[40] The images that Hernandez foregrounds in this panel, however, seem inconsistent with Miller's assumptions. Starting from the left of the panel, Hernandez depicts a young couple leaning into each other and holding hands, then a trio of children playing with a ball, and, finally, a young woman reading a volume of Victor Hugo's *Les Misérables* while a tear drops from her left eye. Such images of romance, playfulness, and sadness—to name just some emotions a reader might interpret as represented here—belie a sense of Palomar as impoverished. Though largely rural and lacking certain technology, Palomar does not lack these aspects of human life. Too, the fact that these images are foregrounded, while the actual image of Miller (if not his thoughts themselves) appears relegated to the middle—if not in fact the background—of the image, conveys a sense of their relative significance. The larger size and greater detail of the images in the foreground give them a greater weight and thus significance within the panel, as if to say that what they represent about Palomar is more indicative of its reality than Miller's already established limited perception. Even sharing the foreground as they do with the representation of Miller's actual thoughts, these images occupy roughly the same amount of space as the thoughts: each takes up approximately one half of the vertical dimension of the panel, and both take up the same space horizontally.

Meaning, then, depends on the juxtaposition of these elements within the panel, and not just between panels. Though Pratt earlier designated, alongside other elements, spatial arrangement and positioning as outside the complexities of meaning, here these elements possess a significance and meaningfulness stemming from their juxtaposition. The same is true about other aspects of this panel. Miller, for example, as he walks and thinks, faces the right edge of the panel and thus does not look at those elements highlighted for the reader in the foreground. Hernandez thus positions him to not see them, or to turn a blind eye to them, visually echoing the blinkered perception he possesses all story line long toward Palomar and its inhabitants. In fact, by foregrounding these elements, Hernandez actually ensures that the reader perceives what Miller fails to see. If, to take McCloud's own definition, "closure" is to observe the parts but perceive the whole, then this panel from *Heartbreak Soup* demonstrates how that operation occurs not just between panels but also within them, to generate "ideas" or meaning. There is not just a "gap" to be bridged between this panel and those that precede and follow it; there is also a "gap," a significance, between not only what appears in the panel but where each element appears, which creates a significant and meaningful contrast to be "closed."

In *Heterocosmica*, Lubomír Doležel explains, "[I]n the act of writing, the author produces a text and thereby constructs a fictional world; in the act of reading, the reader processes the text and thereby reconstructs the fictional world. Both the author and the reader perform communicative acts."[41] Like Phelan, Doležel describes a dynamic process between text and reader. He expands upon this process via a metaphor of musical composition:

> The author is responsible for text production and world construction; his text functions as a kind of score in which the fictional world is inscribed. The reader's text processing and world reconstruction follow the instructions of the score. To be sure, nobody can prevent actual readers from reading however they please and from using the text for whatever purpose they wish. But an individualistic ethics of reading, which grants the readers this license, is not a theory of reading.[42]

In this conception, author and reader play individual and contrasting roles in relation to each other via the text. The author creates a text that is the reader's by-no-means-wholly-prescriptive guide to processing its narrative and meaning. Readers thus act on texts, but texts—and their authors via them—act on readers.

It is this role of the author and text that comics criticism has largely neglected in its understanding of how narrative unfolds in the medium. From McCloud and on, readers, to greater and lesser extents, have been granted precisely the "license" that Doležel above discounts. McCloud explicitly dismisses the contents of the comic panel in *Understanding Comics*, declaring, at one point, "Whatever the mysteries within each panel, it's the power of closure between panels that I find the most interesting.// There's something strange and wonderful that happens in this blank ribbon of paper."[43] Such a declaration locating the power and wonder—and thus the narrative—of comics outside their panels diminishes one side of the interactive process between authors/texts and readers to generate and perceive narrative. It stands in sharp contrast to what Aldama and González described in their introduction to this volume as the working together of individual panels and the gutters, the movement and rhythm achieved in Latino comics. It has likewise constricted how such elements of narrative as time and meaning have previously been understood and explained as existing and operating in comics.

As with so much else, the work of Jaime and Gilbert Hernandez—as well as Latino creators in general, as represented by those discussed in this collection—demands that the understanding and possibilities of comics be expanded. The few panels discussed here from each brother's ever-expanding oeuvre demonstrate in particular how the preeminence of sequence has narrowed the ways comics have been understood to work. If, as their critics have argued, Los Bros Hernandez expand what is possible for the comics page to achieve, then so too do they implicitly require the explanation of comic narratives and how they function to grow beyond and thus out of the limits of sequence.[44]

NOTES

1. Derek Parker Royal, "Palomar and Beyond: An Interview with Gilbert Hernandez, *MELUS* 32.3 (2007): 221.

2. Charles Hatfield, "A Broader Canvas: Gilbert Hernandez's Heartbreak Soup," in *Alternative Comics: An Emerging Literature* (Jackson: University Press of Mississippi, 2005), 68.

3. Todd Hignite, *The Art of Jaime Hernandez: The Secrets of Life and Death* (New York: Abrams Comicarts, 2009), 29.

4. Frederick Aldama, *Your Brain on Latino Comics: From Gus Arriola to Los Bros Hernandez* (Austin: University of Texas Press, 2009), 84.

5. Henry John Pratt, "Narrative in Comics," *The Journal of Aesthetics & Art Criticism,* 67.1 (2009): 107.

6. Will Eisner, *Comics and Sequential Art: Principles and Practices from the Legendary Cartoonist* (New York: W.W. Norton, 2008), xi.

7. Scott McCloud, *Understanding Comics: The Invisible Art* (New York: Kitchen Sink Press, 2009), 9.

8. Greg Hayman and Henry John Pratt, "What Are Comics?," in *Aesthetics: A Reader in Philosophy and the Arts,* ed. David Goldblatt and Lee B. Brown (Upper Saddle River: Pearson, 2005), 423.

9. Robert C. Harvey, "The Aesthetics of the Comic Strip," *Journal of Popular Culture* 12 (1979): 641.

10. David Carrier, *The Aesthetics of Comics* (University Park: Pennsylvania State University Press, 2000), 10.

11. Aaron Meskin, "Defining Comics?," *The Journal of Aesthetics & Art Criticism* 65.4 (2007): 369.

12. Similarly, Christopher González draws on Jaime Hernandez's work to suggest the need for scholars of comics "to move away from predominant terms that privilege temporal aspects of narrative," among which he includes "sequence." See Christopher González, "Turf, Tags, and Territory: Spatiality in Jaime Hernandez's 'Vida Loca: The Death of Speedy Ortiz,'" *ImageTexT: Interdisciplinary Comics Studies* 7.1 (2013): n. pag.

13. David Herman, *Story Logic: Problems and Possibilities of Narrative* (Lincoln: University of Nebraska Press, 2002), 223.

14. McCloud, *Understanding Comics,* 104, original emphasis. Here, I have adopted the convention used elsewhere of designating breaks between panels with a double slash ("//"). I have also regularized the font, which on the original page appears in all capital letters, and left in boldface text that appears so on the original page.

15. Ibid., 70–72.

16. Nor is it possible to subsume such transitions under McCloud's final category of the non sequitur. He defines such transitions as "offer[ing] no logical relationship between panels *whatsoever!*" (72, original emphasis) and, though neglected in the logic behind McCloud's other categories, shifts from scene to moment or aspect, or subject to action, do seem logical. At the very least, the ability to imagine such shifts as possible suggests the need for a seventh category of "mixed" or "hybrid" transitions.

17. Johanna Drucker, "Graphic Devices: Narration and Navigation," *Narrative* 16.2 (2008): 128.

18. Eric Rabkin, "Reading Time in Graphic Narrative," *Teaching the Graphic Novel,* ed. Stephen E. Tabachnick (New York: Modern Language Association, 2009), 37.

19. Ibid., 37.

20. Brian McHale, writing about time in postmodern and experimental narratives, critiqued as similarly narrow the ways in which "literary theory has for the most part limited itself to "a narrowly mimetic framework" (Brian McHale, "Beyond Story and Discourse: Narrative Time in Postmodern and Nonmimetic Fiction," *Narrative Dynamics: Essays on Time, Plot, Closure, and Frames,* ed. Brian Richardson, Columbus: The Ohio State University Press, 2002, 58). Specifically, he criticizes how understandings of prose narrative have equated their temporality with "human time," the former taken for granted as mimicking

the latter. In a sense, theorists of comics have demonstrated a similarly problematic mimesis, taking for granted how time in comic narratives mimics the temporal experience of reading comics (i.e., following sequentially from panel to panel).

21. Brian Richardson, "Introduction: Narrative Temporality," *Narrative Dynamics: Essays on Time, Plot, Closure, and Frames*, ed. Brian Richardson (Columbus: The Ohio State University Press, 2002), 10.

22. Jaime Hernandez, *Maggie the Mechanic: A Love and Rockets Book* (Seattle: Fantagraphics Books, 2007), 39.

23. Ibid., 49–50.

24. Ibid., 63.

25. Ibid., 43.

26. Ibid., 52.

27. McCloud, *Understanding Comics*, 63.

28. Ibid., 66.

29. Eric Berlatsky, "Lost in the Gutter: Within and between Frames in Narrative and Narrative Theory," *Narrative* 17.2 (2009): 163, 174.

30. Pratt, "Narrative in Comics," 110.

31. Ibid., 111.

32. James Phelan, *Living to Tell about It: A Rhetoric and Ethics of Character Narration* (Ithaca: Cornell University Press, 2005), 18.

33. In both the hardcover *Palomar* and paperback *Heartbreak Soup* collections most recently published by Fantagraphics Books, "Chelo's Burden" is listed as the first story in the Table of Contents, followed by "Heartbreak Soup." In previous collections, "Chelo's Burden" was not distinguished as a story from "Heartbreak Soup."

34. Gilbert Hernandez, *Heartbreak Soup: A Love and Rockets Book* (Seattle: Fantagraphics Books, 2007), 9.

35. Ibid., 7.

36. Ibid., 11.

37. Ibid., 11.

38. Ibid., 6.

39. Ibid., 185.

40. Ibid., 186. Earlier scenes display the source of Miller's disappointment in Palomar. He opens the story by casually discarding the Palomarian delicacy, the *babosa*—a fried slug (170)—and he later laments the lack of a nearby telephone and television on a call back to his editor (180).

41. Lubomír Doležel, *Heterocosmica: Fiction and Possible Worlds* (Baltimore: Johns Hopkins University Press, 1998), 203.

42. Ibid., 205.

43. McCloud, *Understanding Comics*, 88.

44. This essay's genesis began at the 2010 Project Narrative Symposium held at The Ohio State University and is indebted to directors Jim Phelan and Robin Warhol, as well as my fellow participants in the symposium. Early versions of the discussions of Gilbert's and Jaime's works were presented, respectively, at the 2011 and 2012 International Conference on Narrative, and comments from both presentations were important in revising these sections. Finally, I thank Dr. Allan Austin of Misericordia University, who read drafts of both conference presentations and this essay and, as always, provided invaluable feedback.

TWO

RECREATIVE GRAPHIC NOVEL ACTS IN GILBERT HERNANDEZ'S TWENTY-FIRST-CENTURY NEO-NOIRS

FREDERICK LUIS ALDAMA

PAGING THROUGH Gilbert Hernandez's stand-alone graphic novels—*Chance in Hell* (2007), *Troublemakers* (2009), and *Maria M.* (2014)—I was struck by how these at once stand on their own *and* interface with one another. They differ from his earlier graphic narrative threads in that they are published as self-contained units—unlike those *Love & Rockets* story threads that were published over long periods of time. At the same time, they speak to one another—and, with a gossamer thread, connect with some of Gilbert's other storyworlds, including *Birdland, Poison River*, and *Speak of the Devil*. They interconnect through the continual appearance of the buxom Latina character Rosalba "Fritz" Martinez—she plays the film role of an unnamed prostitute (*Chance in Hell*), Nala (*Troublemakers*), and Maria (*Maria M.*), with the latter self-reflexively referring to Fritz's own mother Maria. (Recall, too, that in the Gilbert greater universe, Maria is mother to Luba and the shrink-turned-actress, Rosalba "Fritz" Martinez. And in these pulp fictions, Fritz plays the role of Nala and Maria.)[1]

The triptych stand-alones also connect through shared generic convention: pulp fiction. Gilbert sidesteps his trademark multiplotted, temporally zigzaggy, hugely abundant character-filled narrative (*Palomar* as case in point) to use the shaping devices of pulpy noir genre fiction (film and novel). By participating within the conventions of the noir, Gilbert necessarily creates three stand-alone graphic novels that follow only a few protagonists and only a handful of secondary characters.

While the story arcs are more straightforward and the characters fewer than seen in Gilbert's earlier work, we find complexity in a different way. As we read and reread the three graphic novels, they ask—demand, even—that we entertain a secondary level of interpretation. That while we are obviously reading/viewing graphic novels, they are graphic novels that *star* (as in films) "real" figures like Fritz *as* fictional film characters such as Nala or Maria. That is, Gilbert asks that we at once relish reading his graphic novels with all the wonderful visual means of storytelling that he uses *and* create a mental palimpsest of sorts that lays a pulp-cinematic sensibility over our appropriation of the graphic novels as such. Namely, we are to keep constantly in mind the fact that Fritz is an actor playing the roles of pulpy B-films titled *Chance in Hell*, *Troublemakers*, and *Maria M*. We are to keep this metalevel awareness in play as we experience Gilbert's will to style in his giving shape to a world filled with the gratuitous profusion of violence (blood and gore), violation (physical and ethical), and vile character type that we have come to expect from the pulp fictional format.

In this essay I first take a few steps back to consider the creative and recreative processes generally at play in the mind of an author like Gilbert. I therefore consider how causal, counterfactual, and Bayesian reasoning mechanisms work generally in the making and consuming of this triptych of pulp graphic fictions. I then discuss how our emotions (intense and short in duration) and mood (blanket-like and long in duration) function generally and how Gilbert's visual and verbal shaping devices, or his *geometrizing* of story, create emotion blueprints for us to follow and experience. These geometrizing devices include panel size, layout, angle of vision, line and ink density, object shape, and balloon and lettering shape. It is this geometrizing of story that creates the mood that blankets each of the graphic novels. It is this mood that functions to direct the reader toward identification of the graphic novels as participating and bending the noir, pulp fiction conventions. Finally, I show how taken as a whole, Gilbert's triptych pulp graphic novel system demystifies capitalist ideology and its straightjacketing of social relations (family and coupling conventions, for instance). Taken as individual parts and as a whole, all three graphic novels criticize a decrepit capitalist system that has ripped apart our social tissue, disallowing the healthy development and flourishing of youth today.

READER PACTS

When we step into Gilbert's triptych storytelling system of pulp graphic fictions, we do or do not sign on the dotted line. That is, we either allow the stories (in form and content) to educate us as to the best way to read them, or we don't. And all this text–reader contractual business starts even before the story proper begins. On the inside front and back jacket covers to all three books there appears a series of silhouetted images of a busty female figure in various posed positions in a variety of square-shaped panels: Bond-style with a gun, knife poised to kill, space-suited and armed to the teeth, and so on. Across each of these panels run titles such as: "For Sinners Only," "Tame," and "Love From the Shadows." Whether we read these as film posters or book covers, the fact is that the stylized poses and exaggerated titles identify the conventions of the pulp fiction and exploitation genre so prevalent in yesteryear's cinema and genre novels. Gilbert wants to immediately anchor our reading experience in a different era of culture production and consumption. Clearly, however, if we fail to notice these signposts or simply decide to read these graphic novels more along the lines of Gilbert's earlier work, like the magical realist *Palomar*, we will not be signing the pact and thus *not* step into the shoes of the ideal reader of these novels. Only by signing the pact will we more likely get its layers of meaning—straightforward, self-reflexive, and metatextual.

Not all have signed the pact and made for ideal readers. Several critics either failed to identify these signposts of pulp fiction making or simply didn't get them. For instance, while *Entertainment Weekly* recognized the "undeniable power" of *Chance in Hell*, the reviewer asked if "it is an incisive character study or just crafty cynicism?" and considered the surreal ending to be "a copout" (85). An equally less forgiving Gordon Flagg considered *Chance in Hell* as lacking the "scope or resonance of his epical Palomar stories," identifying its "artificial setting [as] possibly less convincing than the similarly elliptically told *Sloth*" (68). Clearly missing the signposts of how one is to read these graphic novels, other critics responded in similar ways to *Troublemakers* and *Maria M.*

Indeed, this initiating of the reader pact only just begins with the appearance of the pulp covers that feature a curvaceous female action figure. For instance, with *Chance in Hell*, after the reader thumbs past these cover images, she encounters the title in caps, "CHANCE IN HELL," and, underneath the title, "From the story 'Empress of the Known Universe.'" Gilbert throws us a bit of a mental puzzler.[2] Is *Chance in Hell* a pulp graphic novel recreated from this story? Is the graphic novel (pulp and all) meant to be experienced as a film that is recreated from a story? Whatever it is, Gilbert wants us to be aware already of how his distillation of the building blocks of reality in the making of *Chance in Hell* comes from the social and physical real world (we recognize his drawings as distillations of human shape, action, and behavior as well as objects generally that make up the world) *and also* from things that we have created, such as a story titled "Empress of the Known Universe." When opening the jacket cover to *Maria M.*, we read the following:

Gilbert Hernandez continues his metafictional realization of the film career of his troubled heroine Rosalba "Fritz" Martinez, who abandoned her psychotherapy practice to become queen of the Z-grade exploitation movies. Now she's starring in the role she was literally born to play, in a dramatization of her own mother's life! The "true" story of Maria M. was told in Gilbert's classic *Poison River*, collected from the pages of *Love and Rockets*; this original graphic novel embodies the first part of the film version. Maria's life consorting with the underworld makes for a sordid tale of sex, drugs, violence, and power that fits right in with Fritz's other film credits. (jacket cover)

The jacket-cover description spells out the pact between text and ideal reader: the graphic novel participates in the conventions of pulp fiction (noir and exploitation) storytelling—but with a self-reflexive, intertextual, and metafictional dimension. Here, nothing is left to chance or guesswork when identifying the text–reader pact. And, once we turn the cover page to the title within the book proper, it reads, "Maria M. by Gilbert 'Beto' Gilbert," only then to play with the expectation that this is fiction (and it is, of course) by including in the bottom left corner: "Based on a True Story." It is based on a "true" story—but a true story in that a biographically fleshed-out character from Gilbert's other storyworld (*Poison River*, for instance) appears here as the person, Fritz, who *acts* the role of Nala and Maria M.

WILLFUL RECONSTRUCTIONS

Before I move into an analysis of the specifics of Gilbert's three pulps, let me take a few steps back to identify what is going on in his mind as the creator. This is not a question of my mind-reading Gilbert. Rather, it is taking what we know from advances in research in the cognitive and social neurosciences to understand how artistic creation (here realized in the metafictional pulp graphic novel format) takes place. It is also bringing this knowledge to bear on what it is we do as readers when we consume fiction (here realized in the metafictional pulp graphic novel format).

Like all artists, Gilbert distills then reconstructs those building blocks of reality that include natural, social, and biosocial features of reality as well as cultural phenomena; in this case, it would be the pulp, noir novels and exploitation B-flicks of yesteryear. In the distillation-then-reconstruction process, Gilbert imports from the building blocks of reality elements that we recognize as coming from the conventions of pulp fiction, such as the femmes fatales and villain gangster types. However, what gives this material its freshness is Gilbert's mental (shaping in the imagination) and then physical (drawing and writing) work. In using his mental mechanisms and eye–hand coordination, he gives shape to a series of graphic novels that make *new* pulp fictional conventions. I already identified one way that he does this: his building into his stories these layers of metafictionality whereby we are to read a graphic novel that is based on a "true" biography of an actress who plays various roles in various pulp B-flicks; one of these roles is of the fictional mother, Maria, of the actress playing the roles. Gilbert uses his mental mechanism and skill at drawing to not only create a metafictional puzzler for us, the readers, but also flaunt the artifice of his graphic fiction making. He flaunts the fact that in fiction, anything goes—as long as it is done well and its parts cohere within the fictional world created. He exposes the device, foregrounding how his graphic novel fiction is *creation* that adds something new to the world. His reconstruction of the building blocks of reality make fresh the pulp genre and announce that what he is doing is inventing and *adding to* reality—and not *imitating* reality.

We can understand what Gilbert is doing with even greater specificity. In the making of his pulp graphic fictions Gilbert exerts what I call a "will to style." That is, his willful use of all variety of mental mechanisms and technical know-how work to distill and reconstruct the building blocks of reality with a specific teleological aim and result in mind. He uses his mental, emotional, and physical faculties to work on and give *shape* to the content of these graphic novels, aiming to communicate new sensations, thoughts, and feelings to the reader. That is, these graphic novels are the product of an activity moved by a goal, a *will to style*, a desire to achieve a form, a shape that will elicit aesthetic reactions and experiences in us, his readers. (For more discussion on the use of the creator's will to style, see my books *A User's Guide to Postcolonial and Latino Borderland Fiction*, *Mex-Ciné*, and *Conversations on Cognitive Cultural Studies*.)

COUNTERFACTUAL MECHANISMS

If we keep at this same level of abstraction, we can understand Gilbert's making of a triptych of pulp graphic fictions as his exercising of a series of causal, counterfactual, and probabilistic mechanisms. Like Gilbert, all of us are born with certain innate capacities that grow as we *grow* in our social environments. These include our capacity for language, reason, emotion, perception, taste, and all other mechanisms that inform who and how we are as unique entities living and transforming (and being transformed in turn) in the world. More and more of today's cognitive development research and neurobiology confirms (a) that the social informs directly the manner in which the brain develops its capacity to fully explore the world *as it is* (causality) and the way(s) it *might be* (counterfactually) and (b) that the social from birth through adulthood shapes the basic *neurobiological* and *neuropsychological* mechanisms required for further and deeper knowledge of the world as it *is* and as it *could be*. It is this *could be* that is interesting when it comes to Gilbert's visual/verbal–fiction-making activities—and our consuming of these visual/verbal–fictional acts.

From the day we are born, we begin growing our capacity for causal, counterfactual, and probabilistic thinking, doing, and behaving in the world. In our constant interaction with the natural (organic and inorganic) and social (people and institutions) world, we imagine and work through in our minds possible and probabilistic outcomes to actions, and we actually do the work to modify our environments and/or our expectations. As we modify our natural, personal, and social environs, we also get to know our own abilities better.

All this results from the healthy growing of our causality mechanism (whereby we learn that A leads to B, then to C, and so on) and our counter-factual process (whereby we learn that *if* I do A, I will achieve B and not C or D). Namely, these capacities allow for the following: *if* A produces or is the cause of B, we can formulate a hypothesis that A might (as a possibility) *cause* C. Or, conversely, we can move from effect toward the cause: maybe the cause of C is A.

Another, arguably more foundational mental mechanism (likely initially reserved for solving particularly important ecological problems at an earlier stage of our evolution) also comes into play in Gilbert's creating of his trip-tych pulp fictions. This is known as our capacity for probabilistic reasoning (or what some have identified as Bayesian probability).[3] This is a tool so useful for human beings that it is at the basis of many of our most important mental faculties, including those just discussed, such as causality and counterfactu-ality. We use this mental tool in our everyday activities, including in such banal actions as looking for our lost keys. For instance, in this case, we create mental grids to circumscribe the space where they were lost and then divide and conquer: the space becomes a series of squares whereby we assign arbi-trarily a probability; then, when nothing is found, that square is crossed off the grid, assigning a higher probability that the keys will be in the next set of squares.

Gilbert's probabilistic reasoning capacity is not unique to his brain as a graphic novelist or to his brain as an adult. He shares this capacity with all others; it is just that he chooses to focus his gridding and probabilistic thinking on the making of comics. And the growing of these mechanisms began early for Gilbert—as with all of us. Those working in early childhood cognitive development have created ways to measure the development of this probabilistic reasoning in the creating of make-believe play situations. Pretend play for children provides an opportunity to practice and perfect the skills of reasoning from, and learning about, a causal model, just as play fighting or hunting allows animals to perfect complex motor skills. Through the use of our causal, counterfactual, and probabilistic mechanisms we can create art and by creating art create universes that are not identical to the physical world in which we live and of which we are a part. Namely, such mental mechanisms allow us to interface, discover, and explore the world we inhabit. They also allow us to create and transform this world that we inhabit. Gilbert happens to choose to use his capacities to create graphic fictions.

Our capacity to formulate or perceive relations of causality and to perceive and formulate counterfactual hypotheses, arguments, and thoughts generally allows us to develop and sharpen our capacity to create maps—of the physical (natural) and the human (social) world, including Theory of Mind, whereby we read the interior states of mind of others built on approximations and successive guesses. That is to say, these cognitive mapping mechanisms (comprising causality, counterfactuality, and probabilistic reasoning) feed all Gilbert's creating of counterfactual characters like Fritz in his graphic novels. Thus, when Gilbert creates his graphic novels and we read them, we exercise our causal, counterfactual, and probabilistic mental mechanisms—and to specific ends: to experience a roller-coaster ride in reading something that Gilbert intended to trigger fear, shock, anger, and horror in us.

Like all humans, then, Gilbert has grown his innate counterfactual capacity within the social—but with a crucial difference. Unlike those of us who simply consume graphic novels, at a certain point in Gilbert's life—and according to an interview in *Your Brain on Latino Comics*, he was a young teen living in Oxnard, California—he decided to direct this reason system (causal, counterfactual, and probabilistic) in the imagining, writing, and inking of visual–verbal stories. That is to say, Gilbert's graphic novels are a deliberate and precise expression of our everyday reasoning mechanisms used to map ourselves and others in our natural (physical) and social (people) world.

At this level of reduction, then, his three stand-alone graphic novels are the highly willed and deftly controlled results of these processes. Gilbert *imagines* and then puts into play a whole series of violent, seemingly blank-slate, non-readable (interiority) characters whose actions lead to specified outcomes. His counterfactual as expressed in the graphic novel form allows readers like myself to *imagine* what such a set of characters *might* be like as well as what *might* be the consequences of such characters' actions. Put otherwise, random bashing in of heads, shooting out of eyes, rooftop voyeuristic excursions, and rompy-pompy bedroom action, to name but a few events threading through these three stand-alone graphic novels, are an amped-up, carefully orchestrated reorganization of the building blocks of reality—we recognize the events, even if they might not be a part of our own lived everyday experience—to create something new: a counterfactual in the form of a visual–verbal story with an affective intent.

EMOTION, MOOD, AND GENRE

Unlike our counterfactual mechanism that arrives with us in the world less developed, we arrive with an emotion system at full throttle. We cry and scream when hungry or neglected, smile and coo when satiated and attended to. For those of us (fewer and fewer) who didn't grow up in a dump like Gilbert's Empress (*Chance in Hell*), there is a social network of caregivers (typically parents) who not only provide for us but also function as our surrogate reason systems (causal and counterfactual inclusive) until we develop our own. They soothe and inhibit so we can *think* instead of reflex emote. As we grow, our emotion and reason systems become more in balance—we even begin to *think* about the emotions we experience. Working together, the emotion and reason systems allow us to ponder, assess, and modify our actions—and sometimes in ways that run counter to our basic reflex emotions. We learn to direct our emotion system—and not just in deciding *not* to run from a baseball-bat-marauding Empress or knife-wielding gangsters who castrate and stab eyeballs without much ado, but as a storyteller like Gilbert, to use specific devices to channel the reader's emotion system in carefully directed ways.

Put otherwise, carefully exercising his reason system (causal and counterfactual inclusive) Gilbert chooses a series of geometric visual shaping devices (perspective panel layout, angle) and plot devices (themes, characterizations, dialogue) that together create emotion blueprints for the reader to follow, gap-fill, and feel. For instance, Gilbert uses six stretched panels to describe one of the many gruesome episodes brought on by Maria's presence in the story; remember, this is a film character that is being played by the character Fritz—the biological daughter of Maria, the character she is playing.

Moving from a medium close-up to a medium long shot (p. 130), we are made privy to a variety of interior domestic spaces: the extraordinarily violent and mundane. The shift in perspectives and careful placement of the word balloons lead us from shock and horror of the torture of "El Doctor," the mob boss's doctor who had been slowly poisoning him, to a calm, casual phone conversation scene. The layout of the page into four panels—from rectangular to square stretched panels then two square panels at the bottom—provides the eye with a change in perceptual rhythm just as we move from emotions of fear and shock at the violence of plucked eyeballs and castration to the phone conversation. The choice of shots, from close-up to long, also provides a perceptual rhythm that at once allows the reader to gap-fill the location of the action and intensifies the juxtaposed horror and calm of the moment.

Gilbert intuits well that his readers' brains are not built to experience emotions for a long time; if we did, we would simply short-circuit. So, as we follow the emotion blueprint offered by *Maria M.*, we experience a series of peak emotions (intense and short in duration) that are held together by what we call *mood*—feelings generated as a residual afterburn, say, of the predominant emotions (negative or positive) that make up the emotion blueprint. Gilbert intuits that mood is derived from emotion, that it is a sub-product of emotion. And peak emotions work in an accumulative sort of way to orientate our emotion system (limbic) toward a mood; reciprocally, the persistence of mood is only possible with the periodic presence of emotional jolts—otherwise the mood extinguishes itself. He intuits how moods create certain expectancies and thus create a favorable terrain for the eliciting of emotions. (Quite often, a jacket-cover description, if done well, will describe the key emotion-tagged events in the plot to reduce any given graphic novel to its emotion blueprint essence.)

In *Chance in Hell, Troublemakers*, and *Maria M.* the mood generated is one of an ominous fear, anxiety—boding evil. So while there are, to varying degrees, moments of calm, comfort—even happiness, believe it or not—they are few and far between. In all three stand-alone graphic novels, these positive emotions are subordinate to the negative emotions that accumulate over the totality of each of the respective stories, creating a mood of tragedy and despair that blankets the atmosphere of each. Stated otherwise, the triggering of negative emotions overwhelms the positive, and we begin to install ourselves in the mood of tragedy—or the tragic mood.

When we finish reading any of these three graphic novels, we might recall the panel or page details of those instances when we experienced, say, fear, but usually what we remember most after closing the final page is the *mood*. Indeed, we very often remember this for a long time after; years after reading *Chance in Hell* I remember feeling a general sensation of upset, anxiety—a sense that this story was deeply tragic.

Emotion blueprints create mood, and mood directs us toward classification: comic, tragic, epic, for instance. Years after reading *Chance in Hell*, I remember having read a tragedy—and not a comedy. This felt mood, if looked

2.1. Nala as the femme fatale in *Troublemakers*.

at critically, can be seen to take me one step further toward establishing the perimeters of my engagement with and evaluation (likes and dislikes) of *Chance in Hell*—or *Troublemakers*, or *Maria M*.

This is only part of the story. Of course, Gilbert uses a series of devices, plot structures, mise-en-scènes, and characterizations to orientate his readers toward the type of emotion filter he wants us to use in interpreting the events and characters in the respective stand-alone graphic novel. With this filter in place, there is a further refinement of our classification that happens.

While Fritz starring as the buxom prostitute character in *Chance in Hell* functions as too much of a background character to have any real presence as a femme fatale, in the other books that make up the triptych she comes into her own. For instance, in *Troublemakers* Gilbert gives Fritz center stage as a femme fatale in her role as the film star Nala. (See figure 2.1.) In Gilbert's portrayal of Nala he chooses to give her a shapely hourglass figure, a gentle, seductive facial expression (hair across one eye), and absurdly high heels, all while ready to pull the trigger of her gun. In shape, demeanor, and gun-readiness, Nala *is* a femme fatale.

Fritz appears again as Maria in *Maria M.* and plays the same type. In an odd, self-reflexively playful way, Gilbert typecasts Fritz to play only femme fatale roles. It is in *Maria M.*, after all, that her actions—her faked kidnapping in order to get out from under her Mafioso boss husband's thumb—lead to all sorts of violent murders. Again, even before we have begun the story proper, Gilbert readies us for her role with the cover art (see figure 2.2). And, on the very first page and very first panel of the story proper, Gilbert writes the date of the story's setting (1957) and an image of a building with a sign that reads "Exploitation begins here" (see figure 2.3). Gilbert inscribes the story within the Exploitation genre format popular during this period. The late 1950s was a time, of course, when breasts were allowed out of the closet, so to speak.

And, once the story unfolds, we see even more clearly than in *Chance in Hell* and *Troublemakers* how Gilbert is careful to use the big-breast conceit in ways that resonate within a larger cultural context. What was still rather underground and marginal during World War II—soldiers using pinups of big-breasted women as masturbatory aids, for instance—was becoming more

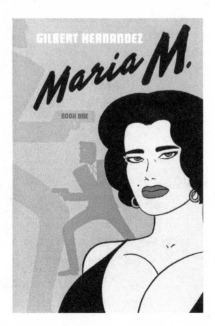

2.2. Cover of *Maria M.*

2.3. Panel from *Maria M.*: "Exploitation Begins Here."

and more *out* in the mainstream in the late 1950s and early 1960s. This was a time when you could pick up magazines at public newsstands that had big-breasted women on the covers; in fact, it became so much the case that women with regular-sized breasts were not to be seen on magazine covers. This was the epoch of movie stars such as Sophia Loren, Martine Carol (France), Anita Ekberg (Swedish actress popular with Federico Fellini and who appeared on huge billboards advertising milk), and Gina Lollobrigida (who even appeared nude in some films). It was the period of other curvaceous female stars such as Marilyn Monroe, Zsa Zsa Gabor, Jayne Mansfield, and Jane Russell. They starred variously in lowbrow and highbrow-reaching films, appealing to all kinds of audiences. This was the period when *Playboy* appeared with its nudies—and its purportedly highbrow stories and interviews. It was the era of films like *Some Like It Hot* (1959) as well as the steamier European neorealist films such as *Riso Amaro* (1949), starring the buxom Silvana Mangano, and *Helen of Troy* (1956), starring Rossana Podestà in various states of undress. Fritz's breasts, then, allow us to fill in an entire historical epoch where breasts had emerged from the underworld and become more a part of the mainstream as an important feature of popular culture.

Gilbert's use of big breasts, then, becomes a signpost for us to fill in a huge blank of cultural, historical context not given in detail within the graphic novels. Their inclusion directs our mind to gap-fill an entire epoch. They also function as a narrative conceit. As we follow, for instance, Fritz as Maria M.'s journey through life (we meet her when she is in her twenties and the story ends with her in her late thirties), we see how important her breasts are as agents of change in her life. It is a result of her chest that she transforms from prostitute to pampered mafia wife.

That is, each of the pivotal events that shape the plot of her life revolves around her breasts. They function both as a positive and negative asset in her life. In a patriarchal, sexist world where she tries to find work in regular jobs, her breasts seem always to get in her way: she is fired constantly because she won't put up with lascivious employers drawn obsessively to her large breasts. This eventually pushes her to take certain forms of employment: the prostitution and pornography ring. This in turn puts Fritz as Maria in contact with the underworld and its *capo di capi*—whom she marries—and his two oddball, sociopathic mafia sons, Gorgo and Herman.

Gilbert uses Fritz's large breasts as the main generative motor of the narrative. The presence of the large breasts determines Fritz's life, pretty much, and does so all the way till the end of *Maria M.*, when she is raped and impregnated. The breasts propel the narrative forward as we read the story. They also propel the story forward in our mind as we turn the final page. We wonder what will become of the child that is yet to be born—the child that will grow up to be Fritz, the actress who plays Maria.

The big breasts, along with the noir conceit, situate these graphic novels within another tradition of the femmes fatales. Fritz playing the role of Nala and Maria M. functions as yet another way to direct the reader's gap-filling mechanisms: to fill in the blank of this tradition of the femmes fatales in comic books like Eisner's *The Spirit* such as Madam Minx (February 1942), Lorelei Rox (September 1948), P'Gell (October 1946), and Dulcet Tone (1973). And, we see much cross-fertilization between film and comic book with the femme fatale figure itself: Will Eisner's Sylvia "Silk" Satin (*The Spirit*, 1942) is inspired by Katherine Hepburn, and Skinny Bones (*The Spirit*, 1950) is inspired by Lauren Bacall, for instance.

On the cover of *Maria M.* and the panel with Nala from *Troublemakers*, Gilbert coordinates his mise-en-scène elements to situate Fritz in her various roles within a long tradition of the femme fatale characterization—all while eliciting an emotion of suspense, anxiety, and thrill. In content and form, he creates an instant in the larger emotion blueprint that directs the reader toward the dark, fatalistic mood that typifies the noir genre.

And Gilbert knows well that when we gap-fill from one panel (gutter) to the next, his strategic use of devices to cue emotion are ultimately directed to create the mood that will create the genre (tragedy) and sub-genre (noir) in our mind. In this sense, his emotion blueprint provides important information about the way he wants a graphic novel like *Troublemakers* and *Maria M.* to be experienced and evaluated: as per its participation within genre (tragedy) and sub-genre (noir). It tells us much about how he would like his ideal reader–viewer to receive and interpret this graphic novel. It also reminds us that genres and sub-genres are a more formal way of understanding the mood established in his triptych of pulp graphic novels.

NEO-NOIR AESTHETICS

While several of us certainly missed the boat in our first reading and evaluating of Gilbert's twenty-first-century stand-alones, others appeared to have been on the money, astutely picking up Gilbert's use of device to create stories (emotion blueprints) that lead to specific mood outcomes and that give compass direction to its (sub)genre participation. The reviewer for *Publisher's Weekly* considers how *Chance in Hell* takes us "on a harrowing journey that examines the damage done in childhood and how it affects the individual as she moves on through life" (45), concluding with an identification of its subgenre ingredients: it "fills B-movie situations with real drama" (45). Likewise, Gordon Flagg mentions of *Troublemakers* how the former magician's assistant Nala, ex-rocker Wes, and scammer Vincene are all "wily" and "none-too-bright" grifter types who pile on the double-crossings that culminate in an "over-the-top, apocalyptic" end. Moreover, Flagg identifies a congruence between this content and the formal techniques used, including the use of "uniformly sized panels [that match the] proportions of a wide-screen film" and that direct us toward its "B-movie" influences and "pulpy fun" (25). In response to *Troublemakers*, the reviewer for *Publisher's Weekly* attends to the content of various mise-en-scènes as well as to the panels that vibrate with the "frenetic, desperate energy of the characters as they try to pull off their cons" (January 4, 2010: 36).[4]

Attending variously to device, plot, and characterization, each of the above reviews ably identifies each graphic novel's participation within "B" or pulp-fictional genres, including most importantly that of the noir. Recall that noir fiction (along with its gumshoe or hardboiled generic sibling) were published by houses specializing in paperback originals known as "pulps."[5] That is, the attentive reviewers move from (emotion) blueprint to evaluative classification, pointing us more formally in the direction of the B-genre fictional mode. This makes absolute common sense, at the level of both form and content. Noir unsentimentally represents violence and sex—and even uses these elements as kernels to the advancement of the plot. Noir also typically follows a self-destructive protagonist (unlike the eleventh-hour redeemable hardboiled dick), at once victim then perpetrator of the crime. Noir casts a shadow of gloom–doom fatalism over its entire storyworld.[6] Gilbert's *Chance in Hell*, *Troublemakers*, and *Maria M.* fit the bill. So to evaluate them on their own terms, we must necessarily inscribe within the tradition of the noir, and Gilbert makes sure that we do this along multimedia (novel, film, and comic book) registers.

Within the novelistic tradition, Gilbert wants us to put his three graphic novels alongside the, say, higher-brow noir authors such as seen in the fatalistic, hard-hitting, gritty realism of Jim Thompson (especially his genre-defining 1952 *The Killer Inside Me*) and David Goodis; other US authors might include James M. Cain and Elmore Leonard. This means that we would do well to trace Gilbert's twenty-first-century stand-alones within a tradition not just of Thompson and Goodis's noir fictions, but also those that gave initial shape to the worldview of noir: the fatalistic, behaviorist, social-Darwinian sensibility that informs the storytelling of Theodore Dreiser, Frank Norris, and their predecessor, Émile Zola—all arguably the *abuelos* of the noir genre. In each we see the creating of protagonists who are fatally flawed from the get-go—fated to become alcoholics or perpetrators of violence or moral reprobates (Dreiser's, Norris's, and Zola's prostitutes) whose only motivation, behavior, and action in the world seem to spring from some sort of genetically driven social-Darwinian base.

As I mentioned earlier, Gilbert wants his readers to also situate his stand-alone graphic novels within the B-movie tradition. Indeed, in a Möbius-strip-like fashion, the governing conceit of *Chance in Hell*, and *Troublemakers*, and *Maria M.*, is that they are graphic novel versions of movies that featured Fritz. This metafictional conceit—the graphic novels are different adaptations of movies that only exist within Gilbert's world of fiction—is most clearly and cleverly identified within the respective inside jacket covers. For instance, *Troublemakers* includes a whole series of poster art that feature Fritz in a number of B-movies: "King Vampire," "For Sinners Only," "Chance in Hell," "Black Cat Moon," "The Earthians," "Maria M.," "The Troublemakers," and so on.

Gilbert's ontologically interpenetrating B-movie conceit directs us to his attraction to a chop-shop storytelling aesthetic. In fact, Gilbert's trademark clean line drawing, efficient panel layout, and temporal cuts that are very cinematographic could be used as a storyboard to make a film; perhaps this adds yet another layer of metatextuality to his triptych of pulp graphic fictions. Each of the graphic novels indicates with such detail through his drawings what is going on—the action—that a good director could just follow his book to make a good film. While conveyed clearly on the graphic novel page, it is confirmed in his reflection on his practice.

In an interview in *Your Brain on Latino Comics* Gilbert discusses his attraction to yesteryear's Classics Illustrated Comics because they were "butchered versions of classic novels funneled into forty pages" (174). And he mentions the influence of "those comic-book adaptations of movies where the artists never saw the film, and worked only from stills. So they had to make up their own story that sometimes went other places than the original movies" (175). In this huge circular recycling within which Gilbert situates his stand-alones, we see how US noir novelistic tradition became an important repository for film adaptation by French directors like François Truffaut. Indeed, Gilbert embraces yesteryear's B-genres that were adapted, chopped, and spliced to vital ends. Much like these directors (and also, of course, today's Robert Rodriguez), Gilbert's skilled crafting of the characteristics of the noir genre—fatalism, resistance to providing psychological depth to character, and so on—ups the ante and brings new vitality to these "B-genres."

It is worth mentioning briefly here that Gilbert is not just doing with graphic novels what the French did with film, but that he does so very much in the same spirit as Latino film director Robert Rodriguez—another of

Gilbert's self-acknowledged influences.[7] We see in Rodriguez a like creative will to style where he seeks in his final product to have fully absorbed the non-mimetic spirit of the comic book; of course, Gilbert is already working within a medium where conventions allow more of a suspension of everyday physical laws (gravity, say) and codes of behavior (ethics, say). But it is precisely Rodriguez's attraction to this that makes his films so successfully of the comic book mode, and conversely it is Gilbert's absorption of the B-movie that allows him to absorb so well the cinematic mode.

Gilbert's noir pulp fiction graphic novels are rich in multimedia cross-pollination, influence, and allusion—and this includes the very visual–verbal B-genre storytelling tradition his graphic novels exist within. Not only do Chester Gould's B-genre detective comic strips of the 1930s, such as *Dick Tracy*, and Dashiell Hammett's *Secret Agent X-9* (1934) come to mind, but more centrally the work of Will Eisner—a comic book author–artist inspired centrally by Fritz Lang's hard-edged darkness, close-ups of violence, and hard-angle shots. We also see much influence from 1950s EC Comics, especially their nonhorror lineup that included, for instance, Bernard Krigstein's classic noir "Master Race" story (that appeared in *Impact* in 1955) and its masterful use of panel layout and sizes to create dramatic storytelling tension, as well as Johnny Craig's early 1950s bimonthly *Crime SuspenStories*, which adapted several Ray Bradbury stories and exerted a co-influence on the likes of James M. Cain.

GILBERT'S COUNTERFACTUAL NEO-NOIR ITERATIONS

The noir move is not new to Gilbert. At the beginning of his career, Gilbert (along with bros Jaime and Mario) wrote and inked *Mister X: Series 1* (issues 1–4, June 1984–August 1985)—a storyworld inspired by Fritz Lang's *Metropolis* (1927) and that follows the mysterious doings of the noir-inspired architect protagonist, Mister X, and his long-suffering ex-girlfriend, Mercedes. While a first incursion into the noir genre, *Mister X* didn't have the same emphasis on violence—or the emphasis on how social conditions and specific kinds of environments create the psychological conditions for the unhealthy growing of mind/brains often expressed in an unmotivated kind of violence.

This is not a Quentin Tarantino emotion blueprint. Gilbert's stand-alone storyworlds depict a violence that is not intended to be seen or read as humorous—and least of all as parody. In this sense, Gilbert shares again much with Robert Rodriguez. Where Tarantino's dark and violent films, such as *Kill Bill Vol. 1* (2003) or *Inglourious Basterds* (2009), establish a tongue-in-cheek emotion blueprint, those of Robert Rodriguez are to be taken with a straight face; terribly violent things are done to people in *Desperado* (1995), for instance, but we are not to read these with anything but a straight face. Likewise, there is extreme violence in Gilbert's *Chance in Hell*, *Troublemakers*, and *Maria M.*, but it never tips into the register of tongue-in-cheek hyperbole. Gilbert's situating the emotion blueprints firmly within the conventions of the noir acts as our guide; we read the eruptions of violence as predetermined consequences of growing up and living in a shredded social tissue.

Gilbert embraces the noir conceit: action, especially violent action, has no motive. But there is more to say on this score. In noir, the, say, sociopath is usually the femme fatale figure. It is the presence of the femme fatale that alerts us to the genre—several such voluptuous bombshells I mention above—and also provides a ready package for understanding motive when one is never given within the narrative itself. The noir genre justifies such sociopathic acts. In noir storytelling these sociopathic types are usually products of a capitalist, patriarchal society that has thrown them to the gutter; their violence is often directed *against men*—and if not, it is depicted as the consequence of having to live in a violent, sexist, patriarchal society. In this sense, we might consider the femme fatale figure as a precursor to today's strong, liberated female character as seen in all variety of storytelling media.

Out of the triptych of pulp stand-alones, *Chance in Hell* is the graphic narrative that offers the most, say, explanation of the violent acts. When the story begins we meet the young Empress living in a dump along with other children trying to survive. We don't know why she lives there, who her parents are, or where they live. But we do know that she is orphaned and calls any adult male that passes her way "my daddy." Except for presence of a few random pedophilic and parasitic adults—some of whom are killed by the children—the first third of the graphic narrative focuses on the children's interaction with one another and their protection of one another. We are also introduced to the first of a series of male figures who care for Empress and whom she latches onto. In this instance, her guardian is a teen armed with an assault rifle who wants to protect her from being raped or kidnapped; in the panels that follow we learn of the growing affection between Empress and her guardian as well as his disappointment ("sigh") that her affection is not exclusive, that he is not special: "Everybody's your daddy, Empress."

In a powerful move, Gilbert then offers a panel with Empress in bed with another character she calls "my daddy." He tells her: "I'll take care of you, Empress. Nobody'll rape you no more." The gap-filling leads us to imagine, as one possibility, that she was just raped by this character, but that her innocent outlook prevents her from understanding this action as anything but a show of affection. How tragic is that?

A series of violent events unfolds, including the murder of her guardian, and she is taken away. Like in *roman noir*, one way or another Gilbert gives us a backdrop—and here it is Empress's early days, whereas in the other stand-alones it is society in general—to make sense of what will follow in the graphic narrative. She moves from the dump to be taken under the wing of a poet figure who lives in the nearby vice-ridden city and who frequents the brothel for a kind of S/M therapeutic play; a series of nuanced details allows us to infer that he is struggling with being in love and sexually attracted to the now adolescent Empress; she befriends a pimp and his "Hearts of Gold" multiethnic prostitutes; then, after she unknowingly smashes her poet guardian's head to a pulp, she escapes to the care of a Catholic home for girls; she grows up to meet a goody-two-shoes justice-seeking lawyer. The events that move the plot all revolve around her eruptions of violence that one way or another eliminate permanently any possibility of comfort and affection.

Gilbert once again carefully builds the story along the conventions of the noir plot. As mentioned already, it is this behaviorist, say, framework that allows us to understand the accumulation of corpses and violence in the graphic novel itself. So, we see, for instance, a moment of calm when Empress's poet guardian describes the act of creating his poetry, then with a turn of the page, we're at the brothel, the poet is awaiting his S/M sex play, and Empress suddenly, without knowing that it is her guardian, swings the club wildly at his head: "Whok, Whok, Whok."

She hits to kill—and does kill him. And this is just the beginning of the train wreck she becomes, killing willy-nilly all who come into her life. Gilbert ends the story with Empress returning to the dump, finding the doll she left behind, and then gifting it to the next little girl, sealing the girl's fate just as Empress's was.

In bringing this essay to a close, I would like to mention a stand-alone pulp graphic fiction of Gilbert Hernandez's that doesn't fit squarely within the triptych just analyzed but that does expand somewhat our sense of his pulp sensibility. Just after the publication of *Chance in Hell*, in 2008 Gilbert published *Speak of the Devil*. In this stand-alone—*really* a stand-alone, as it doesn't seem to have much connection to the Fritz triptych—Gilbert continues his trademark storytelling whereby he subtly conveys to us the social context in which the characters exist. When we meet his buxom protagonist, Val, she is an angsty young adult living in a topsy-turvy world. In this world, as the character Paul remarks, a "guy gets twenty-five to thirty years for drug possession" and another "guy goes in for rape and manslaughter, but gets out after doing just nine years." And we meet Val's friend Zed, who simply states, "The world's going to hell." We don't need Gilbert to give us any more background filler. It is just enough for us to gap-fill a social context to understand better Val's behavior: her out-of-the-blue murderous rages. It is enough that she lives in a world where nothing makes sense and its youth have given up imagining a future—and doing what it takes to realize this future.

The more the story unfolds, the more Gilbert escalates the frequency of Val's violent, gruesome eruptions. As we saw with his triptych of pulp graphic fictions, Gilbert carefully orchestrates our eye movement across the page, building ebbs and flows of emotions as we viscerally gap-fill the action, thought, and feeling of his characters in his oft-silent panels. In the following sequence, we see in the first panel Paul announcing that he knows Val killed his parents—an abusive father to boot. In the following, we have a silent panel, and in the third, Paul is stabbed and only the TV is heard.

In the close-up of Paul we read his extraordinary response to his discovery of Val's killing spree, which includes many members of his family. Not so much upset that she is a murderer, he remarks on how she will be able to go home to her "Daddy" and that he now has "no home to go to." Gilbert uses a medium shot to silently portray a scene with Val with her back turned to Paul and a nonplussed facial expression. In a medium-close shot, the next panel shows Paul stabbed deeply with a knife and blood running down his chest. Why did she suddenly stab Paul? No verbal ingredient here fills in any blanks; no words establish a motive. Gilbert knows well that if a motive were established, the coherence of genre would break down; his graphic fiction would no longer be recognized as noir.

Like the other pulp graphic fictions discussed, the further the story progresses, the more violent it becomes. At the stepmother Linda's inciting ("You took your father away from me") Val once again violently explodes, killing the stepmother. Spread over four pages (113–116), Gilbert moves carefully between different shots, silent and sound panels, and layout to depict a similar eruptive violent behavior in the parent.

It is a fight to the death between stepmother and daughter—and seemingly out of nowhere. But it is also a fight to the death whereby Gilbert's strategic use of panel layout, size, and shot, as well as rhythmic move between sound and silence that directs our gap-filling process, intensifies our emotive engagement and response to the violence.

I end this essay with a brief mention once again of Gilbert's effective use of the noir storytelling conventions. There are many author–artists of graphic novels that use the genre: Carlos Trillo and Eduardo Risso (*Chicanos*), Brian Azzarello (*100 Bullets*), Rafael Navarro (*Sonambulo*), author–artists of those EC comics mentioned above, and many, many more. And in each we see the use of the *key* ingredients to the genre: the strong female figure along with a behaviorist and/or social-Darwinian outlook, among others discussed above. However, it is difficult to pull off a good noir—it can easily slip into clichés of romance and melodrama—but Gilbert does pull it off—and with a difference. We see with Gilbert's stand-alones his very careful dosage of B-fiction elements coming from the romance and crime novel as well as the nuanced depiction of the sociological (environment/family) and biological (family) background that shapes the characters and that crucially demystifies capitalist ideology and capitalism as a socioeconomic system.

In retrospect, then, it is no wonder that Gilbert chooses to envelop his stories in the noir fictional mode. Gilbert is deeply attuned to our world that disallows any future, and the noir mode with its social-Darwinian and behaviorist worldview is an apt way to package stories about characters like Empress or Wes or Vincene or Valentine—all of whom are fated to live a life in a futureless world, characters who live in places (urban or suburban) devoid of imagination and where life—even of one's grandmother as happens in *Troublemakers*—means nothing.

The careful redeployment of noir—and other related B-genre fictional modes—in Gilbert's stand-alone graphic novels conveys in a powerful, nonsentimental message the impossible struggle for the "healthy" growth of an ethics and emotion faculty in youth today living in a world governed by a rotten-to-the-core capitalism. He chooses to express his counterfactuals in the making of aesthetic blueprints that powerfully move readers to consider the consequences of capitalism; represent forcefully the historical involution of a decrepit and senile capitalism that sells itself as the road to success and happiness, but that in actuality divides and lays to waste the Haves and Have-nots; and portray well those environments destructive to the emotion and reason systems of all people.

Finally, what is powerful about Gilbert's twenty-first-century pulp graphic novels is *not* that they tell ageless tales of love, violence, and sometime sacrifices made for the restoration of social harmony. No, what is powerful and compelling about *Chance in Hell, Troublemakers*, and *Maria M.* is Gilbert's deft use of verbal–visual devices to aesthetically reconfigure our world today—a world that increasingly only fosters the growing of a stunted counterfactual mechanism built on fear, anxiety, and anger.

NOTES

An earlier version of this essay appears in *ImageText* 7.1, 2013.

1. In a further Möbius-strip move, Gilbert ends *Maria M.* with Fritz as Maria walking to who knows where. She is pregnant from a violent rape. It is at once a cliff-hanger—we don't know where she is going—and a moment of completing the circle. If Fritz is playing

Maria—she is playing the mother she never knew. According to where the story ends with *Maria M.*, we don't know what her future will be as a mother. Yet, if we are familiar with Gilbert's larger storyworld that includes *Birdland*, *Poison River*, and *Luba in America*, we do know where this story ends.

2. Notably, when the respective titles *Chance in Hell*, *Troublemakers*, and *Maria M.* appear within each of the book's covers in all three of the graphic novels, there appears, "A Love and Rockets Book." Gilbert reminds his readers that not only do the stand-alones act as individual wholes and wholes that make up a triptych, but that there is a further reach into the larger *Love & Rockets* storyworld universe.

3. Bayesian probability has the advantage over classical probability theory in that it is not restricted as much by the necessity to start not only with empirical evidence but also with successful evidence. Points of departure can be speculation and even arbitrary attribution of probability value to an empirical situation and from there on advance toward real, true knowledge based on findings by an ever-increasing probability of getting things right. While starting from a great deal of ignorance, it can advance toward a great deal of knowledge. This approach is one of ever-increasing, continuous approximations toward the *legality* of the universe. A Bayesian approach opens the possibility for counterfactual reasoning: it allows us to imagine things that don't exist, as with examples given with children or the millions of artistic creations in the world. But we can also imagine alternative pasts—that the treasure was buried 500 years ago in grid 33—and imagine the future: dig grid 33 and at the same time be thinking what I would do with the treasure—a whole series of futures can be imagined.

4. Another of Gilbert's recent stand-alones, *Speak of the Devil*, also falls into the category of a B-flick-style graphic novel also set in a dark and cynical world. For Gordon Flagg this lowbrow format allows Gilbert to create "expressive opportunities [such as] over-the-top violence" (26). For Flagg, *Speak of the Devil* suggests "a cannily knowing, slightly tongue-in-cheek slasher film" (26).

5. Notably, the Sunday newspaper supplement was not the only origin of comic books; pulp magazines ("pulps") also played a central role. While popular literary magazines printed on cheap paper derived from wood pulp were already in circulation in the second half of the nineteenth century, it wasn't until the 1930s that they became a venue for the publishing of popularized adventure dime novels that were cranked out by hacks paid by the word. It was the low cost of publishing pulps that suited well those moving into comic book production; there was also cross-fertilization of pulp and comic book authors. By 1936 pulp publishers were publishing comic books: "Reprinting newspaper strips in cheaply manufactured magazines was essentially an easy means for syndicates to cash in on previously used material" (15), Jean-Paul Gabilliet informs us. Comics Magazines Company published the first themed comic book, *Detective Picture Stories*, in December 1936. It broke with reprinting of funnies, offering crime and detective narratives. And in February 1937 DC published the first issue of *Detective Comics*.

6. For a discussion of how Latino novelists use the gumshoe genre to demystify myths of Latinos as well as how they allow for the complex reimagining of Latino subjects, see Ralph Rodriguez's *Brown Gumshoes*. Rodriguez considers how Latino authors such as Lucha Corpi, Michael Nava, Rudolfo Anaya, and Rolando Hinojosa are drawn to the hard-boiled form and its alienated other—a subjectivity that "resonates especially well with Chicanas/os, who though subjects of the nation are often represented as alien to it" (6). For Rodriguez,

"the project of self-evaluation and of understanding the discourses that shape identity remains at the heart of their novels" (8).

7. Rodriguez's *Sin City* is an adaptation of the violent and lurid pulp vision of Frank Miller (comic book author influences include William Gaines of 1950s EC Comics, Wallace Wood, and Will Eisner), a comic book author who revitalized the crime genre in his unsentimental portrayal of a fractured world filled with good and evil. Rodriguez's film is arguably the most successful comic book adaptation. Shot on high-def. video in front of a green screen, he takes his stock of comic book *actors* and, well, turns them into comic book characters: Detective Hartigan (Bruce Willis), hulking Marv (a not-so-made-over Mickey Rourke), Bob (Michael Madsen), Nancy (Jessica Alba), Goldie (Jaime King), and her twin sister Wendy (Jaime King). For more on Rodriguez's comic book worldview, see my *The Cinema of Robert Rodriguez*.

THREE DECADES WITH GILBERT AND JAIME HERNANDEZ: AN ODYSSEY BY INTERVIEW

CHRISTOPHER GONZÁLEZ

FOR OVER THIRTY YEARS, brothers Mario, Gilbert, and Jaime Hernandez have continually worked to shape the comics art form with their critically acclaimed *Love & Rockets*. The formative years Los Bros Hernandez, as the brothers have come to be known, spent in Oxnard, California, would ultimately become a crucial ingredient in the comics they would later create. Their passion for the drawn image/text was truly a family affair even when Los Bros were children. Their mother, who had once had a stout collection of comics along with the talent to draw, and their father, a painter who would urge the boys to practice creating the drawings they saw in comic strips, both fostered a love of art in their children.

As Los Bros continued to explore and develop as comics artists, the culture scene of the Los Angeles area greatly influenced their artistic sensibilities and, later, directly impacted *Love & Rockets*. Music, and punk rock in particular, gave a raw vitality to their comics. The defiant, in-your-face attitude of the bourgeoning music landscape of the late 1960s made its way into how Los Bros approached making comics. Coupled with their Latino culture, Gilbert and Jaime found a way to fuse the two elements in their work, abetted by heavy influences of other giants in the comics industry, such as Charles Schulz, Hank Ketcham, Steve Ditko, Jack Kirby, Robert Crumb, and others.

Initially taking it upon themselves to publish their own comics, Gilbert and Jaime would come to be significant artists of alternative comics, with *Love & Rockets* as their magnum opus. With a wide cast of characters that spans many storyworlds, such as Palomar and Hoppers 13, Gilbert and Jaime have created a robust contribution to the study and enjoyment of comics. They have given Latinos a thunderous voice in the comics landscape, so that now any discussion on the development and history of this form of storytelling must necessarily include their work.

In November 2013 I met with Gilbert and Jaime Hernandez in Columbus,

Ohio, where they were featured speakers at the Grand Opening of the Billy Ireland Cartoon Library and Museum and its Festival of Cartoon Art at The Ohio State University. I spoke with Gilbert and Jaime about their work, the process of creating their stories, their engagements with Latino culture, and much more.

STYLE AND AUDIENCE

CHRISTOPHER GONZÁLEZ: How do word and image balance in your work? Is it a constant battle when creating the story?

GILBERT HERNANDEZ: Often it's the silent panels that are the most powerful. The roaring silence is often preferable, but it's a cheat if you do this all the time. You need the dialogue (people talking) to contrast the quiet moments. Where one discovers the balance comes from a gut feeling.

JAIME HERNANDEZ: Often you come to the point where the story doesn't need words. Sometimes it's easy because it's a person who's not talking to anybody; they're just observing.

GH: Sometimes I will write the quiet scenes, and they're perfect, but find that I have to add words. For instance, I've had a quiet character do this or that, look around, leave, then I think, "It's going to kill this scene to put words to it, but I don't have enough information." I always think of the reader. The reader's more important. Let it kill me then. So I make those compromises because my work specifically is made for reproduction and to be in the reader's hands. I'm looking to connect with the reader. That's what's important to me.

JH: I'm very mindful of the reader. It's the goal; it's the final frontier. Like Gilbert was saying, you go through all these thoughts. You've come to a block. You figure a way around it. You say, "Well, maybe I can do it this way," and in the end it doesn't matter. As long as it's communicated to the reader, that's where it ends.

CG: How much work do you put into the, say, prefabrication of the story before you come to the page? Do you find that there's discovery as you're creating?

GH: A lot of the beginnings of my stories are simple indulgences. I may feel like drawing a setting, a set of clothing, a particular character, and a particular look of a character. Sometimes that's how it starts. You just want to draw something. It's not like something you have to do. Because if it's something you *have* to do, you'll get a block. Go first for something you *want* to do. And then it transmogrifies. It changes. It evolves.

At other times I have to erase it all. Erase all those words that I loved writing. And it may work perfectly, but I'll realize, "This is not the story. This is not what I want to say here." If I'm feeling energetic enough, I will literally go make a photocopy of that page just to save the work. And then, even later on, I may revisit it and think, "I could use this!"

CG: How do you know what to keep and what to shelve or toss?

GH: You have to trust your instincts. Trust that you know what you're doing. Oftentimes I've written things that I wrote years prior, and I'll implement them in a new story because it works with only a little change. There's so much preparation that is unconscious or through the subconscious. I used to make mistakes all the time. Ink the work too quickly, and then I'd have to fix it after. Now I try to discipline myself to keep it at pencils and then ink it when I'm done.

CG: Jaime, does your work take unexpected turns and directions that surprise you?

JH: Some of my stories come by accident or because, like Gilbert was saying, I inked too fast. And then I spend countless hours using those images, and I rewrite the story. It takes the story where I didn't expect it to because I was just too lazy to redraw it or to get rid of something I worked so hard on to finish. Take *100 Rooms*, for instance. It started as one thing, and it became something else because of several drawings I created that I didn't want to get rid of. Instead, I rewrote the reasons for those drawings. It took the story in a totally different direction than it was originally.

At other times I might write a story with a specific goal in mind. *The Death of Speedy Ortiz* was like that. I had the title first: "The Death of Speedy." I wanted him to die. What went on in those forty-something pages before was all filled in just to get me to the end of how he dies. There's a lot of discovery in the process and a lot of surprises. As long as I still know that in the end Speedy has to die.

CG: It sounds like some ideas have a will of their own . . .

GH: At other times you'll come up with an idea because you think, "Okay, I really need to fill in these last six pages with something. There's got to be something." Often those moments are the most fun because you know they're not important. And sometimes it makes the story so much better because you didn't sweat it. That doesn't happen all the time. When you don't sweat a story it's not strong enough because you just let yourself do it. You always have to sweat somewhere in the story. But those times are really great when you don't have to and you've got six pages to just bullshit and you have a great time. And sometimes you add even more than you wanted to originally. And it doesn't ruin the ending.

JH: Yeah, sometimes the filler is the most fun. And it works within the story because the story sometimes needs a break. It needs a lightening up.

CG: Let's come back to the reader. Both of you have had a career that has spanned thirty-plus years and still is going strong. Do you find that you have become cramped by your own success? Do you have readers who expect certain things because of their devotion to the early Palomar work or the early Maggie and Hopey stories? Do you find that it's hard to break from those reader wants and expectations?

GH: Lately, I've been able to deal with it by using the old [Federico] Fellini *8 1/2* thing: if you don't have an idea, create a story about *not* having an idea. But you don't want to repeat that. You want to do something different but along those lines.

I did have the pressure to return to Palomar. I was putting the pressure on myself, actually. And I tried to do it. I realized that what I was coming up with was that I don't have a reason to go back there. Often what happens to artists when they go back to places they don't really belong is that they start to trash it. They criticize what they did before. I wanted to avoid that, even though that sort of thing encroaches. So, I pulled back and started making fantasy versions of those earlier moments—having a couple of movie versions of things that have already happened. In the end I can trash it in the fantasy, but I don't want to trash it as it happened.

CG: You're doing that now . . .

GH: I have a character who is Luba's granddaughter. She wants to go back to the Palomar that we all know, the one we all grew up with. The '80s Palomar. Well, she wants to do that, but everybody's moved on. We've moved on. You can read it in the reprints. You can read the stories. You can want more, but it's done. I'm going to be fifty-seven years old. It's done. I was twenty-five when I started Palomar. It's done. But it doesn't mean I can't ever go back; it's just that I'm not there right now. So, I have a character going back looking for *that* Palomar that's not there. And when the story ends, she'll have accepted that *she's* the new Palomar. She doesn't know that yet.

CG: This is a not-so-subtle message to the reader, right? The desire to have Gilbert go back and create more and more stories from that time—that '80s Palomar, as you put it. I think of that old Thomas Wolfe line, "You can't go home again."

GH: Yeah, but I don't want to criticize the readers for their desire. They don't want to go back and wallow in nostalgia. They want to go back for good reasons. These stories were vital to the reader. They were vital for me when I was doing them. They meant a lot to my work in those days. So, it's not nonsense that they want to go back there. It's just that it's not there right now for me. I have to deal with that.

I wondered, how do I do that without trashing it? I figured, that will be my story. Let's try to go back to that Palomar knowing you can't. I might change my mind in two years if I've got a Palomar story! You never nuke the place. You let it live.

CG: What do you make of your readership these days, Jaime? Do they want the early Jaime stuff?

JH: I'm not trying to diss my readers. I've learned along the way that readers say things like, "Oh, I want Maggie and Hopey!" And I ask myself, "Okay. Maggie and Hopey. What are they doing right now?" Well, they're pretty boring right now. Well, they *are* boring, right? So, I make their lives . . . pretty boring! [*laughter*] And I've noticed a lot of responses where readers will say, "Oh, my god! I was totally blown away by this Maggie and Hopey story because I had no idea! I didn't expect . . . " And I wonder, "Did they want nostalgia? Did they want me to go back to fun Maggie and Hopey?" But I showed them a different Maggie and Hopey, and their response was, "Whoa! I didn't expect this. This is pretty good." I've just noticed hints along the way that suggest the older I get, the older my characters get.

GH: Young people act different from people getting older. We can't expect Maggie and Hopey in their late forties or whatever to crawl through windows again and steal beer. And it's not that for us either. I don't want to say, "It's over," that I'm abandoning a return to those early stories. But it's like asking, what am I doing hanging out with twenty-five-year-olds!

CG: You get older. Your characters get older . . .

JH: Yeah. I've got a new Maggie and Hopey story I'm working on right now, and they're like grandmas. I think, "But people like the whole exuberant stealing beer Gilbert mentioned for Maggie and Hopey." Well, guess what Maggie and Hopey are reflecting on in the story? They think, "Remember when we were young?" It's there because they are these old ladies talking about, "Remember when we were dumb and carefree?" It's just old people like me talking about the past.

GH: It's not always easy to be reminded of that. Oh, I am older and I want to look at things differently. I actually think my characters are sexier, my women, when they're older. So I like doing that. But then I remember, young people want to read about young people. And if I want new readers I have to consider that.

CG: Growing your readership?

GH: We always want new readers. Our original readers are fine, but they're getting older. You always want younger readers, and they're not going to want to read about old people.

JH: I've introduced young teenagers—sixteen-year-olds—in my newest stuff. Yet I've got a lot of fans clamoring for Maggie and Hopey, still. And I think, "So, you don't care that they're old people as long as it's Maggie and Hopey." Something in there can be worked out. I can have both parts of it.

Writing stories about young people is hard. I ask, "What do you guys *talk* about?" I don't remember a lot of stuff I thought about when I was young, or how I reacted to certain things. Now I watch my daughter react to certain things and think, "Why are you making such a big fuss about *that*?" I realize, "Oh, yeah. That was natural to make a big fuss about nothing when I was young."

KINETIC CHARACTERS

CG: Related to this issue of age, an early decision in both of your works was to have the characters grow, age, and die, whereas many serialized comic characters remain in a stasis. One readily thinks of Schulz's *Peanuts* and Matt Groening's animated series *The Simpsons*, where it's as if a reset button is pressed at the start of every installment.

GH: That's true. Bart's been nine years old for twenty years now.

CG: Was the growth of your characters a reflection of your own observations of getting older?

GH: I learned as a kid that longevity was important; as little kids we would watch movies from the forties with our mom and I would think, "These people are still a big deal." I loved superhero comics, but when I learned about comic strips and how long they lasted—*Blondie* started in the late twenties and it's still in newspapers—I understood, "That must make it important."

CG: Strips do have a different relationship with time and continuity . . .

GH: The closest example of what I was looking for was *Gasoline Alley*. That was a strip that started in the thirties. It was just about a garage and a guy named Walt Wallet. He was a doofus shuffling around this little town. Then one day somebody left a baby on his doorstep. So what the artist, Frank King, decided to do was age the kid in real time. Now, you have to be careful because "in real time" means you're doing a daily strip. So King had to balance it. You'd actually see the baby turn into a little boy, then into a teen, and so forth. Skeezix the character grew as we grew. They didn't rush that. There weren't flashbacks or flashforwards or anything. I was amazed.

CG: Skeezix had a life that unfolded over time, just like the readers of *Gasoline Alley*.

GH: That really fascinated me as a kid. I wanted something like that, but I knew I had to do it differently. I wasn't doing comic strips. How could I do this in a comic book? I thought, I would age the characters as *I* get older but maybe not as fast. Of course, when you have a large cast of characters, the other characters have to age, too. The ones that should stay eleven years old, like my Venus character, should be eleven years all the time. Well, she's not now; she's in her thirties now. And if this doesn't work for me, that's why she's not in the strip. Right now, anyway. And my wife always complains, "Well, why did you age her?" And I answer, "Because *nobody* can age if Venus stays eleven." All my other characters can't age.

CG: It shows how the cast is connected in time. That must present a host of difficulties in the stories you want to tell.

GH: What I do now is balance it out by removing characters that you want to stay the same from the stories so you don't see or think about them while the other ones are aging. I'm okay with the idea of just throwing in a story where Venus is still eleven. But once I age a character I don't want to go back. Except when information is needed to bolster a new story. In the next issue of *Love & Rockets* I'm working on now featuring Fritz, I'm actually showing her as a fifteen-year-old again. Because it's in the service of what's going on now. I'm willing to do that, but I won't go back and do it for a series. I like moving forward, but you can't move forward too fast because you'll age your characters too fast!

JH: If you want to keep somebody young, you'd better do it all in one chunk because they're going to have to catch up with the rest of the characters. There have been times in the past when I wanted to replace a character with a young person. I can't do Maggie at seventeen anymore unless it's a flashback. So I come up with a new seventeen-year-old. It doesn't always work. You can't replace Betty and Veronica, as much as you try and argue, "Oh, Betty and Veronica, they've gone on to better things. Let's create a new character!"

CG: They've become too iconic at that point to be replaced.

GH: Yeah. You can't make a new Hopey. She is so defined. You can make approximations, but it doesn't work. They might work in the plot of a story, but they aren't the characters. That's not going to be Hopey. Hopey is Hopey, and that's it.

CG: I think it might be interesting to have you comment on each other's signature characters. Jaime, what does Luba mean for Gilbert's work, for Palomar?

JH: It's hard to describe Luba. She is almost more Palomar than Palomar is. She is what everything returns to. Even if originally she was the outsider coming into Palomar, she became that base character that everything revolves around—even when she's not doing anything major to turn the plot. She bones her boyfriend and is happy. That's basically her role at that moment. Yet all these things revolve around her.

GH: I've been fighting myself with this Palomar stuff forever and Jaime just nailed why I can't go back. Because Luba's not there. I never even considered that idea.

JH: I didn't either.

GH: I never considered that I can't go back to Palomar because Luba's not going back. The characters will dictate where we go. And if the characters are so well defined like Luba for me and Maggie and Hopey for Jaime, they will control us. Not all the characters will because we can boss them around. But there are certain ones that will not let us do stuff because they're right and I'm wrong. Luba can't go back to Palomar, so *I* can't go back to Palomar. She's the one that's blocking me.

CG: Luba and her hammer, blocking Gilbert . . .

GH: Now, that could just be a neurotic thing in my head that I don't fully understand yet, but I have to go with that. Fighting it would disrupt the space-time continuum for me.

JH: And it would also take away from her personality. Her character.

GH: It's almost like I'd be saying, "Just kidding! She's going back to Palomar." It doesn't work for me that way. Luba's done with Palomar. She's in America. She doesn't want to go back.

As a matter of fact, I have a story coming up where one-time favorite characters are getting married, and they're in Palomar. It's another gathering of people going to Palomar, but Luba's not there. She's made all these excuses for why she can't be there. She should be there. She's the mother. But I can't take her back there. She doesn't belong . . .

JH: It's almost like the town was really born when she arrived.

GH: Exactly. The town was born when she arrived.

CG: I've often thought that exact same point—that Luba shows up like Athena, fully formed, and that's when you have Palomar. And when she's gone, Palomar's out of mind.

JH: Well, she obviously changed a lot of people's minds in Palomar when she arrived . . .

CG: Gilbert, maybe you could comment on Maggie and Hopey . . .

GH: What's interesting is that I consider myself a Jekyll-and-Hyde artist. Dr. Jekyll will do the *Marble Season*, *Julio's Day*, and the easier-going stories in Palomar. But I do have a Mr. Hyde in me: the Fritz stories.

Jaime is not always aware he's Jekyll and Hyde. Hopey is Mr. Hyde and Maggie is Dr. Jekyll. But sometimes there is a period where Dr. Jekyll is so mean that you didn't even notice it. That's not where you wanted to go. You didn't want to go make Hopey mean just to be mean. You wanted to make her abrasive for the story's sake. And Jaime doesn't like to go to the darker side. There was a period when Hopey went to the darker side, just a little bit. I'm not sure Jaime is aware of this, even. I hear people say, "Wow. Why is Hopey doing that?" And Jaime will answer, "Oh, I didn't notice." I think his unconscious starts to put it down on paper without him being aware of how dark it's getting.

CG: You're unaware of the darkness?

GH: We've gone through periods where we thought we were having fun, and people say, "Why is *Love & Rockets* so dark and mean and bleak?" And our reaction is, "Huh? What? What are you talking about? I was happy doing this story!" I think I'm a little bit more aware of the darkness because I wallow in it. Jaime doesn't so much.

CG: I wanted to ask you about the academic interest now in comics that has surged in the last decade or two. In comics generally, but, lately, in Latino comics. How do you engage with Latino identity in your work? Do you attempt to normalize it? Or, like the darkness, are you unaware of it?

GH: For me, it was about humanizing Latinos. A *conscious* effort to humanize Latinos. Back when I used Luba, originally in the throwaway science fiction *BEM* story, she was a part of the imagery of trash comics and trash cinema, like a voluptuous woman from a Russ Meyer movie. When I started developing the story and developing making comics, my needs for myself were more humanistic. I'd rather just have people hanging out and talking. So I started to pull away from that other stuff, but I still thought characters like Luba worked. I thought, let me humanize what was originally a character grown from trashy roots.

CG: Does it often happen that you find yourself somehow redeeming a throwaway character?

GH: A lot of my work has come from that. I would start from a trashy angle, then I would take this to a better place. Luba was actually a trashy icon, but she wasn't a throwaway. When I brought her to Palomar, she still had that aspect—you'll notice there are little moments in the early Palomar stories where I'm hinting toward the old Luba—but I left it in the dialogue because it just worked for the story. She's actually referring to *BEM* and things like that, but I dropped all that because it was unnecessary to continue.

I also liked picking on the audience. Back then, I was still in my punky attitude. The fact that people scolded me about Luba just made me want to do more stories with her at the center. But the more I did her, the more I humanized her. And the more I liked doing Luba, after a while she was my character. You want characters to express yourself in places where you don't normally in real life. Somebody like Luba was all over the place and she had a temper because that was fun for me to express. But I always reined her in to keep her human. Much of her excesses were simply her flaws. But when you browse a comic and see a woman with humongous tits like that, you just think, "What's this about?" I consider this automatic criticism to be a challenge for me to create a story that asks readers to read carefully what she's saying and to focus on the complexity of the story.

CG: Maybe I could ask you, Gilbert, about Fritz. We talked about Luba. Fritz now seems to be reaching that kind of Luba status. Her character is continually growing. . . .

GH: So to speak.

JH: It's like me talking about Maggie: She's a well-rounded character!

CG: [*To Gilbert*] It seems that Fritz has opened up more avenues to experiment with different kinds of storytelling, such as the use of B-flicks.

GH: Well, Fritz was one of the first characters I ever created, but she never had a personality. I just liked drawing her; I liked putting her in situations. So that's what she became: the character who goes into situations but is more or less a blank slate. As it turns out, she's one of my most screwed-up characters. Give me screwed-up characters and I'm on my way!

Fritz was a born actress and knows how to hide it. She's very pleasant. She can talk to you nicely. She has high-paying jobs, including as a well-paid psychotherapist. Now she's an even higher paid actress. She divorced a millionaire. She's got so much money that I just put that in the background. I didn't even want her dealing with it. She's the most neurotic of all my characters. She also accepts abuse, which makes her very difficult for readers. Whereas Luba wouldn't take shit, Fritz will take it and just smile pleasantly or cry about it. The only time she's real is with her wife, Pipo, but she can't talk to Pipo without crying all the time. Pipo found that sexy at first. Now, she's sick of it.

It's because Fritz was a blank slate that I could give her all these attributes, including her neurotic impulses. It's this blank slate that allows me to take her into unexpected places. She goes anywhere. In the next Fritz collection where she plays her mother, *Maria M.*, she confounds readers. That she portrays her mother displeases the *Love & Rockets* family. So while Fritz is no longer in the comic book, she's spoken of; the characters talk about her like she's some kind of legend. Making this connection between *Maria M.* and *Love & Rockets* can be difficult for readers.

CG: In that sense, Fritz is an extreme character.

GH: Fritz started out in porn! She was in *Birdland*. Like a lot of my characters, like Luba, they start out in a trashy environment and then develop into fuller characters.

LOS BROS RECEIVED

CG: How does Latino culture infuse your work, Jaime?

JH: Like Gilbert, in the beginning it was just about an impulse to humanize. Just showing what I knew. I thought, "I'm not seeing this on TV. I'm not seeing this in movies. Or I'm not seeing it done correctly." I wanted to draw these comics of how it was for me as a Latino growing up. As I was humanizing my Latino characters and my Latino world, creating my own little version of my growing up, I got criticism from some Latinos: "Why are you not exploring the Latino cause? Why are you not doing that?" Part of me wanted to respond, "I was getting drunk with my friends!"

GH: How empowering is that?

JH: I was sorry I didn't go to marches but our life was about day-to-day survival, sometimes leading to getting drunk with friends. I'm not putting down the cause. It's just that I was creating from what I knew.

As the years passed and the response to our comics started coming, I realized that my comic is like history. History's not written while it's happening. It's written down after it's happened. I'm giving you this comic about *my* Latino cause—*my* world, how these people interact, how they relate to the larger world. Now *Love & Rockets* is history because of the stories we did. So, I treat the trials and tribulations of Latinos growing up in Southern California as events that happened—as history. It's history like the "Sleepy Lagoon murder" of José Gallardo Díaz, Reuben Salazar getting killed.

CG: You both received criticism for not being political enough—not *Latino* enough. Yet, having these Latino characters you've created on the page being so *humanized* does important work in the complex shaping of how people conceive of Latinos. They aren't always necessarily activists or stereotypes. They are just regular people that struggle to overcome challenges like everybody else, even if those challenges may be different.

JH: It's like the argument about the Catholic church. You hear the political side that the Catholic church [is] against women and so on. Yet, who is going to tell that ninety-year-old lady who goes to church and prays for hours every Sunday that she shouldn't be doing that? Sure, I understand the political argument, but I understand hers, too. I'm not going to tell my mom not to go to church.

GH: With the your-work's-not-Latino-enough argument I accept the part that I didn't emphasize the Latinoness in the imagery—on covers, especially. Sometimes we would get into a kick and say, "Okay, I'm going to give them a Latino cover." But we'd only do it once in a while. Maybe I should have emphasized it more.

JH: It's kind of like your hip-hop cover, Gilbert. With Junior Brooks on the cover. You're just yelling at the reader in that cover.

GH: And it was time to do that. And it got a good response, so why didn't I do more of this? It's not a big regret, but I do see the argument to represent. We had covers and we were out there in the stores. So why didn't I make it clear that these are Latinos?

We were looking at comics more as art, as storytelling. I wouldn't say we would forget being Latino, but we just weren't thinking that that should be emphasized.

JH: Sometimes you have to clobber them over the head.

GH: I think I just missed some opportunities for that. That's why I want to reconsider doing covers now for *Love & Rockets*. We only do them every two years now! So, I got to think, what do I want to represent now?

CG: You receive criticism, and you criticize yourself as well . . .

GH: Twice I heard that Will Eisner (*The Spirit*) and Burne Hogarth (*Tarzan* comic strip) were critical of how [my work] started out with a Latino focus, but that I dropped this and became boring; that I should go back to making it about Latino culture. It was like they thought [my work was] not Latin enough, but I asked, what do you mean it's not Latin enough? I'm Latin enough!

I suspect both of Eisner and Hogarth were criticized for being racist. After all, Will Eisner created one of the most racist, idiotic characters in comic book history—Ebony, for *The Spirit*. He had to apologize for the rest of his life for that. Hogarth was criticized for Tarzan, which is essentially a racist character. Here's this white guy running the jungle when there's a bunch of locals who could be doing the same thing.

JH: Running a whole continent.

GH: Right! A whole continent! This aside, both strips are brilliant. And maybe Eisner and Hogarth were critical of my work out of guilt for their own racist screw ups. Will Eisner became the Jewish cartoonist, remember? All his stories were just about being Jewish and Jewish people. And Hogarth became a teacher.

CG: Over time you both become the mantle bearers for all things Latino, and it has to be explicitly rendered in your comics. It can't be subtle. It can't be matter-of-fact as part of daily life.

GH: I wonder if we *had* been more militant how it would have gone. I'm talking about the covers and the stories focused more on being Latino. Would that have died? Would that have killed the comic? One thing we always wanted to do was never alienate the readers, no matter what culture they're from.

We invite the readers no matter their background. Sometimes when you just get too militant, all of a sudden your readers drop off and you've got twelve readers left. I need to make a living, so you make some compromises.

JH: But there's nothing wrong with putting in little stabs once in a while. I notice in the past, Gilbert and I have made little, tiny quips about white people.

GH: In one of my stories there was this little kid who was complaining about how she'd never met a white person. She's a little Palomar kid, and she remarks, "Oh, I heard they smell like pee." I heard this garbage growing up and knew it wasn't true. But I put that in the story, and it read so badly! I turned it into, "I hear they dance like ducks." That's bad enough, but at least it's not evil. So, I would restrain myself.

CG: So it wouldn't become a little too real?

GH: You have to cut out reality sometimes if you don't want to alienate your readers. Especially the readers we had at the time. Some realities you just keep behind the door, man. It's just ugly to spread.

JH: At times you wonder: do you want to start a fight or don't you? I don't think *not* starting a fight is weak. It's just maintaining a certain balance so your work can do its job without you throwing in a quip here or there.

TELLING, SHOWING, AND THE X-RATED BROS

CG: Quite often both of you create your stories out of order. It's a non-linear style. For someone who is now discovering *Love & Rockets* for the first time, it might be hard for them to find an entry point. Could you talk about the process of creating these stories knowing that you've already covered certain topics, making sure you don't step on or contradict an earlier story line.

GH: That would be the only reason I'd look at my old stories. I don't look at my old stories for entertainment anymore—to experience again what I felt when I made them. I only look for references to establish continuity. As we're getting older, Jaime and I, we *are* forgetting what we did in the early days. We are forgetting details of information you don't want to mess with.

I realize that character already said that 25 years ago or that they already dealt with this issue and I realize that I screwed up. I don't want to make those mistakes.

When I read a bunch of the old serialized Marvel comics in one sitting I realized that they screwed up the information, but I let it go. It's hard for me to let it go when I screw up information like that. Like when you, Jaime, were talking about the number of brothers or the number of people in a family.

JH: Yeah. I created whole epic stories just to correct mistakes. Sometimes it works out for the better.

CG: *Birdland* follows a tradition forged by Robert Crumb and others who pushed that explicit sexual content in comics. What do you make of academics who are considering something like *Birdland* from a scholarly perspective?

GH: That's kind of funny to me. To me, porn is porn. Whether it's funny, sexy, or whatever, it's still porn. I make no illusions. So when you talk about it in a serious way, I can see how you're looking at how the story is handled, how it was drawn, how the intensity was here or there. This I can accept. But as anything more than that, I'll let you guys take care of that.

CG: But isn't *Birdland* more than just porn?

GH: It's really just an over-the-top action comic using sex. Instead of using superheroes and violence, I decided to make the most intense sex comic—without the violence. American artists tend to mix violence and sex together. This is okay. I do this with the Fritz books. But with *Birdland* I wanted to drop all that and create a work that depicts sex in the most in-tensely physical way I could without hatred. Now I look at it and think that I could have drawn it better. I can't believe how many hard-ons I drew! I don't know if I could even do that again.

CG: Did you fear it would affect how people see your larger *oeuvre*?

GH: I worried a little that it might hurt my reputation. After *Birdland* was published, *Love & Rockets* started getting more serious attention. Oddly enough, it hasn't bitten me in the ass. After all, Robert Crumb is a national treasure and he's done the most disgusting porn you can imagine in his stories. If it didn't hurt him, how's it going to hurt me?

CG: Jaime, within the past few years you've really played with the super-hero trope in your comics on the Ti-Girls. Could you talk about this turn in your work?

JH: *Ti-Girls* came along because I just wanted to breathe. The continuity of *Love & Rockets* was going at its usual, intense pace. I just wanted to draw sexy girls in tights. Seriously. It's funny you guys talking about *Birdland* because *Ti-Girls* was just supposed to be a fun romp, socking through walls and the like. I was happy to create a world outside of *Love & Rockets*, even if at times Maggie was involved.

Obviously, *Birdland* had structure to it. It did have Gilbert inside it. He didn't just throw it on autopilot and let it fly. He put a lot of hard work into what might be considered fluff. That's how the *Ti-Girls* turned out. It became something because I couldn't let it leave my grasp. There's always got to be something underneath all the fluff for me to finally feel satisfied and let it go.

GH: It's interesting what Jaime's saying. You start out wanting to just make a goofy romp, or fluff, as he says, and then it becomes really intense no matter how much you try to avoid that. *Birdland* became this intense, overly complex story. To the point where every panel had to have a gag—a funny quip. That's a gag for six panels a page. Like Jaime said, you want to just have fun with it, then it becomes this intense story.

OTHER MEDIA RECREATIONS

CG: Palomar has been discussed as having the makings of a great film. Arguably, TV is able to do certain things in storytelling better than Hollywood. Do either of you envision the Maggie and Hopey stories or the Palomar stories as working perhaps better in the television medium rather than in film?

GH: While my dream was to see Palomar as a movie, I'm willing to see it as a TV series. It would have to be a pretty faithful version of Palomar. I don't see a transformed Palomar. I think a lot of *Love & Rockets* is simply stuff we wanted to see as it is, not as we dream it to be something else. I don't see Palomar as working as anything else but what it is. How do you sell to producers the making of a show that's about a small town with Latinos where nothing goes on? They'd likely ask if it has to be a small town and if they all have to be Hispanic and not get what the story's about.

Did you know there's a resistance to Luba? The media industry doesn't know what to do with her.

JH: She's your Wonder Woman.

CG: Hollywood couldn't handle her.

GH: After all, we have the bombshell Sofia Vergara on *Modern Family*, but notice all the Latinas that end up getting a name all have to be bombshells. There are no Latinas that are seen as great actresses. No, they're always bombshells. Then they get noticed. *Then* if they go on to do other things, that's fine. But they're only let in if they're bombshells.

CG: Could Maggie and Hopey work in a TV series, Jaime?

JH: I guess it depends on what I want to tell. Part of me likes a movie—two hours beginning to end, and it stands by itself. Another part of me thinks this is a serialized comic and do I want to tell certain stories as I'm going along? The older I'm getting, the less interested I am in adapting it. Like Gilbert was saying, it is what it is. *Love & Rockets* was created because of something missing.

GH: Jaime's stuff is easier to approximate on screen than Palomar. Palomar is a small town with dark-skinned people, with Luba, and all that stuff. Whereas Maggie and Hopey, even though they are Latina, producers could change it so that they're white girls; there are plenty movies with these two types of white-girl characters, or combinations of the two types, such as in the movie *Juno*. Jason Reitman's *Juno* is the Hopey movie 25 years later. This said, what would be important in making the film adaptation of *Locas* would be to keep them as Latinas. We've seen the types with white girls, but not with Latinas.

CG: Both of you have incorporated different genres in your works. You've brought in the superhero, science fiction, porno, and B-flick exploitation genre. What remains untapped for you both?

JH: The short answer is that all my energy goes into *Love & Rockets*. I'm not sure I have the strength to explore other genres and stories. I might want to do a Western, but I don't have the energy to research it. I don't draw horses very well, and I don't want to learn to draw horses well. But every once in a while I get the idea of creating a hundred-page story about the Mechanics characters without Maggie, like taking one of the characters when they were young and creating a whole epic along the lines of *The Wages of Fear*, where these guys have to do this impossible job and keep getting into danger. I've always wanted to do the story of these space mechanic guys—maybe they're not even space mechanics anymore.

CG: What would it take to make the Mechanics story happen?

JH: The way I work is, whatever ideas come first get the job. I don't work as fast as Gilbert. And I need to fill the pages. I respond to whoever comes to me with a story first: "Okay, what do you guys got for me? Okay, Maggie. You got something? C'mon. Let's go. Show me a story." It's usually Maggie that comes first because she writes her own material.

I can't wait for the Mechanics story to gel. One day I might wake up and have a *reason* why I'm creating the story.

CG: What genre remains for Gilbert Hernandez to tackle?

GH: I've never created a single story, let's say graphic novel, for intelligent, educated grown-ups. They've always had some element of trashiness, genre elements, or over-the-top comedy. I've never created a straightforward story that features adults dealing with adult things without the distraction of violence or crime or whatever. It doesn't have to be a dry, humorless story, but it does have to be about people that have a life. I rely so much on my interests from the past—beautiful, sexy women and scary monsters, for instance—that I don't want these to become a crutch; these elements can spice up the story, but I want it to be a story for intelligent grown-ups that stands on its own two feet. Even something like *Julio's Day*, which might be the most serious story I've ever created, has a lot of genre aspects to it, including magical realism. I wonder, when am I going to do a story that doesn't rely on those things?

PART II

CUERPO COMICS

FOUR

BIOGRAPHIC CHALLENGES: WILFRED SANTIAGO'S
21: THE STORY OF ROBERTO CLEMENTE

CHRISTOPHER GONZÁLEZ

THE LIONIZATION OF Roberto Clemente commenced upon news of his death on December 31, 1972.[1] Clemente, who would later become the first Latino professional player to be inducted into the Major League Baseball (MLB) Hall of Fame, had just taken the final step into the pantheon of superlative baseballers just three months prior. With his three thousandth hit — an achievement only ten other players had managed at the time — Clemente was bound to become immortalized in the eyes of a game that so loves and relies upon its history and statistical records.[2] That he did not live to attempt even one more hit makes his career and life all the more moving, and the seeming inevitability of what he was poised to accomplish had he not died so abruptly and unexpectedly has helped make Clemente a colossus in baseball lore. Little surprise that numerous biographies have attempted to bring Clemente's life and death to account.

In 2011 Wilfred Santiago, illustrator and comics artist, added to this list of books on Clemente's life in graphic novel form. *21: The Story of Roberto Clemente* (2011) is an intriguing contribution to both an understanding of Clemente's life as well as the comics medium itself. As a matter of biography, Santiago's book does not seek to reshape our understanding of Clemente's life by providing new insights gleaned from, say, newly found or previously ignored information. Santiago is not a journalist like David Maraniss, whose well-received biography on Clemente — written in narrative prose — was published in 2006.[3] Indeed, the medium of comics, the unique interplay of the visual and verbal text that cohere to weave a narrative, plays a crucial role in Santiago's take on Clemente's life story. The book uses elements of narrative fiction as well as comic book storytelling that yank Clemente ever so slightly from a fact-based reality. He is, in short, rendered as a cartoon image. Consequently, Santiago's Clemente has an otherworldly feel to him, particularly when his physicality is represented on the page.[4] In effect, Santiago's graphic

4.1. Pittsburgh Pirates fans literally have their hearts ripped out, from *21: The Story of Roberto Clemente*.

biography of Clemente is not literal; it is metaphorical, yielding an effect that cannot be replicated in a traditional biography[5] that constantly strives to adhere to the historical record. For instance, at one point in the book Santiago plays on the metaphor of having your heart ripped out (i.e., "disheartened") when something does not go your way (see figure 4.1). In this case, Santiago depicts the Pittsburgh Pirates fans with their hearts literally wrenched from their bodies after Mickey Mantle's New York Yankees crushed the Pirates 15–1 in 1960. The game that was played is a matter of historical record. However, the historical record also shows that no human hearts were removed from any fans' bodies on that day in Pittsburgh. Indeed, as Paul Buhle observes, "Comic art can, of course, be used to tell a very different kind of history, aimed closer to a narrative beyond personal or family experience, distant from oral history and thereby closer to the historian's familiar art."[6]

What is it about a biography in comics form that allows for a malleability of storytelling unfettered by a devotion to the mimetic? While there have been many robust explorations of autobiography in comics by a host of scholars, there are too few investigations in the area of graphic biography, or what I am calling the "biographic" in this essay. In their structure, biographics are inherently different than "autographics" or "autography."[7] For example, in an autobiographic there is a consistent type of narrator that is a reflection or projection of the author, most often as a retrospective narrator. That is to say, both the images and the verbal text on the page emanate from the author, who narrates some slice of his or her own life. Not only are such authors writing a narrative derived from their own life events, but they literally turn themselves into a cartoon image on the page. Someone like Alison Bechdel renders her father, her mother, and herself as the subjects of her books. *Fun Home* (2006) and *Are You My Mother?* (2012) are each a manifestation of the interplay of Bechdel's memory and artistic creativity, and each is called into service in creating her narratives. Conversely, in a biographic the author has had no personal interaction with the narrative subject, and in that sense so much more of the process of characterizing becomes a function of imagination and interpretation rather than memory.

This essay will explore the formal elements in biographics using *21: The Story of Roberto Clemente* as a case study. I assert that a biographic can do something, narratively speaking, that biography cannot—that they are inherently a different kind of narrative activity. Though biographies and biographics appear to engage in the same sort of narrative activity, their respective media enable them to weave different types of narratives. Second, despite using what is ostensibly the same mode of storytelling (i.e., the image/text), autographics and biographics have different structural underpinnings as well. I lay out the historical and theoretical contexts for a sharper accounting of the biographic form in contrast to biography and autographics. Next, I situate Santiago within Latino/a comics as well as examine his general use of formal elements such as color, panels, and narration. Finally, I demonstrate how Santiago's careful use of form in *21: The Story of Roberto Clemente* embodies a significant contribution to Latino comics as well as to our understanding of both biography and comics.

BIOGRAPHICS

Challenges to traditional literary forms inevitably cause scholars to scramble for an explanation. As the comics art form continues to be used by its practitioners in a myriad of ways, scholars of conventional forms such as biography and history are suddenly confronted with understanding the implications of such a cross-pollination of genres. For instance, Mary Louise Penaz closes her essay, "Drawing History: Interpretation in the Illustrated Version of the *9/11 Commission Report* and Art Spiegelman's *In the Shadow of No Towers* as Historical Biography," by calling the graphic historical biography "that genre monstrosity."[8] Penaz excoriates the writer and the illustrator of *The 9/11 Commission Report*, Sid Jacobson and Ernie Colón, respectively, for their adaptation of the actual 9/11 commission report in the comics medium, characterizing it as "an important, yet troubling, historical biography."[9] Noting the graphic adaptation of *The 9/11 Commission Report* as "signal[ing] a new direction for biographical studies," Penaz faults Jacobson and Colón for adopting many traditional conventions of comics artists, though she calls them "spurious truth claims and problematic use of voice and perspective."[10] As a result, Jacobson and Colón's version of *The 9/11 Commission Report* cannot hope to meet Penaz's standard of a biography because her standard is established by the convention of the *traditionally written* biography. On the other hand, Penaz views Art Spiegelman's *In the Shadow of No Towers* in a positive light for its attempt to "undermine or complicate 9/11."[11]

Anyone who has read either of the biographies Penaz examines will immediately recognize that they are vastly different texts that have vastly different aims in terms of an ideal reader. Spiegelman's text is personal, and there are many elements that make his book much more *auto*biographical than Jacobson and Colón's book. For instance, Jacobson and Colón never reference themselves in their narrative, while Spiegelman does. While I agree with Penaz that there are shortcomings to the graphic narrative version of *The 9/11 Commission Report*, I do not ascribe those shortcomings to some agenda or deficiency on the part of the author and illustrator. Rather, it is the comics medium itself (in this case its use in the service of a government report) that undergirds its faultiness. Because there can never be a one-for-one correspondence in any adaptation across media, Jacobson and Colón's version ought not be held to the same standard as the original report. It is also unfortunate that such limitations impinge on such a weighty and somber document.

Nevertheless, Penaz's issue with the graphic adaptation of *The 9/11 Commission Report* is important, for it exposes a crucial fault line where biography and comics meet. In biography there is what I call a devotion to historical fact, and any deviation from historical fact makes the biography suspect. This, I argue, is Penaz's major criticism with Jacobson and Colón's adaptation. Unfortunately for Jacobson and Colón, they constantly emphasize their effort in adhering strictly to the official record. But this is an impossibility in a biographic that is inextricable from the medium itself. Such intractability comes from the difference between prose and graphic narrative.

When readers reconstruct storyworlds from narratives they read, there are always characteristics of the narratives that go a long way in determining what is ultimately constructed in the reader's mind. Narrative voice, focalization, time, space, and so on are factors to be considered in shaping the narrative within the mind. Significantly, what is left unsaid, the gaps within the narrative, are those aspects that lie squarely in the reader's discretion. Whereas prose narrative uses words alone to suggest a storyworld, graphic narrative employs two-dimensional images (that simulate a three-dimensional space) in service of its narrative. The implications of this fact are crucial. In reading the prose version of *The 9/11 Commission Report*, the reader is undoubtedly reconstructing the narrative in his or her mind using *photorealistic* images, perhaps based on memories of the various broadcasts, not cartoon versions of, say, Rudy Giuliani or the World Trade Center or the Pentagon. Thus, because Jacobson and Colón's adaptation is graphically rendered as cartoon images, it is separated from reality by default. It is an issue inherent to the medium.

On the other hand, why criticize the medium for something it never claims to be able to do? Jacobson and Colón are constrained by the official report. For example, Colón, as the illustrator, could not use a style that would make the human figures look like, say, an Art Spiegelman–drawn figure from *Maus*. Colón could not make the firefighters look like mice or cats. Nor could he use other tropes and techniques of graphic narrative in his illustrations that would similarly stretch the bounds of realism. Out of respect for the victims of that catastrophic day in 2001, Colón had no choice but to use a style that always did its best to cling to reality-based representations.

Here we have a distinguishing feature between biographics and autographics. When an artist creates a comic book or strip based on his or her own life, he or she is free to put the conventions of the medium to good use in service of the narrative. Spiegelman can use anthropomorphic figures in *Maus*, and the resulting effect, in his hands, is superb. An artist such as Wilfred Santiago, however, writing about a baseball player revered not only in the United States but in much of Latin America, must navigate the possibilities of cartooning amidst a devotion to the historical Clemente. This is the path Santiago must tread with care. He must work to do Clemente's life and memory justice while using the conventions of comic art to capture the ineffable quality of Clemente's greatness on the page. In short, Santiago has to make Clemente a superhero without making him a cartoon, a seeming paradox.

Thus, not only are biographics different from biographies, they are different from autographics as well. To be sure, they are not Künstlerromane, as Rocío G. Davis observes.[12] The author is in no way intimately connected to the subject of the narrative. The key difference, I argue, rests in the flexibility of the biographic storytelling mode and its ability to swerve into the terrain of the novelist—what might be called creative representation.[13] Because its readership inherently knows the biographic does not bear the onus of one-for-one correspondence to the historical record as a biography does (i.e., it announces its fictionality in its artist's rendering of people from history), the biographic has the capacity to allow its readers to "see" the represented subject as never before. Santiago uses this characteristic of the biographic to great effect. That is to say, a biographic does not confront the problem of "authenticity" in the way Charles Hatfield notes regarding autobiographical comics, about which he notes:

> Protean in form, it applies the narrative techniques of fiction to stories implicitly certified as "true," insofar as they defer to a level of experience "outside" the bounds of text. The tacit rules of the genre demand fidelity to such experience, yet storytelling demands license; narrative needs shaping. Thus autobiography inevitably mingles the factual and the fictive (even among the most scrupulous of practitioners). This blurring of boundaries presents a conundrum that criticism has been able only to turn over and over, never to resolve: what has storytelling to do with the facts?[14]

Because the life of another person, even of people conspicuously in the public eye, is always subject to interpretation, an adherence to the facts is much more pliable than autobiographical writing. To rephrase Hatfield's question, what has *biographic* storytelling to do with the facts?

Clearly, there is something about the biographic form that attracts Santiago, as in recent years he has created a pair of such works in rapid succession: *21: The Story of Roberto Clemente*, which is discussed below, and *Michael Jordan: Bull on Parade*, about another revered athlete, published in 2014.

CONSIDERATIONS OF LATINO/A COMICS

Little by little, with each passing novel, film, television series, and graphic novel, there is an accretion of a complex *latinidad* that is being formed in the American consciousness. As Frederick Luis Aldama observes:

> The final decades of the twentieth century and the first decade of the twenty-first century witness the rise of what we can strictly call a Latino/a literature, that is, a rich, varied and complex body of literary works that covers all genres, all formats—and all tastes: from lowbrow to middlebrow, to highbrow novels, short stories, poetry, drama, and comic books.[15]

This steady accretion occurring across media, across forms, and across genre conventions is manifest in the interstices of Latino/a literary and cultural production—spaces that serve as a kind of nursery for the proliferation of Latino/a literature itself. Latino/a comics in particular are shaping the way both comics art and Latino/a literature are now encountered:

> In the Latino graphic narratives, a whole field of artistic accomplishment is being built before our very eyes. Comic books appeared in the United States in the 1890s, and their so-called golden age—at least for those of the mainstream variety—took place between the 1930s and the 1950s. Now, in the twenty-first century, ethnic comics, and particularly their Latino components, are witnessing the arrival of their own golden age.[16]

Certainly, comic art is but one of many areas in this surge of Latino/a literary and cultural production, but it is a significant area precisely because, as Aldama notes above, this area is in its own golden age. Comics' importance is partially located not just in their historical context but also in the very form of the medium itself. Because of their adherence to the visual form of storytelling (the prominence of static images configured within panels is arguably the medium's defining feature), comics can often convey certain aspects of a narrative through a direct visual channel. Whenever a reader is confronted with an image in a comic, he or she has less control of the image. Unlike a verbal description, the visual image in a comic can be impactful or unsettling because there is little mediation. Since an image can be read without the sort of piecemeal assembly of verbal narrative where details slowly and steadily accumulate into an image within a reader's mind and at the reader's discretion, images in comics arguably have a direct route to the emotional systems of the reader as they bypass reconstruction of the narrative by matching the reader's personal compendium of signifier and signified. The image in comics remains consistent across readers, resisting the type of variability of storyworld reconstruction that occurs when narratives use words alone.

To be clear, I am not suggesting that comics are a superior form of storytelling. Throughout their history they have been pronounced as being exactly the opposite. On the other hand, if comics aren't inherently superior or inferior to other types of literary endeavors, we should at least acknowledge that they are a *different* form of storytelling, that our baseline ought to be different when engaging with comics. They are neither word-only blueprints for recreating storyworlds nor multisensory filmic experiences that allow for relatively little mediation on the part of the audience. Visual and verbal narrators shape the narrative discourse in comics through the creative interplay of image and text, and readers grapple alternatively with word and icon as they work their way to the end of a graphic narrative. If we can accept that comics are a different form of storytelling, then it strikes me as exceedingly useful to ask and examine how comics authors create narratives that are refracted through the experience of the marginalized subject. In fact, one of the reasons comics—as a literary art form—began to receive sustained study and recognition, beyond small, devoted audiences, is that they began confronting the problems faced by racial and ethnically Othered experiences.

The exemplar here is Art Spiegelman's *Maus*. This story of a son's attempt to understand his father by uncovering the traumatic experiences of having survived the Holocaust has become required reading in many high school and university English classrooms throughout the United States. And though the story is compelling and heartbreaking, its use of various animals as human stand-ins is easily Spiegelman's masterstroke. By casting the Jews as mice and the Nazis as cats, Spiegelman allows readers to approach the Holocaust from a different direction. In short, *Maus* is not a simple cat and mouse cartoon.

There are many quality examples of how the comics form of storytelling can grapple with serious issues that are inherently bound with identity, though several deserve mention here. Howard Cruse's *Stuck Rubber Baby* (1995) takes to task racism and violence during the Civil Rights Movement in the American South. Its depiction of a lynching, though fictional, nonetheless has the power to leave a reader shaken. *Palestine* (1996), by Joe Sacco, recounts the author's experiences in Gaza and the West Bank in the early 1990s. And Gene Yang's irreverent confrontation with the Chinese American stereotype in *American Born Chinese* (2006) powerfully interrupts understandings of race in America in an unabashedly direct style.

Latinos, too, have crafted important forays into the comics form, as Aldama's *Your Brain on Latino Comics* and the contributors to this very collection of essays demonstrate. Authors such as Gilbert and Jaime Hernandez, known as "Los Bros," Frank Espinosa, Javier Hernandez, Ilan Stavans with Lalo Alcaraz, and many more have spun Latino/a-infused graphic narratives. In the remainder of this essay, I examine the work of Wilfred Santiago, a Puerto Rico–born comics artist who has contributed two significant works to this area of Latino/a comics: *In My Darkest Hour*[17] and his biographic *21: The Story of Roberto Clemente*. A brief analysis of Santiago's will to style and depiction of *In My Darkest Hour*'s protagonist's body will inform my exploration of his use of the biographic form to cast new light on Roberto Clemente.

EMBODIMENT IN *IN MY DARKEST HOUR*

In My Darkest Hour, Santiago's first graphic novel, is a highly stylized, glossy-paged book that (in form) is atypical of the medium. The images of the text are not in the traditional black and white such as one finds in the vast majority of comics. Like the comics artists Lance Tooks and Ho Che Anderson, Santiago often employs photorealistic and corporate logo images to create a collage aesthetic that carries his narrative forward. His use of the photorealistic image is itself a key aspect of Santiago's work. As Scott McCloud theorizes in *Understanding Comics*, a reader is less apt to associate himself or herself with a photorealistic image, while an iconic image (McCloud cites the example of Charles Schulz's Charlie Brown) can more readily serve as a stand-in or Everyman with which readers may identify.[18]

If McCloud's notion of the photorealistic/iconic image holds true, then Santiago's protagonists resist a reader's ability to see himself or herself in the character, keeping the image always at arm's length throughout the comic. However, Santiago does not limit himself to the photorealistic. In fact, his protagonist, Omar Guerrero, is drawn in any number of ways that fall in highly distinct categories according to McCloud's diagram of the triangle with three vertices (The Picture Plane, "Reality," and Language) that "represents the total pictorial vocabulary of comics or of any of the visual arts."[19] Because of Omar's shifting image on the photorealistic/iconic gradation, reader identification with Omar's sliding image will also be in flux throughout the narrative progression. Unlike the constancy of how characters are represented in many comics, Santiago refuses to settle on one standard styling for Omar. (Incidentally, the same holds true for Clemente in *21*.) Thus, as the protagonist literally appears differently to a reader depending on the time space within the narrative, *In My Darkest Hour*'s thematic construction enables a similar movement of reader identification, ranging from disgust with to sympathy for Omar. It is no accident that a reader's "relationship" with Omar changes as his own image on the page changes. Santiago's protean depiction of Omar's physiognomy and body are thus highly consequential.

As a result, Omar's complexity affects readers' identification with him. Readers will likely be repulsed at his womanizing yet will sympathize with his struggles with substance addiction. Not only does Omar develop as do most protagonists in fiction, but his visual image, that is, Omar's body image as drawn by Santiago, undergoes significant changes via weight loss/gain, hairstyle, and emotional states. Indeed, at times Omar seems like a different character altogether (a manifestation of his bipolar disorder) not only because he "acts" differently, but because his visual image is also rendered differently. The collision of mixed media in Santiago's novel, according to Aldama, "blur[s] the boundary between the interiority of his Latino character . . . and the post-9/11 American collective psyche."[20] Indeed, Nicholas Hetrick has examined the psychological aspects of *In My Darkest Hour*, arguing that the novel's formal innovation lies in its representation of consciousness.[21] I support Hetrick's assessment, but I also find it difficult to ignore Omar's very embodiment within the pages of the book as being intertwined with his psychological travails. His body—at times unremarkable; at times grotesque during dream sequences—mirrors Omar's fragile sense of self. Put another way, Santiago's willful manipulation of Omar's body is a crucial ingredient to the narrative progression. To have Omar's body remain in static form would undermine the violent psychological trauma he experiences throughout *In My Darkest Hour*.

While the form of Santiago's innovative first novel complements the narrative content found within its pages, we might ask how a similar approach would work when the subject is an actual person, such as Roberto Clemente? How would a blending of media and a shifting of how Clemente's body is depicted affect how Santiago tells Clemente's already well-known life story? Here the considerations of the biographic come into play.

FROM MOMEN[22] TO EL MAGNIFICO

Published in 2011, Santiago's biographic of Clemente furthered the type of challenging storytelling he initiated in his stunning debut. Through his use of color, collage, fractured panels, and mixed media, Santiago tells Clemente's story in a manner that reflects the complexity of the Puerto Rican baseball legend. Santiago re-creates Clemente's life in the pages of his biographic, taking him from childhood to professional baseball player, and ultimately, to sacrificial Latino hero. There is no doubt that Clemente mystified many baseball fans in the United States. According to David C. Ogden:

> [Clemente's] reputation varied from culture to culture and from country to country. In his native Puerto Rico, his growing prowess on the field was a point of national pride. In the United States, however, he was an enigma: talented but erratic and sometimes not dependable. But toward the end of his playing days and in the years following his tragic, albeit storied, death, social forces and the insatiable hunger for heroes and legends have resculpted Clemente's reputation while recasting Clemente within the framework of new social and cultural perspectives.[23]

Indeed, not only is Santiago interested in Clemente's physicality as an athlete, but he also is eager to articulate Clemente's life through complex, careful design and depiction of his body—whether as an eager child, an emotionally distraught young man, or a man at the height of his success.

Here I return to my opening issue regarding what a biographic can do that a traditionally written biography cannot. Undoubtedly, Santiago's book on Clemente is distinctive from David Maraniss's biography. Each author approaches Clemente's life with all the conventions their respective medium affords. Maraniss is a well-respected biographer by trade; Santiago writes and illustrates comics. Maraniss weaves his stories with words alone, adhering closely to the historical record; Santiago uses the visual–verbal mode of storytelling where text often is used to underscore the image rather than the reverse. There is a personal component at play here that surfaces as well. Unlike Maraniss, Santiago shares his Puerto Rican heritage with Clemente. As John Seven notes in his *Publishers Weekly* piece on Santiago's biographic of Clemente, "Santiago felt that he might be able to tackle the baseball star's life from an angle usually not taken by other biographers—that of a fellow Puerto Rican."[24] Thus, not only does the comics medium lend itself to Clemente's preternatural physical gifts as if he were a superhero, but Santiago's own connection to Puerto Rican culture manifests in the shape—both literal and figural—he gives Clemente's story within the pages of his biographic, as well as in the care he takes to include excerpts from historical and encyclopedic sources.

Santiago's decision to take up the challenge of Clemente's biography told via comic art is a significant development. Without question, *21* marks a new direction in Latino/a comics, to say nothing of Latino/a literature in general. Take the relatively straightforward convention in comics whereby the narrative is broken into distinct parts via the panel. Los Bros Hernandez, who have dominated Latino/a comics for the last thirty years, rarely stray from the more traditional modes of graphic storytelling that employ black-and-white, rectilinear panel configurations. Thierry Groensteen and others have argued that the panel on a comic page is the essential unit of graphic storytelling.[25] But while the panel is a convenient organizing unit, more and more comics artists such as Wilfred Santiago are pushing against conventional usages of the panel in order to tell their stories (see figure 4.2). Indeed, Santiago's imaginative use of the panel, or even his decision at times not to use panels at all, or to overlap them haphazardly, as in the example above, ensures that his portrayal of Clemente's life will be unlike any other biography of the baseball player published heretofore.

This tradition and devotion to the panel as a building block of graphic storytelling and a convention of comics is essential in understanding Santiago's relationship with his audience. Breaking with tradition or convention, or at the least moving away from it, is surely a risky business for authors and publishing houses, but especially Latino/a or other so-called minority writers who are most often pigeonholed by publisher and audience expectations. For Santiago, his biographic of Clemente is unconventional in genre (what I am calling a biographic); is not exactly sportswriting or outright biography (unlike Maraniss's book); and defies expectations for graphic storytelling, as well as biography, in its formal structure. In this sense, we might call *21: The Story of Roberto Clemente* a challenging text in a dual sense. It is a challenging read, and it also challenges readers' understanding of Clemente's life.

Let me return once more to the kind of graphic storytelling predominantly found in the comics of Los Bros Hernandez by way of example. Gilbert and Jaime both employ a panel configuration that is essentially rectilinear. Invariably, a reader will encounter a page that is composed of boxes that are read from left to right and top to bottom. Los Bros rarely, if ever, deviate from this pattern of storytelling, which is a convention of the majority of American and European comics.[26] In terms of structure, their comics conform to established reading practices. This is not to say that the comics of Los Bros don't challenge readers; they do. It is just that their challenges are often presented to readers through the explicit nature of the stories they tell and to a lesser degree at the level of the panel.

Yet when storytelling convention is disregarded, be it through panel configuration or other formal devices, readers must suddenly grapple with the break in expected storytelling practices. (Consider figure 4.2 once more in this respect.) Signposts are critical—signals that help orient readers as they navigate through the storyworld. Put another way, when an author takes the risky move of compelling readers out of habitual reading practices, he or she must also guide readers through the process of learning how to read differently. It is an empowering authorial decision to change how the reader "reads" a book and, thus, how he or she engages with the subject of the narrative. This issue may help explain why there are readers who cannot make themselves comfortable with reading graphic novels; the free-flowing nature of reading comics produces a sense of discomfort within them, especially those that are experimental (or at least unconventional) in form. It is precisely this sense of discomfort that Santiago exploits in his depiction of Roberto Clemente's life.

AN ANALYSIS OF *21: THE STORY OF ROBERTO CLEMENTE*

Santiago's biographic on Roberto Clemente uses a variety of comic book conventions while focusing on key moments in the baseball player's life. What is undeniably his greatest moment as a baseball player occurred on September 30, 1972, when Clemente achieved his three thousandth hit before his home crowd in Pittsburgh. How did Clemente manage this rare achievement? This is the question Santiago sets out to address in his book, mostly through flash-back. Everything in the book works with Clemente's singular accomplish-ment in mind. When Santiago depicts Clemente as a small boy in Puerto Rico, readers are meant to feel how these seemingly small moments in a boy's life resonate with his future three thousandth hit. When Clemente leaves his family to play baseball in the United States, struggles with a foreign language (English), and experiences the racism of the Jim Crow South, it makes the poignancy of that September day in 1972 all the more powerful. And when Clemente's life is tragically cut short, which Santiago does not depict directly, it actually puts the three thousandth hit in proper light. Though many re-member Clemente as a Hall of Fame baseball player, Santiago reminds us that Clemente, however flawed he may have been in life, ultimately died in an attempt to help suffering people he had never even met. Charitable acts, it seems, are not deemed as worthy of tally as MLB hits are.

In terms of the source material for Santiago's book, there are many simi-larities with Maraniss's biography, an unsurprising fact because they rely on many of the same events in Clemente's life. However, if one reads both books, one gets a different sense for Roberto Clemente, as both a baseball player and a person. Such a difference is a function of each book's medium. For instance, Clemente's preternatural skill in throwing a baseball was a result of having, according to those who knew him, "hands so magical they were said to have eyes at their fingertips."[27] It is a metaphor equally descriptive and puzzling, and Maraniss here reports what was commonly said of Clemente. The spirit behind the metaphor indicates a preternatural awareness in Clemente's hands, as if his hands knew where to direct the baseball even if Clemente himself did not. It is the kind of attribution that often elevates the average to the level of greatness, the sort of unfolding mythopoesis that is all too common among certain sports heroes.

As *21: The Story of Roberto Clemente* opens on the day Clemente reaches his three thousandth hit, Santiago chooses to begin with Clemente in his position at right field, leaving the all-important hit until much later in the book. Santiago relies on the technique of representing motion and action typical of comic art. As Clemente begins his run to field the ball, we see the repeated "CHK" sound of his cleats digging into the ground, the "Wamp!" of the sound of the ball being hit. Here Santiago employs certain elements in order to give Clemente a superheroic bent that only a comic book can convey. Specifically, Santiago manipulates and represents Clemente's body in ways that a biographer such as Maraniss, working with words only, cannot possibly achieve. Santiago, alluding to that saying about Clemente having eyes at the

4.2. Santiago makes a metaphor literal, from *21: The Story of Roberto Clemente*.

ends of his fingertips, gives us just such an image in this scene showing Clemente fielding the ball in right field (see figure 4.2). In this moment, Clemente is introduced as a kind of baseball player for the ages. There are four panels on the page; the borders between each panel create a zigzag that implies motion. Moreover, it is Clemente's body that unites the action within the panels. Santiago has broken the sequence of motion into still frames that highlight Clemente's body and physicality as a rare athlete.

The top three panels work as a constellation that underscores Clemente's physical prowess. The top image is not unlike those found in architectural friezes in bas-relief from Ancient Greece, wherein a figure is captured in a static pose in midaction. The bottom of this panel slopes slightly to the right, in the direction our eyes are reading and complementing the direction Clemente is moving in. But this is an illusion; there is no motion in the image. Clemente is in an impossible body position were he not moving. His body alignment, like overt direction arrows, leads us to the ball in his glove. In the second panel, Clemente has turned to fire the baseball, presumably from right field to third base. It is a long throw that requires exceptional arm strength and accuracy. Clemente seems to be opening the very panel itself with his left arm, as if the panel cannot contain him any longer. Prominently displayed is his number on the back of his jersey, a clear indication that this baseball superhero is the subject of the book's narrative. In the third panel, Clemente has released the baseball—the end of his arm obscured in an explosion of power, the smoke appearing to emanate from a lightly sketched volcano—a foreshadowing of the seismic violence that will ultimately lead to Clemente's death. Again, the panel itself, structured as an acute angle, denotes the speed and power exerted from Clemente's body.

This third panel also makes visible what would ordinarily be a metaphor. We wouldn't expect to see huge plumes of dust and smoke appearing at the end of Clemente's arm when he releases a baseball. Santiago makes the most of the comic book convention of seeing the hero's body as malleable and capable of unrealistic transformation. While I stop short of saying it is impossible for verbal narration to replicate what is accomplished within the mind of the reader in these three panels, I would argue that it is extremely unlikely. The reason is that in a biography, even when invoking metaphors such as "His arm was a cannon," the reader will envision Clemente as an actual human being and will recognize that the phrase operates as a metaphor. And when readers of Santiago's book arrive at the fourth and final panel on the page, the metaphor is made flesh. As the three panels culminate in the striking image at the bottom of the page, we see that Clemente literally has eyeballs at the ends of his fingertips. It is a haunting and somewhat disturbing image that shocks readers out of their comfortable expectations.

How do we read such an image, especially when we know we are reading what is ostensibly a biography of an actual person? Unlike Maraniss, Santiago doesn't explain the visual metaphor in the panel, though he does contextualize the metaphor much later in the book; the textbox above it, narration supplied by an unnamed narrator, reads, "There was something odd about him. . . ." Unless one already knows Clemente's story, a reader may be left wondering how the bottom image relates to the top three panels of the page. By withholding a verbal description of the "eyes at the tips of his fingers" metaphor, Santiago forces readers to stop and dwell on the constellation of images as if they were an intricate puzzle, the solution of which rests in Clemente's graphically drawn body on the page. The narrator's observation of Clemente's preternatural qualities coincides with the fantastical images concerning his body. Santiago converts Clemente's body into a figure more at home in a superhero comic book than a sports biography. The images carry the burden of expressing the ineffable nature of one of Puerto Rico's greatest baseball players. In short, where words fail, comics succeed.

21: The Story of Roberto Clemente is broken into several sections interspersed along different years in Clemente's life. The opening pages occur on the day of his three thousandth hit in 1972, and Santiago returns to this day later in the book. The scenes depicting that day in 1972 are identified by the overt yellow tinge to every panel as well as the character narrator, later identified as a young woman who was at the Pirates game on that day. Her narration boxes are also recognizable because of their grayish-blue color. Santiago gives this unnamed woman a position of privilege in the book, as she is the only character to narrate any scene. She is an observer and witness to Clemente's baseball greatness. She is the one who calls Clemente by his moniker, "The Great One." She is the one who calls Clemente a hero, "because of the way he lived." Of course, she is a loyal, if biased, baseball fan. As an unnamed fan and narrator, she serves as a stand-in for likeminded Clemente fans everywhere.

His greatness, though statistically verifiable, was ultimately difficult to articulate. Santiago's book works to make manifest this indefinable greatness, as well as to provide for Clemente something that every great superhero has — an origin story. If the day of his three thousandth hit was Clemente's greatest day as an athlete, the day of his death proves to be the apex of his humanitarian spirit. The sacrifice of oneself in order to help the unfortunate resonates with Clemente's own religious teachings and tenets of faith. In the book, for example, Santiago takes the unusual move to focalize from above a car accident involving Clemente, his brother Matino, and a drunk driver. Using the type of artistic license unavailable to traditional biographers, Santiago embeds the unmistakable image of a crucified body, ostensibly that of Jesus Christ, created by the intersection of two roads. It is a reminder of Clemente's religiosity and his relationship to the concept of sacrifice for the greater good. In sport Clemente used his body to achieve great levels of success; in death he died in pursuit of helping those he did not know. Santiago weaves these two aspects throughout the book with skill, yielding a much more complex portrait of Clemente beyond the baseball headlines of 1972.

The book concentrates on four major points in Clemente's life: his childhood from 1942 to around 1953; his early baseball career from 1954 (the year of his brother Luis's death) to the last day of 1960; his courtship and early years of marriage to his wife, Vera, from 1964 to 1969; and finally, the apex of his baseball success from 1970 to September 30, 1972. The final seven pages cover the last two days of Clemente's life, until the moment his plane disappears forever from radar. Each of these sections works to provide the reader with a *visual* articulation, an embodiment of a now-mythic Roberto Clemente, and more importantly, a sense for how this seemingly superheroic baseball player came from humble origins fraught with tragedy and loss. The result yields a more human, a more approachable Clemente.

Early in the book, Clemente's mother punishes Roberto for tarrying too long in coming home. Though he is at times seen in his school, Clemente's thoughts are preoccupied, like those of most of his country, on the sport of baseball. But in this scene his passion for playing baseball has gone too far, and in a series of wordless panels, his mother tosses his homemade bat, inscribed with his nickname, "Momen," into a fire. Unlike the scenes of Clemente playing baseball in the major leagues, here Santiago refrains from any of the traditional conventions of superhero comics, such as motion lines and exaggerated body poses. Roberto is but a child here, and he is too small to prevent his prized possession—his bat—from being destroyed in the cooking fire. It is an altogether different storytelling technique than the scenes with Clemente as a baseball player. Here he is young and helpless to prevent the corporal punishment he receives. Still, it is a defining, poignant moment for several reasons. Not only does Santiago show Clemente's early passion for baseball, but also the makeshift bat in the fire hints at the tragedy of Clemente's older sister, Anairis, who died of severe burns after her clothing caught on fire.[28] Though Anairis died when Clemente was only an infant, Santiago uses the burning image of the makeshift bat tossed into the fire to transition to that earlier moment when Clemente's father, Melchor, learns of Anairis's death as he worked in a cane field. As biographers and commentators of Clemente have noted, Clemente's otherworldly sense of connection with the world of the dead originates with Anairis's death. Santiago, leaving conventional graphic storytelling aside, depicts young Clemente's encounter with his deceased sister via a dream. Anairis appears in one of the smaller panels as a winged angel, and in a later panel, engulfed in flames. As she urges Clemente to "keep moving," Clemente falls off a cliff. Upon waking, he is consoled by his mother, who explains to him the story of the three kings and notes a triple star configuration in the sky that represents them. Santiago, who initiates the inclusion of Anairis's story with Clemente's mother as disciplinarian, closes the scene with a mother's tender consolation of her terrified boy. The three-star configuration indicative of the three kings of the Nativity appears throughout the book; indeed it is the final image and is intended to bring readers to Clemente's maternal and religious connections once more.

Only a few pages later, Santiago invokes another key moment in Clemente's life. Previewing Clemente's penchant for helping others, Santiago depicts a car accident in which Clemente navigates down a cliff on a bike to pull a man out of a burning car. Again, Santiago does not exaggerate Clemente's body or physical feats in this scene. Save for the top panel, which shows Clemente in close-up, he appears as a tiny figure on a bicycle—far from the dominant physicality of the athlete shown in figure 4.6. Rather, Santiago shows Clemente as a realistic twelve-year-old racing to pull a grown man out of a wrecked car. Thus, Clemente's physical gifts are subservient to his greater need to help others. He is not an impervious Superman. As his death shows, Clemente was all too mortal.

In the middle of the next page, Santiago jumps forward in Clemente's life from the moment he pulls the man from the burning car to an older Clemente on the cusp of signing a contract with the Santurce Crabbers. Here Santiago takes readers into a classroom, and further, into a textbook, that invokes the multiracial heritage of the Puerto Rican people—being an amalgamation of Spaniard, Taino, and African. In less than half a page of space, Santiago sets the stage for the struggles Clemente will endure when he later plays baseball in the United States. His African heritage, never an issue in Puerto Rico, would lead to tremendous self-doubt and anxiety as he played baseball in the United States. A later page reveals Buzzie Bavasi of the Brooklyn Dodgers concerned that Clemente, as a "colored . . . could be a problem for the white players." As David Maraniss says of the time, "It was so different in Puerto Rico from in the United States in that period. If you were black Puerto Rican or black American, you could eat wherever you wanted to, you could sleep wherever you wanted to, you could date whoever you wanted to, there wasn't this constant reminder of the color of your skin" (*American Experience*).[29] Santiago emphasizes Clemente's struggle with racism, for instance, by portraying the segregation of restaurants—a concept Clemente cannot fathom (see figure 4.3). Despite his physical gifts on the baseball field, with his dark skin and generic suit, he is simply another black man in the American South.

Throughout the book Santiago foregrounds Clemente's Afro-Latino heritage as he rises through the baseball ranks in the major leagues. While today

4.3. Clemente experiences racism in the American South, from *21: The Story of Roberto Clemente*.

Afro-Latinos are a prominent demographic among MLB players, Santiago time and again stresses the difficult path broken by Clemente, who, in the 1960s, was in many ways breaking a path similar to Jackie Robinson's, only Clemente had also to negotiate a language barrier as well as a color line. In a sport that records the actions of great bodies as statistics, Santiago reminds readers of the physicality Clemente embodied as a man of color. Robinson could not have prepared the sports media for a player who looked African American but spoke Spanish. Just as starkly contrasting skin color serves as a

4.4. Dreaming in English, from *21: The Story of Roberto Clemente*.

4.5. Shattered helmets, fractured panels, from *21: The Story of Roberto Clemente*.

visual marker of difference, Santiago further renders the cultural difference in visual contrast by using the bright yellow-orange speech bubbles to denote English against the "natural" white speech bubble, which represents Spanish. During a photo shoot for the Pirates, the sports reporter exaggeratedly speaks English to Clemente, who asks him to stop shouting, that he understands. In truth, though Clemente may have understood some English, he was never at ease speaking it.

In reality, Clemente's limited facility with the English language was a fact that shook his confidence and self-esteem for most of his time in the United States. Santiago sporadically uses the bold yellow-orange speech balloons to signal the use of English, until this device threatens to overwhelm Clemente on the page (see figures 4.4 and 4.5). In this two-page spread, he unites Clemente's struggle to learn English with his frustrations playing baseball. Figure 4.4 depicts Clemente's near-desperate desire to learn English. With each successive panel, Clemente becomes more desperate—first reading an advertisement for a "scientific process" of learning English in his sleep, then falling asleep and being bombarded by English in his dreams. As in many moments in *21: The Story of Roberto Clemente*, this is a page that calls for careful reading. If one follows the panels in traditional fashion, it is evident that there is a break right in the middle of the page. The fourth panel disorients a reader by asking him or her to discern its relation to the preceding three panels. It is not until the bottom row of panels that Santiago clarifies that the yellow panels are occurring in Clemente's dreams. In revealing the dream to us, Santiago allows us to glimpse Clemente's frustration. By making it visually striking, Santiago's decision is to configure the panels in a way that reveals Clemente's psychological stress, as it manifests in his dreams, in a way a conventional biography cannot. This technique, used to powerful effect in Santiago's *In My Darkest Hour*, here gives readers a sense of what it is like for Clemente as he struggles on and off the field of play. It helps give reason to why Clemente struggled with insomnia. And the mention of an advertised program for learning a language while you sleep, a passive process, one assumes, provides an opportunity for Santiago to explore Clemente's struggles even while he sleeps. In his dream, tinted in the bright yellow that denotes his linguistic discomfort, the advertisement print he encounters every day now dominates, his frustration at its incomprehensibility signaled by the word "ENGLISH" seemingly pasted over the words. An advertisement featuring Bob Hope's face makes no sense to Clemente, and neither do any of the other snatches of English text. The words fall apart as Clemente's dreamscape renders everything one word, said over and over in frustration: "ENGLISH!"

While Clemente is plagued by his linguistic insecurity in the quiet of his sleep, Santiago shows that the problems with language carry over into Clemente's career. On the page that faces figure 4.4, Clemente is caught in a slump as his problems with English merge with his frustrations at the plate (see figure 4.5). The bold yellow speech bubbles of the umpire repeatedly calling, "Strike!" and "Out!" are visually connected to the dreams regarding English that haunt Clemente. They are English words Clemente has learned the hard way, unlike the unbelievable promise of learning the language while he sleeps. His emotional volatility is made manifest in Santiago's choice of panel shape, size, and configuration at the bottom of the page as thin slivers emulate the shards of his helmets shattered in frustration. In his baseball environment, Clemente's arms are stretched impossibly like those of a comic book hero, smashing helmet after helmet in dissatisfaction. Santiago, using an economy of space, at times even a thin shard of a panel, manages to express Clemente's frustration during his initial MLB career through mostly visual representation without the aid of verbal narration. This technique of allowing the mode of visual and verbal storytelling to blend as the narrative progresses is emblematic of Santiago's book as a whole. Indeed, the two-page spread that comprises figures 4.4 and 4.5 is a telling example of the power of the biographic to express Clemente's struggle and irritation during his early career with the Pirates, before he took his iconic number 21—all accomplished in a mere two pages.

It is important to remember that throughout the book, Santiago deliberately takes the time to stress how baseball is infused with other aspects of Clemente's life. It is a reminder that Clemente ought to be remembered as much more than a great baseball player. As a child in Puerto Rico, with his family suffering hardship and heartache, his relationship to baseball had already made a mark on the impressionable boy then known as Momen. Later, as Clemente struggles with racism and English, his baseball suffers equally. And during his happiest moments with his wife, Vera, Clemente is garnering the greatest baseball accolades of his career. Rather than compartmentalize these different facets of Clemente's life, Santiago blends them at every opportunity—even invoking Clemente's dream of creating a "sports city—a place where children can come and play." Unlike his aggravating dreams wherein English taunts him, his dream of building a place where Puerto Rican children could revel in play would ultimately come to fruition two years after his death.[30] In contrast to the panels in figures 4.4 and 4.5 where struggle in his social life yielded struggle on the field, here Clemente is at the apex of his personal well-being and the edge of baseball immortality, with his three thousandth hit within reach. Santiago rejects rectilinear panel boxes here once more, instead using curves, circles, and hearts to convey this joyous period in Clemente's life. With the date of his death already a matter of history, readers encounter the years on the page both as milestones and as markers that bring them closer to the moment of Clemente's untimely and tragic death. On this page Santiago unites the more realistic portrayal of Clemente in his social life with the more exaggerated pliability of his body when in his superhero's costume, his baseball uniform. It is a contrast made visible, without words, in a way that lends the biographic much of its heft and power.

CONCLUSION

I close by reasserting how this graphic articulation of Clemente's on- and off-the-field struggles and achievements provides readers with a different means of understanding the revered baseball player than traditional biographies afford. From the perspective of the comics medium, Santiago's use of the formal elements available to him make him a decidedly unconventional storyteller. Like fellow Latino comics artist Frank Espinosa, whose Eisner-nominated comic *Rocketo* also eschews traditional comic art conventions,[31] Santiago makes bold use of color, page space, and body representation. Because of the pliability of the comics medium, Santiago's use of formal elements is unconventional within a biography. In part, this is what imbues his work with such a

4.6. Clemente seems capable of flight, from *21: The Story of Roberto Clemente*.

striking relationship to his audience. However, there are two implications that thrust *21: The Story of Roberto Clemente* into an upper echelon of storytelling.

First, Santiago uses the medium of comics—the creation of narrative by using a combination of image and text—to tell a biographical story. With the images of Santiago's book carrying the storytelling load, readers have significant narrative gaps to negotiate, and more of them. The various images of Clemente dominate the majority of the book's pages, and readers are urged to "see" Clemente rather than imagine him in the way a traditional biography would.

And there lies the second implication of Santiago's biographic. In either a biography or a biographic, readers must use their capacity for imagination when visualizing the events recounted in the narrative telling. In *21: The Story of Roberto Clemente*, readers are confronted with a cartoon rendering of Clemente. Further, Santiago employs a variety of Clemente "bodies" ranging from playful drawings of Momen as a child with a larger head (think Charlie Brown), to exaggerated body poses and flying figures more at home in DC or Marvel comics (see figure 4.6), to more photorealistic renditions (see figure 4.4). This formal decision to have a continually reshaped Clemente throughout the book contests with a reader's intuition that Clemente was decidedly not a cartoon figure in real life and results in readers' constant rethinking and refor-

mulating their understanding of who this legendary baseball player was. Santiago's incorporation of these storytelling techniques and his interpretation of
Clemente as a figure, as a *body* in repose as well as in action, as a child and as a
man, as a hero and as a martyr, provide a fresh take on Clemente and his life.

Santiago's biographic on Clemente is a significant addition to Latino/a literature. It adds to a literature about Latinos written by Latinos. In a larger
sense, we interpret such unconventional or groundbreaking works of Latino/a
literature in all its manifestations as signaling a change in audience expectations for what Latino/a literature can be. Wilfred Santiago, working in a
medium that has long been derided as lowbrow, shows how a careful design
of visual and verbal storytelling can create new understandings of how biography is told, how Latino/a literature is perceived, and how authors can be
confident that readers can rise to meet them at the level of their challenges.

NOTES

1. For a concise overview of Clemente's struggle against racism in the United States
during his rise in professional baseball, his connections to his native Puerto Rico, and the
aftermath of his death, see Samuel O. Regalado, "Roberto Clemente: Images, Identity, and
Legacy."

2. According to MLB.com, the nine players to achieve three thousand hits before Clemente are, in the order they achieved this milestone, Cap Anson (1897), Honus Wagner
(1914), Nap Lajoie (1914), Ty Cobb (1921), Tris Speaker (1925), Eddie Collins (1925), Paul
Waner (1942), Hank Aaron (1970), and Willie Mays (1970). As of 2014 there have been only
28 players to amass at least three thousand hits in an MLB career.

3. David Maraniss, *Clemente: The Passion and the Grace of Baseball's Last Hero* (New York:
Simon and Schuster, 2006).

4. According to Andrew J. Kunka, "The juxtaposition of the historical text and cartoon image resembles the postmodern use of intertextuality in historiographic metafiction—
fiction that metatextually comments on and critiques the written historical record—as
described by Linda Hutcheon in *A Poetics of Postmodernism*." See Andrew J. Kunka, "Intertextuality and the Historic Graphic Narrative" 169.

5. Henceforth when I refer to biography, I mean traditional biographies that are written
using narrative prose.

6. Paul Buhle, "History and Comics," *Reviews in American History* 35.2 (2007): 317.

7. Unsurprisingly, scholars are divided on what to call comics that are about the writer
who creates them. Gillian Whitlock and Anna Poletti suggest the term "autobiographics,"
while Robyn Warhol has made a case for the term "autography." My own sense is that "autobiographics" works better vis-à-vis my own deployment of "biographics," for the same taxo-
nomical maneuver on "autography" yields "biography," which is not helpful in my case as
I am attempting to show a difference between biography in comics form (biographics) and
traditional biography. See Gillian Whitlock and Anna Poletti, "Self-regarding Art," *Biography* 31.1 (2008): v. See also Robyn Warhol, "The Space Between: A Narrative Approach to
Alison Bechdel's *Fun Home*," *College Literature* 38.3 (2011): 1.

8. Mary Louise Penaz, "Drawing History: Interpretation in the Illustrated Version of the *9/11 Commission Report* and Art Spiegelman's *In the Shadow of No Towers* as Historical Biography," *a/b: Auto/Biography Studies* 24.1 (2009): 109.

9. Ibid., 94.

10. Ibid., 94.

11. Ibid., 96.

12. Davis specifically argues that texts by Will Eisner and Yoshihiro Tatsumi "are, on one level, *künstlerroman*, but crucially, they also engage the history of graphic art and publication, as they consider the ways comics and manga have been produced and consumed in the twentieth century. Thus, they not only engage their authors' artistic lives, they also assess the development of an industry." See Rocío G. Davis, "Autographics and the History of the Form: Chronicling Self and Career in Will Eisner's *Life, in Pictures* and Yoshihiro Tatsumi's *A Drifting Life*," *Biography* 34.2 (2011): 255.

13. Similarly, Lan Dong makes the assertion about Will Eisner's *Life, in Pictures* that "this collection of autobiographical fiction provides an intriguing example of the intersection of life writing and the graphic novel. Instead of telling the tales as fiction or autobiography, Eisner presents selected episodes that are related to 'aspects' of his life, career, and people surrounding him." See Lan Dong, "Thinly Disguised (Autobio)Graphical Stories," *Shofar* 29.2 (2011): 16–17.

14. Charles Hatfield, *Alternative Comics: An Emerging Literature* (Jackson: University Press of Mississippi, 2005): 112.

15. Frederick Luis Aldama, *The Routledge Concise History of Latino Literature* (New York: Routledge, 2012): 127.

16. Frederick Luis Aldama, *Your Brain on Latino Comics: From Gus Arriola to Los Bros Hernandez* (Austin: University of Texas Press, 2009): 5.

17. Wilfred Santiago, *In My Darkest Hour* (Seattle: Fantagraphics Books, 2004).

18. Scott McCloud, *Understanding Comics: The Invisible Art* (New York: HarperCollins, 1994): 51.

19. *Ibid.*

20. Aldama, *Routledge Concise History of Latino Literature*, 145.

21. Nicholas Hetrick, "Chronology, Country, and Consciousness in Wilfred Santiago's *In My Darkest Hour*," in *Multicultural Comics: From Zap to Blue Beetle*, ed. Frederick Luis Aldama (Austin: University of Texas Press, 2008): 190.

22. As a child, Clemente earned the nickname "Momen" for his habit of saying *momentito*, or "wait a moment."

23. David C. Ogden, "Roberto Clemente: From Ignominy to Icon," in *Reconstructing Fame: Sports, Race and Evolving Reputations*, ed. David C. Ogden and Joel Nathan Rosen (Jackson, MS: University Press of Mississippi, 2008): 16–17.

24. John Seven, "History, Identity and Baseball: Wilfred Santiago Tells 'The Story of Roberto Clemente,'" *Publishers Weekly*, Feb. 22, 2011.

25. Thierry Groensteen, *The System of Comics* (Jackson, MS: University Press of Mississippi, 2009).

26. While the Japanese comics form known as manga reverses the direction of reading, it also is essentially rectilinear in its panel arrangement.

27. Maraniss, *Clemente*, 4.

28. Rob Maaddi and Susan Nuaddi Darraj write,

The Clemente family had endured tremendous suffering during Roberto's childhood and adolescence. For one thing, poverty, and the fear of it, always loomed in the background. Tragedy was another: when Roberto was still a baby, his sister Anairis died when her clothing caught on fire. While she was playing near the large outdoor oven that Luisa used to cook meals for Melchor's workers, gasoline spilled on the flames and ignited the little girl's dress, causing serious burns on over 90 percent of her body. She died in the hospital a few days later, after suffering tremendous pain. The family was devastated and haunted by her horrible death.

See Rob Maaddi and Susan Nuaddi Darraj, *Roberto Clemente* (New York: Chelsea House, 2009): 23.

29. David Maraniss, "Roberto Clemente," *American Experience*, directed by Bernardo Ruiz, PBS, aired April 21, 2008, transcript, http://www.pbs.org/wgbh/americanexperience /films/clemente/.

30. Founded in 1974, Roberto Clemente Sports City (RCSC) is, according to its website, an

organization dedicated to providing athletic opportunities and life lessons for young people throughout Puerto Rico and beyond. Sports City occupies 304 acres in Carolina, on the outskirts of San Juan, consisting of baseball, football and soccer fields, a swimming pool, tennis courts, training facilities and meeting rooms . . . There are few better ways to transform the despair of marginalized young people into confidence and optimism than allowing them to play their games and using those games as instructional vehicle for positive life lessons. RCSC has pursued this path since its inception.

See http://64.78.33.77/rcsc21/index_en.cfm.

31. Espinosa employs a horizontal page layout, that is, the longer side of the page is horizontal; eschews panel borders; utilizes bold pen lines; and relies on color washes to bring his fantastical world, set 2,000 years in the future, to stunning reality. See Frank Espinosa, *Rocketo Vol. 1 & 2: Journey to the Hidden Sea* (Berkeley: Image Comics, 2006–2007).

FIVE

WRESTLING WITH COMIC GENRES AND GENDERS: *LUCHADORES* AS SIGNIFIERS IN *SONAMBULO* AND *LOCAS*

ELLEN M. GIL-GÓMEZ

THE WORLDS OF professional wrestling—with or without the masks of Mexican *lucha libre*—and graphic narratives share some common ground as they both vascillate between popular "low" and elite "high" cultures and their forms and signs. Though the birthplace of the freestyle masked wrestling, which ultimately evolved into *lucha libre*, is in the eastern United States, it was enthusiastically embraced by early twentieth-century Mexican culture and has since been translated and reshaped in its national image. This process has been so dramatic that masked wrestling generally, and the *lucha* mask specifically, have become one of the most prominent symbols that signify Mexican cultural authenticity and community identity. (Notably, I use *lucha* here to indicate the mask generally and broadly within the sport rather than that of a specific *luchador*. I use it more as a catchall for the world, the sport, the traditions, the costumes, and the participants.) As American inheritors of this complex adoption and retranslation process, Chicano comic book author–artists Rafael Navarro and Jaime Hernandez have put their own spins on wrestlers and wrestling as tropes within their comics for very different purposes and with different effects. Interestingly, however, both author–artists use their *luchadores/as* to disrupt traditional comic genre forms—specifically the detective, superhero, and science fiction comics. Hernandez's and Navarro's comic book narratives diverge, however, in the ways their wrestlers operate within and push upon the boundaries of male and female gender roles and expectations.

THE ORIGINS AND DEVELOPMENT OF *LUCHA LIBRE*

A complete history and explanation of *lucha* is not necessary here. However, in order to make clear the significance and interplay of the meanings in the *luchador/a* characters within Hernandez's and Navarro's comic book narratives, some background and details of its forms, styles, and meanings, along with its cultural significance in its specific Mexican history and communities, are necessary.

In *The World of Lucha Libre*, Heather Levi charts the course of professional wrestling: beginning with the so-called "collar and elbow" style from nineteenth-century Vermont, popular with Civil War Union soldiers, and then as a means to drum up customers in saloons and bars in New York City. P. T. Barnum next incorporated wrestling as a part of his famous circus, where matches included direct audience participation; at first Barnum wrestlers fought untrained members of the audience, and then the spectacle shifted to fights with a plant posing as a part of the audience (6–7). Levi claims that this shift to "fixed" entertainment created a new form of professional or exhibition wrestling and "[w]ith this innovation, the performance changed from a contest to a representation of a contest" (7). These performances grew in popularity in both urban and country settings: the county fair circuit gave birth to intercity wrestling clubs. In the early twentieth century both American and European promoters organized wrestling tours and wrestlers began to include elements in their performance to "mark themselves as memorable characters" (7). For example, in the United States immigrant wrestlers were marked by their national origin as a definition of their character.

Mexico's most popular sports—soccer, baseball, boxing, and wrestling—were brought from North America or Europe and embraced as part of Mexico's broader pursuit of the modernization agenda enforced by dictator Porfirio Díaz. This valorization of American and European sports also brought its opposite: the denigrating of popular activities like cockfights and bullfights. Wrestling has walked the line of these designations of "sport" and "entertainment" for the Mexican government's cultural valorization and support through a developed patronage system. *Lucha libre*, on the other hand, rides the line between the two—sport and entertainment—because its predetermined ending seems to indicate its fraudulent nature while there is no doubt that any wrestling match is a physical contest. Levi argues ultimately that through this balancing act, *lucha libre* "posits a different moral universe than do conventional team sports. . . . it mocks the very terms of the discourse of modernization in the Mexican context" (17).

Although Mexican *lucha libre* started as an import from these American roots, it is now perceived, inside Mexico and out, as a uniquely Mexican genre, a fact that grew soon after its introduction. After its beginning matches in the 1930s, both local support and participation grew and "[i]nnovations in costuming, character and technique further Mexicanized the genre" (22). While evidence is mixed on the class status of early audiences, the general shift of perception toward *lucha* has been first as a popular form for mixed audiences—if not for the sophisticated, then at least for the urban—and with television came the middle class. Many of these details also signal allegiances that separate whom we might call the "posers" from the "aficionados," and thus feelings are strongly held. These rather shifting sands to some degree indicate the unique and fine balance that *lucha* navigates within equally shifting Mexican national and local cultural constructs.

Levi argues that *lucha* has historically been an important location wherein a range of sometimes contradictory narratives about Mexican national and local culture play themselves out or that "lucha libre is a story that Mexicans tell themselves about themselves" (50). She points to the use of the mask as its defining characteristic and symbol of cultural currency. Interestingly, many "both in and outside the family *luchística*, have called attention to the connection between the use of masks in *lucha libre*, and their ritual use by indigenous peoples in Mexico. By connecting *lucha libre* to the indigenous world, the mask is seen as central to the Mexicanization of the genre" (105). She points out that while the actual origin and creation of the first *lucha* mask does not come directly from indigenous ritual culture, what is important is that the *story* of that connection is vital and continues to be salient.[1] What *is* true is that "[m]asks, masking and unmasking are themes that pervade not only lucha libre, but also Mexican cultural discourse in general" (105). Thus the development of the mask in *lucha* linked it with this discourse and "associated the wrestling performance with the idea of a unified Mexican national culture rooted in a pre-Hispanic past" (113).

While Levi's useful project focuses on explaining how *lucha libre* is contextualized for Mexicans, it is reading the Chicano translations of these meanings that I focus on here. She argues that the context of Mexican nationhood is twofold: "Two themes have been central to twentieth century discourse of Mexican national culture. The first has been that of mestizaje, the relationship between the indigenous and Iberian aspects of Mexico's culture and population, and their relationship to themes of modernity, civilization and urbanization. The second is the complex relationship between Mexico and the United States" (67). While these factors can be seen operating within Chicano *lucha libre* signification, the level of detail in the particulars is quite different. For my purposes in this essay, it is an understanding of the development and function of *lucha libre* (with the mask and without), and its operation as symbolic of Mexican culture and identity, that is of primary importance.

From a Chicano context, *lucha libre is* Mexican culture. Indeed Carrillo and Mackinney describe the use of the "*lucha libre* motif" as "advanc[ing] the aesthetics of self-representation of Mexicanos and Chicanos" (226), thus fusing both identities within one representational process. I believe that it is by reading Hernandez's and Navarro's use of *lucha* characters and symbols in their comics through the history, operational structures, and symbolic meanings of *lucha libre* from within Mexican tradition that their distinctive Chicano comic translations can be best appreciated.

RAFAEL NAVARRO'S *SONAMBULO*: NOIR *LUCHA* ACTION HERO

In the introduction to this volume, Aldama and González effectively describe how the noir-style detective fiction inherently "takes us back to the origins of comics in the pulps of the 1930s and 1940s and their inclusion of crime noir stories" and more specifically that "Navarro ch[ose] to envelop [his story] in the noir fictional mode—a mode with its social-Darwinist, behaviorist, fatalistic worldview—as a way to comment on a world ripped apart at the seams and where characters are fated to live a life in a world that offers no real options." Both of these descriptions of noir and the resulting impacts on *Sonambulo* are perfectly true; however I also find that these noir elements are sharpened and made distinct by how *Sonambulo* places them in specific cultural contexts. David Schow's introduction to Navarro's *Sonambulo: Sleep of the Just* positions the protagonist within the worlds of the noir detective and superhero genres, though he claims that the comic "challenges them" (n. pag.). His description of the noir-style detective story is most focused on its iconography of "trenchcoats and fedoras, big buglike vintage autos, femmes fatale[s], the cigarette smoke unreeling towards the ceiling, the half empty bourbon bottle, the half-closed office of private investigation, the betrayals and the mournful darkside music," whereas his version of the superhero story is focused on the qualities of the hero—"the social misfit with oddball powers or goofy Spandex costume"—and the conflict and action that ensue (n. pag.). While these generalizations are broadly true, I find that *Sonambulo* is more conversant with the noir genre, and its masked *lucha libre* detective who has kept, and is inseparable from, his *lucha* character name resonates more as a Chicano action hero than as a comic superhero. Thus I find his mask evokes the nature of his cultural heroism more strongly than as equivalent to a superhero mask. As Navarro has said:

> Sonambulo is this giant burrito that wraps up all the things I've always loved, either from my culture or just stories in general. From Mexican luchadores, folklore, to horror, sci-fi, and noir films. . . . He's Mexico's equivalent of the

U.S. superhero, the luchador: an ordinary person that becomes larger than life once they put on their mask. . . . Creating a luchador superhero was also a way to bring in rich indigenous and folkloric Mexican culture. (Aldama, pt. 3, "Rafael Navarro")

Sonambulo uses a noir style in its artwork: black and white, strong contrasting geometric shapes—window blinds, stairs, rain, sections of buildings—simplified facial features, expressive stark lighting, and a generally dark and compressed atmosphere. While Navarro does use some of the perspectives that typify film noir—both high angles and low angles, some hallucinatory imagery through various minor characters' "dreams," and extreme close-ups, mainly of eyes—though he does not use skewed angles, blackouts, or flashbacks in any major way. In figure 5.1, both noir visual style and content are clearly demonstrated, as is the effective inclusion of subjective imagery in the extreme close-up of eyes representing an internal dream view or the speaker's "mind's eye" rather than as a concrete external image.

Navarro explains his interest in noir style in terms of both point of view and film-like "shots" and lighting and mood. He discusses his interest in mixing both traditional shots and more abstract ones, typical of noir film in order to

tell a story in a way where you can cut to those extreme close-ups to show drama and tension and emotion. . . . but there's also the lighting that creates ambience. Film noir is wondrous for that. With small budgets, it was all about lighting: lighting in specific ways a figure standing in front of venetian blinds to convey that striking sense of drama. (Aldama, pt. 3, "Rafael Navarro")

The comic's subject is also typical within the genre: a private detective's investigation of an apparently simple crime—a kidnapping of a senator's daughter—that turns out to be much more convoluted and complex. While the story is dark, because of its violent and criminal content, it is not pessimistic, hopeless, or cynical, nor is Sonambulo himself morally ambiguous as is typical of noir heroes or antiheroes. Instead he is fairly straightforward, as Navarro describes:

I always thought of Sonambulo as a self-educated guy. With this comes a certain confidence in self-experience: he is very comfortable with himself and confident about where he stands on issues. He's this simple, two-fisted guy with a semirighteous view of the world. At the same time, he knows he's

5.1. Visual depiction of a dream view or the speaker's "mind's eye," from *Sonambulo*.

flawed, that he does the best he can then moves on. (Aldama, pt. 3, "Rafael Navarro")

Interestingly, his character is much more reflective of the *luchador* figure within Mexican film. This is true stylistically in terms of Navarro's own artistic vision: "I love telling stories by laying things out like a film: the establishing shot, cut to a medium shot, then pull back, then cut to a close-up, all for dramatic purposes" (Aldama, pt. 3, "Rafael Navarro"). But more importantly, the *luchador* in movies as a symbol who was "a man of the people" who "fought for the common good and always won. . . . the narrative of the luchador promised a vision of stability, an incorruptible hero immune to the ravages of time" (Levi 190). While Sonambulo is in business as a private detective, he ultimately makes his decisions based on what is right. For example, when he discovers that the kidnapped woman, Sylvia Tiscareño, was systematically sexually abused by her father and ran away to marry her sweetheart, he not only doesn't turn her in, even after he learns the couple have been trying to have him killed, but helps them escape together, sending them off with "Be *good* parents" and a hug (chapter 4). The plot of the comic is also similar to one from the outlandish films: the kidnapping is down to a secret cult whose leader wants to bring his lost love back to life through ritual sacrifice by transferring her soul to the kidnapped woman's body. It is also full, of course, with numerous visually flamboyant wrestling moments featuring Sonambulo: a stylish mambo which turns into a fist fight (chapter 1), the subduing of dozens with only a folding chair that he calls "'ol reliable" (chapter 4), and even a brief interlude of him watching a film with "El Gato," trying to save Los Angeles from an insect from outer space (chapter 3). Thus while the trappings of *Sonambulo* are undoubtedly noir, the important content and main character are definitively *lucha libre*. In figure 5.2, for example, Navarro creates on one page and with four panels an impressively compressed transition from the sexy and athletic mambo of Sonambulo and a wrestling reporter Miss Smith to the fight. This series nicely blends representations of Latino and *lucha* cultures and furthers the development of Sonambulo's character traits alongside specific gendered functions. Men are undoubtedly the actors on this page, for good and for evil, whereas Miss Smith's eyes function as the mirror with which our hero sees the bad guys approaching so that he moves seamlessly from mambo to body throw.

The challenge to the genre, then, whether straightforward noir or the detective noir, arises with the combination of these elements: the *luchador* as noir detective action hero. No one in Sonambulo's world ever notices or comments on him wearing his mask; unlike the superhero figure, he has no alter ego. He

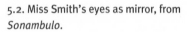

5.2. Miss Smith's eyes as mirror, from *Sonambulo*.

5.3. Visual incongruity of Sonambulo in a *lucha libre* mask, from *Sonambulo*.

wears it constantly, as a true *lucha libre* star would do publicly, but he even wears his when we see him alone. The visual incongruity of a huge wrestler in a *lucha libre* mask while wearing a pinstriped suit, fedora, and wing tips is a startling one. It is the layered meanings of that mask, though, that provide the weight within the story, its main character. (See figure 5.3.)

At the end of the comic we get the only real nod to the superhero genre; the only flashback is the story of how a famous *lucha libre* star named Salomon became Sonambulo inside and outside of the ring with the power to see the dreams of others. We find out that because Salomon would not work as a thug for a gangster wrestling promoter, he is shot, beaten, and buried under a wrestling ring, left for dead, where he "slept the sleep of the dead" and "didn't dream." After waking he could never sleep again and "the ability to lose consciousness [was] lost. And [he was] aware of everyone's dreams and nightmares . . ." (chapter 5). So the *lucha libre* character "El Sonambulo, The Sleepwalker of Death" is cursed with sleeplessness but also the power to know what others dream, which gives him insight into their thoughts and their lives and thus places them in his power. Frederick Luis Aldama concludes that this sleep is symbolic of "his journey to an ancestral, Aztec-identified underworld" from which "he returns with this superpower" (pt. I, sec. 11). Whether Sonam-bulo's cocoon-like slumber, imprisoned under the wrestling ring, signifies an Aztec rootedness in a collective cultural memory is, of course, debatable, but what I find most helpful in Aldama's observation is his nod to the union of the *luchador* with a mythologized and historical indigenous heritage. It follows that this signification occurs at the most mythic moment within *Sonambulo*—his unconscious dream state and transformation into a superhero—and is also where he most embodies the Aztec origins of his Mexican *lucha* culture. Thus Sonambulo's defining characteristics culminate in this final scene, which is a flashback to his origins. Ultimately, then, the change in storytelling modes, from detective comic to superhero comic, coincides with the multiple signi-fiers of mystical Aztec origins and Mexican identity all within the powerful *luchador*.

At the same time as the shift in genre, gender identity remains solidly in place, though at times offered with a wink. Sonambulo is a huge and mus-cular man with hands the size of a man's head; men call him "fat" and "old," and women desire him. He is mainly an upright and physical actor who makes progress on his case because of the actions of others rather than through his own intellectual processes. The only truly powerful woman is a demon figure, who haunts the nightmares of some, who seems to claim the cult leader's life at the conclusion of his story, and, finally, who is revealed to be an old crone or figure of death (chapters 1, 4). The women who are desired are typical hour-glass beauties, such as Shauna Smith, the magazine reporter, and Sylvia Tisca-reño, the kidnap victim (chapters 1, 3), while Sonambulo's secretary, who is efficient, is reliable, and ultimately saves his life, is plain and wears slacks and glasses (chapter 1).

It is the relationship between Sonambulo and his secretary, Xochti, wherein most of the satirical "winking" about gender constructions takes place. In the very first chapter, he is chasing a man through rain-soaked streets and is al-most immediately shot in the shoulder. We see here the initial example of So-nambulo's superpower of hearing and seeing others' dreams as he commands the man he has overpowered, "Tell me your dreams!" After getting the infor-mation that he wanted from the man, he nonchalantly goes back to the office to "patch up." This epic action scene locates Sonambulo as a superhero with typically masculine traits—physical strength, a stoic demeanor, honorable be-havior, and the use of physical power to dominate a weaker man to accom-plish his ends. On his way to the office the noir imagery is highlighted as he walks in the rain toward his prominent geometric building; he proceeds up the staircase and is captured in a high-angle shot with a tilted view. These ele-ments reify his masculinity as he moves against and through his world and is powerfully and physically defined through his rather idiosyncratic individuality. Once he enters his office, though, the tone shifts as we meet Xochti calmly painting her nails while sitting in front of her desktop computer. She soon scolds Sonambulo for getting to work late. He apologizes and she responds: "'S right boss, I've got no life, never go anywhere, do anything, even my goldfish snores when I talk to it. My cat tells me I just need a man and, oh, by the way you're bleeding" (chapter 1). Their lighthearted banter continues while he undresses to tend to his wound, throwing his tie and shirt to the floor carelessly. Messages she conveys—ones that also convey Sonambulo's power and influence (a bank loan has been approved, and a reporter from *Lords of the Ring* magazine has called him for an interview)—are juxtaposed with her jab that "a man of your age should really not be out so late." Sonambulo replies "A man my age! **A man my age!** ¡Que la canción! I'll tell you what chica since you care so much for me, I'll take your advice and rest up a bit before I go home. But if you **ever** bring up my age again, you're fired." To which she teases: "You do and I'll sue" (chapter 1). This interaction with Xochti encourages us to poke fun at his hyper-masculinity because it is juxtaposed with his prior actions, his behaviors, and his stylized noir representation. This is demonstrated nicely as Xochti matter-of-factly teases Sonambulo for his extreme toughness but also minimizes her need for a man by referring to it as a suggestion her cat has made.

This exchange occurs on only two pages, but on these pages Navarro crams thirteen separate panels. He shows Sonambulo barely fitting through the office door, face fully in darkened shadow contrasted with full light on his fedora and shirt. With this entrance to the office and through the first half of the panels, Sonambulo's darkened figure looms over the space, in foreground or background; his is the main physical presence. But as the above dialogue continues, he becomes more and more contained by the panels themselves and more correspondingly paired with Xochti's figure until we see them equally from an extremely high angle. Sonambulo is spread out on the couch, in his undershirt and with his shoes off, his protruding round stomach accentuated while Xochti puts on her coat, joking that she will sue him. As she closes the door to leave, we see only his socks in the darkened room, and this section ends with three small extreme close-up panels of Sonambulo's eye: one eye closed for two panels and the last one showing it opened. By the end of these two pages Sonambulo as "an old-school macho" (Aldama, pt. 3, "Rafael Navarro") is both celebrated and critiqued.

The powerful crone, or death figure, runs like a thread throughout the comic, though it is most firmly situated within the horror genre rather than either the detective or superhero comic genre. The first we see this image is in the dreams of the first henchman that Sonambulo chases. Artistically presented as a typical noir hallucination, in his dream he describes being drawn to a house with an endless series of halls that "reek of slow and feverishly numbing path to death" that leads to a mysterious female figure. As he narrates,

> There **she** is . . . always waiting for me. Her old, wrinkled hand trembles with an ancient evil within her more **powerful** than I could ever dread to imagine. . . . Her crackling, gravel voice consumes me with a great **fear** I've never known. . . . I just pray to the god I have forsaken long ago to please take my soul before she does. (chapter 1)

The hallucination gives us clues to the reason that Sylvia Tiscareño left her father in the first place as the number thirteen is repeated in his dream. (The number thirteen appears later in Sylvia's own dream of her and her father: it could perhaps have been her age when the sexual abuse began, we see it on her cheerleading uniform and in a button, and it is also stamped on her father's head when she sees him as the devil grinding her innocence to dust.)

The image of the woman also appears visually throughout the dream. We first see a close-up of the old woman's skeletal hand distorted and covered in spots. We then see a partial close-up of half of her face; though primarily obscured in shadow, it is full of sagging skin, wrinkles, and pockmarks. The final shot of the woman is almost a full figure, wrapped in the clothes of an old woman standing in front of the flames of hell, the top half of her face darkened in shadow, with glowing inset eyes and an evil grin. She holds a small box in her open hands, offering it to us (through the eyes of the dreamer himself). Consequently, this figure is associated with fear, death, depravity, guilt, and shame, evoking both the pain from specific trauma and bigger mythic and religious concepts of evil.

In Sylvia's boyfriend Condor's dream he first hears Sylvia laughing and sees her like an *Attack of the 50 Foot Woman* poster, legs astride and hands on hips wearing a leopard-print tank dress. He then becomes a clown, seeing her normally sized, walking into a body of water, finally seeing her as a corpse underwater, looking like the old crone from the first dream with similar putrefying skin, though with wide-open eyes and mouth agape, and the number thirteen carved on her forehead. This image of a woman representing death echoes the figure from the first dream, though this time with Sylvia as a potential victim of death, in addition to being a victim of the slow death of her father's systematic sexual abuse, rather than as death herself. (See figure 5.4.)

The final woman as death figure does not emerge in a dream but instead occurs at the climax to the kidnapping narrative. After Sonambulo and Condor

5.4. Sylvia in Condor's dream, from *Sonambulo*.

save Sylvia from Eugene's and the cult's clutches, Eugene scrambles to find the ashes of his lover, whom he calls his great goddess, Elsa Lemper. A female cult member, who looks quite similar to the old woman from the first dream, offers herself "body and soul" (chapter 4) to Eugene and he responds by immediately stabbing her. He then releases the ashes over her dead body, while surrounded by cult members, chanting "mmmmmmmm . . . beloved come to me . . ." in order to reincarnate her. At first her beautiful naked form appears in front of him, quite similar in appearance to Sylvia—though ultimately we see Eugene fall to his knees before the powerful and frightening figure of a desiccated corpse with her legs astride and arms reaching out seemingly to grab Eugene. It is difficult to tell what the corpse's expression is because only the top of the jaw is intact, but it appears at least malevolent if not murderous—certainly not a romantic anniversary. Eugene, eclipsed by the size and impact of the corpse, is laughing and half-crazed with perverse delight so that we cannot be sure of the accuracy of the prior images—did this figure, with striking physical similarities to the old crone, Sylvia, and photographs of Elsa, appear only in his mind or in the reality of the setting? Regardless of the answer, this figure not only has narrative impact on the comic—it is a recurrent thread connecting all the story's levels—but also provides recurrent visual tropes symbolizing fearful and powerful womanhood within these multi-genre comic forms.

The world of *Sonambulo* is repeatedly anachronistic—it appears to be a nostalgic post–World War II past full of classic cars, classic music, and vintage clothing but also includes desktop computers, cable television, and contemporary sedans and buses. Its use of multi-genre elements inset in historical context is also anachronistic but aids the development of its hero, *luchador* Sonambulo. The constructions of gender are equally anachronistic, with bombshells strutting alongside resourceful career women threatening sexual harassment though still managing to serve Sonambulo's traditional macho character. While each of these components stands on its own and speaks to *Sonambulo*'s uses and reuses of traditional forms, all of these features in fusion work together to craft and shape Sonambulo himself.

JAIME HERNANDEZ'S *LOCAS*: THE POWER OF *LUCHADORAS*

Hernandez's use of the *luchadora* is far more vast and diverse than Navarro's Sonambulo, which isn't surprising given that his major contribution to Los Bros Hernandez's *Love & Rockets* series—"Maggie the Mechanic" and *Locas*—spans 20 years and contains dozens of stories and characters. As in *Sonambulo*, Hernandez uses the figure of the wrestler—the mysterious action hero and former star wrestler Rena Titañon—as a way to challenge a specific comic genre. Specifically, the character Rena keeps the originally science fiction comic grounded in "the real" while she closely resembles the action hero Sonambulo. Once Hernandez's work found its footing within the realism of his *Locas* stories—which focus on the lives and dramas of a small group of Chicanas and various mixed-race friends and family in their local neighborhood—the inclusion of the *luchadora* motif develops further. In addition, Rena's life and impact on the arc of *Locas* expand and develop from extraordinary action heroine, bordering on the "super," to the gift of an entire matriarchal world of wrestling wherein Maggie's own aunt Vicki is a leader. This world introduces numerous options and opportunities for Maggie, including a place to live, an income, and a potential career. It also provides Maggie with numerous big and strong women's bodies that challenge her personal pain about her increasing weight and subsequent negative body image. Thus within *Locas* the *luchadoras'* challenge to the superhero and science fiction comic genres is only the beginning.

Rena enters *Locas* with the first major "Maggie" story, the six-part "Mechanics," which is told in epistolary form through letters from Maggie to her friend and sometimes lover, Hopey. It generally takes the shape of a daily travelogue of her adventures in tropical Zymbodia as a professional mechanic who works on rocket ships and battles dinosaurs. In it, Maggie is drawn as a short though otherwise fairly typical hourglass beauty who dances on tabletops, wrestles monsters in the mud while half-naked, inexplicably encounters her topless, buxom friend Penny Century in the jungle, and battles numerous villains. When Rena Titañon enters, Maggie casually states that "the real topping off the cake is that Rena was once a superhero" (43). Interestingly, though, when she is introduced via her wrestling history (44), the panels Hernandez includes constantly shift from her in the present within Maggie's story to flashback images from Rena's life in wrestling. The images are stylized more as still photographs from a newspaper. These photorealistic images portray Rena as a newsworthy and historical heroine with a gravitas worthy of remembrance. When Rena begins to tell Maggie the story of her wrestling career, Hernandez includes two pages full of text and numerous small panels that again shift from the present to Rena's historical though newsworthy past. Each part of the story is punctuated by the image of a wrestling move, Rena raising a trophy or her arm in victory again such as would be included in a newspaper story (57–58). Thus, while Hernandez's narrative constantly celebrates Rena as an action hero or even superhero, these realistic images, though still celebratory, ground Rena's world of fantasy in the honor of the wrestling world. (See figure 5.5.)

"SO FINALLY WHEN I GOT A CHANCE AT THE WORLD TITLE, ROSA NEVER KNEW WHAT HIT HER. IT TOOK A LONG TIME, BUT IT WAS WORTH IT. I WAS NOW QUEEN RENA OF THE LADY WRESTLERS. AND BEING CHAMP WAS FUN. CHALLENGERS CAME IN ALL FORMS. MY BIGGIES WERE AGAINST MAD MALA, SULTRY SIRENA, THE BLACK WIDOW, WHO I UNMASKED, AND KITTY KATZ, THE HOT NEW-COMER I WAS SUPPOSED TO WATCH OUT FOR. HELL, IT LASTED FIVE MINUTES. I WHIPPED 'EM ALL!

5.5. Rena's fantasy grounded in the world of wrestling, from *Locas*.

During Rena's story, Maggie learns that her aunt, Vicki Glori, while once Rena's tag-team partner, became her enemy because of her cowardice in not defending Rena in a match that made them lose their championship belts. Ultimately Vicki "used the ropes" (58) to unfairly defeat Rena in a one-on-one match and used other deceitful "*ruda*" measures to win.[2] Before their rematch, Rena was kidnapped and taken to Zymbodia, where "they loved my wrestling so much that the dick dictators . . . made me their queen!" (58) and where she found her calling as a freedom fighter. Thus Rena becomes a political global power broker as action hero via wrestling. Even though Maggie's aunt was the cause of Rena's championship loss, she welcomes Maggie into her world and encourages her to see that she too could be powerful within it. Maggie concludes that "the people of Zymbodia planned to destroy their self-appointed leader and Rena, whom they call 'La Troña,' was behind the whole thing. What a woman. She shows the people how to think free then moves on. Wild" (68). She agrees with her friend Daffy that "she sounds like some kind of goddess!!"

(69). Nevertheless she understands that "all of these gods I came across were just flesh like me, or were just flat out fears to begin with . . ." (69). With this conclusion, the transition from the "gods" and monsters of science fiction and superheroes to a heroine of women's empowerment is complete.

Interestingly, while the *luchadoras* in Hernandez's work do wear costumes but not masks, there is still an important connection, particularly in charting Rena's mysterious path as a freedom fighter (why did she disappear? where will she turn up and why?), to the secrecy of the mask within the world of wrestling. Levi states that "the 'truth' about professional wrestlers is not really unknowable. Wrestlers are just ordinary human beings in an unusual profession. . . . information about the 'real lives' of wrestlers . . . may say more about practices of self-representation than it does about 'real life'" (51). It is just this kind of mystery and secrecy that gives Rena her "La Toña" persona and power. The importance of this secrecy—not in who Rena is because she does not wear a mask, but how that relates to who she has become—"suggests that secrecy itself is a structuring feature of lucha libre. . . . Secrets are kept secret to generate the energy of secrecy" (47). This energy is certainly an influential component of Rena's character and impact.

As compared to this genre challenge of Rena Titañon's character, the majority of other *lucha libre* elements within *Locas* resemble accurately the culture and features of Mexican wrestling, though because Hernandez creates a wrestling world of women, there is an inherent challenge to gender. One of the most significant elements is the alternative matriarchal family structure that the world of wrestling both symbolizes and provides. The long-term "frenemy" relationship between Rena and Vicki reappears numerous times in the series; we get a number of stories about their histories, both together and separately. While they constantly fight, they are of one mind when it comes to supporting Maggie.

In the story "Locas 8:01 AM" Vicki Glori takes her in when she has nowhere to live—though Vicki Glori claims that it would be Maggie doing her a favor because she is lonely after losing her title (62–63). Once she wins it back in "The Valley of the Polar Bears," Vicki offers Maggie a job to go on a national wrestling tour (167) to play a role as her accountant as part of Vicki's taunt to "insure [her] belt" (170). Even though Vicki forces Maggie, to her dismay, to change her hairstyle and wear a suit in order to find a role to play on the tour, Vicki sees it as the only way to help Maggie. She says:

> Somebody's gotta feel sorry for that kid! I had to take her in years ago
> because her parents had the balls to use her as their excuse for breaking up!
> . . . An' I really tried to be more than just an aunt to the shrimp in those

tough times, but I don't think she ever appreciated it . . . even now she resents everything I try to do for her! Hell, nobody's perfect! I ain't no mother! I'm a wrestler! (172)

While Vicki does clearly try her best, she is continually portrayed as persistently homophobic and abusive of Maggie; in fact we learn that it is Vicki's homophobia that distracted her in the match where she and Rena lost their tag-team championship and not fear of the violent combat, as Rena believed ("Camp Vicki" 152). Maggie ends up getting fired for showing sympathy to Rena's old partner, Pepper Martinez, with whom she eventually joins an East Coast wrestling tour to find her friend/lover, Hopey, who has disappeared in New York. Thus, while the specific women wrestlers, actions, and outcomes are not always positive, the world of wrestling still provides consistent opportunities for Maggie. For example, figure 5.6 shows a television interview of Vicki, playing the *ruda* with her angry taunts and threats, while we see an uncomfortable Maggie in the background pretending to be Vicki's accountant.

The emphasis on kinship is increasingly important through the series as Hernandez develops more background about the relationship between Rena and Vicki, as well as creating new parallel stories of young women who have come to train as wrestlers at "Camp Vicki." In fact Vicki's "origin story" as a wrestler ties directly to Maggie herself: in a flashback where we see Vicki's family gathered to celebrate Maggie's birth, Vicki's father announces, to gasps and laughter, her plan to be a professional wrestler. Perhaps we are also given a hint about Vicki and Maggie's future relationship here when Vicki declares to baby Maggie, "I'll be better than El Santo, Bobo Brazil and Rena Titañon combined, eh, Margarita?," to which Maggie passes gas (144). Maggie is reintroduced to her cousin Xochitl (nicknamed "Xo"), who is training as a *ruda*. Hernandez weaves the flashbacks of Vicki's origins, rise, and conflicts with Rena with the present-day story of Xo and Gina. Gina is in love with Xochitl and also wants to be her tag-team partner, though Vicki keeps them working as individual wrestlers; Gina gives up a chance to win the Texas state title by throwing a match to Xo to make her happy. Thus Gina and Xo are presented as the opposites of Vicki and Rena: a wrestling partnership that emphasizes friendship and cooperation over the glory of winning and individual success. This is certainly an important theme in these later wrestling stories, and it definitely illustrates "the importance of kinship as both a trope and an organizing principle in the occupation subculture of professional wrestlers" (Levi 50).

Xochitl's story develops that even further in "The Navas of Hazel Court," wherein we see her at home with her former wrestler husband and three children. The children are describing their mother's match: "Mommy made the

5.6. TV interview of Vicki playing the *ruda* with her angry taunts, from *Locas*.

lady all bloody" and "And it was so gross!" (164), to which Xochitl, as a *ruda*, celebrates her effect on the crowd: "You should've seen it, Mario. That crowd wanted to murder me! It was great . . ." Her son chimes in, "A man tried to hit Mommy with a chair!" (165). All of this is spoken alongside typical family life—complaints about Barney videotapes and getting ready for school. With their children sent to bed, she and her husband argue about how they both work and watch the kids, but make up in the morning. The short story ends with Xo grinding the eye socket of her next opponent as her husband sits beaming ringside. It demonstrates the normalcy of professional wrestling as labor and wrestling families like any other kind of family along with the whole family's membership in *la familia luchística*, the wrestling family.

The story specifically also demonstrates Levi's argument as to how *lucha libre* creates a unique space for women to be self-supporting, physically strong, and independent from the limitations of Marianismo. In "the discourse of Marianismo, luchadoras should figure as indecent women—committed to a public, money-earning, aggressive activity that may take them away from their husbands or children. . . . Instead, as athletes, performers, and mothers, luchadoras embody a visceral, grassroots, feminist argument that both alludes to and evades the dichotomy of decency and indecency" (170), partially because *lucha libre* itself is given such important cultural currency and also because *luchadoras* in Mexican tradition are usually not sexualized to earn power or respect.

In Hernandez's first post–*Love & Rockets* series story, the extended "Whoa Nellie!" includes all of the above elements—the matriarchal wrestling family, the interweaving of multiple generations, the creation of distinctively strong female roles through support and conflict, the presentation of varied female body types—and adds to them a critique of and challenge to the operational powers of professional wrestling itself. There is a continuation of the earlier story lines between Xo and Gina but in addition an exploration of the business of professional wrestling and its personal and professional impacts on individual wrestlers.

Xo still wrestles mainly as a *ruda* and Gina a *técnica*; at their first match the announcer introduces Gina as "186 pounds . . . from Chickasaw, Oklahoma . . . Gina Bravo!" (4). Afterwards Xo teases her about this implied Native heritage and Gina replies: "I know, Xo. But coach thinks it'll be good for my image to keep up my indian routine" (8). The packaging and development of character is secondary to the larger juxtaposition of good and evil, *técnica* versus *ruda*, where Vicki calls for "more hair pulling, eye gouging and pearl harboring! You guys hate each other remember?" (8). As we see in "Whoa Nellie!" the outcomes of each match are not predetermined, but the relationship of each wrestler to this moral landscape is essential for the broader spectacle and the business of wrestling.

Hernandez nicely pokes fun at these frameworks and dynamics when Xo's children watch her wrestle on television and cannot understand why their mother both is the "bad guy" and wins the match, and later when she plays the *técnica* against Vicki, her son asks, "Then you'll win and everybody will love you??" (13). Her son is even more confused when, playing "the good guy," Xo loses to Vicki and the crowd is against her: "'But she was the bad guy . . . an' you were the good guy . . .' 'Yes, I told you sometimes the bad guys win.' 'But they were cheering her . . . and they were booing you . . . an' you were the good guy?' 'Yes.' 'So how come you didn't win?'" (20). His childish questions effectively capture the contradictions of *lucha libre*: fair competition between individual wrestlers tied into a larger moral paradigm of good guys and bad guys—what Levi calls a wrestler's "ethical identification" or "moral role" (85). Levi sums this shifting landscape:

> Lucha libre portrays a world in which human agency is limited and supplemented by the intervention of (natural and supernatural) forces beyond human control. . . . Lucha libre thus portrays a world-view that recognizes that human agency is ultimately constrained by the forces of history, nature, and the world beyond. (78)

In this story the world beyond is primarily the business of wrestling itself. Vicki is brought into a meeting of the wrestling board and is notified that the Texas state title must be vacated because the champion is pregnant. While Vicki assumes there would be a contest to have a new title holder, the board instead informs her that they want Xochitl to be given the title. While those around hold suspicions about the reasons for this, Xo is ecstatic. However, she loses her first match as champion to Katy Hawk, a *técnica*. Afterwards Gina tells Vicki she wants to challenge Katy for the title, and Vicki explains to her that because of the limits of geography, tied to her moral role, she can't. She says: "'You're not a heel in west Texas they love you there. It wouldn't work!' 'But I was a heel tonight backing Xo!' 'Here in East Texas you're a heel! There in west Texas you're a baby face! Got that? Now forget it Gina!' 'Something is very wrong about all of this!' 'You mean you're just figuring this out?'" (53). Ultimately, Gina learns from the other wrestlers that Xo was set up for these events to draw larger crowds for the upcoming "Super Wrestle Rock Shock" event.

When Gina confronts Vicki about the setup, she discovers that while Vicki did have knowledge of the plan, she has chosen to retire and close Camp Vicki because of her disappointment over them. She tells Gina of her dreams and struggles as a young wrestler:

> Once I had made it all the way to the top, I'd use all my power to protect other gals trying to break into pro wrestling. That's why Camp Vicki was created. I was going to make you all champions. Because everybody deserves to be a champion at least once in their life. A real champion not a hand picked one, y'know? But, as it goes, the harder you beat your head against the wall, the harder the wall gets . . . and after awhile it's not your head that hurts . . . but your heart . . . and then all you can be is disgusted . . . and ashamed. (56)

Finally, the comic concludes with an eleven-woman "over the top rope battle" (58) that Vicki works as commentator. After dramatic action, the last two competitors in the ring are Gina and Xo, and they stare each other down in anger. The announcer provides the following description:

> "Wait a minute! They're both leaving the ring! They're not going to continue! Whoa, Nellie! They deliberately disqualified themselves so now nobody goes home with the two grand! That is the craziest. . . . How do you like that Vicki? The way they're acting you'd think they were just crowned tag team champions of the world!" "Sure looks like it don't it?" (67)

Vicki sits ringside with a satisfied smile. That final panel takes up two-thirds of the page and features the two women hand in hand, arms aloft in victory. The two women chose to put their own conflicts behind them and battle instead the unfair wrestling board, by thwarting the power structure, taking power into their own hands, and presenting themselves as a tag-team through disqualification. This is the most powerful example of how these women challenge the forces of power in their lives, and it is the *lucha* ring itself that elevates these small individual challenges to the level of complex gender representations: "It is a performance that displays many of the elements of machista discourse—male strength, male power, masculinity, as an act of struggle—but places them in a context that disrupts the hegemony of machismo's terms" (178). But as with the *Locas* stories from *Love & Rockets*, even with all of the challenges of the male-dominated world of wrestling, it is that same world that provides opportunity and representational context.

Though *Sonambulo* and *Locas* feature widely divergent *luchadores* and *luchadoras* through characters, genre contexts, and themes, they both provide one consistent element: a challenge to narrative expectations through an essential culture marker of origin and communal identity. In *Sonambulo* this origin and identity gives the title character his purpose and ultimately his power while Navarro uses the same figure and contexts mainly to reify gender expectations. Hernandez, on the other hand, uses the development of complex wrestling narratives in his series as communal, familial, cultural, and gender representations. In both narratives, *lucha libre* signification "is *fundamentally* about the exercise of power, *where physical power stands in for other modes*" (219); the forms of power in these narratives vary wildly, and thus *lucha libre* also functions differently.

NOTES

1. Levi details the creation of the first *lucha libre* mask by Antonio H. Martinez, a shoemaker in Mexico City in 1934:

> Thus, the first wrestling mask was not carried from the villages of Jalisco or Guerrero to Mexico City. It was invented by an urban, mestizo shoemaker at the behest of a North American performing in a genre recently imported from the United States. It alluded not to ritual practices of indigenous Mexican communities but to the Ku Klux Klan. (110)

2. In general, a "*rudo*" or "*ruda*" is the "bad guy," the morally negative role, whereas the "*técnico*" or "*técnica*" is the "good" and morally just role in a match. A wrestler's "moral position" must be communicated to the audience mainly nonverbally through "movement vocabulary: different ways to enter the ring, different preferred techniques, and different orientations of their bodies in the space of the arena" (Levi 85). More specifically, "one aspect of the *técnico/rudo* difference, then, is the contrast between skill and brutality" (87) though this dichotomy is never absolute.

PART III

TORTILLA STRIPS

SIX

LATINO IDENTITY AND THE MARKET: MAKING
SENSE OF CANTÚ AND CASTELLANOS'S *BALDO*

HÉCTOR FERNÁNDEZ L'HOESTE

Economy and culture — it's the same fight.
JACK LANG, FRENCH MINISTER OF CULTURE (1981–1986, 1988–1992)

WRITTEN BY HECTOR CANTÚ and illustrated by Carlos Castellanos, *Baldo* (2000–) is a lighthearted comic strip that narrates the travails of Baldomero Bermúdez, a Latino adolescent of Mexican descent.[1] In the story, the character belongs to a family (his dad, a widower; his sister Gracie, an intelligent and willful child; and scatterbrained great-aunt Carmen, who fails to fit in US culture; see figure 6.1) that, to a certain extent, suggests archetypes of a quintessential Latino household exposed to the constant barrage of the US advertising sector and general media, bent on conquering Latinos as the fastest-growing portion of the national market. In this sense, the comic strip embodies an initial stab at representing the process of acculturation and assimilation of new generations of Latinos into US society and culture. Thus, within the overall context of capitalism, it is possible to argue that Baldo's interaction with US identity takes place chiefly by way of his negotiation with economic imperatives, dutifully mediated by the advertising industry, rather than with strictly cultural ones, borne out of folklore and ethnic or social tradition.

In Baldo's world, economy and culture merge into one, very much along the lines once suggested by French Minister of Culture Jack Lang in his quest to defend Gallic culture from the assault of international media. While the general contexts differ, the actual combination of variables describes a similar process. Amid this setup, Latino identity represents an additional segment that must be engaged, co-opted, and hegemonized by the US economy. This assertion applies equally well to other characters in this volume — in particular, in the case of Latino superheroes, like those covered by Isabel Millán (Anya Sofía Corazón), Kathryn M. Frank, Brian Montes, and Adilifu Nama and

6.1. Hector Cantú and Carlos Castellanos, *Baldo*.

Maya Haddad (Miles Morales). After all, just like Cantú and Castellanos, Marvel seeks to appeal to a growing demographic.

The fact that Cantú, the writer, is someone with a background in the Latino business community (for a time, he worked as managing editor for *Hispanic Business*) plays a significant role in this operation. Cantú has been quite outspoken about how the best comics tend to sneak in messages in a subtle, subversive way, making huge commentary on the US way of life. In turn, Castellanos claims to explore misunderstanding beyond ethnicity, hoping to universalize the nature of the comic strip.[2] Accordingly, many of the story lines in *Baldo* depict the negotiation of identity between the main character and members of his family and the US market. In them, the latter comes across as a setting willing to engage and embrace identities as long as, in accordance with its prerogatives, they appear to bear economic potential. In this sense, many of the circumstances covered in *Baldo* mimic the history of the integration of previous groups into the US mainstream: women, Italian Americans, African Americans, homosexuals, and so on. (See Richard T. Rodríguez's reflections on gay Latino superheroes in chapter 11 of this volume for a sample of this process.)

That is to say, Cantú and Castellanos develop their narratives based on the premise that economic integration into the US marketplace will precede social and cultural acceptance—to this extent, both authors operate as advocates of capitalism and fully acculturated Latinos. As a result, it is vital to prove that Latino identity conforms and corresponds to the theoretical dictates of the US marketing and advertising industry, which will, in due time, vow for its inclusion into the national mainstream, perhaps resulting in a redefinition of domestic identity. For an ethnic group to be fully accepted and integrated into US society and culture—they seem to claim—it must first learn to flex its economic muscle.

In spite of this, my main contention when it comes to *Baldo* is that in the process of proposing a cultural product that models and discusses the various stages of acculturation and assimilation as part of the immigration process, and suggesting as champion of its story line an individual with an apparently complete case of acculturation (Baldo is fully functional in English and very seldom utters expressions in Spanish, seems extremely comfortable and familiar with US culture, and performs like the average suburban teenager), thus validating the successful inclusion of Latinos into the cultural mainstream, Cantú and Castellanos end up passing from one stereotype to another. To be exact, instead of relying on what is considered the stereotypical Latino perception—quite basically, that of a group that has refused to relinquish its culture and blend into the mainstream in a fashion as conceding as previous communities—this pair of cultural actors end up reinforcing certain biases with respect to the way Latinos will eventually integrate into US culture. The way in which they portray acculturation is, to say the least, a tad problematic, for, just as prevailing stereotypes fail to contemplate the Latino community in all its complexity, with a variety of races, national origins, class contexts, and sexual and religious preferences, the version suggested by Cantú and Castellanos contains multiple normative, reductive, and homogenizing denominators.

In the process of pursuing an audience, Cantú and Castellanos have delineated a version of reality that adjusts to prevailing notions in the world of marketing for what a fully acculturated Latino might be like, albeit in the course of negotiating his cultural viability with the advertising sector. While *Baldo* contends that, yes, Latinos will eventually assimilate and become a very functional component of US identity—as discussed in other essays in this volume—it fails to acknowledge that Latinos come in many packages, and, consequently, the degree of acculturation and negotiation of identity, particularly in an age influenced by instant access of information and communication across the globe, will vary significantly from one individual to another.[3] Following Cantú and Castellanos, within difference, there is a denial of difference. Instead, *Baldo* portrays the process of acculturation in a staged, quasi-deterministic fashion.

To come to the point, *Baldo* fails to suggest that the process of assimilation of Latinos will be unlike that of any other previous groups because, at the very moment of its occurrence, it involves a greater number of variables that, unlike previous migratory experiences, have fluctuated significantly. Migration has seldom been as homogenizing as conventional culture tends to portray it—be it the case of Latinos or previous collectivities—but this homogenizing mind-set, proper of individuals seemingly influenced by theories emanating from the marketing sector, is apt for an industry willing to deal with difference in the most coercing, unaccommodating manner available, regardless of its actual level of competence.

It is important to clarify what all the buzz is about regarding Latinos and the US market. In the present century, Latinos have become one of the most sought-after portions of the population within the US market. The year 2007 marked the first year in which Latinos controlled more disposable personal income than any other minority group in the nation. According to the US Census Bureau, the purchasing power of the Latino community was projected to be more than $1.5 trillion (or 10 percent of the US total) by 2015. Having recently become the largest minority population in the country, the Latino population keeps growing at a faster rate than the rest of the general population (while the Latino population grew 43 percent from 2000 to 2010, non-Latinos expanded only 4.9 percent, which means Latinos grew nearly ten times faster; US Census 2010); in fact, it will still account for about 60 percent of the growth of the US population over the next five years.[4] Latinos make up the largest, youngest, and fastest-growing racial/ethnic group in the United States, accounting for 16.3 percent (50.5 million) of the total population.[5] Specifically, nearly one out of every six individuals in the United States is currently a Latino; by the year 2020, one in five Americans is expected to be of Latino origin. By 2035, Latinos are expected to become the majority population in the country.[6]

As the number of Latinos increases, so will the corresponding rate of penetration of the market, so an enormous amount of capital will be at stake. Thus, advertising companies are paying close attention to this segment of the population and studying it carefully, hoping to establish more effective approaches to understanding its patterns in terms of preferences and consumption. Marketing research ratifies the notion that when advertising matches cultural norms, it tends to be viewed more favorably and generate higher levels of purchase intent. In sum, targeted marketing plays a key role in the interaction between mainstream US culture and Latinos. Most notably, targeted marketing can sometimes be perceived as offering legitimacy and validation rather than exploitation, an aspect that would contribute and hasten assimilation into the mainstream.[7]

During the past decades, the US marketing sector has developed a number of theories with respect to Latinos, many of which are supported by quantitative research of varying quality; some of it is superlative, but some of it is far from exhaustive. Hastily digested, this latter research may result in potentially reductive proclivities. Early psychographics for Latinos (or Hispanics, as the group was labeled back then) emphasized the following: they were very proud people with strong family and cultural ties; they were willing to perpetuate their traditions through future generations (particularly through the use of Spanish and conventional religious beliefs); they professed a growing sense of distinctiveness and unity, engendering a feeling of being Latinos first, Americans second; they subscribed to the notion that Latinos are more family oriented than non-Latinos; and, finally, regardless of the actual level of linguistic dexterity, they valued highly the sharing of a common language. In terms of purchase patterns, marketing research was not much more elaborate in its findings. According to studies promoted by the tobacco industry, Latinos tended to believe that the biggest, most popular brands were best; selected name-brand goods over house brands; favored small neighborhood stores; reacted favorably to Spanish-oriented advertising, as long as it was executed properly; and were more concerned with getting value (quality for the price) than US citizens as a whole.[8]

Needless to say, with the passing of time, many of these notions were revised or complexified, in particular, those directly affected by judgments related to a degree of acceptance and interaction with Anglo culture. Such a shift is predictable. Sometimes, otherness pays off a bit. As a more protracted understanding of Anglo culture matured, it was only sensible that a mirror effect took place. In general, Latino consumers were described as sociable (sharing and enjoying pleasure with others was an important factor), emotional (somatically inclined), pleasure-seeking (allegedly, they devoted considerable time and energy to the pursuit of pleasure), polite (negative advertising figured as a definite turn-off), respectful (of others and authorities), and macho (thus essentializing maleness).[9] At the same time, independent of the depth of the assessment promoted by these studies, Latinos' shared cultural values were found to influence consumer behavior consistently. Irrespective of their tangible applicability within a wide spectrum of migratory experiences—that is, failing to consider how these aspects shifted within a variety of contexts (after all, migration is a highly individualized experience, affected by nationality, class, race, gender, etc.)—*respeto* (respect for authority, familiar or societal), *fatalismo* (resignation), *familismo* (family orientation), and *simpatía* (harmonious social relationships) were found to be important predictors of consumer behavior among Latinos.

Within this framework, cultural concepts like acculturation and assimilation became the buzzwords of the day. They were said to play a key role in the definition of marketing models. According to Merriam-Webster, acculturation is the "cultural modification of an individual, group, or people by adapting to or borrowing traits from another culture" or "a merging of cultures as a result of prolonged contact." As understood by the advertising industry, acculturation involves abandoning one's original cultural background and measures the integration of one individual into another culture, two key considerations for anyone willing to influence consumer habits. Following Boaz, a more traditional authority, all people acculturate to some measure since we are all influenced, in one or another way, by a foreign culture.[10] However, each individual develops his or her own style and pace of acculturation; just like migration, it entails an exceedingly personalized process. As acculturation happens, a very selective progression of embracing the host country's culture takes place.

Acculturation is a very multifaceted procedure, and it takes root in a different way in each person, affected by each individual's willingness to embrace the local culture, though at the same time keeping some of his or her own. This much did not escape the grasp of the advertising and marketing industries. However, research does not seem to have focused on effective ways to assess this degree of variability. Instead, a variety of taxonomies surfaced, willing to explain acculturation in a less pliable, more categorical fashion. According to one, acculturation may be conceived as unidimensional, that is, taking place individually when an immigrant travels alone and lacks a context with which to resist the local culture and economy, or multidimensional, in which individuals embrace aspects of the host culture while preserving some of their own (such as language).[11] Current research supports the notion that most Latinos are acculturating into US society according to the latter model, as daily existence in a globally interconnected world renders the former impractical.[12] Then again, acculturation also allows for a segmentation of the market into more empirical categories, such as the unacculturated (at 25 percent, it comprises those who live in Spanish-speaking households and use English reluctantly), the bicultural (at roughly 66 percent, it comprises those who adapt comfortably to both worlds and languages), and the acculturated (at 9 percent, it is English-dominant and consumes primarily English media).[13]

In theory, there are four distinct mind-sets that reflect the varying levels of acculturation among Latinos (though these descriptions are concrete, their nature is not exact): first, the cultural loyalist, who is a foreign-born, Spanish-dependent recent arrival who has been in the country for less than five years; second, the cultural embracer, who, though foreign-born and bilingual, has become resident and prefers Spanish; third, the cross-culturer, who is usually first-generation US-born, bilingual, and bicultural and is equally comfortable in the Latino and Anglo worlds; and fourth, the culturally integrated, who stands as a fully acculturated, US-born Latino, usually belonging to a second, third, or fourth generation—English dependent, she or he may not speak Spanish or speak it well.[14] While practical for the handling of identities through a collective approach, this set of categories apparently fails to contemplate an expanded, more diffuse array of information—for instance, the fact that as their migratory experience has matured, a wide number of foreign-born Latinos have become equally comfortable with the Latino and Anglo worlds, effectively bridging the second and third categories.

Assimilation, on the other hand, refers to the process by which an individual or a group's language and/or culture come to resemble those of another group. From a marketing perspective, this entails an ethnic group's almost complete acquisition of the values and behaviors of a national culture by shedding its own. (Think of the mind-blowing potential in terms of consumerism. There is one key difference, though: in the case of acculturation, minority culture may remain intact; in the case of assimilation, it changes.) Given its extreme nature, assimilation stands as one of the possible outcomes of acculturation, the others being rejection, integration, and marginalization.

As a rule, assimilation tends to have a more definitive and all-encompassing connotation, describing the traditional way in which groups blended into the "melting pot" in the past, through coercion and social–cultural–economic pressure. In other words, when it comes to marketing (and not sociology or anthropology, both of which tend to be more considerate), the difference between full acculturation and assimilation echoes more a matter of kind than quantity.

It is not altogether uncommon to find marketing research suggesting relationships between the degree of acculturation of an individual and the exercise of brand loyalty.[15] A relatively common viewpoint seems to support the idea that brand loyalty is inversely proportional to the degree of acculturation; that is, successfully acculturated individuals are, for the most part, more adventurous in their exploration of new brands, while recent arrivals tend to stick with established brands—US or otherwise—from their home country.[16] Thus comes into play the concept of advertising "in culture" (rather than "in language"); that is, Latinos of various acculturation levels are exposed to advertising in both languages, as this particular variable no longer seems to play a defining role in the outcome of the purchasing experience. As long as Latinos identify with the execution, advertising in English is not out of the question. Mass communication also partakes in this exercise: TV is more effective at reaching unacculturated individuals, while printed media are more effective among acculturated Latinos. Therefore, with these audiences in mind, TV may be in Spanish but the press will tend to favor English (and even this seems to be at play: witness Fusion, Univisión and ABC News' recent joint project, and the number of newspaper editions in Spanish, starting with Miami's *El Nuevo Herald*). Even so, the press in Spanish might abound, but the ultimate goal is to advertise in English.

In *Baldo*, the power of media is always recognized; for the most part, they are portrayed in English, just like the comic strip (despite a translated version). In addition, making things even more arresting, research by advertising powerhouses such as BBDO shows that the acculturated segment of the Latino population is the largest and fastest-growing segment of the community, increasing at an annual rate of 12 percent. By 2010, the number of isolated Latinos—namely, those who prefer to cling exclusively to Latino culture—dropped from 32 percent to 25 percent.[17]

As a cultural product, *Baldo* seems to bear information of this nature very much in mind. As mentioned, the careful segmentation of the family unit into generational groups with very distinct attitudes and approaches toward life in the United States seems closely predicated on some of the previously described taxonomies. In the strip, in one of the clearest examples of the difference in generational tastes—and thus the overwhelming importance of the cultural industry in the segmentation of audiences—Baldo appears discussing choices for his CD mail-order music club (à la Columbia House) with his dad, Tía Carmen, and Gracie. Dad favors Vikki Carr, proper of a cultural embracer. After all, Carr, née Florencia Bisenta de Casillas Martínez Cardona in El Paso, Texas, was one of the first Latina cultural performers to gain widespread acceptance by the US public. Though nowadays she records *ranchera* albums, she epitomizes the immigrant dream. Ever the loyalist, Tía Carmen prefers Tito Puente, a native New Yorker with broad appeal in Latin America. The choice of Puente is particularly strategic. Like Carr, he was born in the United States (to Puerto Rican parents); unlike her, his experience embodies a Caribbean, Eastern Seaboard flavor (rather than Texan), so Tía Carmen's preference suggests a more pan-Latino musical taste, less rooted in an exclusive sense of *mexicanidad*, a very effective measure in terms of developing a feeling of identification with a wider readership. Thanks to her keen critical bent, baby sister Gracie refuses to participate in the CD selection process; she calls it the way she sees it: *el ripo off*, in well-versed Spanglish. A tad clueless, Baldo mistakes her Spanglish expression for the name of a rock *en español* band (*The Lower* 111).

The boundaries could not be clearer. Baldo's familiarity with rock *en español* identifies him as a millennial since most of these acts gained popularity in the United States only toward the end of the previous century and early 2000s, when Latinos reached a critical mass in terms of visibility. And this isn't the only hint at intergenerational contrast. Baldo loves soccer. His dad prefers baseball, harking back to the earlier days of glory of the national pastime. However, when Dad alludes to Alex Rodríguez's $250-million contract with the Texas Rangers (a brief hint at a Texan identity), Baldo immediately agrees to play ball with him (*The Lower* 113).

In yet another strip, when the holidays are approaching, each member of the family appears, looking at a catalog embodying her or his preferences: since she incarnates a loyalist, Tía Carmen goes for a *Catálogo de Hierbas*, in Spanish; culturally integrated, Baldo reads the *Lowrider Holiday* catalog; and Gracie, the youngest and therefore most thoroughly acculturated member of the family (and thus even more in contact with Anglo sensibilities), favors the *PETA Christmas Catalog* (*The Lower* 122).

The fact that they all substantiate their identities by way of consumer preferences only ratifies that which I argue with respect to the strip: *Baldo* is like a guide on how to acculturate successfully, as long as you intend to follow the precepts of the advertising industry. Market segmentation comes to light in the strip in the oddest ways possible. When Tía Carmen listens to the radio, she grapples with Charo, who reached her peak of popularity in the 1970s and, like Carr, speaks to older Latinos; Ricky Martin, the forerunner of the late 1990s Latin pop explosion; La Macarena, a mid-1990s craze if there was ever one; a soccer-match scoring cry, à la Andrés Cantor (which signaled the arrival of Latinos to sports media thanks to the 1994 World Cup); and even "Hasta la vista, baby," Arnold Schwarzenegger's catchphrase from *Terminator 2* (1991), a concession to Mexican-American prevalence in California, acknowledging how a mélange of Latino cues can exemplify comprehensive commercial targeting (*Night* 56). In this case, the object is not to portray her as a member of a group but for the reader to become aware of her or his cultural competence and congruence with a viable commercial premise.

In another instance, once again drawing on generational difference, a vignette displays each decade's corresponding icon, chronicling the further descent into commercialism: while Tía Carmen loves Desi Arnaz from the 1950s and Papi is enraptured with Rita Moreno from the 1970s, Baldo goes gaga over a Gamestation 2000 console (*Night* 59)! As a result, it is pretty clear how, to the extent that Latinos have gained increased acceptance in the mainstream, they have also been co-opted by the entertainment industry. In all, Cantú and Castellanos's portrayal of market segmentation clarifies how they have carefully aligned their characters' profiles according to theoretical delineations guided by marketing prerogatives. While they may be effective for purposes of readership identification, in the end, they pay a disservice to Latinos, given the overall reductionism of their interpretation.

Siblings Baldo and Gracie are both thoroughly acculturated individuals, fully functional in English and comfortable with US culture, despite the fact that Baldo, who is older, seems less mature and intellectually motivated than his prodigious baby sister. Though their preferences seem to point out different approaches to Latino identity—Baldo is obsessed with a lowrider, while Gracie seems infatuated with Frida Kahlo (*The Lower* 112)—when it comes to the market, they both react in analogous ways: once Baldo realizes he only has $19 available for a 1964 Impala worth $9,500, Gracie points out that the major obstacle toward the achievement of his big dream is the size of his wallet, making it clear that, even at such a tender age, she also quantifies success in distinctly economic terms (*The Lower* 11). In effect, thanks to the fact that she has eaten all her Halloween candy, Baldo is able to con Gracie into serving him as a domestic aide in return for a few Tootsie Rolls (*The Lower* 75), which means she is well versed in the exchange value of goods and benefits.

On the whole, her degree of economic literacy is more on par with the pragmatism of Anglo culture than with the abstract sense of worth endorsed by elders from south of the border (as we will see, her dad is one of those). Nonetheless, toying with language in one of their few admissions of origin for the comic strip's *latinidad*, Cantú and Castellanos ascribe Gracie's ambitious nature to Chica Power (rather than Chicano) (*The Lower* 19). In Gracie's context, the word *chica* stands for "girl," as in "Girl Power." However, another acceptation for the word is "small." The joke plays well, since *chica* describes Gracie's minimal height appropriately. The fact that "Chica" could be a shortened version of "Chicano" (just one syllable less) adds to the humor. And when she tries to get rid of El Cucuy (the strip's version of the Boogeyman), Gracie does so by offering a no-compete contract (*The Lower* 20) with concrete allusions to a severance package (*The Lower* 51), a sign of familiarity with a culture obsessed with the rule of law. During Christmas, Gracie is even capable of coming up with a Santa Claus to stand against unfair child labor practices (*The Lower* 124), a concern that does not echo habitual Latino attitudes toward the job market, more oriented in the direction of critiques of the exploitation of illegal aliens. For a child of her age, her level of economic–financial literacy is simply baffling. A Latin American child her age would seldom think of these things. At the same time, Gracie plays the role of hypercritical, rebellious voice in the strip, sometimes giving in to comic relief, as when she grows enraged by what she deems to be a grotesque take on Mexican identity (the traditional campesino hat and outfit forced upon a little body with an enormous head), only to find out that it is her brother in a costume, and he's paid $10 an hour (*Night* 101)! In the greater context of things, despite her flirtations with Zapata and Subcomandante-Marcos-like figures (*The Lower* 97), Gracie seems a lot more acquainted with US society than with her Latino background.

Sergio Bermúdez (aka Papi, or Baldo's dad) owns a small business, and, though he also speaks English well, he clings to his old shirts with a sense of flair proper of anyone fond of guayaberas (strictly speaking, his shirts are not guayaberas, as they lack lower pockets), like Latinos of the olden days. In point of fact, Papi's guayaberas become a matter of discussion between Baldo and his dad, leading to an exchange that elucidates a key distinction between generations: when Sergio reminds his son that money isn't everything and that things ought to be made rather than bought, the adolescent retorts sarcastically that he needs some underwear made, rather than purchased (*The Lower* 5).

Given its early nature—it is at the beginning of the first collection of Baldo strips—this exchange serves as an introduction to the degree of relevance that economic matters will bear in the course of the story. Truth be told, Baldo is not the only one "wanting" things; when Gracie watches the TV commercials for Christmas toys, she suddenly becomes possessed by an alarming sense of greed, with her eyes popping out (*The Lower* 101). Hence, by making light of the distorting impact of capitalism on young minds, the authors disarm any criticism that may suggest a contrast with the generally more altruistic dispositions of older generations.

Tía Carmen, Baldo's great-aunt, is perhaps the most telling character. (In a nod to a hypothetical pan-Latino identity, which is more appealing at the point of marketing, Cantú and Castellanos seldom allude to a particular nationality. In many ways, Baldo comes across as a Texan of Mexican descent, but his ancestry is not a matter of discussion in the comic.) Tía Carmen is extremely devout and fond of old recipes and herbal remedies. Though she is also fluent in English, her sense of social relationship evokes more collective constructs than a nuclear family, as when she goes to the hospital and her friends and relatives pack the place (*Night* 125). Nevertheless, Tía Carmen has made great strides in terms of embracing US prerogatives. When questioned about when she learned to distinguish the bulk of wallets from the size of bottoms (to the unaware reader, her descriptions of men's behinds are the heart of the joke), she replies that it was about the same time she learned the difference between dentures and real teeth, i.e., in her old age (*The Lower* 16). In truth, what the strip implies is that her appreciation of money is a rather belated event, as her earlier context allegedly supported a less monetarily driven approach. In another strip (*The Lower* 16), when Baldo questions her about the fervor with which she prays by her *altar*, the customary homemade shrine with an effigy of the Virgin Mary and countless candles, she explains she is hoping to win the $295 million Lotto with her fifty lottery tickets! In fact, Tía Carmen is so adept at the game of money that soon enough she sets up her own psychic hotline from home (*The Lower* 67).

If this is what is happening to an old lady, the reader might surmise, what is the object of so much resistance to cultural assimilation? Given her idiosyncratic nature, the many nuances of Tía Carmen's behavior enclose precious information about the story. Tía Carmen may have adapted, yet she incarnates the failure to give in of many Latinos. When she rushes back and forth during a meal (*The Lower* 18), it is to avoid the intromission of commercials in her telenovela. At some other point, in a more directed comment at her nationality, she observes the Day of the Dead (*Night* 109), which, though it is gaining a wider following, remains a distinctly Mexican holiday, standing in almost direct opposition to Halloween; thus it is possible to argue that, at least from Tía Carmen's side, Baldo is of Mexican descent.

A low-key counterpart to Tía Carmen is even older great-Abuelita Zoraida (great-grandmother), who drops in for a visit every now and then. Attesting to the number of English-speaking generations in this family, Abuelita Zoraida is also fluent in English. The old matron closely guards the survival of tradition in her great-grandchildren, making sure that Baldo respects the elderly (the much treasured notion of *respeto*, cherished by the advertising sector, as it allows for the endorsement of products through experienced senior advice) and Gracie retains family traditions like the ability to make a good empanada (to be preyed upon by the advances of food conglomerates like Kraft or Goya) (*Night* 48). Once reassured, Abuelita Zoraida sends Baldo a check for $300 (supposedly, so he can purchased a plane ticket and visit her), reiterating that love is best quantified as cold cash, earned at the local bingo (*Night* 49). So, like other members of the family, Abuelita Zoraida has learned well how to conflate ethnic tradition and economic interests.

Within Cantú and Castellanos's portrayals, there are a few significant variables in matters of representation. Baldo's aspirations and desires—even his feeding habits—proper of a culturally integrated teenager, are more in line with Anglo modernity and its accompanying economic paradigm. When asked to illustrate his desires in art class, like any US adolescent, he draws a car: a PT Cruiser, of all things (*The Lower* 63). When he acts older, wearing a suit, his age is dictated by a fondness for fine Colombian roasted coffee, his awareness of the NASDAQ's good performance, and, most notably, the existence of a to-do list in his organizer (*The Lower* 83). Still, his efforts are futile; Dad refuses to give him the keys to the car. Clearly, maturity is defined in terms of access to the market (rather than responsibility in household chores or academic duties), an aspect that definitely encourages consumerism. Seated by his desk, next to one of the first-generation colorful iMacs (sign of an established middle-class status), Baldo answers the reader survey for *Custom Cruiser* magazine, hoping to win a set of tires for his dream car (*The Lower* 96), in a fashion akin to many car-obsessed US youth. At times, his link to the market denotes how his relationship with *norteamericanidad* is more than theoretical. Since he has never seen actual *chicharrones* ("chicharone chips," in the comic strip's Anglicized language)—he holds a bag of them in his hands as proof—he questions his dad about the food. Dad goes on a lengthy description of the product: bite-sized morsels of pigskin boiled in "a big vat of greasy lard" and fried to "a nice salty crisp" (*The Lower* 13). Thoroughly accustomed to the US's aseptic sense of modernity, in which food is seldom portrayed as bearing any relationship to an actual living animal—if it were so, it would hinder a great deal of food consumption in the country, given the dire conditions in which animals are farmed for food—he is revolted by his dad's enthusiasm for lard and fried food.

In occasional instances of self-reference, with more than a slap of irony, the strip spares no effort mocking its own commercially driven ambitions, as when it shows a group of white-collar workers disserting about their highly advanced scientific data–collection process, in which the finest researchers procure market intelligence from dynamic consumers, that is, Baldo and his pal Cruz, expressing their preference for a puke-green- or earwax-orange-colored soda (*Night* 65).

In *Baldo*, food, a key player in market segmentation, is a sore subject. It, or the way it is consumed by the characters, is particularly telling about their degree of acculturation. In a one-frame vignette, Cantú and Castellanos portray the four members of the family sharing a wildly disparate meal, proper of the eclectic nature of many Latino households (*Night* 83). While less acculturated individuals like Tía Carmen and Dad opt for *tamales de lengua* (tongue tamales) and arroz con pollo (rice with chicken), the more acculturated members of the family (Baldo and Gracie, understandably) stick with macaroni and cheese and peanut butter and jelly sandwiches. To Baldo, the mere mention of real bits of jalapeno (rather than *jalapeño*, the difference is key) on the box of spicy-hot sugar flakes is a matter of appeal (*Baldo* 14). To his dad, in turn, the fact that there are nacho cheese Kellogg's Pop-Tarts suggests a cultural transgression (*Baldo* 15). Thanks to the careful delineation of Latino-friendly products, what appears as commercial empathy to Baldo stands as an intrusion into heritage for his father. The trend is so rampant that even Gracie advertises her banana splits as "salsa covered," to which Baldo objects, claiming that his sister is "overestimating the whole *Latino trend* thing" (*Night* 52).

In all three cases, the characters are reacting to the very same thing: the integration of Latino cues and language into quintessentially Anglo food products. Nevertheless, the responses could not be more diametrically apart. The key consideration is that, regardless of their response, the three of them take sugar flakes, Pop-Tarts, and banana splits, all consecrated elements of Anglo gastronomy, as something acceptable, conceding that, to a certain point, they share a degree of acculturation with the US diet. Nonetheless, for the father, food staples are not the only agent of linguistic contamination and interaction. When he invites Baldo and his pal Cruz to the local fast-food joint, he goes crazy with so many butchered Spanish words (*nacheeseburger, tamachile, gordodita, chalupo supremo, fajitaco, buritatoe, questilla, chimichango, hamburrito,* and so on) (*The Lower* 105).

Yet, once again, the normative aspect of the joke resides in the acceptance of the visit to the fast-food franchise as an adequate source of food in the context of US modernity. Even Tía Carmen is affected by the so-called trend. When she visits the local bodega (while the term has a New York origin, they now exist all over the country), she is surprised to find "stress pop herbalized soda" (with chamomile and kava kava!) and laments missing the opportunity to market an herbal product (*Night* 55). Later on, she even disparages Baldo for consuming an energy drink with caffeine and ginseng, when, according to her, any worthy herbologist knows these ingredients are useless without a touch of chamomile (*Night* 86). At other points, food allows the authors to point out how capitalism has gotten the best of the family. When they go to the movies, the four are so concerned about their snacks—in a fitting fusion of Latino and Anglo snacking habits, minty mints, nachos, root beer, water, jay-jay nuggets, popcorn, banana chips, etc., all to the benefit of the food industry—that, by the time they have settled who has what, the film has ended (*Night* 95).

Baldo acknowledges constantly the great influence consumer culture exerts upon constructs of identity, be they gender driven or motivated by particular values. In this sense, despite initial impressions, treatment of identity in *Baldo* is occasionally sophisticated. However, more enlightened readings of identity come by way of Anglo presence, as when Britney, his Anglo neighbor and future love interest, explains to Baldo that "Latino" clothing does not come into being by what it is, as much as by how it is worn (*Night* 121). Dyeing of the hair, painted fingernails, and plucked eyebrows, which his dad identifies with women, are part of the repertoire of accepted male fashion at Baldo's school (*The Lower* 56). When he surveys female friends about their perception of a PT Cruiser, to his dismay, he realizes the vehicle does not project the tough and cool, gender-driven image that he desires (*The Lower* 119). The Cruiser, it seems, smacks of a "chick" car, a pejorative notion to any teenager seeking to boost his machismo. In Gracie's case, being a young Latina, consumer culture's impact on her construction of gender is even more drastic. In the middle of a nightmare, she envisions herself as a skinny, scantily clad supermodel called Graciela Bermúdez, the very image of eating disorders and a determined shopaholic—in short, an utmost incarnation of superficiality, the exact opposite of the child, who hopelessly rejects body commodification, materialism, and commercial manipulation (*Night* 15).

At other moments, identity constructs pertain more to personal values, like concern for animals and individual health. When Gracie defends vegetarianism—not because she is troubled about her figure, but for the mere sake of public health and animal life (the child is a do-gooder)—her clueless dad reminds her that cholesterol, chemicals, pesticides, hormones, antibiotics, and E. coli, all unfortunately present in the current US diet, have been a Bermúdez family tradition for generations (*Night* 35). And when she debates the virtues of a vegetarian diet with Baldo, her dad points out how, in his day, debates sparked from deep-seated convictions, and not from fast-food commercials, as is the case for brother and sister (*Night* 61). Quite clearly, to him, since he has experienced so much change—thanks to acculturation—dietary convictions cannot be so entrenched. Not to be outdone, when he tries to convince Baldo to drop his preference for brands like Fubu, Hilfiger, and Guess (to save some money), the father even writes in the margins of a magazine—customized publishing, he labels it—that teens are getting more clothes at discount department stores (*Night* 78). The irony lies in that while the strip suggests a negative critique of consumerism, it also appeals to the tastes of a young reader audience, extremely fond of these image-conscious brands.

As I have mentioned, Cantú and Castellanos are very comfortable with a more generic sense of *latinidad*, evidently more applicable for any comic strip seeking broad ethnic appeal, so rather than hint at a concrete origin, they make light of it, hoping to take all audiences to one common starting point: the arrival of Europeans, never mind slaves from Africa (true to its Mexican nature, the strip does celebrate a few Amerindians). However, when Baldo imagines his ancestor the conquistador staring at the stars from the deck of a caravel, he turns to Walter Mercado's astrological hotline for advice! And when the conquistador ancestor loots the riches of Amerindians, it turns out to be an allusion to Baldo's wiping out all of the root beer and chocolate-covered cherries in the refrigerator (*The Lower* 65)! In other words, in *Baldo*, history evolves into active consumption.

In *Baldo*, even figments of the imagination give in to the market. When Baldo's fairy godfather shows up dressed as a homeboy, he explains that the change was motivated by the lack of appeal of his previous attire: a business suit, which did not do much in terms of "client retention" (*The Lower* 120). In the end, he transforms into that greatest of cons, the professional wrestler (albeit one dressed as an Amerindian), hinting at the extent of his ductility in pursuit of customers. And so, consumer culture is a part of life that must be accepted, even by apparitions. Nevertheless, the clash between conflicting traditions in the Anglo and Latino worlds is always evident. Negotiation of identity must be acknowledged. It is one thing to benefit from crass commercialism, and an altogether different one to give the impression of being a cultural sellout, the comic strip seems to assert. Before entering the mall and doing her patriotic duty for the good of the country (according to Baldo's dad) — that is, spending money, enacting *norteamericanidad* while energizing the economy through the circulation of capital, a distinctly US prerogative — Tía Carmen splashes herself with some holy water (*Night* 117). That is to say, the best antidote for a reality of factual concerns is a tradition hinged on unearthly affairs, counterbalancing the effects of that most material of ideologies — capitalism — with the import of an allegedly immaterial one: religion. Then again, once inside, approaches to capitalism are influenced by the degree of acculturation: Baldo seems ashamed of an aunt who bargains inside the mall as though she were at the local Flaco's Flea Market, where other rules apply (*Night* 117). By these measures, Tía Carmen's labor of acculturation is yet unfinished.

Language, the great commercial variable, is so intimately tied to identity that it plays a proverbial role in *Baldo*. Though Baldo speaks fluent English, evincing his advanced degree of acculturation, it is also clear that he knows Spanish. At the mall, once he is offered $10 to complete a survey in Spanish, he immediately shifts language (*Night* 100). Also, when telemarketers call, he switches to Spanish to avoid them (*The Lower* 31). His dad then point outs that, being bilingual, one is worth twice as much to telemarketers (culture is always subjected to the market's appraisal), to which Baldo retorts that it also implies receiving twice as many calls (*Night* 7). In this way, as an acknowledgement of the impact of the economy on their identities, telemarketing mutates into a source of fear. Dad, Baldo, and Gracie cringe together in horror when confronted with a telemarketer who knows their name, address, and what they like, and even speaks Spanish (*Night* 8)!

It is quite apparent that, next to the imperatives of a capitalist economy's propaganda apparatus, Latino identity appears very vulnerable. Language might be an asset, but it can also be easily co-opted. This much is clear to Baldo. When he befriends Britney, she acknowledges that she has learned most of her Spanish from watching television, immediately hinting at Univisión's *Sábado Gigante* (*Night* 93). At another moment, he even jokes with Gracie, creating playful phrases (*poo poo stinkeroso, vómito loco*) and trying to make light of his linguistic clumsiness, when Dad, à la academic establishment, reminds them about the importance of bilingualism in the marketplace of tomorrow (*The Lower* 60). By way of humor, Cantú and Castellanos are so bent on showing people that it is not anti-American to speak Spanish and to be proud of your heritage that they tend to stay close to the current models of acculturation coming from the advertising industry, as though placating and assuaging any potential fears of the audience in terms of alterity.

An eminent conclusion for this essay is that, quite obviously, Latino identity is not confined to language and acculturation. In truth, these factors, though important, only play a supporting role in the overall experience of the Latino community within US society and culture. Demographic and marketing studies point to the continued importance of Spanish-language print and electronic media as expanding in market share because of patterns of acculturation that do not conform to earlier rates and vectors of adaptation into US culture. At the same time, cultural consumption patterns that are common to both younger and older generations of Latinos regardless of acculturation patterns remain equally relevant, influencing market share. In this sense, Latino portrayal in *Baldo* is flawed and shortsighted.

For all the buzz they seem to create, language and acculturation are not true markers of Latino identity. To make matters even more puzzling, current research shows that people identify as Latinos well past the point of being unable to perform effectively in Spanish.[18] Ultimately, while certain aspects of Latino identity might be familiar to the advertising industry—the case of collectivism, *familismo*, or *simpatía*—what truly stands as significant is the degree of interconnectedness between these aspects.

In other words, rather than awarding prevalence to these aspects, what must be prioritized is the relationship among them, which makes for a wonderfully complex mix at the time of understanding how Latinos will gradually settle into the US mainstream. Within this scope, the eventual acceptance of English or the number of generations that have lived in the United States plays a lesser role—regardless of what Marvel or other staples of the industry might intuit in their production. Instead, at the heart of Latino identity we may have more relational and broadly defined constructs, such as interpersonal orientation (how Latinos relate to other people), perception of time and space (potentially influenced by constructs of weather and social relations; public vs. private), degree of spirituality (the multiple forms of being a believer/the multiple forms of being a nonbeliever), and discernment of gender (straight, gay, bi, trans, intergender, etc.).[19] In this way, what becomes increasingly evident is that what marketing companies are so desperately trying to understand—What is it that makes a Latino different?—will remain a continually evolving conundrum until the possibilities for definition are exhausted.

NOTES

1. In their interviews in Frederick Aldama's *Your Brain on Latino Comics*, Cantú and Castellanos speak of *Baldo* in general terms, since their work combines Mexican (Cantú) and Cuban (Castellanos) descent. However, as readers will see, in terms of reception, it is possible to assign some descent to the character.

2. See Cantú's comments on p. 136 and Castellanos's response on p. 141 of Aldama's *Your Brain on Latino Comics*.

3. According to John Horrigan of the Pew Research Center (Horrigan, John, *America Unwired*, Pew Research Center, Wireless Internet Use—Pew Internet & American Life Project, http://pewresearch.org/pubs/1287/wireless-internet-use-mobile-access, accessed 1 Nov. 2013), Internet access through a mobile device is highest among Latinos at eighty-nine percent versus eighty-three percent for African Americans and eighty-four percent for whites. In addition, according to Pieraccini et al. (Pieraccini, Cristina, Leonardo Hernandez, and Douglass Alligood, "The Growing Hispanic Market," *International Journal of Integrated Marketing Communications* 2.1 [Spring 2010]: 29–39), online usage among young Latinos is growing at a faster rate than the general market. Online usage in Spanish is also increasing both as Latinos who prefer Spanish increasingly go online and as the number and quality of Spanish online media options increases.

4. Korzenny, Felipe, and Betty Ann Korzenny. "The Composition of the Hispanic/Latino Market." *Hispanic Marketing: Connecting with the New Latino Consumer*. New York, NY: Routledge, 2011. 39–79.

5. US Census Bureau. "2010 Census Shows America's Diversity." http://www.census .gov/newsroom/releases/archives/2010_census/cb11-cn125.html. Accessed 1 Nov. 2013.

6. US Census Bureau. *Statistical Abstract of the United States: 2010* (129th ed.). http:// www.census.gov/compendia/statab/. Accessed 1 Nov. 2013.

7. Washington, Harriet A. "Burning Love: Big Tobacco Takes Aim at LGBT Youths." *American Journal of Public Health* 92.7 (2002): 1086–1095; Smith, Elizabeth A., and Ruth E. Malone, "The Outing of Philip Morris: Advertising Tobacco to Gay Men," *American Journal of Public Health* 93.6 (2003): 988–993.

8. *Spanish USA, 1984 Summary*, RJ Reynolds Tobacco Company, Bates no. 504616837/6839, http://legacy.library.ucsf.edu/tid/wnf65doo, accessed 1 Nov. 2013; and Jones, Yasmin M., *Previous Hispanic Research*, 16 Dec. 1987, Mangini v. RJ Reynolds Tobacco

Company, Bates no. 507129143/9151, http://legacy.library.ucsf.edu/tid/eqz62doo, accessed 1 Nov. 2013.

9. "Exploratory market of Hispanic smokers." Mangini v. RJ Reynolds Tobacco Company. Bates no. 507132498/2425. http://legacy.library.ucsf.edu/tid/tha72doo. Accessed 1 Nov. 2013.

10. Boas, Franz. *The Central Eskimo*. Washington, DC: Bureau of American Ethnology Annual Report, Smithsonian Institution, 1888; University of Nebraska Press, 1964. 631–632.

11. Laroche, Michel, Chankon Kim, Michael Hui, and Marc A. Tomiuk. "Test of a Non-Linear Relationship between Linguistic Acculturation and Ethnic Identification." *Journal of Cross Cultural Psychology* 29.3 (1998): 418–433.

12. Palumbo, Frederick A., and Ira Teich. "Marketing Segmentation Based on the Level of Acculturation." *Marketing Intelligence and Planning*. ABI/INFORM Global 22.4 (2004): 472.

13. Barbosa, Liria, and Angelina Villarreal. "Acculturation Levels Play Role in Marketing Strategy." *Marketing News* 42.3 (15 Feb. 2008): 26–28.

14. McDonald, Kelly. "Relating, Not Translating: Why and How to Market to U.S. Latinos." *Illinois Banker* 1.3 (Mar. 2006): 12–13.

15. See Corona, Ramón, and Mary Beth McCabe. "Acculturation in Marketing to Latinos in the US." *Journal of Business & Economic Research* 9.9 (Sept. 2011): 67–70.

16. Barbosa, Liria, and Angelina Villarreal. "Acculturation Levels Play Role in Marketing Strategy." *Marketing News* 42.3 (15 Feb. 2008): 26–28.

17. See "BBDO Special Reports on Hispanic Viewing." BBDO (unpublished manuscript), 2007, cited in Pieraccini, Cristina, Leonardo Hernandez, and Douglass Alligood, "The Growing Hispanic Market," *International Journal of Integrated Marketing Communications* 2.1 (Spring 2010): 29–39.

18. Liesse, Julie. "The Latino Identity Project: Understanding a Market." *Advertising Age* 78.8 (19 Feb. 2007): A5–A8.

19. Liesse, A7.

SEVEN

THE ARCHEOLOGY OF THE POST-SOCIAL IN THE COMICS OF LALO ALCARAZ: *LA CUCARACHA* AND *MIGRA MOUSE: POLITICAL CARTOONS ON IMMIGRATION*

JUAN POBLETE

THE LATINO GRAPHIC ARTIST Lalo Alcaraz[1] is author of the *La Cucaracha* comic strip—compiled in one volume under the same title in 2004 and still on-going today—and of widely distributed and published editorial comics, many of them gathered ten years earlier in the book *Migra Mouse: Political Cartoons on Immigration* (1994 ; see figure 7.1). In analyzing these two works here, my main claim is that Alcaraz produced an excellent early mapping of what today can be called the post-social moment in the history of Latino migrations to, and Latino populations in, the United States.

By "post-social," I understand a social configuration resulting from the transformation of the welfare state. The latter, with its ethos of the social as a solidarity-based commitment administered by the state, is replaced by a competitive state whose rationality derives from the neoliberal version of the economy, and whose ethos, instead of socializing and distributing risk in solidarity, individualizes and privatizes it. The new space of the neoliberal post-social, affecting migrants in the United States today, is in the process of transforming old spatial extra-national separations. Those divisions between development and underdevelopment, or close First and distant Third World, are now turned into an intra-national coexistence. Although such coexistence profits economically from the same lack of consideration of the racialized labor of others, it has internalized intra-nationally that hierarchically struc-tured bipolar geography.

Borders become internal to the social totality (which can no longer be called a national *community* without qualifications), and fear and distrust among different types of denizens and citizens (another term to qualify) co-exist with a mutual interdependence. This internalization of borders takes place in a political macrocontext in which the state seeks new forms of legiti-mation. If in industrial capitalism the state had found its legitimating narra-tive in the universalizing expansion of welfare and social rights, now that a

7.1. La Migra Mouse
front cover.

relative separation between politics and power has occurred, it requires a different form of self-validation. It finds it not in the provision of a modicum of
security in the form of welfare for *all* its citizens, but in the provision of police
security *to some* citizens and the political exploitation of the fear *of those* citizens
toward other citizens and denizens, excluded or semi-excluded.

Immigrants, and especially undocumented ones, find themselves in the
paradoxical position of providing many of the low-paying services demanded
by the economic restructuring of the economy and its service sectors while,
at the same time, they are the victims of the resentment of the white middle
classes threatened by downward social mobility. Even more broadly, and now
affecting not only Latino immigrants but also Latino residents and their children, a distance and perhaps a break has arisen between a "gray" generation
which tends to be white and older and a younger and ethnic one which could
be called a "brown" generation (Poblete, 2015). The affect that mediates this
seeming distance and hidden interdependence is, more often than not, mutual
fear.

Lalo Alcaraz's comics are a sharp diagnosis of the multiple contradictions generated by this new post-social condition of Latino and Latin American immigrants in the United States. Alcaraz's works explore and exploit some of the key basic mechanisms of what critic Simon Critchley, in his book *On Humour*, calls the best humor. I would like to examine, first, in what sense Alcaraz's comics are an example of such humor and its capacity to explore the contradictions of the social. Then, I will analyze several examples of the textual mechanisms his work uses in order to counter the American socio-semiotic machine for the representation of the Latino other.

In his edited volume *The Philosophy of Laughter and Humor*, John Morreall groups theories of humor into three different types, depending on which central humor mechanism they emphasize: superiority, relief, or incongruity. Superiority-based theories of humor include those of Aristotle, Plato, and Hobbes. They explain, according to Critchley, a basic functioning of humor, especially of the ethnic variety: "Humor is a form of cultural insider-knowledge, and might, indeed, be said to function like a linguistic defence mechanism. Its ostensive untranslatability endows native speakers with a palpable sense of their cultural distinctiveness or even superiority" (Crichley 88–89). In this sense humor functions like "a secret code" shared by all those who belong to the *ethnos*, and it produces a context and community-based *ethos* of superiority, expressed in two ways: first, foreigners do not share *our* sense of humor or simply lack a sense of humor. Secondly, foreigners are themselves funny and worth laughing at.

Alternatively, relief-based theories of humor originate "in the nineteenth century in the work of Herbert Spencer, where laughter is explained as a release of some pent-up nervous energy" (Critchley 3). The most famous exponent of this mechanics- or pressure-based theory is Sigmund Freud. In Freud, humor is a form of economically disposing of energy otherwise used in repression. The net effect for the subject is a feeling of relief.

The third kind of theory Morreall distinguishes corresponds to incongruity-based hypotheses. In this case—Kant, Schopenhauer, and Kierkegaard included—humor is the result of the incongruity between our structure of expectations about a certain situation and the punch line of the joke that surprises us. This cognitive disappointment, this "evaporation of expectation to nothing" (Kant, as quoted in Critchley 5) is the basis of Critchley's philosophical approach to humor that also combines elements of the other two types of theories.

For Critchley, in order for that incongruence effect to take place, there has to be a basic congruence between the structure of the joke and the cultural presuppositions of a particular society (what he calls a *sensus communis*).

While said common sense is affirmed in racist or xenophobic humor, it is also questioned both by the residue of awareness about our own racism the joke produces and, in other types of humor, by a certain critical detachment from that shared "everydayness." In the best humor, Critchley proposes, the subject does not laugh at others but at himself or herself, and the result is not just pleasure but a critical awareness of their contingency, of the contingency of the subject and his or her circumstance. Humor thus produces not simply a confirmation of our belonging to a social group with all its shared certainties, but also an epoché, a bracketing of the naturalized belief in those presuppositions. While acknowledging that a significant portion of humor is in fact reactionary, Critchley proposes what he calls his own *sense of humor*, a counterthesis to explain the self-mockery and defamiliarization characteristic of what he deems the best humor:

> first that the tiny explosions of humour that we call jokes return us to a common, familiar domain of shared life-world practices, the background meanings implicit in a culture. . . . However, second, I want to claim that humour also indicates, or maybe just adumbrates, how those practices might be transformed or perfected, how things might be otherwise. (Critchley 90)

This critical distancing from the known, accepted, and expected is what Critchley calls the capacity of the best types of humor "to project another possible *sensus communis*, namely a *dissensus communis* distinct from the dominant common sense" (Critchley 90).

The projection or even possible imagination of a community based on difference and intercultural dialogue, including the capacity to laugh not only at others but at oneself, is precisely what the graphic humor of Lalo Alcaraz develops.

In order to do so it explores the ideological forms of superiority (including the oftentimes suspicious forms of liberation from taboos) and the mechanisms that highlight the incongruity of that which is, nevertheless, accepted at face value and taken for granted. In this process Alcaraz's humor becomes an example of critical Latino culture in the United States, a culture that potentially forces US national culture (but also Latin American culture) to confront, at a time of cultural globalization and the culture of globalization, its quintessential heterogeneity as a cultural formation and, thus, to accept the inevitability of cultural and linguistic translation as one of its defining traits. In Alcaraz's work the joke is precisely the mechanism or discourse that points to the necessity of such translational dynamics. Moreover, as part of Latino culture, his work aims at transforming a monolingual multicultural reading (which is, in fact, a monocultural American or national reading) into a true intercultural encounter. Such encounters occur in a contact zone in which the results have not been predetermined to be either the unchanging translation or assimilation of difference or its purely commercial exoticization. Instead, through the space for social analysis created by humor, Alcaraz's work proposes to turn those intercultural situations into encounters fully open to change and the true experience of, and in alterity in, a global context. Contrary to a certain still dominant ethnic culture in the United States, the most critical Latino culture and Latino humor want to actively problematize all efforts to reduce their complexity to the clichés of a textual economy specialized in the domestication of ethnic alterity.

In *Brown Tide Rising: Metaphors of Latinos in Contemporary American Public Discourse*, Otto Santa Ana reminds us of the power of discourse to constitute reality. Santa Ana uses cognitive science and, in particular, cognitive metaphor theory as developed by George Lakoff and others to claim, "metaphor is the mental brick and mortar with which people build their understanding of the social world" (Santa Ana xvi). Therefore, the study of the metaphors used to refer to Latinos in the 1960s and 1990s makes clear the differential impact of two different ways of metaphorizing racism. Through these two different metaphoric systems, "the public's concept of Latinos [was] edified, reinforced and articulated" (Santa Ana xvi). Accordingly, "metaphor, as expressed in public discourse, can be studied as the principal unit of hegemonic expression" (Santa Ana 9). According to Santa Ana, if the presiding metaphor to refer to Latinos in the 1960s and before was that of the "Sleeping Giant," during the late 1980s and 1990s the image was that of a "brown tide rising." The image of "dangerous waters" served to dehumanize Latinos and was, and still is, instrumental in the deployment of the two other prominent metaphors organizing American public discourse about Latinos: the nation as body and the nation as house. The waters threaten the house; external agents and disease can infect the body. What these two preconceptual understandings of the nation produce is an organic and individualistic organization of everyday knowledges that privatizes the semantic field of the nation—this at a time when both American individuals and homes, as the "bounded finite space of a nuclear family" (Santa Ana 271), are more connected to and dependent on global flows of people, communications, and goods than ever before. As a result, Latinos are constituted by a set of metaphoric definitions that fix the limits of social identities:

1. Immigrants possess less human value than citizens.
2. Citizen is defined, not in legal terms, but culturally as follows:

a) Be a monolingual English speaker,
b) Have an Anglo-American cultural orientation,
c) Consent tacitly to the U.S. racial hierarchy.
3. Latinos are immigrants. (Santa Ana 285)

In this way, what Santa Ana reminds us of—the need to be vigilant about the language mainstream journalism, policy makers, and public opinion use in describing Latino populations—defines one of the main facets of Alcaraz's work. In this vein Alcaraz devotes significant energies to a systematic deconstruction of dominant discourses in all their contradictions and xenophobias. While the almost invisible power of language to "produce" social reality may not easily be changed at the level of preconceptual understanding, it can certainly be faced and challenged once its constitutive mechanisms are known and rendered visible. The other side of Alcaraz's work understands that if dominant representations have the almost invisible power of defining and "producing" social reality, it is imperative not just to analyze and deconstruct them but also to generate a set of counter-representations that range from transformative appropriation to the fullest and freest exercise of liberating creativity in the humorous cartoon or comic. This frequently involves the capacity to laugh at oneself.

In *Tropicalizations: Transcultural Representations of Latinidad*, Frances Aparicio and Susana Chávez-Silverman propose two very useful concepts for moving on to the analysis of Alcaraz's work. Tropicalizations denote "to trope, to imbue a particular space, geography, group, or nation with a set of traits, images, and values" (Aparicio and Chávez-Silverman 8). As far as Latin America is concerned, hegemonic tropicalizations—Aparicio and Chávez-Silverman emphasize—produce and reproduce "a mythic idea of *Latinidad* based on Anglo (or dominant) projections of fear" (Aparicio and Chávez-Silverman 8).

The second useful concept for my purposes in this essay is the group of variants, introducing a more dynamic multilateralism, which the authors identify in their effort to avoid the static binarism of the orientalist model. More specifically, they refer to three important variants. First, the idea of *tropicalizing from* (Aparicio and Chávez-Silverman 11) inside or outside the object of study; secondly, the idea of *strategic tropicalization*, in which the resistance is joined by a resemanticization of dominant codes (Aparicio 199; Aparicio and Chávez-Silverman 12); and, finally, the logical danger of the latter: *acritical or failed self-tropicalization*, in which the effort of reappropriation founders in a form of reception that confirms the cultural prejudices of the reader or spectator and worsens or promotes the stereotypes defining the dominant representations of Latinos and Latin Americans in the United States. With this set of conceptual tools, I would like to move to the analysis of some relevant features of Lalo Alcaraz's work.

Alcaraz deploys, as it was to be expected, a sharp awareness of the codes and forms of social representation itself. He does so in order to carry out a double semiotic work: first, on the codes of dominant culture for the hegemonic representation of Latinos, and, secondly, on the forms of self-representation of the Latino community, including the representations of the relations between these two groups. His comics use two basic mechanisms. First, reading and then transforming the thought of Caribbean critic Frantz Fanon, he makes explicit, and gives his version of, the psychosocial drama of the colonized. Eddie, one of the central characters of *La Cucaracha* and the alter ego of its author, is a young Latino (Mexican-American, to be precise) who draws comics. Eddie himself has an alter ego, Cuco Rocha, whom he created one inspired night: "Late one night, yet another comic strip is born" (*La Cucaracha* 7). This double game of others who inhabit the subject results in a divided ethnic subject who, perhaps as a result, is highly self-conscious.

The division of the ethnic subject has in this case two aspects: on the one hand there is Cuco Rocha, who is, like he himself states upon jumping from the page into Eddie's life, his politically radicalized alter ego but also that which is repressed by Eddie's daily life in the United States. There is, on the other hand, a second aspect of the divided ethnic subject or perhaps a double valence of the first. The radicalized *latinidad* or "brownness" of Cuco Rocha is, simultaneously, the ensemble of political aspirations of the Latino American people in the United States and that which is repressed in daily life "by the [White] Man"—a liberating impulse and also the place in which the ethnic subject internalizes the perception the dominant other has of her or him. Such ambivalent dual functioning sometimes confirms the Latino subject in its unity while on other occasions subverts it from within. In this intermediate and, by definition, interethnic space it becomes possible to produce a humor that looks as often toward the ethnic inside (the I) as it does to the extra-ethnic outside (the other).

The second basic mechanism of Alcaraz's comics is metalinguistic. It is the frequent use of representation itself as the material scenario in which his humor unfolds. Thus, the newly arrived Cuco tells Eddie, "As your alter ego it's my duty to explain that I've leapt off the page and right into your boring life" (*La Cucaracha* 7). To which Eddie replies, "What a cheap story device!" This mechanism, which pays direct attention to the materiality of semiotic representation itself, is here metalinguistic in at least three senses. First, the comic refers to its own constitutive elements: characters, narrative devices, and humor. Secondly, the meta-commentary ("What a cheap story device!") criticizes this device from the external viewpoint of an impartial reader or observer. Finally, as Cuco suggests ("Eddie you are Latino, right? Just say it's 'Magical Realism . . .'"), those mechanisms and narrative devices are always used in sociocultural contexts that integrate them into more comprehensive discourses (in this case, the American discourse on the Latin American narrative Boom of the 1960s and 1970s) which themselves are part of dominant and reductive perceptions of the culture of the Latino American other (the American reception of the aforementioned Latin American Boom and the post-Boom literature, a reception that has privileged "magical realism" qua form as a defining element over and above other issues, such as the socially revolutionary impulse, to name just one). A potential fourth, and perhaps final, metalinguistic sense in this example is the already obvious reference to the situation of the real reader and his or her relation to what he or she reads. Like Cuco, the reader ends up trapped within a semiotic machine that transforms him or her into a discursive effect or, to be clearer, reminds the reader that an important part of his or her social existence is determined by such discursive webs. Of course, such a semantic grid affects as much the white as the Latino reader.

The two central mechanisms for the representation of Latinos in the US mass media, especially on TV, are exclusion and stereotyping. In the first case, it is an issue of a deficit in representation, while in the second case, it is an issue of an excess or surplus of representation. Commenting on the names of the four dominant broadcasting TV networks, Cuco reimagines and translates their names as follows:

> ABC (American Broadcasting Company) becomes "Anything But Color."
> CBS (Columbia Broadcasting Service) becomes "Can't Beat Segregation."
> NBC (National Broadcasting Company) becomes "No Brown Characters."
> FOX becomes "Full On Xclusion." (*La Cucaracha* 20)

Cuco Rocha, who has sent a TV pilot to a production company, receives the reply shown in figure 7.2 (*La Cucaracha* 115).

Humor here comes from the discursive unmasking of the clichés that often organize the relations or contact between Latinos and their others, between white Americans and their others of color. The only representable Latinos for this dominant semiotic machine are those who reproduce ethnic characters who are immediately and stereotypically narrativizable. The gang member, the undocumented, and the recent immigrant easily generate a limited, but sure, fast, and stable, textual yield within hegemonic discourse. They do their

7.2. Cuco Rocha receives reply regarding his TV pilot, from *La Cucaracha*.

semiotic jobs in the most economical way, and they lend themselves, without much resistance, to their full exploitation. At another point and returning to the issue, Cuco complains: "Why do they call them reality shows? They never have Latinos on them! They should be called 'Unreality Shows'" (*La Cucaracha* 20).

Along with exclusion or representational deficit, there are, in this dominant representation of the ethnic other, plenty of mechanisms of controlled representation or what could easily be labeled a superficial and dominant multiculturalism that coexists with directly racist stereotypes. In a recent strip from October 16, 2013, Eddie and Cuco Rocha summarize this state when referring to the celebration of Latino Heritage Month. Eddie wonders: "What happens when Latino Heritage Month is over? We aren't allowed to celebrate our Latino heritage anymore?" Cuco, always sarcastic, replies, "The whole country turns into Arizona" (gocomics.com, October 16, 2013). In other words, when the moment of multicultural celebration and exclusively symbolic inclusion is over, what dominates is the moment of inclusion qua relative exclusion that characterizes both the state of Arizona and, potentially, the whole country at the post-social moment.[2]

In the Clinton years Alcaraz had already mordantly and concisely alluded to the ideological limits of that acritical, blindly liberal, and superficial, but extraordinarily effective, multiculturalism. (See figure 7.3.)

Uncle Sam reads the newspaper on the ethnic genocide in Bosnia and comments, "Why don't people respect other people's culture?" Cuco Rocha responds to this in Spanish: "¡Sí *verdad!*" Uncle Sam replies abruptly, "Hey! English Only!" (*Migra Mouse* 20). In this way Alcaraz highlighted the exclusive and narrowly "cultural" nature of a multiculturalism based on limited recognition, a multiculturalism that can acknowledge difference only if it can neutralize it and completely assimilate it. He thus revealed the ideological operations of a domesticating and "light" multiculturalism.

The dominant representation of Latinos reduces them, therefore, to a series of stereotypes attempting to semiotically control the proliferation of ethnic alterity, perceived as a threat in what amounts to a cocktail of affects — combining fear, anxiety, and mutual dependency — that defines my concept of the post-social. In a brilliant cartoon from 1994, Alcaraz allows us now to see to what extent the propagation and exploitation of the anti-immigrant hysteria, based on fear, constitute not only a discourse of high political yield and long-duration effectiveness for conservative and ultraconservative Americans, but also one of the basic mechanisms that have affected, for over two decades now, US representations of Latinos and regulated the contact between that population and the white majority.

In the cartoon shown in figure 7.4, a conservative politician shows an insect-killing spray named not Raid but "Fraid." This new product that eliminates annoying plagues, on the one hand, has a long-duration effect and high political yield ("Keeps on working for up to two elections") and, on the other, as indicated by the neologism of its brand name, is based on a potent combination of thanatic impulse and visceral fear. The product is so effective that "nine out of ten politicians prefer it" (*Migra Mouse* 71).

Similarly, in another cartoon from the same years, 1995 this time, a wealthy white couple of Republican delegates to the Republican National Convention in San Diego wonder, while they rest poolside at their hotel, at what time the anti-immigration Republican meeting might be, while around them, unbeknownst to them, the waiter, the housekeeper, and the gardener, all Latinos, do their job to allow the couple their pleasant stay at the hotel. (See figure 7.5.)

As in many other of Alcaraz's creations, this cartoon effectively distills that weird but frequent and crucial mix of co-dependence and reciprocal fear that is at the bottom of the American post-social condition — a condition that was beginning to make itself felt twenty years ago and continues today, doing its effective biopolitical job of regulating inter-ethnic contact.

CHAPTER 3:
ENGLISH ONLY, POR FAVOR

Hey! English Only, 1994

English Only is a divisive issue that is completely intertwined with the anti-immigration issue, which is why I've included it in this collection. Cynical politicians appeal to the fear and xenophobia of monolingual Anglo voters despite overwhelming evidence that bilingualism is a positive contribution to society.

7.3. Critique of multiculturalism, from *Migra Mouse*.

FRAID, Anti-Immigrant Border Spray, 1994

I was inspired to do this cartoon after reading about a nascent "Border Enforcement Technologies" research program at a Northern California State University. The program was an attempt to get federal research dollars for creating technologies that might deter unauthorized border crossing, but I felt the results sounded literally like a "Roach Motel" for immigrants. One project was a powder developed to stick to "illegals" as they scampered across the kitchen floor—I mean, the U.S./Mexico border. The powder somehow then lit up the culprit to Border Patrol detection devices.

On another note, I made posters of this toon, and was chastised by an angry Chicano concertgoer who said I shouldn't use the word "spick." I explained to this big, tough homie that I wasn't saying this word, this racist politician was . . . He pondered this and said, "Well, in that case, I salute you, homes!"

7.4. Eliminate annoying plagues with "Fraid," from *Migra Mouse*.

San Diego Republican Convention, 1995
The GOP delegates enjoy another Southern California morning, thanks to immigrants.

7.5. Cartoon that mixes a sense of co-dependence and reciprocal fear in American post-social condition, from *Migra Mouse*.

Fear or xenophobic feelings are exacerbated when, as happens in the post-social condition, they are combined with a rather diffused "certainty" or an emergent evidence that Latinos do a good deal of the hardest jobs: from the most physically demanding tasks to the most dangerous, including the affective labor of taking care of the children or caring for the elderly and whole families. This intensification results, then, from the discovery of a cognitive and affective dissonance. Such dissonance makes what is ideologically felt as most foreign, external, and threatening in the lives of many Americans (including those who hold militantly anti-immigrant positions) so internal, intimate, and crucial for the production and reproduction of their quotidian and familiar lives. These jobs, performed by immigrants and their descendants, extend—in a way that is only superficially surprising—to other labors considered decisive for the production of life in the United States, including military service. In a cartoon reproduced in *La Cucaracha*, Cuco and Eddie observe the slogan "An Army of Juan" presiding over the front of an Army recruiting office, while they ask themselves whether the Army is running out of poor and willing-to-be-conscripted Latinos (i.e., those who in the last two decades have been one of the highest growth populations for the Army efforts) (*La Cucaracha* 32).

In 1997 a cartoon in *La Migra Mouse* already pointed out, with devastating clarity, that contrary to the racist prejudice that blames immigrants for the alleged decadence of the American Dream and the lack of well-paid jobs, the real way in which Latino immigrants could ruin the life of many Americans would be by disappearing or refusing to perform all the jobs that are badly paid but crucial for the development of the new everyday life of and in the post-social (*La Migra* 91).[3]

In a more recent cartoon, on October 21, 2013, ten years after the publication of his book *La Cucaracha*, Alcaraz charges again in the same direction. This time he criticizes American politics in the era of Republican opposition to Barack Obama and the virtual paralysis affecting the work of Congress. Characteristically, he does it by using the figure of the undocumented immigrant: Cousin Memo, who is undocumented and, in this scene, dressed very formally, is picked up at a big box store parking lot and now works doing those jobs "Americans refuse to do." The punchline: "Call me Congressman" (gocomics.com, October 21, 2013).

In order to show the degrees of continuity that even positive change may mask, Eddie, Cuco, and the same Cousin Memo remark that for the first time in twenty years undocumented immigrants can obtain a driver's license (they are referring in this case to the historical decision by the state of California to create a driver's license for undocumented people). Closing at least temporarily a cycle that Alcaraz had begun as early as 1992, Memo sarcastically comments, "I'll have to mention this at my valet parking job." More concisely but equally effective in its capacity to critique dominant discourse, Memo states on Labor Day, "It's hard stealing jobs nobody wants to do!" (gocomics.com, September 2, 2013).

This deconstructive work on the dominant forms of discursive metaphorization or tropicalization of Latinos is, as already stated, only one type of cultural work developed by Lalo Alcaraz's work. Another connects with his capacity to produce critical autotropicalizations and involves a willingness to perform two basic operations: on the one hand, to discover and undo the forms in which dominant discursive modalizations penetrate Latino identity discourse itself, and, on the other, to be able to laugh at oneself.

Turning our attention from the dominant to the dominated gaze, Alcaraz reminds us that, at least in part, racism is often also a self-inflicted injury and not the exclusive prerogative of the dominant sectors. "Why Chicanos shouldn't say wetback," a 1994 two-image cartoon, shows, in the first image, a couple of Chicanos derogatorily calling out "wetback" to a passerby, who, from his clothes and hat, seems to be Mexican. In the second image, though, the two Chicanos plus the alleged Mexican are observed from a distance by Uncle Sam who complains, "Good Lord! Look at all those wetbacks!" (*Migra Mouse* 82).

In an extended series of strips in *La Cucaracha*, Eddie and Veronica (a Latina teacher who is a feminist), on the one hand, and the same Veronica and her cousin Dolores, who aspires to become a Hollywood actress, on the other, exchange comments and observations on the typical forms of tropicalization affecting Latino actors and actresses in Hollywood. They also, however, indicate the acritical forms of self- or auto-tropicalization, and, sometimes, of strategic tropicalization that said context produces. In one of those strips, since blondes are supposed to go extinct by the year 2028, says Veronica, an ecological preserve has been created to protect them. Where? asks Memo. Veronica's punchline: "Spanish language TV" (*La Cucaracha* 26). In this way, they are alluding to the intra-ethnic tensions of the pan-Latino ethnic project that América Rodríguez, studying the history of Spanish-based media in the country, has highlighted (Rodríguez 77–84). In another strip Veronica and Dolores, the two Latina cousins, get together at a café to chat after a long hiatus. Dolores says she was afraid because the neighborhood was "so 'Latin.'" Veronica reminds her that she (Dolores) grew up in that barrio and that, being Dolores Sanchez, she is as Latina as the neighborhood. Dolores responds, "Please call me Dolly St. James, that is my stage name" (*La Cucaracha* 94). In the culmination of this heavily metadiscursive series, Dolores comments, in another strip, that if she wanted to try her luck as an actress by auditioning as a Latina, she would have to dye her hair back to its original blackness, get rid of the blue contact lenses, and stop avoiding the sun to prevent a darkening of her skin. She concludes by sighing, "It's hard being a Latina. How do you do it?" To which Veronica retorts, "I wake up and put on my sombrero one leg at a time, just like everybody else" (*La Cucaracha* 94).

In a recent series of *La Cucaracha* titled "Non-lyin' Mayan prophecies," it is announced that "the CIA will develop a new invisibility technology by using DNA from Latino actors in Hollywood" (gocomics.com, January 11,

2013). What is thus acknowledged is how difficult the formation of the identity of the subaltern is when it is permanently devalued by dominant culture. Eddie answers the phone and after listening to the message says, "Somebody just stole [electronically] my identity." To which Cuco replies, "Was that the cops on the phone?" "No," says Eddie, "It was the identity thief begging me to take it back" (*La Cucaracha* 55).

In order to show how little things have changed in the last twenty years and how powerful the ideological machine of dominant assimilation still is, another recent strip shows the Republican corrections to an immigration reform bill in Congress. The path to citizenship section in that revised bill includes article 12, which reads "You promise to discriminate against the next wave of immigrants" (gocomics.com, February 20, 2013). It reminds us that even if the centuries-old Chicano populations of the United States have been and continue to be the objects of multiple forms of racial discrimination, in what Tellez and Ortiz call *Generations of Exclusion*, they themselves oftentimes actively discriminate against their ethnic immigrant kinfolk.

Sometimes, in what Aparicio and Chávez-Silverman would call strategic tropicalizations, the stereotyping perception of the other by the other may be strategically mobilized for their own benefit or in order to acknowledge their own faults and laugh at themselves. Thus, when Veronica reminds Dolores, who has just asked her cousin to call her Dolly St. James, that there is a TV audition that day for actresses of a "Latino type," Dolores replies very quickly that her name is "Dolores Rosario María Conchita Alonso González Sánchez" (*La Cucaracha* 94). In another, similar strip, Veronica asks Eddie where he is going so hurriedly. He responds, "I'm late for my Latino time management seminar!" (*La Cucaracha* 47).

In another recent strip series, Cuco Rocha has decided to write a manual: "La Cucaracha: Latino Employee Diversity and Sensitivity Manual." In it he writes, "Remember: not all people [Latinos] eat tacos and burritos" and then adds, "but they are crazy if they don't" (gocomics.com July 23, 2013). In a final example, the terrific and laconic street vendor of tacos—one of the most endearing and funniest recurring characters in the *La Cucaracha* series—places a street sign next to his cart in order to promote his tacos. The sign reads "Mexico is now the world's fattest nation . . . Discover their secret" (gocomics. com August 3, 2013). Making these necessary concessions, being able to laugh at oneself, of course, also allows a laugh at and with the dominant other in more effective and perhaps mordant ways.

According to Arjun Appadurai, ethnic minorities have a deconstructive effect on the claimed purities of nation-states and are a constant reminder of their unfairness. They affect the neatness of social taxonomies, "blur the boundaries between 'us' and 'them,' here and there, in and out, healthy and unhealthy, loyal and disloyal, needed but unwelcome" (44).

It is the latter feature that matters the most in our context. For Appadurai helps us recognize that Latino immigrants function as a paradoxical reminder of the unavoidable global condition of American life in times of post-industrial capitalism and neoliberal restructuring (i.e., what I have called here the post-social). It is this capacity of the immigrant to embody both the anxiety-producing fact of the global nature of the present (they are needed; Americans depend on them for many aspects of their lives) and the concomitant uncertainty of the status and future of national life (they are unwelcome and feared; they must be expelled) that makes them such powerful elements in the national psychic life. Attacking globalization is bound to be difficult given the abstract nature of the object of hatred. The immigrant provides a physically available representative for such anxious political impulses and affects. Appadurai names the political positions thus created predatory identities, to the extent that, focusing their energies on a minority population to be destroyed or expelled, they grow out and enact a fear or anxiety of incompleteness, "an intolerable deficit in the purity [and autonomy] of the national whole" (53).

Latino immigrants, as shown by the brilliant work of Lalo Alcaraz, have been the object of such predatory identities and their discourses in the past twenty years. Alcaraz's work also shows that Latinos and Latino artists have responded to those and other dominant tropicalizations with a wide set of counter- and auto-tropicalizations, transforming, deconstructing, and countering those xenophobic discourses. In that process, they have reclaimed and rebuilt a place for themselves in the national space and, especially, their own right to laugh not only at and with others but, as crucially, at themselves.

NOTES

1. Lalo Alcaraz—award-winning editorial cartoonist and Latino journalist—has produced editorial cartoons for *LA Weekly* since 1992 and also creates cartoons in Spanish for *La Opinion*, the oldest Spanish-language newspaper in the United States. His work has appeared in *The New York Times*, *The Village Voice*, *Los Angeles Times*, *Variety*, *Hispanic Magazine*, *Latina*, *La Jornada* in Mexico City, *BUNTE* (Germany's equivalent of *People* magazine), and many other publications.

2. In the last few years Arizona has defined itself by its growing ultraconservative radicalization against legal and undocumented Latinos in the state. Two examples are the "legal" measures of Sheriff Joe Arpaio and Arizona's state law SB 1070.

3. This is precisely the premise of the film *Un Día sin Mexicanos*. See Poblete, "U.S. Latino Studies in a Global Context."

EIGHT

MY DEBT TO RIUS

ILAN STAVANS

I SEE MYSELF AS A by-product of the Mexican *historieta*, and, tangibly, as a stepchild of Eduardo del Río García, aka Rius (Zamora, Michoacán, 1934), in my eyes its most innovative, rebellious practitioner. My relationship with Rius is equally refractory: his reader for over a decade, I admire his style; I also see him as my Virgil in my understanding of a number of thorny issues connected to Mexican culture; but I take strong issue with his political stance.

First, I want to say a few words about the *historieta* as a genre. It is indeed a most peculiar artifact. I realize the word, in certain quarters, is taken as a substitute for *tira cómica*, what in Spain is known as *tebeos* and in Mexico as *monitos*. Another term is *los comics*. To me these aren't synonyms. *Historietas*, at least in the way the term was used among my peers in the 1970s, is a reference to autochthonous products, mostly Mexican but also from other parts of Latin America. For instance, we talked of *Mafalda* (1964–1973), by the syndicated Argentine illustrator Joaquín Salvador Lavado, also known as Quino, as a *historieta*, even though it is really a political cartoon made, for the most part, of a multi-panel strip unified by a specific theme.

The standard *historieta* is more developed and also less belligerent. It is designed to entertain, not to provoke. Still, it isn't quite like the graphic novel as it is understood in the English-language world, say, Will Eisner's *A Contract with God* (1978), in that it is shorter in size (an average of between twenty-four and thirty pages). It might be in sepia or in black and white, although its tendency is to appear in color. It is rather inexpensive. And it features a set of characters who reappear in weekly adventures.

During my adolescence, I would save a handful of pesos to buy, at the newsstand on Sunday morning, a batch of *historietas*. Although I disliked Walt Disney and Hanna-Barbera comics, at times I would buy a copy of *Archie*. It had been translated into Spanish, but it never dealt with Mexico, which is what I always looked for. I was a sucker for the autochthonous items. I liked

Kalimán, an Egyptian superhero—as seen through the Mexican lens—who is a descendant of the Pharaohs. It began publication in 1965, after a radio show on Radio Cadena Nacional turned the character into a staple in the popular imagination. Kalimán fights all sorts of mythical enemies alongside his companion, Solín. By the time I started reading the *historieta*, in the early 1970s, there were a bunch of movie adaptations, like *Kalimán, el hombre increíble* (1972).

There was also *La familia Burrón*, started in 1948 by Gabriel Vargas. And *Condorito*, drawn by Chilean illustrator René Ríos Boettiger, known as Pepo. It was launched in 1949. In a series of conversations with Frederick Aldama (*¡Muy Pop!: Conversations on Latino Popular Culture* [2013]), I reflected on the way these characters—Kalimán and Solín; Mafalda, Felipe, and Manolito; Condorito and Yayita; Don Regino Burrón and Doña Borola Tacuche de Burrón—shaped not only my personal identity but also my sense of self as a Mexican, given that I had been raised in a small immigrant Jewish enclave that kept itself rather aloof from what took place in the country on a regular basis. Among them, Kalimán was my ticket into a sense of belonging: having Middle Eastern roots, or at least imagining them, I wanted to be like him, to fight enemies seeking to undermine Mexico. To a lesser degree, *La familia Burrón* enabled me to peek at the way a traditional non-Jewish family behaved, an opportunity I seldom had in real life.

By far my deepest, most lasting interest was in *Los Supermachos* with Juan Calzónzin, a shrewd indigenous inspector. (*Caltzontzin* [or *cazonci*], in the language of the indigenous Purépecha people, is the word for "emperor.") Rius started it in 1965. Unlike other *historietas*, this one felt haphazardly produced. The story line was never fully clear. It purported to have a detective-story kind of plot, but its author at times forgot to develop it. Other members of its cast are Calzónzin's close friend Chon Prieto, the cacique and municipal president Don Perpetuo del Rosal, the bartender Fiacro Franco, the bourgeois Don Plutarco, the nun Doña Eme aka Emerenciana "La Bigotona," and the policemen El lechuzo y Arsenio. I enjoyed these characters, but seldom did it appear as if they were at the service of the narrative. What Rius intended to do, in my view, was teach his readers to be unsettled by Mexico's political landscape. It denounces racism, illiteracy, injustice, and sexism. The status quo, in the author's eyes, was rotted. Urgent change was needed. Except that no solution was ever offered.

There was something deliciously subversive in *Los Supermachos*. No sooner did I finish an installment than I already began to fantasize about the next. I didn't know anything about Rius then, and, to be honest, I know little about him today. Every source I find offers the same superficial information—

including his official website, rius.com.mx: that he started drawing political cartoons in the 1960s, that he is an atheist as well as a vegetarian, that he was a staunch opponent of the Partido Revolucionario Institucional, known by its acronym, PRI, that he attacked the neoliberal policies of the 1990s, that he collaborated on important humor magazines such as *El Chamuco* and *El Cha-huistle*, and that his anti-clerical views have turned him into persona non grata in the Catholic Church. He has been awarded twice Mexico's Premio Nacional de Periodismo. And his work has been featured in a handsome retrospective exhibit at the Museo del Estanquillo, a venerable institution devoted to pop culture. I also know the nation's intellectual elite looks down on his *historietas* as mundane, even unworthy.

Actually, I like being ignorant about Rius (whose oeuvre has been analyzed by critics such as David W. Foster [*From Mafalda to Los Supermachos*, 1989] and Ana Merino [*El Cómic Hispánico*, 2003]), for what attracts me to his work is the effectiveness of his art. When I first encountered him, Mexico remained under the thumb of the PRI, as it had been since the late 1920s. The one-party rule created the mirage of fostering a democratic atmosphere although it functioned through a regimen of censorship. While it was clear to my generation that ours wasn't a dictatorship like those in Argentina, Uruguay, and Chile, repression was frequent, and it acquired multiple forms, from controlled exposure to certain news items to political prisoners, targeted assassinations, and *desaparecidos*.

I was born in Mexico City in 1961. Less than a decade later, the student massacre in Tlatelolco Square took place in which the government attempted to quiet the dissatisfied, rebellious youth manifesting itself as the Olympic Games were about to take place. My family lived in the southern part of the city, in Colonia Copilco, a few blocks away from the Universidad Nacional Autónoma de México, the largest, most important public university in the nation. I don't much remember the episode, although I do recall my parents saying that "a river of blood was coming down the street."

It is unlikely that I started reading Rius then. He belongs to a latter period of my education, sometime in my late teens, when I became fully conscious of the fragile ideological equilibrium I was surrounded by. Every six years, Mexico voted for a new president. But even before the first voter reached the booths, newspapers had already announced the election winner because the PRI was able to orchestrate a democratic mirage that didn't fool anyone. In fact, by popular vote the uncontested presidential winner, election after election, was Cantinflas, the popular movie comedian.

Not too far from my home in Copilco was the Librería Salvador Allende, a hotbed of activism. I remember wandering into it about once a week to read copies of *Mafalda*. It was there that I came across some of Rius's books in what later came to be known as the *For Beginners* series. Only recently, thanks to my friend N. Christopher Couch, a historian of comic strips, have I come to understand Rius's overall impact. His path-breaking booklet on Karl Marx was published in English as *Marx for Beginners* (2003). I had first seen it at Librería Salvador Allende in its original Spanish version, titled *Marx para principiantes*, which came out in 1972. In a loose, thought-provoking fashion, it juxtaposes text and images to deliver a crash course on Marxism, one written with an anarchist perspective. Its style was quickly imitated by Richard Appignanesi, Donald D. Palmer, and others. Rius did several others, like *Lenin para principiantes* (1975), *ABChe* (1978), *Mao en su tinta* (1979), and *El diablo se llama Trotsky* (1981). Today one is able to buy just about any "serious" topic in the *For Beginners* series, from Sigmund Freud to Ronald Reagan. For those of us who first got a glimpse of the approach, they all feel like Rius imitators.

Since pre-Columbian times, Mexican culture has been visually driven. From the hieroglyphics-based languages to the iconography of civilizations like the Aztec and Maya, images are the preferred currency. Rius fits squarely into this practice. His direct predecessor, and a source of constant borrowing for him, is the engraver José Guadalupe Posada, who chronicled the *Revolución* in engravings that made fun of social types, like the aristocrat, the *politico*, and the *soldadera*. Posada is credited for popularizing the *calavera*, the skull, as Mexico's symbol. That symbol is an integral part of folklore today, especially in *Día de los Muertos*. His famous characters include the *Calavera Zapatista* and *Calavera Catrina*.

Posada used cheap material to mass-produce his art. His audience was the masses, not the elite. The same might be said of Rius. Not arbitrarily, Posada has come to represent the Mexican soul, and famous artists like Diego Rivera included him in their paintings, like "Dream of a Sunday Afternoon in Alameda Central," where Posada stands not far from Frida Kahlo and child-looking Rivera himself. In one *historieta* after another, Rius has done the same, incorporating his *calaveras*. He also wrote *Posada, el novio de la muerte*, where he describes the engraver as less progressive than previously thought. In fact, according to Rius, whose opinion is based on a study by cartoonist El Fisgón, Posada was rather reactionary in his ideological views and close to the regime of Dictator Porfirio Díaz, against whose dictatorship the Mexican Revolution rose.

When I think of Rius, a couple of idols in the Mexican pop culture pantheon come to mind. The first is Cantinflas. His real name was Mario Moreno. (Mexican pop artists have a penchant for pen names.) Years ago, when I wrote a reflection on him as an enigma (included in my collection of essays

The Riddle of Cantinflas [1998, rev. ed., 2012]), the Mexican elite suggested I was overemphasizing his influence. This isn't surprising. The elite dismissed his movies—close to fifty—as trashy, but therein lies, in my opinion, his revolution: he made the masses laugh by portraying the rich and powerful as pompous. In plot after plot, Cantinflas, unable to hold on to a stable job, lives at the mercy of others; yet he allows the downtrodden to find pride in their condition. This is clear in my favorite movie, *Allí está el detalle* (1940), in which he is accused of a crime he didn't commit. In most of the story, he is in a bourgeois house as an intruder, an impostor. Cantinflas's seditious, destabilizing tool to undermine the prosecution against him is his language: his Spanish is rowdy, nonsensical, and verbose; it builds astonishing circles through which he confuses, and thus undermines, those around him.

The other idol is Chespirito, aka Roberto Gómez Bolaños, the TV comedian who created *El Chavo del Ocho*, *El Doctor Chapatín*, *El Chapulín Colorado*, and other irredeemable characters (all names starting with a "Ch"). I am in awe of the reach of Chespirito throughout the Spanish-speaking world. While based in Mexico, his programs were seen, on a weekly basis, from Argentina to Venezuela, from Peru to Puerto Rico. Unlike Cantinflas, his humor is rather simplistic, not linguistically based but rotating around social stereotypes, such as the humble kid in the neighborhood, the rambunctious medic, and the weak superhero. There is something quasi-religious in Chespirito's fame: people in the Hispanic world watch the same episode time and again, as if it is a ritual, a rite of passage.

In spite of Cantinflas's subversive language, neither he nor Chespirito were opponents of the Mexican establishment. On the contrary, their work was rather complacent; in fact, they numbed the public, making it forget the nation's urgent problems. In contrast, Rius was tolerated. I have asked myself why countless times. The answer, I believe, is that his type of humor endorsed no party line. He surely wasn't seen as a Communist. And his public was elusive. How many of his readers were there? In truth, there were a great many. Later on, I found out that the number of copies sold of a single Rius *historieta* was close to 250,000, a huge amount for a country where illiteracy is rampant. But Mexico has another problem: there is no difference between a person who can't read and a person who won't read.

In Rius's case, it wasn't the number of followers but who they were and where they came from that matter. Mexicans of all social strata poured into his work because we found in it courage, which was altogether absent from other types of pop-culture artifacts. In time, his *historietas* were adapted into movies, although the process represented a dramatic watering down of Rius's style. For instance, in 1974 Alfonso Arau, who later was in charge of *Like*

Water for Chocolate (1992), directed his own cinematic adaptation, co-written with Rius, of *Los Supermachos*. It was called *Calzónzin Inspector*. The movie, with Héctor Ortega, Carmen Salinas, and Virma González, dealt with corruption in a small fictional town. To be kind, it was mediocre. (A couple of years before, Arau did *El águila descalza* [1971], about a superhero à la Kalimán, except this one was based in Mexico. The result was more estimable.) Still, it allowed Rius's fans to envision his reach beyond the weekend newsstand.

Truth is, the best work produced by Rius wasn't *Los Supermachos* but another series: *Los agachados*. In translation, the term means "the bending ones." Using mestizo types, he elaborated a sophisticated assessment of the Mexican inferiority complex by exploring, in this case thematically and not by means of fiction, various aspects of the nation's life, from the role of Catholicism to the half-improvised ways capitalism found its grounding in Latin America. This is where his influence is most obvious, and it reaches far beyond the country's borders. It is impossible to know exactly how many titles in *Los agachados* there have been. On the official Rius website, the list is incomplete. I have seen estimates that range from three to five hundred. I know of collectors who have around two hundred. Unfortunately, as a first-time reader, in the heat that is the teen age, it never crossed my mind to save them: once I read them, I lent the *historietas* to some neighbors. I never saw them again.

Again, the production quality of *Los agachados* was rugged. A better word might be *distressed*. It is difficult for me to describe what the content is. As before, it makes use of a set of characters, in this case mostly "dumb" mestizos and Indians, vis-à-vis their oppressors from the ruling class. Together they explore a topic (the Echeverría presidency, drugs in the United States, Protestantism) in an irreverent, questioning fashion. The rest is half *historieta*, half didactic manual. This gave place then to a number of *How to . . .* booklets designed to demythologize a topic. Take *La panza es primero* (1973), *El yerberito ilustrado* (1975), or *Cómo dejar de comer (mal)* (1989). All three belong to a theme Rius was passionate about: vegetarianism. He hammered that message repeatedly: Mexicans eat poorly—and it's their fault. He also stresses the frequency with which people, especially children, drink soda at all times, announcing that after the United States, Mexico is the largest consumer of Coca-Cola.

My career as a Rius reader spans into my adult life. In general, his drawings are far less developed than the standard ones the reader comes across in *The New Yorker*. They are made of only a few lines of text. In *El yerberito ilustrado*, an Indian says, *"Pregúntenle a Hernán Cortés quién le curó la sífilis . . ."* (Ask Hernán Cortés who cured him of syphilis).

Only the cover is in color; the inside content appears in black and white.

Each page is made of between one and eight panels creatively distributed, in asymmetrical fashion, to allow for a certain unharmonious rhythm that rejects the baroque visuals that are omnipresent in Mexican art.

As I continued my weekly readings, I remember experiencing a growing discomfort. I admired Rius, but something about his *historietas* made me cringe. I realized he was a reactionary. And I began to see through the veil. His obsessions were Chomskyan: anti-American, anti-Israel, anti–centralized government, and anti–organized religion. He abused stereotypes, and his tendency was to simplify, not to complicate in order to explore contradictions, for that is what true thinking is about. It also became clear to me that Rius borrowed without remorse. He took lines from others, or else entire arguments. An example: his *Juicio a Walt Disney* (1991) was an indictment of Disney animation. Much of that approach had already been stated—more convincingly—by Ariel Dorfman and Armand Mattelart in *How to Read Donald Duck* (1975), released in Spanish in 1971.

He has also dealt with trends and currents like jazz, AIDS, and feminism. His views are often libertarian, verging on the nearsighted. I remember being shocked by them. For instance, in *De aborto, sexo y otros pecados* (1993), he champions an openness toward changing sexual mores while also making fun of the inherent, biological weakness of women and of the threat that homosexuality posed to the "normal" family. As I look back, it seems to me that Rius was an engine of collective reflection. I don't believe his views were those of his fans. Instead, he made them think.

Another favorite Rius theme is sex. He has a delicious booklet called *Kama Nostra* (1987), an obvious reference to the ancient Indian classic *Kama Sutra*, which, Rius argues, is the perfect manual for young lovers in a country like Mexico, restrained by Christian mores. He attacks the Catholic Church for hypocrisy for prohibiting free love while its priests are sexual predators. The *historieta* isn't altogether visually explicit. It makes reference to male and female genitalia while showing them only in the most scientific form. The fact that such artifacts would be available for anyone to purchase on the street is a statement of Rius's grasp.

When I came across *Hitler para masoquistas* (1983), a tutorial on the Third Reich, I was flabbergasted by his quiet endorsement of certain Nazi policies, such as ethnic cleansing. The *historieta* didn't quite condemn it: not in the case of Jews, not when dealing with gypsies either. These impressions were verified when, already an adult, I read two more, *Palestina, del judío errante al judío errado* (1982) and *Los judíos* (1998), on the Jews from biblical times to the present. Anti-Semitism in Mexico then wasn't different from what it is now: a tacit force sponsored by left-leaning parties as well as the Catholic Church. On the surface the country is pluralistic. Yet these xenophobic sentiments serve as an undercurrent. In the case of the Jews, the minority was minuscule: some 30,000 in a country with a population of almost 100 million. The strategy these and other minorities took was to sit tight, not agitating the waters.

Two more recurrent topics that defined Rius's work have been close to me: one was language, the other atheism. The two had a strong impact on me. I perused *El diccionario de la estupidez humana* (1978), *El libro de las malas palabras* (1980), and *Lexikon Ekonomikon* (1983). In the former, he makes fun of human stupidity, not through words per se but through historical missteps. I liked the way he poked fun at excesses among Greek philosophers like Aristotle, in the Bible, by the French Encyclopedists like Voltaire and Rousseau, and so on. And in the latter he reflected on the etymology of ubiquitous Mexicanisms such as *chingar, pendejo, cabrón*, and *la hueva*. In the 1940s, a series of intellectuals, including Samuel Ramos, had begun exploring the meaning of these expressions. Octavio Paz, in his book *The Labyrinth of Solitude* (1950), continued this line of thought. A decade later, Armando Jiménez released the book *Picardía mexicana* (1960), in which he analyzed jokes, faux terms, and Freudian slips, as well as graffiti—statements written on bathrooms and public spaces. Rius continued this tradition by rehashing the topics in his popular graphic style.

Along with Mexican politics, atheism is Rius's fundamental subject. This topic permeates his entire oeuvre. I loved *El mito guadalupano* (1981), where he ridiculed the myth of the Virgin of Guadalupe, the country's matron saint, although I also was conscious of the extent to which he had failed to see religion as a driving force in organized society.

This *historieta* felt much more dangerous than anything else I had read by Rius because Guadalupanism is taboo in intellectual circles: to critique it is to undermine Mexicanness. Even though I am an assiduous reader of the Bible as narrative, I also enjoyed *La Biblia, esa linda tontería* (1996), where he argued that everything in the Bible was sheer lies. In *Con perdón de Doré* (1979) he laughed at the religious imagery portrayed by the French romantic lithographer Gustave Doré. And in other booklets (*Cristo de carne y hueso* [1972] and *Puré de Papas* [1993]), he talked of Jesus Christ as a concoction of the Catholic Church. His argument reminds me of a segment in Dostoyevsky's novel *The Brothers Karamazov* (1880) known as "The Grand Inquisitor." In it Jesus Christ comes back to earth in Seville at the time of the Holy Inquisition and he is imprisoned in order not to agitate the masses.

Perhaps Rius's best book on atheism was *Manual del perfecto ateo* (1981). I am not sure I am an atheist; I am more of a skeptic who dwells in atheism in times of despair. Not long ago, I delivered a series of eight lectures called *God:*

A History (2014). In them I argued that believing in a supernatural force is a psychological need but the transformation of that belief into a religion has resulted in a sequence of devastating atrocities. The uses of God are connected with morality. We need to organize our lives according to the parameters of good and evil. Yet transforming those parameters into excuses for violence is, in my view, shameful. That, if I remember right, was also Rius's take. Of course, any atheist organizes his or her arguments along these same lines. My point is that I first came across that line of thought, later supplemented by thinkers like Bertrand Russell, Richard Dawkins, and Christopher Hitchens, while reading Rius.

When Los Angeles–based cartoonist Lalo Alcaraz and I made *Latino U.S.A.: A Cartoon History* (2000), my own objective was simple: to use lampoons in order to reflect on the development of a historical tradition among Hispanics. I had been living in the United States for fifteen years. In that time, I began seeing myself less as a citizen of Mexico and more as an immigrant undergoing a process of acculturation. Honestly, I wasn't thinking of Rius when I wrote the book, which, as a result of its length—some 180 pages—isn't quite a *historieta*. His impact had trickled down to me through Posada and through the *For Beginners* series. It was only when it was released that readers suggested a direct link. Then, as Alcaraz and I decided to collaborate again, this time on *A Most Imperfect Union: A Contrarian History of the United States* (2014), that inspiration was fully conscious. This second title has a more sparse style that shies away from excess and strikes me as closer to Rius's. It also has a more irreverent, anti-establishmentarian approach that pays homage to him.

Except that I have resisted simplification. Of course, producing a history of the United States in 250 pages packed with images cannot avoid sweeping statements. Yet I am allergic to unrefined thinking, which means that even when I engage in stereotypes I encourage the reader to debunk them. Indeed, the two books in collaboration with Alcaraz have as their two protagonists the Author and the Cartoonist. The two spend the entire narrative discussing how to avoid shortcuts that result in pigeonholing.

In sum, my debt to the Mexican *historieta*, and to Rius in particular, is substantial: they taught me how to laugh while questioning the world I live in.

PART IV

A BIRD, A PLANE . . . STRAIGHT AND QUEER SUPER-LATS

THE ALIEN IS HERE TO STAY: OTHERNESS, ANTI-ASSIMILATION, AND EMPOWERMENT IN LATINO/A SUPERHERO COMICS

MAURICIO ESPINOZA

WHILE LATINO/A COMICS are perhaps better known for Los Bros Hernandez's alternative storytelling modes and Lalo Alcaraz's political cartoons, the superhero genre has been a significant force behind the growing presence and popularity of Latino/a characters and narratives in the US comic book universe, especially in the past 20 years. Latino/a comic book superheroes date back to the 1970s, when Marvel introduced its first Hispanic caped crusader (White Tiger, 1975) and Texas judge Margarito Garza self-published the first Latino/a superhero comic independently created by a Latino/a (*Relámpago*, 1977). Mainstream comic book publishers—who had for decades excluded minorities from the exceedingly white and masculine realm of superheroism— created a few Latino/a superheroes during the next two decades, but they generally played minor roles and relied on stereotypes.[1] In the 1990s, Latino/a artists sought to address this representational imbalance by publishing their own comics and by creating complex characters whose Latino/a culture was central to their heroic personas. Examples of this trend include Richard Dominguez's *El Gato Negro* (1993) and Javier Hernandez's *El Muerto* (1998). The "indie Latino comics explosion of the mid-'90s"[2] continued into the twenty-first century, with new superheroes seeing the light of day via self-published or print-on-demand comic books, as well as web-based comics and graphic novels. In the 2000s, mainstream publishers found a renewed interest in Latino/a superheroes, creating characters and story lines that complicated Latino/a identity and experience, even turning Latinos/as into main protagonists. Among this new generation of Latino/a superheroes are the new Blue Beetle (DC Comics, 2006), Spider-Girl (Marvel, 2010), and the new Ultimate Spider-Man (Marvel, 2011), which are explored in detail in this collection by Isabel Millán, Adilifu Nama and Maya Haddad, Kathryn M. Frank, and Brian Montes.

With very few exceptions, Latino/a superhero comics published since 1993 (which are the focus of this essay) share the characteristics of contemporary

US horror and science fiction narratives. Many of these comics feature super-heroes who are themselves monsters, or whose powers or mutations have given them a strange or supernatural appearance. Additionally, these narra-tives almost universally exhibit elements of "otherness" or "alien-ness" asso-ciated with their Latino/a characters and the worlds they inhabit. In some instances, the alien is an actual extraterrestrial force that comes to Earth and alters the lives of the protagonists. In other cases, the element of otherness is represented by a magical, spiritual, or cultural power that originates from out-side the United States or from within an ethnic community and is, therefore, alien to US-dominant, Anglo-centric culture. Whether these comics feature a monstrous hero, an alien force, or both, a common theme permeates them all: the superhero's powers and the story's plot development are dependent on an element of otherness that is or becomes ethnically and culturally specific.

What happens when the representation of Latinos/as in both indepen-dent and mainstream superhero comics is marked by the salient presence of monster-ness and/or alien-ness? Scholars have in the past recognized and criti-cized the dangers of such portrayals in US media and popular culture, arguing that they represent a continuation of the long-standing tradition of negative stereotyping to which Latinos/as have been subjected in all manner of public discourses. Charles Ramírez Berg claims that there is a connection between late twentieth-century American science fiction narratives and the issues of immigration and ethnic/cultural difference, indicating that the alien monster featured in popular US films embodies "a narrative pattern that identifies for-eign intruders as threats to national order and socio-ideological coherence."[3] Commenting on the work of Robin Wood, Ramírez Berg advances the idea that the "Other" represented by these monsters is the projection of something a culture has repressed in order to discredit, disown, or exterminate it.[4] In this context, Ramírez Berg sees immigrants—and particularly Latinos/as—as the main "Others" that US-dominant culture both oppresses and represses, and which have made their way into science fiction and horror films personified as dangerous creatures that stand for "the un-American Other."[5] Ramírez Berg claims that this process of signification is even worse than stereotyping, in which Latinos/as are portrayed as one-dimensional characters such as crimi-nals, buffoons, or harlots. What we encounter in these narratives, he writes, is representational "distortion," as Latinos/as are now depicted as "nonhuman Aliens."[6] Whether these movies employ "sympathetic aliens" or "destructive monsters" to portray the immigrant "Other," the result is always exclusion: those creatures must be eliminated "either lovingly, by returning them to their native environs . . . or violently, by destroying them."[7]

Ramírez Berg offers several explanations to try to make sense of this repre-

sentational distortion in recent US cinema, including "the perceived height-
ening of political and economic stakes placed upon the system by the new
immigrant,"[8] which leads to more hostile forms of stereotyping due to the
threat embodied by newcomers and the contestation of power that this entails. However, he sees the roots of the immigrant distortion in horror and
science fiction films as going beyond a mere competition for finite resources
between an in-group and an out-group, indicating that the "new immigrant
'invasion' calls into question the very identity of the nation itself, and the rejection of the Alien in SF films is projected, mass-mediated nativism" that re-
affirms the dominant view that "the status quo can be maintained only by exclusion."[9] In other words, the alien Other of these films reenacts a profound
contradiction at the heart of American history and national identity: one in
which the country's immigrant roots (Melting Pot metaphor) and diversity
(*E Pluribus Unum*) are celebrated, while simultaneously new immigrants and
their cultural differences are rejected. However, Ramírez Berg notes that some
"sympathetic" aliens, including superheroes such as Superman, are allowed to
stay, but only because their powers and services are of extreme benefit to the
United States and only after they have gone through a complete process of
acculturation and naturalization that more or less erases their differences.[10] In
the end, Ramírez Berg concludes, the transformation of the Latino/a immigrant from a stereotype to a monstrous distortion is a reaction by the dominant (Anglo) in-group to fear and anxiety over losing what it considers authentic "American" culture and the legitimate US nation: "We distort through
fear of losing our national self."[11]

I bring up Ramírez Berg's analysis of monster and science fiction narratives not to imply that Latino/a superhero comics engage in the same type of
oppressive and repressive representational distortion observed in films such
as *The Terminator* and *Blade Runner*. While these narratives do make use of
the Latino/a as a monster or alien "Other" image, I am more interested in exploring how this image is turned on its head within their pages. In the comics,
the Latino/a protagonists (already marked by their ethnic and cultural otherness) are initially represented according to the alien–monster–threat distortion formula, as they gain potentially dangerous powers from exotic sources
and in the process acquire new appearances that range from outright monstrosity to masked-and-costumed peculiarity. However, their abilities, heroic
deeds, and moral decisions quickly overwrite this initial, apparent distortion
and serve to contest traditional stereotypes about Latinos/as—giving a new,
resistant meaning to their portrayals. In other words, what I posit here is
that Latino/a superhero comics appropriate the alien distortion pointed out
by Ramírez Berg, nullifying its negative representational effects. They do so

by taking the two sources of otherness associated with Latino/a protagonists (ethnic and cultural difference and superpowered alien-ness/monstrosity) and employing them to assert Latino/a cultural specificity as well as to combat threats to their communities' full realization as human beings and as valuable members of the nation. Two transgressive acts can be identified in this process of appropriation and resignification: resistance against the forces of cultural assimilation and superheroic activism aimed at cultural empowerment and self-determination. By enacting these two transgressive acts within their storyworlds, Latino/a superhero comics immerse themselves in the controversial history and politics of immigration and cultural citizenship in the United States. In doing so, their superheroes become metaphors of Latino/a power and agency, reflecting the ongoing real-life struggles and aspirations of the ethnic and cultural communities that they represent and for whom they deliver a sort of poetic justice. In the next few pages, I will explore how representative superhero comics deal with Latino/a stereotypical and distorted portrayals through resistance to assimilation and active cultural empowerment.

TRUTH, JUSTICE, AND THE ANTI-ASSIMILATION WAY: THE HYBRID SUPERHERO STRIKES BACK

Mirroring dominant US nation-building discourses about immigration and acculturation, the narratives contained in American superhero comics have been traditionally imbued with the cultural assimilation impulse advanced by the myths of the "Melting Pot" and the "American Dream." The very first superhero comic, *Superman* (1938), has been interpreted as the narrative of both an extraterrestrial and a Jewish immigrant pursuing the American Dream but hiding his alien and ethnic origin under the identity of Clark Kent, driven by a desire to achieve complete cultural assimilation.[12] Writing about *Wonder Woman*, Matthew Smith claims that her character has been written "to fulfill expectations associated with the melting pot metaphor," which works to deny "her strong ethnic and cultural ties to her native people" and erase difference and ambiguity by emphasizing "her devotion to [dominant] American ideals."[13] Recent Latino/a superhero comics have defied this assimilation impulse, particularly by emphasizing cultural hybridity both as an essential characteristic of the Latino/a experience in the United States and as a visual and narrative tool for affirming and celebrating new Latino/a identities—identities that are fluid, complex, and ambivalent and thus negate any attempts at stereotyping, simplifying, or essentializing. Latino/a literary and cultural studies scholars have written extensively about hybridity as a strategy long used by Mexican-Americans and other Hispanics "for expressing cultural change

without losing cultural specificity."[14] Because Latinos/as are "positioned between cultures, living on borderlines,"[15] they constantly borrow and learn
from Latin American, Indigenous, African, European-American and many
other traditions. The resulting cross-cultural meldings "are not the sign of an
assimilation impulse, but evidence of an acquisitive and adaptive culture, ready
to use the tools at its disposal to forge new . . . identities."[16] Hybridity is thus
inextricably linked to an effort by Latinos/as to resist complete assimilation
into US-dominant culture in their literary and artistic production, as well as
in the traditions, celebrations, and other aspects of their everyday life. In this
essay, I view hybridity as one of several strategies used by Latino/a comic book
artists to engage in what I call an "anti-assimilation" effort aimed at resisting
cultural disintegration inside America's overheated melting pot.

The comics *Blue Beetle* and *El Muerto* are perfect examples of how hybridity
and anti-assimilation go hand in hand. In both series, the story begins with
an ordinary young Latino whose destiny is inadvertently and irremediably
altered by forces that are alien to his everyday existence. In *Blue Beetle*, Jaime
Reyes[17]—a Mexican-American high school student from El Paso, Texas—
stumbles upon a small object shaped like a scarab, which becomes imbedded
in his spine and turns him into a grotesque beetle-looking cyborg with spectacular skills and powers. Seeing himself in the mirror for the first time after
the transformation, Jaime acknowledges the nature of his new appearance:
"¡Carajo! I look like a freakin' bug-monster!"[18] He also recognizes that if the
government were to find out about his powers, he would be swiftly taken
away from his family just like the aliens of science fiction films, telling his
mother: "Next thing you know, I'm all 'E.T. in the ice cream cooler.'"[19] The
scarab is later revealed to belong to The Reach, an extraterrestrial race that
sends these artifacts to many planets in order to establish "infiltrators" that
will assist in the conquering of new worlds. In the various story lines of the
new *Blue Beetle* published by DC Comics since 2006, the scarab is said to have
been found in an Egyptian pyramid[20] and in a Mayan temple,[21] further adding
to the alien-ness and hybrid origin of the object and its powers. Meanwhile, *El
Muerto* tells the story of Juan Diego de la Muerte, a Mexican-American comic
book author from southern California. On his way to a Day of the Dead party
on his twenty-first birthday, he crashes his vehicle and wakes up in Mictlan,
the Aztec underworld, as the god of death, Mictlantecuhtli, is getting ready
to sacrifice him so he can become his avatar on Earth. The ritual turns Juan
Diego into a zombie with incredible godlike powers, forever looking like the
scary undead mariachi he disguised himself as for the party.

In addition to initially portraying the young Latinos as alien in nature
and monstrous in appearance, both comics present the future superheroes as

potential foreign threats to world and US national security. Because of the origins of the scarab and its mission, Jaime as the Blue Beetle is essentially a superpowered illegal immigrant and invader who crossed planetary and national borders (from outer space, from the Middle East, and from Mexico into the United States) to facilitate violent colonization and impose an alien way of life. To reinforce this image, the comic shows Jaime, after his first transformation and first extraterrestrial outing, naked and stranded along the US–Mexico border in the middle of the night, trying to find his way home. A gas station worker (who at first glance fits the stereotype of the redneck, anti-immigrant, gun-happy American) confronts the boy, assuming he is just another illegal trying to sneak into Texas: "You cross tonight. You habla muy bien."[22] The comic quickly reverses this stereotype, as the redneck turns out to be a Good Samaritan who helps Jaime reach his house after telling him he once was in the Peace Corps in Guatemala. Notwithstanding this challenge to traditional stereotyping, the scene serves the purpose of reinventing Jaime, an American citizen, as an illegal border-crosser/terrorist who carries in his spine (like a suicide bomber of sorts) the ultimate weapon of mass destruction that could annihilate the United States. In *El Muerto*, Juan Diego is also initially portrayed as a menace to his country, particularly to those people descended from the Europeans who conquered the lands once controlled by the Aztec Empire. Mictlantecuhtli wants to turn the young man into the "grimmest reaper of all time!"[23] using him to destroy the European "plunderers" and carry out his plan for *reconquista*: "You will place my name once more upon the lips of the world that dared reject me a half-millennium ago!"[24] Just like Jaime, Juan Diego returns to his home in the United States as a border-crosser, being magically transported from Mictlan (which is located, at least mythologically speaking, somewhere in Mexico) after his transformation into a would-be agent of destruction.

While the early stages of both comic book series point to Jaime/Blue Beetle and Juan Diego/El Muerto as being foreign threats to the United States, the narratives quickly subvert the alien/monster distortion by having their protagonist resist assimilation in a variety of ways. In *Blue Beetle*, Jaime engages from the beginning in a furious struggle to keep the scarab from controlling his mind and body. As the "organic host" of the alien technology, Jaime is supposed to follow orders and advance The Reach's mission of universal domination. However, when he is urged to kill even meta-humans and monsters that threaten his life, Jaime finds different ways to redirect the scarab or manages to control it and orders it to use nonlethal force instead, because "my mother didn't raise me like that. It's wrong."[25] Jaime's efforts to avoid assimilation into the violent alien culture of The Reach are so successful that he becomes the first to retain the scarab's powers and control them at will, even after the object is removed from his body. Instead of being absorbed by and lost to his newfound powers and the oppressive culture where they originated, Jaime employs them to assist other superheroes in a variety of intergalactic battles and also to help people in the border communities where he has family and cultural ties. As a Latino teenager growing up in a working-class family (his father is a mechanic and his mother a nurse), Jaime also faces a variety of more earthly threats, including the influence of street gangs. Driven by his parents to stay in school and avoid bad influences, Jaime also manages to avoid becoming assimilated into the barrio's gang and crime culture, which has consumed many of the people around him—and even led to his father's being shot in the leg because of a gang-related dispute involving his shop's troubled employee, Luis.

Similarly to what happens in *Blue Beetle*, in *El Muerto* the protagonist also faces the daunting task of subduing an exotic force that has turned his life upside down and is trying to control his destiny. Instead of taking part in Mictlantecuhtli's *reconquista* and being lost to death, Juan Diego travels back and forth across the border searching for a way to lift what he considers to be a curse. Along the way, he employs his powers (which include the ability to bring the dead back to life) to help people in need and stop bad guys, contesting the traditional portrayal of the zombie as a mindless, ravenous creature. Although he has been forced to spend his days as an undead outsider, Juan Diego is a highly moral character who is constantly seeking to reclaim his humanity both through his noble actions and through his refusal to admit that (physically speaking) he has morphed into a heartless monster: "I'll fight to get the God of Death off my back, and rejoin the *living* once again. When it really is my turn to die, I'll accept my fate. But until then, I want to walk amongst the living . . . *truly* alive."[26] In any of the supernatural narratives analyzed by Ramírez Berg, El Muerto could had been easily portrayed as a demonic, alien Aztec zombie that crosses the border from Mexico to take over the American Southwest. But that is not the case in Hernandez's comic, where El Muerto's humanity is stronger than his monstrosity and the thing that makes him different is also the source of his heroism. By resisting assimilation into the oppressive alien powers of The Reach, street gangs, and a vengeful Aztec deity (all of which are characterized by the use of violence), Jaime/Blue Beetle and Juan Diego/El Muerto effectively challenge and reverse the stereotypes and distortions associated with Latinos/as in mainstream media and popular culture. They also provide powerful representational counterdiscourses that emphasize positive attributes of Latinos/as—something that is still seriously lacking in US media and popular culture. Additionally, since

Jaime is also a good son and a good student, *Blue Beetle* puts forth a role model that urban youth of color can relate to and aspire to emulate.

In both comics, the protagonists acquire a new hybrid identity as characters as a result of their accidental encounters, which will define the way they see themselves and are regarded by others for the duration of their stories: the Texas teen is at once Jaime and Blue Beetle, human and alien, extraordinary and ordinary, while the California artist is both Juan Diego and El Muerto, human and monster, alive and undead. The comics abundantly reflect this complex identity in visual terms. Several panels show Jaime half as a human accompanied by his family and half as the beetle armor-clad superhero joined by fellow do-gooders or against an outer-space background.[27] Meanwhile, the various aspects of Juan Diego's new identity are brilliantly shown on a page from *El Muerto: Dead and Confused* (see figure 9.1), as he lies in bed pondering his fate—his body shows the chest scar, sunken eyes, shriveled lips, and skull tattoo that mark him as an Aztec zombie, while he also displays a cross on his forehead, a cross necklace, and a crucifix clasped between his fingers that represent his devotion to Catholicism as an important aspect of his former existence among the living.[28]

Assimilation into the alien forces that tried to absorb Jaime's and Juan Diego's identities as humans for their own selfish purposes would have resulted in the complete elimination of those identities, rendering the characters unidimensional and stereotypical. Conversely, resisting such assimilation made the protagonists' identities even more hybrid and multifaceted, as they were able to retain the superpowers that now make them special without losing their former selves in the process.

Finally, it is important to point out that the processes of anti-assimilation and hybridization that resulted in the creation of the superheroes in *Blue Beetle* and *El Muerto* do not take away from their Latino-ness. In fact, they actually enhance the protagonists' construction as fundamentally Latino/a superheroes with visible signs of the type of cultural heterogeneity and capacity for adaptation that Alonzo has referred to. In addition to having complex superhero identities, Jaime/Blue Beetle and Juan Diego/El Muerto are represented in the comics as individuals who possess extremely hybrid identities as contemporary Mexican-Americans—with the storyworlds in which they exist also expressing such variegation (see figure 9.2). In *Blue Beetle*, Jaime and his family code-switch between English and Spanish, as do many of the other Latino/a characters in the comic. The series even includes an all-Spanish issue, no. 26, in which Jaime goes to visit his extended family, all of whom speak Spanish among them, thus reflecting the linguistic realities of many Latino/a families in the United States. Additionally, Jaime's Blue Beetle suit

9.1. El Muerto's hybrid and syncretic nature in Javier Hernandez's *El Muerto: Dead and Confused*.

9.2. New Blue Beetle's mask resembles that of a Mexican *luchador*, yet Latino identity is largely absent when Jaime becomes the superhero.

includes stylistic elements that mark the superhero as Latino, especially the mask, which resembles that of a Mexican *luchador*.

As Jonathan Risner has noted, Blue Beetle's insect-like appearance also brings into dialogue the intertext of the cockroach, which has become a metaphor of Latino/a resilience in works such as Oscar Zeta Acosta's *Revolt of the Cockroach People*.[29] The superhero's *latinidad* is consolidated even further in the story line that shows the scarab as having come from a Mayan temple, thus making Mexico an important source of Jaime's superhero and cultural identities and inextricably conjoining both of those identities. The comic also presents the US–Mexico borderland not as a zone of division but as a fluid space that Blue Beetle and other characters constantly cross, and—as Jaime's grandmother states—he is identified not as a national but as a transnational hero: "El Escarabajo protege a la gente de El Paso y Ciudad Juárez. Él protege a la gente como nosotros sin pensarlo dos veces."[30]

El Muerto is also constructed as a hybrid creature in a hybrid storyworld. Even before his transformation, Juan Diego is shown as an individual whose identity is marked by a lot of cultural influences. He is obsessed with Aztec culture, even sporting a tattoo of the skull of Mictlantecuhtli on his shoulder; at the same time, he is also highly influenced by Catholicism, as previously indicated; he displays a fascination with both Mexican and American popular culture; and he is deeply marked by the religious and cultural syncretism expressed through the Day of the Dead celebration, which represents the day of both his birth and his symbolic death. (For more on this and an analysis of the reculturation process in *El Muerto*, see David William Foster's "Latino Comics: Javier Hernandez's *El Muerto* as an Allegory of Chicano Identity.") El Muerto's moniker connects him with the history of Mexican *mestizaje*, as Juan Diego was also the name of the Indian to whom the Virgin of Guadalupe appeared, symbolically merging Spanish and Indigenous cultures. Just like in *Blue Beetle*, in *El Muerto* the US–Mexico border is not presented as a point of invasion but rather as a site of cultural exchange and narrative flow. As a metaphor of contemporary Latino/a culture, Juan Diego/El Muerto travels back and forth across borderlands (geographic, ethnic, cultural, spiritual) as he brings the Indigenous, Spanish, and American aspects of his cultural makeup together, refusing to sacrifice one in favor of the other. Despite the fact that Mictlantecuhtli has eternally changed Juan Diego's life and seeks to destroy people with whom he shares ethnic and cultural ties, he validates the deity's anger and motivation for vengeance, often meditating on the injustices caused by the Spaniards to his Indigenous ancestors.

Ultimately, El Muerto's heroism is expressed via his commitment to sustaining his hybrid Latino/a identity and protecting his fellow Latinos/as from a variety of forces (Mictlantecuhtli, racist zombies) that threaten to harm them. As David William Foster has indicated, the inclusion of the zombie, a figure derived from African lore, in the already hybridized universe of El Muerto makes for a "decidedly unconventional" mix at first glance, as there is no historical or cultural connection between zombies and Aztec mythology.[31] However, such cultural confluence makes sense within the comic's storyworld when considering the syncretism of religious beliefs that is at the heart of this story. In that regard, Foster argues that by creating an "Aztec zombie" who lives as an average Chicano in a contemporary America marked by renewed nativism and resistance to multiculturalism, Hernandez may be making a political statement: that Chicanos/as, and other Latinos/as, struggle as "nuisance zombies in the background of American society."[32] However, despite his "lifeless" condition, El Muerto fully embraces his hybrid and ambivalent nature and becomes a metaphor for resistance against the assimilationist impulses of Anglo society.

SUPER-POWER TO THE PEOPLE: COMICS AND LATINO/A EMPOWERMENT

Comic book scholars have argued that superhero stories are ultimately and most basically "fantasies of power and success"[33] that have become ingrained in American consciousness because they are "so closely tied to the idea of the 'American Dream.'"[34] In this fictional reenactment of the American Dream, the superhero becomes "an icon of empowerment through transformation, changing from an ordinary person to a superpowered being, making some kind of 'extra effort' to demonstrate his or her superior physical or moral power."[35] For the longest time in the history of US comics, however, the superhero-as-American-Dreamer was essentially white, suggesting that the aspirations of heroism as well as of power and success were beyond the grasp of minorities. Recent Latino/a superhero comics have helped to reverse this trend, emerging as resistant narratives that put forth alternative forms and styles of heroism — and which also portray Latinos/as as empowered individuals at a time in which this ethnic community is rapidly growing in terms of population and influence in all aspects of US life and culture. Just like *Blue Beetle* and *El Muerto*, the more politically engaged Latino/a superhero comics also feature elements of alien-ness and/or monstrosity in the construction of their protagonists and challenge stereotypical or distorted portrayals of Latinos/as.

The authors of these comics frame the struggle of Latinos/as to gain rights and recognition as an outright battle against radical, discriminatory forces that seek to oppress them. They do so by infusing their stories "with a cultural and historical specificity" that seeks to open the "reader's eyes to social, political injustice and outright racism," as Aldama and González posit in this volume's introduction. In Laura Molina's *The Jaguar* (1996), East LA law student Linda Rivera endeavors to protect minorities in an alternate timeline in which Proposition 187 turned California into a police state ruled by right-wing fundamentalists. At first, Rivera employs her education to do "what is necessary to see that justice is done."[36] But when the legal system is not sufficient to achieve results, she engages in vigilante justice by invoking the powers of Huitzilopochtli, the Aztec god of war, and her *nahual*, or animal spirit, the jaguar. In one such mission, Linda encounters a pair of neo-Nazi men, who accuse her of "destroying white people's property."[37] The superheroine easily defeats the skinheads, telling them that they were lucky this time because "my ancestors used to eat their enemies."[38] The Jaguar's unapologetic Chicana feminist identity is reflected in the comic's fight scene, which challenges the historical oppression and discrimination of Mexican-Americans and of women in the United States by staging the superiority of a woman of color over white, racist males (see figure 9.3). Stylistically, The Jaguar's physical and moral predominance is evidenced through the way Molina draws her characters: the heroine has chiseled muscles, she is athletic, and her facial expressions are depicted in great detail, while the villains are shown as weak and their faces are generically drawn, signifying anonymity and lack of representational importance.

The book's cover also highlights the importance of cultural hybridity in Molina's comic: English, Spanish, Spanglish, and Nahuatl are used throughout, while The Jaguar's outfit combines the skintight, full-body spandex suit traditionally worn by American superheroes with elements from ancient Aztec warriors, such as a feather headdress, gold jewelry, and, of course, jaguar prints.

Another superhero who faces intolerant, anti-immigrant antagonists is Javier Hernandez's Weapon Tex-Mex, a hybrid man/longhorn bull character with tremendous physical strength. In the webcomic *Destroy all Mexicans!* (1997), the hero foils the evil plans of Android 197, a robot-encased former "angry ol' governor from the West"[39] who kidnaps immigrants to protect jobs "for God-fearing Americans."[40] In *Weapon Tex-Mex vs. El Muerto* (2011), the two Latino superheroes team up against Mr. Smith, a mysterious Anglo Texan who turns out to be the zombie of a nineteenth-century Texas Ranger, Jedediah Hellinger, who "killed one too many Mexicans in my private time,"[41] was hanged, went to hell, and has been wandering the Earth since. Hellinger manages to take over El Muerto's immortal body and his Aztec powers so he can rule the world. Weapon Tex-Mex comes to the rescue, obliterating the ranger zombie but dying in the process. In the end, however, El Muerto is able to revive himself and his new friend. The way Hernandez pits his two Latino superheroes against an evil, Mexican-phobic, Anglo force is a good example of postcolonial cultural resistance—as the comic book artist flips the discursive coin of power by giving agency to a historically discriminated ethnic group and assigning the role of villainy to the traditionally dominant group. In fact, this narrative rewrites a dominant heroic story in which Texas Rangers such as Hellinger did play the role of nationalist American heroes during the time of US Western imperialist expansion, upholding a dominant system of legality that undermined the rights of Mexicans and other subalterns who were regarded as foreigners and subhuman. In this narrative, Hellinger tries to literally "revive" his reign of terror in contemporary Texas by, once again, stealing something that belongs to Mexicans—in this case, El Muerto's Aztec-giving powers and his very own brown body. But the comic flips the script by giving two Mexican-Americans the role of heroes while highlighting the despicable nature of the Anglo lawman, whose decaying body and backward racist ways disintegrate into the oblivion of history (see figure 9.4). The Jaguar

9.3. Latina dominance as the protagonist confronts a pair of neo-Nazis in Laura Molina's *The Jaguar*.

9.4. Hernandez flips the US historical script by representing Weapon Tex-Mex as a vastly superior hero who protects Mexican-Americans from menacing Anglos.

and Weapon Tex-Mex are heirs to a long-standing tradition of Latino/a cultural heroes (Joaquín Murrieta and Gregorio Cortez among them) who have risen up to defend their communities from Anglo oppression. In this case, their rebellion takes place during a time of exacerbated nativist sentiments and the ongoing struggle of undocumented immigrants to achieve legal status and better living conditions in the United States.

Other superhero comics promote discourses of Latino/a empowerment by creating storyworlds in which Hispanics and other minorities are no longer victims rebelling against dominant forces but assume control of the spaces they inhabit and protect. Meanwhile, the superpowered Anglos in these stories are presented either as inept or unwilling to fulfill their crime-fighting missions or as weaker outsiders who require the minorities' help and must assimilate in order to fit in. In Marvel's *Daredevil: Father* (2006), then editor-in-chief Joe Quesada created a team of multiracial, Cuban-American superheroes known as the Santerians, who have managed to obtain the powers of the orishas (Yoruban spirits) they summoned in religious rites. The team is led by Nestor Rodriguez, a New York City entertainment magnate who, as a young man, had organized a neighborhood watch group known as the Street Angels to protect the city's Latino/a community from rising crime rates and drug activity. Seeking a more effective way to fight crime, Nestor discovered Santeria and transformed himself into the powerful Eleggua, later recruiting former members of the Street Angels to join him in his superpowered vigilante activities. One of them, Ogun, is among the first black Latino/a (or "Blatino") superheroes to appear in US comics. As Adilifu Nama and Maya Haddad indicate, Blatino represents a contentious identity category in popular culture that requires careful analysis, which they have done in their essay in this collection. Tensions between the Santerians and Anglo superhero Daredevil arise after he has cleaned up his neighborhood, the historically Irish-American Hell's Kitchen, pushing crime elsewhere in the city—including the Latin quarters defended by the Santerians. The superhero team confronts Daredevil, defeating him. Eleggua recriminates him for his unwillingness to protect everyone else in New York City, a task that the Cuban-Americans have now taken on: "I'm sick of cleaning up your sloppy seconds," to which Daredevil replies: "'s none of my business."[42] The relationships among race, ethnicity, class, and neighborhoods in the New York City comic book universe are discussed at length by Brian Montes in this collection.

During another confrontation between the heroes, when Eleggua is again unsuccessful in convincing Daredevil to join him, the chief Santerian tries to belittle him and show his moral superiority: "Come, *orisha*, let's see if we can make a difference in this city. Someone's got to do it."[43] Nestor also resents the fact that, years before, Daredevil had shown up too late to save Nestor's father from being murdered by criminals. While the two crime-fighting forces never reconcile, Daredevil is forced to rethink his position after a serial killer that had been targeting people all over the city, except for Hell's Kitchen, turns out to be a friend of his from his neighborhood. Through the confrontation between Daredevil and the Santerians, *Daredevil: Father* points to the dangers of ethnic and racial segregation, in this case represented by an Anglo superhero unwilling to help anyone outside of his mostly white neighborhood—which effectively becomes a gated community shielded from crime to the detriment of others, especially minorities. The comic also presents a challenge to the superiority of traditional Anglo superheroes, highlighting their inadequacy to stop crime (the killing of Nestor's dad) and their refusal to protect an increasingly diverse city. At the same time, the comic underscores the growing influence of Latinos/as and their diverse culture in the United States, represented by Nestor's rise to power as a rich and influential entrepreneur and as a superhero who acquires his super-abilities by tapping into Afro-Caribbean religious beliefs. In the end, Nestor effectively takes over Daredevil's former duties and protects New Yorkers regardless of their race or ethnicity.

A similar, though less gritty, scenario is enacted in Jules Rivera's graphic novel *Misfortune High*, whose Book 1 was published in late 2013 following a successful online crowdfunding campaign. This comic tells the story of a multicultural group of teenagers with special powers attending an inner-city school called Fortuna High 189, in the fictional western town of Las Fortunas. The graphic novel's two Latino/a protagonists are Johnny Cuervo, an avian shape-shifter, and Sonia, an illusion-maker. In this story, Will Bicksford, a spoiled rich white brat, is expelled from his elite Phoenix Magic Academy for cheating. Hoping to teach him a lesson, his father sends him to Fortuna High 189, whose building abounds with graffiti as well as cracked sidewalks and walls. The outsiders' assumptions about the kids attending Fortuna High 189 are infused with stereotypes, as Will's dad tells him that this is "a public school filled with ruffians and offenders,"[44] while Will himself assumes Johnny is one of those "outer rim citizens [who] don't speak English."[45] Johnny complains to his friend Sonia about the way people on their side of town are perceived, echoing the realities faced by Latinos/as in the United States today: "Outer rim guy with anything resembling a tan? Of course he no speaky Ingles. That's how a lot of inner circle people see guys like me. We're just a bunch of illiterate workhorses to them."[46] The graphic novel plays with other Latino/a stereotypes, initially portraying Johnny as a bad guy through his rough, mysterious appearance and his propensity to become angry and violent when provoked. However, Johnny is later revealed to be a sensitive and smart kid who hides behind his bad-boy look and attitude (see figures 9.5a and 9.5b). As Rivera has indicated, this character "was created to invoke a stereotype and then punch it in the face."[47]

Misfortune High not only debunks stereotypes but also hints at the superiority of minorities in a changing America. In one scene, Warren, an African-

9.5a and 9.5b. The stereotype of the violent Latino is invoked through the character of Johnny Cuervo, only to be challenged later in Jules Rivera's *Misfortune High*.

American boy, tries to explain the nature of Johnny's powers to Will: "Cuervo means 'crow,' get it? Oh . . . I guess you don't speak Spanish."[48] After being pampered in his former school thanks to his father's influence, Will is now forced to adapt to the multicultural and multilingual realities of the world outside his sheltered existence just to survive. Finally, the graphic novel highlights the powers derived from the protagonists' Latino/a cultural heritage and thus their hybrid identities. A series of panels on page 23 shows Johnny's transfiguration from a crow into his human form, making an intertextual connection with the Mesoamerican belief of the *nahual*, or animal spirit that is said to inhabit each individual (see figure 9.6).

At the end of Book 1, we learn that Johnny uses his power to protect Las Fortunas from its many threats, including a dragon that has been terrorizing schools on the rich side of town. Here, the graphic novel also contrasts Johnny's superheroism and superior physical presence with Will's selfishness and scrawny appearance.

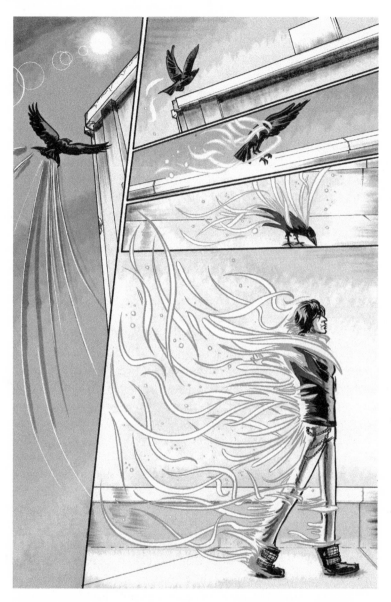

9.6. Johnny Cuervo's shape-shifting powers and the Mesoamerican belief in the *nahual*, or animal spirit, in Jules Rivera's *Misfortune High*.

While they may be easily dismissed as fantastical, escapist stories anchored in the pop-culture tradition of horror and science fiction narratives, recent superhero comics are quite effective at performing and commenting on many of the realities and challenges facing Latino/a communities, as well as at expressing their aspirations for cultural and political empowerment. Latino/a superhero comics created by independent Latino/a authors in the past two decades, as well as those produced by mainstream comic book publishers in the twenty-first century, have managed to dethrone many of the stereotypes often associated with Latinos/as in US media and popular culture, portraying Hispanics as courageous and smart heroes instead of criminals and dimwits. Latino/a superhero comics have fought these stereotypes with the same tenacity that their protagonists employ to obliterate bad guys and planetary threats. First, these comics reflect efforts on the part of their characters to resist assimilation into alien, oppressive cultures, thus enacting the real-life struggles of Latinos/as and other minorities to retain their cultural specificity while adapting to US culture. Second, the comics' characters and story-worlds make explicit and celebrate the rich, hybrid culture that US Latinos/as have developed and seek to maintain, mixing Indigenous, Latin American, European, African, US, and other influences. Finally, Latino/a superhero comics combine this anti-assimilation impulse and the exaltation of cultural hybridity to create transgressive narratives in which Hispanics become empowered by (1) fighting back against discriminatory policies and racist villains and (2) establishing moral and cultural superiority by taking over the role of city or national superheroes from fading or inadequate Anglo crime fighters and praising the values of multiculturalism in a rapidly changing America.

As a significant contribution to contemporary Latino/a narrative media, superhero comics offer a counter-discourse to the dehumanizing distortion carried out in recent US science fiction films—which portray immigrants as invading monsters or aliens that threaten national security and must, therefore, be excluded, as noted by Charles Ramírez Berg. Instead, the "otherness" and "alien-ness" that are very much a part of the Latino/a superheroes' hybrid, contestatory identities become their source of power and cultural pride, as they fight for truth, justice, and their communities' Latino-American way of life. In these narratives, the aliens are no longer excluded to protect an Anglo-centric version of the "authentic" America—becoming instead active, engaged forces that help to shape a new, more plural version of America. In Latino/a superhero comics, the alien has arrived and is here to stay.

NOTES

1. Frederick Aldama, *Your Brain on Latino Comics: From Gus Arriola to Los Bros Hernandez* (Austin: University of Texas Press, 2009), 31–38.

2. Javier Hernandez, e-mail message to author, 5 Sept. 2013.

3. Charles Ramírez Berg, *Latino Images in Film: Stereotypes, Subversion, and Resistance* (Austin: University of Texas Press, 2002), 155.

4. Ibid.

5. Ibid., 156.

6. Ibid.

7. Ibid., 158.

8. Ibid, 159.

9. Ibid., 162.

10. Ibid., 166–168.

11. Ibid., 165.

12. Danny Fingeroth, *Disguised as Clark Kent: Jews, Comics, and the Creation of the Superhero* (New York: Continuum, 2007), 24.

13. Matthew Smith, "The Tyranny of the Melting Pot Metaphor: Wonder Woman as the Americanized Immigrant," in *Comics and Ideology,* ed. Matthew McAllister, Edward Sewell, and Ian Gordon (New York: Peter Lang, 2001), 130.

14. Juan J. Alonzo, *Badmen, Bandits, and Folk Heroes: The Ambivalence of Mexican American Identity in Literature and Film* (Tucson: University of Arizona Press, 2009), 138.

15. Ramón Saldívar, *Chicano Narrative: The Dialectics of Difference* (Madison: University of Wisconsin Press, 1990), 25.

16. Alonzo, *Badmen,* 138.

17. Reyes is the third individual and the first Latino to incarnate the Blue Beetle, following Dan Garrett (1939) and Ted Kord (1967). Blue Beetle is one of several mainstream superheroes who have been "Latinized" in the past 25 years, including El Diablo (1989), Spider-Girl (2010), Spider-Man (2011), and Ghost Rider (2014).

18. Tony Bedard, Ig Guara, J. P. Mayer, and Ruy Jose, *Blue Beetle: Vol. 1: Metamorphosis* (New York: DC Comics, 2012), 53.

19. Keith Giffen, John Rogers, and Cully Hamner, *Blue Beetle: Shellshocked* (New York: DC Comics, 2006), 78.

20. John Rogers, Keith Giffen, Cully Hamner, and Rafael Albuquerque, *Blue Beetle: Road Trip* (New York: DC Comics, 2007), 38.

21. Bedard, Guara, Mayer, and Jose, *Metamorphosis,* 19.

22. Giffen, Rogers, and Hamner, *Shellshocked,* 35.

23. Javier Hernandez, *El Muerto: The Aztec Zombie* (Whittier, CA: Los Comex, 2002), 19.

24. Ibid.

25. Rogers, Giffen, Hamner, and Albuquerque, *Road Trip,* 48.

26. Javier Hernandez and Mort Todd, *Mark of Mictlantecuhtli* (Whittier, CA: Los Comex, 2007), 7.

27. Rogers, Giffen, Hamner, and Albuquerque, *Road Trip,* 16; 18; 26.

28. Javier Hernandez, *El Muerto: Dead and Confused* (Whittier, CA: Los Comex, 2008), 12.

29. Jonathan Risner, "'Authentic' Latina/os and Queer Characters in Mainstream and

Alternative Comics," in *Multicultural Comics: From Zap to Blue Beetle*, ed. Frederick Aldama (Austin: University of Texas Press, 2010), 49.

30. John Rogers and Rafael Albuquerque, *Blue Beetle: End Game* (New York: DC Comics, 2008), 165.

31. David William Foster, "Latino Comics: Javier Hernandez's El Muerto as an Allegory of Chicano Identity," in *Latinos and Narrative Media: Participation and Portrayal*, ed. Frederick Aldama (New York: Palgrave Macmillan, 2013), 235.

32. Ibid., 227.

33. Bradford W. Wright, *Comic Book Nation: The Transformation of Youth Culture in America* (Baltimore: Johns Hopkins University Press, 2011), 1.

34. Christopher Murray, *Champions of the Oppressed? Superhero Comics, Popular Culture, and Propaganda in America during World War II* (Cresskill, NJ: Hampton Press, 2011), 8.

35. Ibid.

36. Laura Molina, *The Jaguar* (Arcadia, Calif.: Insurgent Comix, 1996), 4.

37. Ibid., 8.

38. Ibid., 9.

39. Javier Hernandez, *Destroy All Mexicans!*, Javzilla: The Official Site of Javier Hernandez, accessed 22 Nov. 2013, http://www.javzilla.com, 1.

40. Ibid., 2.

41. Javier Hernandez, *Weapon Tex-Mex vs. El Muerto* (Whittier, CA: Los Comex, 2011), 11.

42. Joe Quesada, *Daredevil: Father* (New York: Marvel, 2006), chapter 2.

43. Ibid., chapter 3.

44. Jules Rivera, *Misfortune High: Book 1* (Los Angeles: 2013), 10.

45. Ibid., 12.

46. Ibid., 26.

47. Jules Rivera, e-mail message to author, 24 Sept. 2013.

48. Rivera, *Misfortune High*, 22.

TEN

ANYA SOFÍA (ARAÑA) CORAZÓN: THE INNER WEBBINGS AND MEXI-RICANIZATION OF SPIDER-GIRL

ISABEL MILLÁN

Añya Corazon[1] is special. She didn't fall into the web like so many others. . . . She truly was chosen, for a destiny I cannot foresee. . . . One she may not live to fulfill. She is reckless. Fearless. Beautiful in her flaws. But she's so young. . . . It's a miracle she survived this long. MADAME WEB[2]

ON MAY 3, 2013, *Latina.com* published "10 Superheroes You Never Knew Were Latino."[3] The first two, Miles Morales and Anya Sofía Corazón, possess mutual affiliations with spiders. Morales topped the list as the Latino[4] and African American Spider-Man debuting in 2011. Seven years prior, in 2004, Corazón entered Marvel's Universe as the Mexican and Puerto Rican Spider-Girl, Araña. Not to be confused with Peter Parker's daughter, May "Mayday" Parker, who is also known as Spider-Girl,[5] Corazón's superhero powers were inherited from her mother, Sofía Araña Corazón. Writer Fiona Avery created Araña for Marvel's *Amazing Fantasy*, vol. 2,[6] depicting her as a fifteen-year-old freshman at Milton Summers High School in Brooklyn, New York, who is neither popular nor a stellar student, often getting herself into trouble. Madame Web's observations above accurately portray her as both reckless and fearless, common character flaws of young superheroes that make her appealing to her audience. Corazón's first day of school begins with a hallway altercation whereby she steps in to defend her friend, Lynn, who is being confronted by an older jock. Within the scrimmage, Corazón suggests they settle their dispute "tonight at nine, the bridge at Fort Greene Park."[7] The occurrences of that night transform her from average high school student to covert superhero. At the park, she meets Miguel Legar, who becomes her initial guardian, and together they form a bond as Mage and Hunter for WebCorps, the Spider Society. Corazón's training consists of surviving a harsh desert climate entirely on her own.[8] This desert symbolizes both danger and a source of great power if she can wield it to her advantage. Of all the possible deserts at their disposal, WebCorps chooses one within "the undisclosed wilderness of the Yucatan Peninsula."[9] Notably, this region of Mexico usually invokes lush vegetation and tropical weather rather than a hot and arid climate. The Marvel Omniverse is, of course, fictitious, as are its characters, some of whom transgress parallel universes, such as Araña's friend, Nomad (Rikki Barnes). It may well be that there is a desert region known as the Yucatan Peninsula within one of Marvel's variations of Earth. The peril, however, occurs when cultural products such as comics are created and read as authentic representations of marginalized others within the logics of contemporary politics. After all, Araña exists within the primary Marvel Universe, Earth-616.

Marvel strategically incorporates marginalized identities throughout its comics in an effort to appeal to a wider audience. Araña is meant to target a Latina/o niche market evidenced by this promotional blurb: "a magical fantasy starring Marvel's first Latina hero—as featured on the WB, Fox News, CNN, and Telemundo."[10] This is purely a marketing ploy since Latina superheroes such as Firebird appeared as early as 1981 within Marvel's *The Incredible Hulk*, vol. 2, issue 265.[11] According to her origin story, Firebird's real name was Bonita Juárez. She was a devout Catholic from New Mexico who worked as a social worker by day. By claiming Araña as their first Latina hero, Marvel is contributing to the erasure of prior Latina superheroes, even within its own comic franchise.

Marvel Entertainment began as Timely Comics in 1939 and is now owned by the Walt Disney Company.[12] The popularity of superheroes and villains such as Spider-Man, Captain America, Storm, Wolverine, Hulk, and Elektra account for Marvel's continued commercial success. Jeffrey Brown observes that "superheroes reveal some of our most basic beliefs about morality and justice, our conceptions of gender and sexuality, and our attitudes towards ethnicity and nationality."[13] Undoubtedly, Corazón is a cultural product and commodity meant to "appeal to a fast-rising middle-class Latino demographic (young and old)."[14] Unlike Firebird, who primarily served as a secondary character, Corazón has appeared in her own series, including *Amazing Fantasy*, vol. 2 (2004–2005); *Araña: The Heart of the Spider*, issues 1–12 (2005–2006);[15] *Spider-Girl: Family Values* (2011); and *Spider-Island: The Amazing Spider-Girl*, issues 1–3 (2011). She also co-starred in special issues, such as *Spider-Man & Araña: The Hunter Revealed* (2006) and *Young Allies*, issues 1–6 (2010), and made regular appearances in *Ms. Marvel* (2007–2008), *Captain America* (2010), *Avengers Academy* (2010–2011), *Fear Itself: The Home Front* (2013), and most recently, *Avengers Assemble* (2013–2014).[16] Despite these appearances from her initial creation in 2004 to the present, Corazón remains a relatively marginal character within the larger Marvel comic industry. Her character's instability is evidenced through her constant negotiation of names, languages, racialization, superpowers, costumes, and even the actual comics or fan art in which she appears. If, as Derek Parker Royal asserts, "comics—by necessity—employs stereotypes as a kind of shorthand to communicate quickly and succinctly," then it is the responsibility of the "comic artists to tell her or his story as effectively as possible without slipping into the trap, even inadvertently, of inaccurate and even harmful representations."[17] My goal is not to determine which aspects of Araña's character or world are either authentic or inauthentic, but rather to critically examine these slippages within a broader discussion of comics as a literary and visual art form and a consumable product. Within comic culture, fans know and even come to expect different variations of their superheroes. Araña's variations, however, are at times so extreme that she becomes almost unrecognizable. Therefore, although comics may rely on stereotypes for short-term or quick comprehension, an analysis of Araña's character development over time challenges static stereotyping; unlike *Panlatinidad*,[18] which attempts to reduce differences by exploiting their greatest common factor, Araña is constantly shifting. Rather than seeing this as a limitation, I am interested in how Araña's variations more closely resemble our contemporary understandings of the nuances around language, citizenship, race, gender, and sexuality.

FROM ARAÑA TO SPIDER-GIRL: THE POLITICS OF NAMING

Corazón's name has generated some confusion within Marvel's Universe, which her character has attempted to explain since her first appearance in 2004. Upon taking attendance, her high school teacher calls out, "Ana Corazon." "Anya. Present," corrects our young protagonist. "Anya? Oh yes, I see," acknowledges the teacher who has presumably noticed the tilde over the "n" in *Aña*. Corazón elaborates further, "Everyone gets it wrong, so I just spell it with a Y. That's how I turn in my papers. A.N.Y.A." "Thank you, Anya." On her birth certificate then, her name might appear as *Aña Corazón*, or *Aña Araña Corazón*, given her mother's maiden name. However, we soon learn that although *Araña* is not on her birth certificate, her mother's name, *Sofía*, is also her middle name. Corazón's birth certificate, as depicted within a panel in *Araña, Vol. 2: In the Beginning*, reads "Aña Sofia Corazon." Notably, *Corazón* has never appeared with the accent mark over the second "o" whereas *Aña* has been spelled *Anya*, and even *Añya*.[19] On a production level, these variations reflect each author's personal preference and have no direct bearing within the plot. In contrast, Corazón's character appears most concerned about her superhero moniker, Araña, which in addition to being her mother's maiden name, means *spider* in Spanish. Corazón constantly struggles between this chosen moniker, Araña, and the one others attempt to impose onto her, Spider-Girl. In *The Amazing Spider-Man: Grim Hunt*, for example, Spider-Man dives in to push her aside and away from trouble: "Move it, Spider-Girl." Corazón, seemingly unaware of the impending danger, corrects him: "Dude, it's Araña." "No time! Just . . . RUN!" She eventually reacts, calling out "Santa Maria . . . ," Spanish for Virgin Mary. Toward the end, even after Arachne (Julia Carpenter) gifts Araña her own Spider-Woman costume, she insists on her chosen moniker:

SPIDER-MAN: By the way, I like the new look . . .
ARAÑA: Yeah, I don't know. Something . . . changed y'know? After the past few weeks, a t-shirt and cargo shorts just didn't feel heavy enough.
SPIDER-MAN: . . . The bad's gonna come, Spider-Girl. . . . Just don't let it define you, okay?
ARAÑA: Thanks "Dad," I'll work on it. And if you don't mind . . . I'm not going by **Spider-Girl**. It's totally corny and makes you want to puke. Name's Araña . . . and it's gonna stay Araña. No offense.
SPIDER-MAN: None taken. . . . Sounds perfect.[20]

Following this exchange, and at the bottom of that same page, Araña asks, "So, what is next?" "Next? Just life. . . . Life is next," responds Spider-Man. "Thanks, 'Dad.'" "Shut it, Spider-Girl."[21] Throughout this playful exchange, Spider-Man teases Corazón about her moniker precisely because he knows she dislikes the English version, Spider-Girl, regardless of the large spider symbol on her new costume.

Araña continues to insist she is not Spider-Girl in *Young Allies*, where she is introduced with the following description: "Anya Corazon. Araña. No longer super-powered. Not Spider-Girl." Her first attempt to combat crime in this series is met with a "Thank you, Spider-Girl!" "Oh. My gosh. I am NOT Spider-Girl.*" The asterisk then directs readers to ASM no. 634–637 "for the webbed truth."[22] However, toward the end of *Young Allies*, Corazón has a change of heart. At the end of a battle against The Superior and his followers, The Avengers (Captain America, Thing, Luke Cage, and Spider-Woman) emerge to haul away the villains. Corazón becomes starstruck by the original Spider-Woman (Jessica Drew), who congratulates her with a handshake while acknowledging, "So, you're Spider-Girl." Araña initially attempts to clarify, "Actually, I'm. . . . Well, really, it's . . . I," only to be followed with the next panel where she utters, "Yes. I'm Spider-Girl." Not entirely convinced herself, *Young Allies* ends with "A Change of Mind" whereby she is introduced as

"Anya Corazon. Spider-Girl." However on that exact page, Corazón stands in front of her bedroom mirror, trying out various poses and potential self-introductions. The page is divided into nine panels, with four on top, four in the middle, and one elongated panel at the bottom. "Spider-Girl," she says in the first panel, standing upright, serious, with her hands beside her. In the second panel she repeats to herself, "I am Spider-Girl. I am Spider-Girl." This time with more confidence and her hands on her hips. It is followed by "Aww yeah, bad guy! You just got schooled by the spectacular Spider-Girl!" Now we see her jumping, fully energized, and almost laughing. Next, in panel four, "Wanna know who I am? Wanna know my name? That's right, punk. I'm the gosh-darned Spider-Girl." This time her shoulders are hovering forward with hands clenched as if ready to attack her prey. Corazón's confidence is short-lived, retracting in panel five, "Uchh . . . No. No No No." Panels six through eight depict her with various facial expressions and body language suggesting she is clearly not content. Her anxiety over her name is verbalized as she answers her cell phone, "Yeah, it's Arañ..Spid..Anya here."[23] Whatever doubt Corazón possessed over her moniker seems momentarily appeased within her own comic book series titled *Spider-Girl*, issues 1–8, as collected in *Spider-Girl: Family Values* and published in 2011. A police officer thanks her for capturing Screwball and realizes, "Hey. You're a kid. . . . Just a girl." Corazón proudly proclaims, "I'm not just a girl. I'M SPIDER-GIRL." She will also refer to her fans as "Spider-Girl fans" and, by the end of issue 8, regains the superhero powers she lost in *Spider-Man & Araña: The Hunter Revealed*. Most recently, Corazón has made guest appearances in *Avengers Assemble*. A dialogue with Spider-Woman reveals her ongoing uncertainty over her superhero identity: ". . . I put on the mask because 'Spider-Girl' doesn't exactly strike fear in the hearts of the cowardly. Look, don't be mean. I'm still new at this . . . Nobody ever pronounced 'Araña' properly anyway."[24] Notably, even ten years after her first appearance, Corazón is still being portrayed as an amateur superhero grappling with her public persona, costume, and moniker—although now she speaks frankly about the challenges of choosing a moniker such as Araña. She had to decide between having her moniker continuously mispronounced or replacing it with something more palatable to a mainstream audience. Unfortunately, this assumes she is mostly interacting with non–Spanish speakers, which dismisses the prominence of Spanish as the most widely spoken language, after English, in major cities such as New York City.[25] Araña need not be discarded quite yet, and even if within an alternate universe, Corazón does make it to adulthood with her original moniker, Araña.[26]

Like the variations in her name, Corazón's place of birth and citizenship status are also contentious. According to *Araña, Vol 2: In the Beginning*, she was born on June 17, 1989, in Fort Greene, New York, within the United States, whereas *Araña, Vol. 3: Night of the Hunter* depicts her as a child living in Mexico. Amun (Jon Kasiya), a hired assassin, seeks information on Corazón in order to find her weakness. He discovers it within her family by investigating her father, Gilberto Corazón. Additional information below his New York State driver's license reveals his social security number, crime record, education, previous residences, and properties owned. Under education it lists MS in Journalism from Columbia University in the City of New York. Under previous residences it lists Puerto Rico and Mexico. We do not know at this point where her father was born or if he is Puerto Rican, Mexican, or both. All we know is that he has a social security number and received his MS while in New York. Corazón's mother, Sofía, appears to be more of a mystery. Assuming Corazón was born in New York, one possible scenario may have been that her parents met there and then relocated to Mexico City immediately after her birth. Corazón's vivid memories of her childhood in Mexico City include her mother's death, which leads to her father and her moving to New York: "Once upon a time in Mexico, there lived a little girl named Anya. She cried a lot because her mother died, leaving only her father to make the big move to a new country called America." This narrative, an assignment she has to submit for class, is paired with fragmented childhood memories merged with a black backdrop of silhouettes such as shrubbery. Unlike the other pages, which are divided neatly into rectangular panels, this page overlaps temporal and spatial delineations by encircling them within a larger border around the entire page (see figure 10.1). This page also suggests a common migration story whereby violence in one's home country, in Corazón's case caused by a tyrant who "made the people of . . . [Mexico] suffer," leads to a death and a move to the United States. However, unlike most migration narratives, Corazón's is one of returning to her place of birth, even if it is unfamiliar to her. Over time, New York will become her permanent home.

While Corazón's attachment to Mexico is represented through her childhood memories, her identification with Puerto Rico is verbally stated and at times used to challenge common stereotypes about Latinas and Latinos in the United States. For example, during a battle scene in *Young Allies*, Araña fights with Ember, whose powers include the manipulation of fire. Ember attacks her physically while crassly attempting to also attack her verbally: "'samatter, chica? Figgered you were missin' that Mexico heat." Rather than engage with whether or not she may miss Mexico, Araña replies, "I'm Puerto Rican dipsti—." This exchange allows her to prioritize Puerto Rico in order to momentarily challenge common stereotypes about "hot Latinas" or Mexicans as default Latina/os.[27] Unfortunately, this utterance is all too brief, belittling

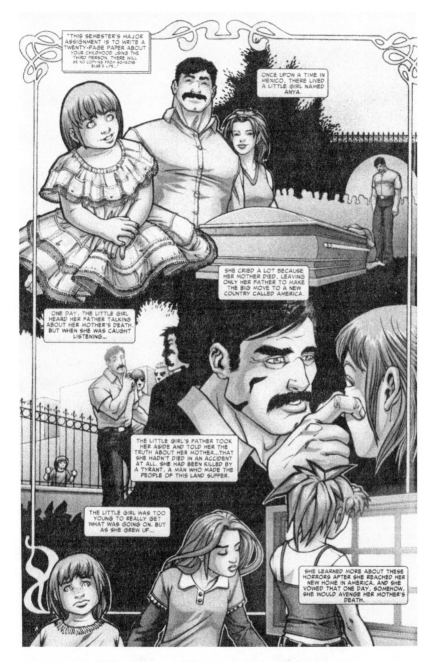

10.1. Corazón's childhood memories, from *Araña, Vol. 3, Night of the Hunter*.

the complexity of Puerto Rico's history, and the Puerto Rican diaspora.[28] Dismissed by Ember, he persists with the racial and ethnic slurs such that even a member from his own villainous team refers to him as a "dyed-in-the-wool racist." In a later battle, Ember furiously yells, "Oh hell no. Cheap. You are so cheap! Prepare to become fajita meat, you cocky little —." Ember is eventually defeated and detained, however, not because of the racial slurs he retorts, but because of the threat he poses in wielding fire.

Corazón is not the only character who is racialized, nor is she the only one who speaks Spanish. Within *Young Allies*, and similar to translations in *Ms. Marvel*, words stated in Spanish and communicated among Spanish speakers are not always translated into English. For example, when Toro (Benito Serrano) first saves Araña, she thanks him with: "¡Dios mio! ¡Dios mio! Gracias. . . . Gracias . . ." "De nada," he responds. While they include the corresponding inverted exclamation mark, the text misses the accent marks in *mío*. Moreover, anything translated from Spanish to English is placed within < and >. For example, while Araña is looking up information at an Internet café, the dialogue between Toro and her is visually marked off as Spanish. We know Nomad cannot understand because all she is able to catch from their conversation is her own name: "What? What about me?" Toro's response, now in English, is much more restrained since he is not fluent: "This is no good. I go." His vocabulary diminishes as he attempts to speak in English, and in later scenes, it becomes almost impossible for Toro to communicate with the other superheroes because of the language barrier. It also gets him into trouble with a group of young men of color who demand he leave their "turf." His "No English" is met with "'No English?' Don't you know you in America?" which quickly escalates to a fight. Throughout this collection, we learn Toro is from Colombia and was taken from his family at a very early age, brainwashed, trained to be a solider, and selected for an experimental genetic enhancement. In the process, he recovers some of his childhood memories and flees the country. Although it is unclear why he chose the United States as his new home, there is no mention of his migration narrative, Toro serves as another reminder that Latinas/os in the United States come from many parts of Latin America. As the only other Spanish speaker within the Young Allies, Araña serves as both a language translator and a cultural translator. However, Toro and Nomad will each attempt to learn each other's language in order to better communicate without always imposing on Araña.

In addition to her name, citizenship, and language, Corazón is racialized through illustration. She is drawn and shaded by a handful of artists, each providing his or her own variation to her skin tone, body structure, height, and wardrobe. Even her hairstyle, hair length, and hair color constantly change. At

10.2(a). Hair variation, dark brown.   10.2(b). Tattoo variation, arm.

times we may spot her with long, dark brown hair either flowing behind her or braided. Other times her hair is light brown, orange, or even blond. In *Ms. Marvel*, for example, Anya's hair is cut at shoulder's length. She also appears with short, light brown or orange-tinted hair in a cameo within *The Amazing Spider-Man*, no. 611. In other variations her tattoo shifts and changes form from her arm to her back. Corazón's depictions are at times so drastically different readers need to be told who she is (see figure 10.2a, b, and c).

Two of her most drastic cover variations are depicted in figure 10.3a and 10.3b. On the one hand, these covers challenge stereotypical representations of Latinas in the media by not pigeonholing Araña into any one body. My concern, however is that these two covers create a dichotomy whereby the second one risks erasing the first. *Spider-Girl*, volume 2 issue 1, tells readers, "Warning! The only things standing between you and the most synapse-shattering super hero debut of the decade are your hands and this cover!" Thus, similar to Marvel's erasure of prior Latina superheroes by proclaiming Araña as their "first Latina hero," Marvel invisibilizes Araña's origin by trumping it

10.2(c). Tattoo variation, back.

with a new "debut." Marvel Entertainment and Panini Comics, a publishing house in Italy, signed an agreement whereby the latter produces translated copies of Marvel comics for Europe (including Spain) and Latin America (including Argentina, Brazil, and Chile).[29] In 2011, Panini Comics published *Spidergirl: El corazón de la araña*. Although it is primarily a Spanish version or translation of *Spider-Girl: Family Values*, its title is the Spanish translation of *Araña: The Heart of the Spider*. Globally, then, and for her Spanish audience, Corazón's genealogy begins with her more mainstream image, Spider-Girl, and not her original depiction as Araña.[30]

Like any young teenager, Araña's relationships with her parents can also tell us something about our conceptualization of youth and the fine line between youth and adults. Corazón's relationships with both her mother and father are tested throughout her superhero trajectory. Not knowing if she is hallucinating, dreaming, or actually speaking to her mother's spirit, Araña welcomes any rendition of her deceased mother, Sofía: "Mama . . . if you're a dream . . . or an illusion . . . or even a ghost . . . I'm happy that I saw you . . . even for a fleeting moment."[31] However, her mother tasks her with doing something that would directly contradict Miguel Legar, Araña's first superhero partner and mentor. While her mother wants her to release the Hunter within, Legar warns her against this because doing so causes her to lose con-

10.3a. Corazón as Araña (2004).

10.3b. Corazón as Spider-Girl (2011).

trol of herself. During a heated dispute, Legar confesses that Araña may not be the Spider Society's chosen one and that her carapace was not given to her by him:

ARAÑA: You're always telling me to ignore my vision, to ignore my own mother telling me to release the hunter. Well, maybe you should ignore your visions too! . . . So, I'm just a backup hunter. A replacement . . .

LEGAR: Anya . . .

ARAÑA: I thought the hunter was in my blood. I thought it was my destiny . . .

LEGAR: Everything happens for a reason. Our paths were destined to cross.

ARAÑA: What about my mother? If I'm not the rightful hunter, why did my mother give me the power to unleash the hunter?

LEGAR: Your mother gave you something powerful, but it wasn't the hunter. Your carapace didn't come from me, or from the blood of the Spider Society.

ARAÑA: What?

LEGAR: In all the generations of hunters, not one of them has had a carapace like yours. While you do share some of my powers, you also received something unique and unexplainable from the spirit of your mother. And that is why you are not a true hunter.

This exchange solidifies Araña's mother as her original source of power. To date, readers are still unaware of, but can speculate about, Sofía Corazón's own ties to supernatural forces. In chapter 9 within this edited volume, Mauricio Espinoza links common Latina/o superhero tropes with contemporary US horror and science fiction narratives, arguing that otherness or alienness is "represented by a magical, spiritual, or cultural power that originates from outside the United States or from within an ethnic community and is, therefore, alien to US dominant, Anglo-centric culture." In this manner, Sofía Corazón, and by extension, her daughter, are unlike other spider-affiliated superheroes. Instead, we might situate them in conversation with indigenous mythologies or iconographies, such as the Teotihuacan Spider Woman in present-day Mexico or Native American accounts of grandmother spider.[32] "Metaphorically," states Esther Pasztory, "spiders represent weavers and are symbols of women and feminine activity from Mesoamerica as far as the American Southwest."[33] For example, when describing why she titled one of her edited volumes *Spider Woman's Granddaughters*, Paula Gunn Allen said it was "because it contains all through it the light of intelligence and experience that, in the Cherokee account, Grandmother Spider brought to the people."[34] Araña eventually accepts her supernatural ancestral ties and new fate by reinterpreting her mother's words. Upon Legar's death, she releases the hunter and transfers its powers to Nina Smith, Spider Society's true hunter. In this manner, her mother serves as her spiritual guide or conscience, pushing her to do good, in alignment with the common trope of good over evil: "The colorful stories of comic book superheroes have always been concerned first and foremost with parables of justice, of basic cultural values about heroism, and of good triumphing over evil."[35] Her mother, however, is not always around to guide her, and Corazón must also learn how to make her own decisions.

Araña's bond with her father, Gilberto, is equally strong but will get tested when he discovers her superhero abilities. Gil is an investigative reporter for the *New York Herald*. He bakes his daughter a cake in celebration of her sixteenth birthday, only to be interrupted by Ms. Marvel (Carol Susan Jane Danvers) and Wonder-Man (Simon Williams), who escort them to the Stark Tower, where Araña must decide if she will agree to register under the new Super Hero Registration Act.[36] Gil protests: "Mi Arañita, you are not old enough to make this kind of complicated decis . . ." His attempt is futile since his initial opposition is met with strong resistance from Araña, who declares her desire to register with S.H.I.E.L.D. and join their training program. Gil eventually agrees but warns Ms. Marvel that she will have to deal with him should his daughter get hurt. Araña and Gil reconcile, embracing each other in a tight hug. Through this narrative arc, Ms. Marvel comes to serve as a type of role model and maternal figure for Araña. This is threatened when, on a mission against the human–robot, Doomsday, who tears off Araña's carapace and leaves her unconscious, Corazón is hospitalized, and, during her recovery, Gil places a restraining order on Ms. Marvel, creating tension between father and daughter:

> GIL: You almost died! Carol Danvers almost killed you!
>
> CORAZÓN: No! The giant freaking crazy Doomsday man robot thing nearly killed me! The only reason I'm even still alive for you to yell at is because Carol saved me!
>
> GIL: Mi Arañita . . .
>
> CORAZÓN: Stop! Stop calling me that . . . that stupid little pet name!
>
> GIL: Carol Danvers put you in harm's way. You cannot expect me to forgive her for . . .
>
> CORAZÓN: She was teaching me how to grow up, dad. . . . All you seem interested in doing is treating me like a little girl.

Gil does not want anything to happen to his daughter; however, Corazón is growing up and he cannot always be there to protect her. This realization must bring back memories of his wife's murder and his inability to avenge her death. Corazón, on the other hand, wants to disassociate from her childhood by rejecting the pet name Arañita. In a moment of frustration, she leaves home, and Gil reports her as missing. Araña, despite her recovered strength, has been captured along with numerous other superheroes. They are being held in Puerto Maravilla, Chile, under mind control by Puppet Master (Phillip Masters). As Araña is coming out of mind control, Puppet Master orders her to kill Ms. Marvel. "I . . . I won't . . . ," strains Araña, ". . . I won't kill my mother, I . . . I won't hurt Carol!" Whether or not it was a trick of the mind, Corazón accidently referred to Ms. Marvel as her mother. This triggers something profound in Ms. Marvel; evading standard protocol, she finds Puppet Master and rather than detaining him, murders him by not preventing his suicide. She admits to herself, "Yes, I killed a man today, but . . . he'll never hurt anyone again." Death, however, haunts Corazón, and in *Spider-Girl: Family Values*, she must face the death of her beloved father, who is poisoned by a member of Raven. The tragic loss of both of her parents cements Corazón's origin story as one parallel to that of many superheroes, such as Spider-Man.

LATINA SUPERHEROES: MEDIUM AS MESSAGE

Araña turned ten in 2014 and continues to make guest appearances in Marvel series, such as *Avengers Assemble*. Many of Corazón's variations across this time span mirror some of the challenges in producing collaborations such as comics. The individuals who make up the comic book industry bring to it their own agendas, ideas, and experiences while also being shaped by the market and popular trends within the production and distribution of their products.

Marvel's first *Araña* series came into fruition under Editor in Chief Joe Quesada, and writer Fiona Avery, who is trained in anthropology. Avery attempted to create a mixed-race bilingual character by "people watching."[37] In another interview, she described her thoughts on branding and marketing when discussing her new company: "We are creating a product for people to enjoy and people want to rely on getting it on time and for it to be entertaining."[38] Her descriptions of her skills and success as a writer are notably different from those of Tania del Rio, who wrote *Spider-Man & Araña: The Hunter Revealed* (2006). In an interview with *The Pulse*, she was asked: "What did you enjoy the most about working on this?" Del Rio responded as follows:

> Most of all, I really like Araña's character. I love the fact that she is a young, Latina female—something I can relate to. I love her sassy personality and she reminds me of one of [my] other . . . favorite Marvel characters, Jubilee, only with a deadlier streak. I love reading stories with brassy girl characters, but I think I like writing them even more.[39]

Del Rio does not simply write *brassy girl characters*; she simultaneously illustrates them. Her depiction of Araña and the characters around her is starkly different from Jonboy Meyer's. Whereas his are extremely hypersexualized, hers appear less so, and more reminiscent of manga.[40] Meyer uses darker colors with greater contrast between light and shadow, whereas del Rio utilizes pastels.

The creative teams behind Araña are also responsible for depicting her as a tech-savvy individual. In earlier issues she shows off her online research skills, and in *Avengers Academy: Giant Size* it is her hacking skills that save the day. Marvel is able to capitalize on Araña's tech skills through social media. In a Spider-Girl "Preview" revealed at the end of *The Amazing Spider-Man*, no.

10.4. Corazón's superhero Twitter feed.

648, readers are asked to follow Spider-Girl on Twitter using @The_Spider
_Girl (see figure 10.4). Her first tweet, posted on October 20, 2010, read: "This
will be my new diary. It's weird that diaries have gone from 'nobody look!'
to 'EVERYBODY look!'"[41] "I look good in black," reads her second tweet.
Her third one, however, parallels her tweets from *The Amazing Spider-Man*
no. 648, where she describes to her fans how she helped Spider-Man. On
November 7, 2010, she tweeted "So I TOTALLY helped Spider-Man today."
These exact words are published in the print version of the issue, as are many
of her other tweets. Additionally, whoever at Marvel created Corazón's account is also responsible for interacting with her followers, and it is quite
possible multiple people may respond on her "official" behalf. This may explain inconsistences in tone or use of Spanish, including a declaration that
"Mi español es muy malo, últimamente."[42] Followers knew they were not
actually interacting with Araña, and yet even that generated comments such
as "This is so fake. But I cant help say HI!!!!!!! :D lol [sic]." The first person
to interact with her even suggested a costume change and included a link
to a sketch. Corazón's response inspires him to draw another costume for
Anya; this one evidently took more time, given the greater attention to details in penciling and coloring. Others simply said, "Hi" and welcomed her
to Twitter, whereas there were also many who asked questions ranging from

her abilities to her relationships. And while most of her followers were from the United States, some revealed locations outside the country: "Following you from México![sic]." "From Mexico?," she replies, "Excellent! Thank you so much!" While Corazón's superhero Twitter account may provide some lighthearted entertainment for some of her most devout fans, it is also important to think of it in terms of Marvel's marketing and distribution campaigns. Disney purchased Marvel Entertainment in 2009, which explains why Disney appears under Marvel's official Partner List.[43] However, Verizon is also listed, which may explain why the New York City Verizon building is visibly identifiable on the left-hand side of the photograph used as Corazón's original Twitter backdrop.

Superheroes such as Araña remain confined within popular discourses of normativity or what constitutes acceptable deviance. Corazón may waver in her blasé attitude toward school, or may have hid her true identity from her family and loved ones, but these are framed within acceptable character flaws, meant to boost her as a better-rounded superhero. "Certainly material that favors the dominant ideology appeals to a common denominator in a society and is, consequently, often the safest bet in terms of marketing a product, regardless of genre," suggest Duncan and Smith. In considering superheroes and subgenres within comics, they add:

> Romance comics almost always end with promise of a heterosexual union. Horror comics feature stories where punishment is meted out to social deviants. Thus it becomes not only uncomplicated but commercially beneficial to "play it safe" and support society's hegemonic concepts.[44]

Within Marvel's official universe, Corazón is presumably heteronormative. Reptile (Humberto López) serves as a possible love interest for Araña in *Avengers Academy*, whereas in an alternate universe she is romantically involved with Black Tarantula (Fabian LaMuerto). Where queerness is suggested for Araña, it borders on the side of insult.[45] I have already noted Ember's racist slurs above; however, he also embodies homophobia. As Araña goes to Nomad's rescue, for example, Ember shouts: "Aww, so cute. You think you're gonna protect your girlfriend when the truth is you're BOTH good as fried . . ."[46] Fortunately, Nomad is able to put up an energy shield just in time to conceal herself and Araña from Ember's fire. Within this exchange, *girlfriend* is used as a pejorative term.

While Araña and Nomad are only friends within the official Marvel Universe, and in her original, alternate universe, Nomad's love interest is Toro, fans can rewrite narratives by creating their own variations of Marvel's comics,

10.5. Araña and Nomad.

stories, or illustrations. A Google search for "Spider-Girl" or "Anya Corazon," for example, revealed a number of illustrations created by fans, including one by Deviant Art member CABurroughs[47] titled "Nomad and Spider-Girl: lesbros" (see figure 10.5). Nomad sits on what appears to be a steel beam, leaning forward with her eyes closed, and boots slightly tilted upward. Araña crouches in front of her, with one hand over Nomad's, eyes equally closed and lips puckered. The shades of orange surrounding their kiss invoke warmth and a certain tenderness. The light in the backdrop is also positioned so that it appears as if it is either sunrise or sunset, and perhaps this is either a kiss hello or a kiss goodbye. Below the image the illustrator explains: "I just wanted to draw something cute. It's pretty rough, but I like the feel of it. Rikki Barnes and Anya Sofia Corazon are marvel's, forever [sic]."[48] The comments to this illustration are equally supportive, ranging from "They are lovely together" and "Seems like a perfect pair to me," to "Super cute!" and "Awww, I love this."[49] Thus, what was meant as an insult by Ember within the official Marvel Universe became the inspiration for a fan-created romance within the unofficial Marvel Universe.[50] Sexuality, then, like Corazón's name, language, ethnicity, or superhero abilities, is varied—adding yet another dynamic to Araña's characterization.

Araña's multiple variations make it nearly impossible to answer the question: Who is she? From her own appearance to the superhero groups she vacillates in and out of, Corazón embodies a form of fluidity or flexibility that makes it difficult for one to confine her to any given category or identity. With the added possibility of alternate universes and time travel narratives, Araña may face her own death, such as in *Marvel Team Up: League of Losers*, or face another Spider-Girl, such as in *The Amazing Spider-Girl* series. As of this writing, Araña's character is in an exciting place. She helped the Avengers solve a major crisis and security breach and can be seen dancing atop her bed to the lyrics: "I'm standing on my own, but now I'm not alone. Avengers! Assemble! Alllways we will fight, as one till the battle's won, with evil on the run, we never come undone. Assemble, we are strong. Forever fight as one. Assemble we are strong. Forever fight as one . . . [sic]" Unless Marvel decides to discard her, Araña's full character and narrative arc remains to be written. Her relatively marginal status within the larger Marvel universe also makes her more open to pushing boundaries. Coupled with fan fiction and artwork, her many variations more closely resemble the nuances, complexities, and contradictions of our current sociopolitical context.

NOTES

1. Araña's first name has been spelled numerous ways, including Aña, Anya, and Añya. With the exception of direct quotes, I refer to "Anya Sofía Corazón" as her full name and "Araña" as her superhero moniker, which I discuss in greater detail later in this essay.

2. Joe Kelly, "The Grim Hunt: Chapter Two." Collected in *The Amazing Spider-Man: Grim Hunt*.

3. See http://www.latina.com/entertainment/movies/superheroes-you-never-knew -were-latino.

4. Latina.com lists Morales as Cuban and African American whereas other news sources list his mother as Puerto Rican and his father as African American or as "Black and Hispanic," "Black and Latino," or *Blatino*. In an interview dated August 8, 2011, Axel Alonso, Editor in Chief of Marvel, does not clarify whether Morales is Puerto Rican, Mexican, Dominican, or Cuban but instead states that he is Hispanic as opposed to Latino (see http://www .latinrapper.com/axel-alonso-interview.html). For more on Morales, see Kathryn M. Frank, Brian Montes, and Adilifu Nama and Maya Haddad within this edited volume. Latina.com's list also failed to include Marvel's Spider-Man 2099; introduced in 1992, Miguel O'Hara was "half-Irish, half-Mexican" and held "the distinction of being the first Latino to use the Spider-Man identity" (see Kathryn M. Frank herein).

5. Spider-Girl debuted in 1998. There have also been several Spider-Women, including Jessica Drew (1977), Julia Carpenter as Arachne (1984), and Martha "Mattie" Franklin (1998).

6. Vol. 2 was published in 2004. Vol. 1 debuted Spider-Man in 1962 (issue 15) and with him, the famous line "With great power comes great responsibility." See Robert M. Peaslee and Robert G. Weiner, *Web-Spinning Heroics: Critical Essays on the History and Meaning of Spider-Man* (Jefferson, NC: McFarland & Company, 2012), 5.

7. *Araña, Vol. 1: The Heart of the Spider* (collects *Amazing Fantasy*, vol. 2, issues 1–6).

8. Ibid.

9. Ibid. When discussing Jaime Reyes as DC's Blue Beetle in chapter 9 of this volume, Mauricio Espinoza notes that Reyes's otherness or alien superpowers originate from a Mayan temple, centralizing Mexico as his source of power intertwined with his sense of cultural identification. Similarly, the desert within the Yucatan Peninsula serves not only as a training ground for Araña, but as a marker of her cultural identity.

10. See the back covers of *Araña*, vols. 1 to 3.

11. Frederick Luis Aldama, *Your Brain on Latino Comics: From Gus Arriola to Los Bros Hernandez* (Austin: University of Texas Press, 2009), 31.

12. *Marvel Comics* no. 1 was published on August 31, 1939. See Sean Howe, *Marvel Comics: The Untold Story* (New York: HarperCollins, 2012), 14.

13. Jeffrey A. Brown, "Panthers and Vixens: Black Superheroines, Sexuality, and Stereotypes in Contemporary Comic Books," in *Black Comics: Politics of Race and Representation*, ed. Sheena C. Howard and Ronald L. Jackson II (New York: Bloomsbury, 2013), 133.

14. Aldama, *Your Brain on Latino Comics*, 38.

15. Collected in *Araña, Vol. 2: In the Beginning* and *Araña, Vol. 3: Night of the Hunter*.

16. Additional reoccurring appearances include *Marvel Team-Up, Vol. 3: League of Losers*, issues 15–18; *The Amazing Spider-Girl*, issues 14, 26, and 27; and *Onslaught Unleashed*, issues 1–4, as well as cameo appearances such as in *Spider-Man*, issue 611.

17. Derek Parker Royal, "Drawing Attention: Comics as a Means of Approaching U.S. Cultural Diversity," in *Teaching Comics and Graphic Narratives: Essays on Theory, Strategy and Practice* (Jefferson, NC: McFarland & Company, Inc., 2012), 68.

18. For an overview of ongoing theoretical debates between *latinidad*, Latinization, Pan-Latina/o, and *Panlatinidad*, see Agustín Laó-Montes and Arlene Dávila, *Mambo Montage: The Latinization of New York* (New York: Columbia University Press, 2001); Juana María Rodríguez, *Queer Latinidad: Identity Practices, Discursive Spaces* (New York: New York University Press, 2003).

19. "Corazón" has appeared with an accent mark over the "o" in *The Marvel Encyclopedia* and in the Spanish translation of *Spider-Girl: Family Values* titled *Spidergirl: El corazón de la araña*.

20. *The Amazing Spider-Man: Grim Hunt*.

21. Ibid.

22. ASM refers to *The Amazing Spider-Man*. Within this narrative arc, the Kraven family attempts to murder all spider-affiliated superheroes in order to weaken and defeat Spider-Man.

23. *Young Allies*.

24. *Avengers Assemble*, issue 23 (January 29, 2014).

25. See Ricardo Otheguy and Ana Celia Zentella, *Spanish in New York: Language Contact, Dialectal Leveling, and Structural Continuity* (New York: Oxford University Press, 2012).

26. See *The Amazing Spider-Girl*, issues 14, 26, and 27. For an overview of Marvel's multiverse as it relates to alternative narratives for Latina/o superheroes, see Kathryn M. Frank's "Everybody Wants to Rule the Multiverse: Latino Spider-Men in Marvel's Media Empire" within this edited volume.

27. Brian Montes more closely examines statistical data on Puerto Ricans in New York in "The Paradox of Miles Morales: Social Gatekeeping and the Browning of America's Spider-Man" within this edited volume. For a broader discussion, see Frances Negrón-Muntaner, *Boricua Pop: Puerto Ricans and the Latinization of American Culture* (New York: New York University Press, 2004).

28. See Jorge Duany, *The Puerto Rican Nation on the Move: Identities on the Island and in the United States* (Chapel Hill: University of North Carolina Press, 2002).

29. See "Panini and Marvel Renew Master Comic Book Agreement for Europe and Latin America," *Panini Online* (March 2006), http://www.paninionline.com/collectibles /institutional/ea/USA/news.asp?idNews=228.

30. For a discussion of other female characters and nationalist discourse, see Mitra C. Emad, "Reading Wonder Woman's Body: Mythologies of Gender and Nation," *The Journal of Popular Culture* 39.6 (2006): 954–984. Within the Marvel universe, the new Ms. Marvel (Kamala Khan) has also contributed to this dialogue since her debut in 2013 as a female, Muslim, and Pakistani-American superhero.

31. *Araña, Vol. 1: The Heart of the Spider.*

32. Contemporary debates question the significance or accuracy of Karl Taube's (1983) description of Teotihuacan's Spider Woman. See Zoltán Paulinyi (2006). It is unclear whether she was a goddess of life or of war, and she may have encompassed both.

33. Pasztory, 86.

34. Allen, 1–2.

35. Brown, 134.

36. The act is also referred to as the "Superhuman Registration Act" or SHRA. *Ms. Marvel*, vol. 2.

37. Quoted in Sequential Tart: http://www.sequentialtart.com/archive/mar01/avery .shtml.

38. Quoted in Four Color Commentary: http://fourcolorcommentary.blogspot.com /2005/06/interview-with-fiona-avery.html.

39. Interview on Comicon.com (March 27, 2006): http://www.comicon.com/ubb /ubbthreads.php?ubb=showflat&Number=359625. Last accessed 9 Feb. 2014.

40. For a discussion of the influence of manga in the United States, see Toni Johnson-Woods, ed. *Manga: An Anthology of Global and Cultural Perspectives* (New York: Continuum, 2010); Leonard Rifas, "Globalizing Comic Books from Below: How Manga Came to America," *International Journal of Comic Art* 6.2 (2004): 138–171.

41. See https://twitter.com/The_Spider_Girl.

42. "My Spanish is really bad, lately."

43. See http://marvel.com/news/comics/2009/12/31/10809/disney_completes_marvel _acquisition.

44. Randy Duncan and Matthew J. Smith, *The Power of Comics: History, Form, and Culture* (New York: Bloomsbury Academic, 2009), 263.

45. Such is also the case with transgender characters who are mocked because of their gender identity. See *Fear Itself: The Home Front*, issue 7, and *Ms. Marvel*, vol. 4. Some of the comics in which Araña appears also include queer characters who are struggling with their gender or sexuality, such as Striker in *Avengers Academy*. For a broader discussion of queer characters in comics, see Ben Bolling, "The U.S. HIV/AIDS Crisis and the Negotiation of Queer Identity in Superhero Comics, or, Is Northstar Still a Fairy?" in *Comic Books and American Cultural History*, ed. Matthew Pustz (New York: Continuum, 2012), 202–219; Valerie Palmer-Mehta and Kellie Hay, "A Superhero for Gays? Gay Masculinity and *Green Lantern*," *The Journal of American Culture* 28.4 (2005): 390–404.

46. *Young Allies*, issue 5.

47. This illustration was originally created and uploaded by an anonymous user on

Deviantart.com: http://www.deviantart.com/art/Nomad-and-Spider-Girl-lesbros-196377 702. Last accessed 9 Feb. 2014.

48. Ibid.

49. In the following essay, Richard T. Rodríguez analyzes audience participation by incorporating quotes from letters addressing gay Latino superheroes such as Marvel's Miguel Santos (Living Lightning) or DC's Gregorio de la Vega (Extraño) and Hero Cruz. Rodríguez is able to document how audience suggestions were eventually incorporated within later renditions of gay superheroes.

50. While none of Marvel's out, queer characters were Latina prior to Araña, DC Comics introduced Renee Maria Montoya as Batwoman's lesbian Latina ex-lover in 1992. See "Introduction" herein. Recently, Marvel's América Chávez (Miss America) casually announced she was not heterosexual in *Young Avengers*, issue 15 (2014); she also had two mothers, now deceased.

ELEVEN

REVEALING SECRET IDENTITIES: GAY LATINO SUPERHEROES AND THE NECESSITY OF DISCLOSURE

RICHARD T. RODRÍGUEZ

There is no unthreatened, unthreatening conceptual home for the concept of gay origins. We have all the more reason, then, to keep our understanding of gay origin, of gay cultural and material reproduction, plural, multi-capillaried, argus-eyed, respectful, and endlessly cherished.

EVE KOSOFSKY SEDGWICK, *EPISTEMOLOGY OF THE CLOSET* [1]

MOST HISTORICAL ACCOUNTS of gay male superheroes in comic books credit Northstar from Marvel Comics's Alpha Flight as the first to emerge from the closet in 1992. Twenty years later, Northstar would marry his partner, Kyle Jinadu, in a much-talked-about wedding ceremony featured on the cover of *Astonishing X-Men*.[2] Also in 2012, DC Comics, in their New 52 reboot of the original narrative, recast the Green Lantern (né Alan Scott) as an openly gay man. Yet when one considers the presence of Latino gay superheroes, the genealogy of gay heroes in mainstream comic books exceeds this twenty-year time period and is more dynamic than staged campaigns for gay marriage and affirmative visibility.[3] In this essay I will sketch a brief history of gay Latino superheroes in the DC and Marvel universes and reflect on the debates emerging as a result of their appearance in traditionally heteronormative action comic narratives.[4] The figure of the gay Latino superhero, I argue, affords the opportunity to discuss myriad issues that vitally address the politics of sexuality and interrelated concerns.

Controversy has arisen both within and outside the world of comics when Latino male superheroes are queerly depicted (and not necessarily "outed") or willingly come out as gay.[5] Here I wish to make the case that within the comic book world the stakes are very high when Latino heroes are queered, particularly in relation to readers of mainstream comics. Contrary to the belief of scholars who wish to move beyond "identitarian" politics, in the context of popular forms like comics, disclosing "secret" identities matters. Indeed, revealing superhero sexual identities—that is, not simply exposing the identity of the person under the mask but rather making public the hero as gay or queer—has, in many instances, world-saving potential. The revelation of queer origins that are "plural, multi-capillaried, argus-eyed, respectful, and endlessly cherished," to riff on the above epigraph by Eve Kosofksy Sedgwick, illuminates how the "unthreatened, unthreatening conceptual home" of comics from which the Latino gay superhero emerges is critically significant for a range of readers with regard to self-affirmation and self-preservation. As Frederick Luis Aldama and Christopher González argue in their introduction to this volume, comic book creators "craft visual–verbal stories that not only engage their readers/viewers but also expand in new and novel ways the perceptual, emotive, and cognitive capacities of their readers/viewers." In this sense, gay—or, in a broader sense, queer—origins, like the origins of superheroes so fundamental to their characteristic emergence as powerful beings intent on saving the powerless, are the link between the fantasy space of the comic book and the social spheres in which superhero narratives hold representational significance.

IN LOVE WITH A STRANGER

September 1988 saw the publication of DC Comics's *The New Guardians*, a series with a short, one-year run consisting of exactly twelve issues. The New Guardians comprised several individuals with superpowers from around the world who were brought together by the Guardians of the Universe. One of those individuals was Gregorio de la Vega, otherwise known as Extraño. Created by Steve Englehart and Joe Staton, Extraño (Spanish for "strange") first appeared in the second issue of *Millennium* as one of ten people chosen "to advance the human race" (18). Hailing from Trujillo City in Peru, Extraño was, prior to his induction into the New Guardians, a magician who would obtain greater powers ("magick powers," to be exact) upon leaving his current life to enter the future.

What is immediately striking about Extraño is how he might immediately be identified as the classic "flaming queen." As journalist Nick Nadel writes:

Extraño fit every single stereotype of the poorly-written homosexual character. His flamboyant wardrobe, stereotypical lisp, obsession with his hair, outrageous jewelry and penchant for calling himself "Auntie" ("Listen to

Auntie, sweetie!") made him the default "gay uncle" of the New Guardians. Despite having vague, Dr. Strange-esque mystical powers, Extraño really didn't do much besides offer advice and drop sexual double entendres.[6]

Nadel is correct in his reading of Extraño given that his very appearance reveals a fey, effeminate man with a thin mustache who wears one hoop earring on his right earlobe and has his left hand placed firmly on his hip with elbow outwardly bowed. Furthermore, Extraño's speech, as made clear in the Spanish-to-English translation, is also a sign of his queerness. Doubting his selection as one of the chosen ten as informed by original Guardians Herupa Hando Hu and Nadia Safir, Extraño responds: "Puh-lease! The only fruits anybody picks down here are bananas, and for that you go to Ecuador!" (19). Yet despite what might be seen as the "poorly-written homosexual character," Extraño is also a complex representational figure whose denouncement as "embarrassing" is much too easy.

While Nadel maintains that Extraño "never actually came out," the various codes presented to readers of *Millennium* and *The New Guardians*—and not only those seemingly "stereotypical"—point to an undeniable queerness that is understood otherwise by differently positioned readers.[7] In response to letters written by readers of *The New Guardians* and published in earlier issues in the letters section titled "Chosen Words," Joe Woods from San Francisco writes in his letter published in issue no. 9 that while

> some people are having difficulty adjusting to Gregorio and all the implications that go with that character . . . I find it a little hard to swallow that these same people who spend an enormous amount of money reading about demons, junkies, mutants, and other ethnic and stereotypical characters have trouble dealing with a gentle, wise and humorous man like Gregorio. Yes, he is gay and flamboyant, but he is also one of the Chosen . . . that alone should make people look at him with a more educated eye. (25)

In his letter Woods insists that readers see the tremendous value in a character like Extraño. And his decision to refer to him as "Gregorio" for me points to the importance of seeing behind Extraño's superhero persona a remarkable gay man whose genuine comprehension requires an educated view.

However, part of the problem readers had with Extraño was his diagnosis as HIV-positive after a skirmish with a villain (described in issue no. 10 as "a rabid mutant created to be a virulent killer carrying the HIV or AIDS virus") ominously named the Hemo-Goblin.[8] Given the misinformed yet pervasive discourse during the historical moment of the late 1980s that often collapsed HIV/AIDS with gay men, casting Extraño as fighting bad guys *and* the human immunodeficiency virus was deeply problematic. But while some readers were troubled by this easy conflation, others were more perturbed by the way this narrative contributed to misinformation about HIV/AIDS transmission. In a letter published in issue no. 6, Jericho Wilson, a self-identified "openly gay man" from Bellbrook, Ohio, writes:

> Gregorio does not have AIDS. He could not have gotten AIDS. There was no, I repeat NO transfer of body-fluids between Gregorio and the Hemo-Goblin. Neither Extraño nor anyone else [including his teammates Jet and Harbinger, also infected with HIV by the Hemo-Goblin with the former dying from AIDS-related complications] can get the AIDS virus b[y] being scratched by the Goblin unless the creature had blood or saliva on his hands. The Hemo-Goblin had neither body fluid on his hands at the time he scratched Extraño. (25)

These were far from the only responses published regarding Gregorio/Extraño; every issue after *The New Guardians* no. 1 contained letters debating the importance of or trouble with the Peruvian superhero. Taking note of what critics were saying, the writers attempted to remedy what they likely conceded were problems with Gregorio's casting. For example, in issue no. 7, upon discovering a crystalline skull regarded as his talisman, Extraño gains not only "newfound knowledge" but also a muscular and hence masculine physique (the editors respond to a reader's letter in issue 11 by saying that Gregorio "has obviously been beefing himself up"). This new "butch" rendering would continue for the next six issues and lead readers like David May from San Francisco to comment (in a letter published in issue 11) on Extraño's new image as "positive" and "what I want in a gay super-hero, more (for want of a better word) 'masculine'" (26).

Unlike some of his teammates who reappeared in the DC universe after the end of *The New Guardians*, Extraño would persist only as a faded memory. Perhaps this is due to Nadel's belief that DC would prefer that we forget Extraño, "an unfortunate reminder of a less-enlightened time." Yet I want to insist that we remember Gregorio for what he signified for queer and Latino readers at a particular moment in comic book history and how his presence generated urgent critical debates regarding issues concerning race, sexuality, and HIV/AIDS. In a letter published in issue no. 7, Wilson Aguilar from Cicero, Illinois, cherishes "the fact that Extraño is from Honduras, El Salvador (from around there)." Aguilar continues: "My mother is from there, so that makes me half Honduranio (something of the sort). Even though I was not born there, it's in my blood!" (26). While Aguilar misidentifies Extraño as Honduran, he identifies with him nonetheless as a fellow Latin American–cum–Latino. Additionally, Lon Wolf from Maple Shade, New Jersey, writes in issue 11: "In *The New Guardians* #7 we saw Gregorio and Paco hug and then hold hands. Thank you, DC, for taking the first brave steps into the 20th Century" (24). Celebrating the fact that *The New Guardians* has courageously tackled issues that other comic books have not (and thus, as Aguilar puts it, making "this comic better than all the rest in the 'comics wise' industry"), both Aguilar's and Wolf's letters are two of the many which testify to how the disclosure of ethnic and sexual identity is significant for what this might mean for readers struggling with who they are in a world obsessed with and yet simultaneously dismissive of difference.[9]

DOES LIGHTNING STRIKE TWICE?

The September 1997 issue of *Superboy and the Ravers*, a DC project spearheaded by the creative team of Karl Kesel and Paul Pelletier, sees Hero Cruz — an Afro–Puerto Rican from Metropolis — declare his gay identity to Sparx, a female heroine whom he unknowingly led on during shared intimate moments. Hero, however, believed his powers interfered with his true desire for men given that his superhero abilities consist of adopting multiple personas when using the "H-Dial" — popularized by DC Comics's Dial H for Hero feature that has its origins in the 1960s — to spell out H-E-R-O. Unlike the earlier, effeminate characterization of Extraño nine years before, Hero Cruz was fashioned as a character who was unmistakably masculine and who didn't wear his homosexuality on his sleeve. Thus it is quite understandable that Sparx would also be taken aback by Hero's self-disclosure as gay since he did not personify the queer traits evident in Gregorio de la Vega (see figure 11.1).

In the following issue (issue no. 14), Sparx reacts to Hero's coming out by declaring that he will "never have a family and that isn't right" and "It isn't natural" (20). (Sparx even chastises Hero for equating his gayness with her family's perceived difference and oddness "to the outside world.") Yet in issue no. 17, Sparx arrives in the knick of time to save Hero, who is falling from the sky at a rapid speed (and uncertain of his ability to land safely given his poor timing in accessing his power to "dial 'H' for Hero"). While lifting Hero to safety, Sparx confesses she didn't believe him until witnessing him "hanging with Leander." Indeed, it is Leander with whom Hero in the final issue (issue no. 19) of *Superboy and the Ravers* is coupled up (with Leander even finishing one of Hero's sentences). It is both here and in the second-to-the-last issue (issue no. 18) where it is clear that Sparx has not completely resolved her issue

11.1. Afro–Puerto Rican Hero Cruz declares his gay identity in *Superboy and the Ravers*.

with Hero's homosexuality as she refuses to engage him in a joke, declaring before she quickly departs: "Why don't you and Leander just go back to your male bonding." Confused by Sparx's behavior, Superboy asks, "What's her damage," to which Hero replies that their bond was broken when he told her he was gay (20). Superboy himself is dumbfounded by Hero's self-revelation. Trying to play it off that "of course" he "knew that," Superboy's surprise is most likely due to the fact that Hero's conventional male masculinity foreclosed any reading of him as anything but straight.

Unlike the letters section of *The New Guardians*, which featured a letter

230 RICHARD T. RODRÍGUEZ

about Extraño's queerness and HIV-positive status in almost every issue, there is only one letter in the nineteen-issue run of *Superboy and the Ravers* that broaches the subject of Hero Cruz's coming out. In issue no. 18, Steven Leitman from Chicago wrote in to ask editor Mike McAvennie to tread carefully on the sexual terrain the comic book has decided to chart. Leitman writes: "My reasons for this letter, though, are because of Sparx's thoughts and actions." He continues:

> I hope you will soon show her that Hero's homosexuality is not an "illness" or something bad. [B]e careful with how you deal with him and Sparx; too many people are already prejudiced against homosexuals (not that the comics industry is). I'm always glad when a new character who is gay is introduced. When I was younger I always wished one was so it would give me a kind of role model. I commend your efforts. (24)

DC was clearly thinking about how to bring out Hero in a way that avoided the common pitfalls leading to accusations of queer stereotyping. According to the insightful website *Gay League*, "In the promotional ads for the *Ravers* title, Hero was initially called 'Hard Luck,' and was originally meant to have 'bad luck' powers—but The Powers That Be nixed that idea since they knew of Hero's eventual sexual orientation, and decided that it probably wasn't the best idea to have a gay hero with such a 'problem' power."[10]

A little over seven years later and in the Marvel Comics universe, the second, July 2005, issue of Marvel Comics's *Great Lakes Avengers* shows an almost defeated Flatman, who is repeatedly unsuccessful in attempting to recruit a host of superheroes for his Midwest-based team of crime-fighting crusaders. One of Flatman's intended recruits is the East Los Angeles native Miguel Santos, otherwise known as Living Lightning, who possesses the ability to transform into electrical plasma to fly, generate electricity, create lightning bolts, and produce a protective force field made of electricity. Having first appeared in issue no. 63 of *Avengers West Coast*, Living Lightning began his career as a foe of the Avengers given his intent on clearing his deceased father's name. His father, Carlos Santos, was a member of a group of agents intent on conquering the United States of America known as the Legion of the Living Lightning (sometimes identified as the Lords of the Living Lightning) whose fate was sealed at the hands of the Hulk.

When introduced in 1990, Living Lightning was not originally conceived as a gay character. In fact, his coming out would happen fifteen years later in a very brief exchange with Flatman (see figure 11.2).

11.2. Living Lightning comes out in an exchange with Flatman.

Recognizing his confusion about Flatman's invitation to join the GLA (realizing he had misinterpreted GLA as being shorthand for the Gay/Lesbian Alliance), Living Lightning apologizes and speeds off in his disappointment ("'Great Lakes Avengers?' Oh, sorry. I thought you were the Gay/Lesbian Alliance." [13]). In an interview, *Great Lakes Avengers* writer Dan Slott responded to the dubious queer revisionist history of Living Lightning, who, prior to his encounter with Flatman, was previously understood to be straight. Slott maintains: "He's gay. Get over it. Previous girlfriends? Beards. Or relationships that just didn't work — because Miguel hadn't come to terms yet with who he really is. Miguel is a gay superhero and a wonderful role model."[11]

Quite possibly a means to avoid charges of stereotyping gay men as effeminate, DC and Marvel most likely took a cue from the importance of "butching up" Latino gay male superheroes like Extraño by fashioning a character (Hero Cruz) who is unmistakably "manly" (and whose coming out comes as a great surprise), or turning a previously heterosexual hero gay (Living Lighting) without providing explanation for doing so or fully developing his identity. In any case, the value of these heroes coming out cannot be overstated, as Steven Leitman's letter illustrates, for even Flatman — confessing he was inspired by Living Lightning — emerges from the closet in *Great Lakes Avengers* no. 4. However, the age-old critiques of stereotyping gay men would once again surface in 2011 with the introduction of a superpowered openly gay teenager from a Mexican village named El Chilar in the DC Comics universe. But like the many that came before, this one was also more multifaceted than hastily assumed.

DEBUNKED ASSUMPTIONS

In 2011 DC initiated "The New 52," a project (or often called an "event") that aimed to "reboot" their existing line of superhero comic books with refashioned characters and story lines. One of the revamped titles included the *Teen Titans*. Although the rebooted series saw the return of familiar characters like Superboy, Wonder Girl, Kid Flash, Red Robin, and Solstice, two new heroes were added to the lineup. One of these was Miguel José Barragán, also known as Bunker. With the ability to project psionic purple bricks at his enemies, Bunker is arguably the most congenial Teen Titan; he is also described as "quite chatty" and constantly "flabbergasted." Miguel is also a fashion maven, and it is clear that his sense of style when not in purple hero garb matches that of many contemporary young gay men.

Unlike the previously discussed heroes, Miguel's gay identity is a fact shared with and embraced by his family and the community of El Chilar (despite his arrest by the authorities for displaying "metahuman" abilities). And distinct from Hero Cruz and Living Lightning while more closely aligned with Extraño, Miguel is not cast as hypermasculine but rather quite the opposite. According to Miguel/Bunker's co-creator Brett Booth:

> We wanted to show an interesting character whose homosexuality is part of him, not something that's hidden. Sure they are gay people who you wouldn't know are gay right off the bat, but there are others who are more flamboyant, and we thought it would be nice to actually see them portrayed in comics. Did we go over the top? I don't think so. I wanted you to know he might be gay as soon as you see him. Our TT is partly about diversity of ANY kind, it's about all kinds of teens getting together to help each other. It is a very difficult line to walk, will he be as I've read in some of the comments "fruity"? Not that I'm aware of. Will he be more effeminate than what we've seen before, the "typical" gay male comic character, yes. Does it scare the shit out of me that I might inadvertently piss off the group I want to reflect in a positive way, you're damn straight (pun intended!).[12]

Rejecting the impulse that regards associating flamboyancy with gay men as an automatic act of stereotyping, Booth's desire for a "positive reflection" of Bunker does not entail the simple repudiation of femininity to in turn up-

11.3. Bunker comes out to Wonder Girl, *Teen Titans*.

hold masculinity. This indeed reveals much regarding the criticism directed at Bunker from the LGBT community.[13] The frantic demand for positive representations may in fact be a sanitized yearning for normalizing images rather than acknowledging the gender variance reflected in myriad behaviors, gestures, and self-fashioning practices adopted by queers.

Even before issue no. 6 of *Teen Titans*, when Bunker comes out to Wonder Girl (figure 11.3), he is unique from the traditional hardened male superhero, given the affection he displays toward his teammates, especially Superboy and Red Robin.

And when Bunker does disclose his sexual identity, the response is not one of shock and dismay (Wonder Girl, for example, simply confesses to having "the worst gay-dar in the world" and states firmly she is "not judging" [13] like Bunker thinks she is). In fact, more disarming than his sexuality is his desire for a demonstrative sense of camaraderie exemplified by touching and hugging. This is evident in issue no. 3, when Bunker confesses that he "swore if [he] ever met Red Robin [he would] give [him] a big hug" (13) (which he does) and in issue no. 11 of the New 52 *Superboy* starring the Mexican hero, which showcases his growing intimate bond with the eponymous hero (at one point, Bunker puts his arm around Superboy).[14]

Like Extraño, who would return to his country of origin to reunite with his (former) partner, Bunker announces to the other Titans in issue no. 23

that he is going home to see "the love of [his] life," Gabriel/Gabe, awoken from a coma and who immediately asks for Miguel. (We are first introduced to Gabriel in *Teen Titans* issue no. 17, where we witness him bedridden and visited by Miguel's mother, who reveals that Gabriel saved her son's life.) Seeing him depart to Mexico with friend and ally Beast Boy, readers online expressed concern that Bunker may have been written out of the comic. The second-to-the-last issue of the *Teen Titans* (issue no. 29), however, meaningfully brings Bunker back into the fold, with the final issue (issue no. 30) showcasing a glimpse of his hometown, his family and community, and the intimacy shared with Gabriel. Yet after battling and defeating the villain Brutale, instructed to capture Gabe because of his metahuman status, Bunker leaves behind Gabe (similar to how Extraño would leave Paco) because the universe—and his teammates—required saving.

When DC announced that it would conclude the New 52 *Teen Titans* series, many fans expressed disappointment online about how they would miss their favorite team members. Not surprisingly, Bunker was one of the most discussed and singled out for his importance.[15] For example, on his blog "A Less Than Reputable Source," James Ashelford from Reading, England, writes that Bunker "was one of the New 52's greatest shots at originality and a shot they hit."[16] Ashelford continues:

> It certainly isn't just that [Bunker] was gay, though a large amount of the character's appeal for me was that he was gay in a way not usually seen in superhero comics or many other "adventure" genres. Bunker's sexuality was, at one and the same time, absolutely vital to the character and completely incidental. It actually helped him a lot that his boyfriend was in a coma because it instantly cut off all the obvious, immediate ways to take a gay character: relationships were off limits. Yes, this could just as easily be read as cowardice on DC's part in having an openly gay character and not writing him to display his gayness too openly and scare the horses. . . . However, I want to err on the side of optimism and believe that this was a conscious effort by Scott Lobdell to have a gay character with more to do in-story than have "the gay storylines."

While one could argue that the dynamic between Bunker and Gabe is indeed both "in-story" and a "gay story line" that could have very well been developed early on as opposed to saved for the final issues of the *Teen Titans*'s run, I concur with Ashelford's claim that Bunker's sexuality played an "absolutely vital" role. And more than this, it is Bunker's status as a gay Latino superhero that fuels the means to effect change on several levels.

In *Red Hood and the Outlaws* no. 16, during the Titans' battle with the Joker, Outlaw member Arsenal notes that Bunker's powers are stronger than he probably realizes (with "more going on than anyone gives him credit for") and that he could very well "be in the Justice League before he's twenty" (13). One only hopes that he does have such a promising future and does not go the way of the gay Latino heroes before him, disappearing from view or playing such a minor role in the comic book universe that his creation was only to uphold a simplified claim to diversity that Sara Ahmed might call a "fantasy fold." For Ahmed, diversity "is often imagined as a form of repair, a way of mending or fixing histories of being broken."[17] Instead of signifying a politics of "reparation," queer Latino heroes like Bunker should instead reflect the intersectional and composite identities and identifications embodied by the teenagers like the Titans who inhabit the world in all their complexity. And similar to the case of Araña, about whom Isabel Millán succinctly writes in the previous essay, "[her] full character and narrative arc remains to be written," the same can be said of Bunker.

HOLDING OUT FOR A HERO

Jonathan Risner, in his essay "'Authentic' Latinas/os and Queer Characters in Mainstream and Alternative Comics," importantly argues that "in the world of comics, to point to a single character and deem him or her the *real* Latina/o, or the *real* queer figure, undermines the openness of the terms Latina/o and queer" (53).[18] I hope I have made clear in this essay, for as much as challenging stereotypes is a necessary endeavor for drawing attention to the continued ways marginalized people are distortedly conceived in the realm of popular culture, that the demand for "real" or "authentic" Latina/o, queer, and Latina/o queer superheroes may not always align with the way readers of comics relate to characters that on the surface might be read as problematic. To be sure, such characters, with their multidimensional origins, may serve to galvanize readers of comics to stake claims for a gay superhero with whom they may identify or speak out on the queer politics prompting their animation.

However, Risner makes the crucial argument that

> the emergence of Latina/o and queer characters must undergo some scrutiny that should itself be fluid and open without any fixed criteria. Anyone aware of the historical and still contemporary (mis)representation of homosexuals and Latinas/os in media such as television and Hollywood films understands the need to ascertain and contemplate ideas of authenticity; comics should be put to the same test. (53)

One example we can point to with respect to these politics is the case of Ivan Velez, Jr. Velez, a gay Puerto Rican artist who once worked for DC on titles such as *Blood Syndicate* and *Ghost Rider*, played a vital role not only in altering the pantheon of queer (and) Latina/o superheroes (particularly with *Blood Syndicate*'s gay Latino hero Fade, né Carlos Quiñones) but also by participating in the industry as an out gay Latino.[19]

While I was researching and writing this essay, increasingly growing attached to each of the heroes I have written about here (with my deep connection to Bunker delaying me from sending this essay on time to the editors because I refused to wrap it up until the New 52 *Teen Titans* series folded), I couldn't help but ponder whether Latino/a queer comic writers and artists had a hand in designing these characters. For as much as I have come to embrace Extraño, Hero Cruz, Living Lightning, and Bunker, I will continue longing for more gay Latino origins—"plural, multi-capillaried, argus-eyed, respectful, and endlessly cherished," to draw from Sedgwick once more—in the pages of mainstream comic books and also on the artistic teams that draw up the plans for actualizing their superheroic existence.

NOTES

Acknowledgements: I wish to thank Veronica Kann, Martin Manalansan, Rob Barrett, Brian Montes, Noel Zavala, Lito Sandoval, and Mirelsie Velazquez for help and support in writing this essay. I am especially grateful to Frederick Aldama and Christopher González for their encouragement and patience. This piece is dedicated to the memory of José Esteban Muñoz, who was an avid reader of comic books.

1. Eve Kosofsky Sedgwick, *Epistemology of the Closet* (Berkeley: University of California Press, 1990), 43–44.

2. The wedding scene was originally featured on the cover of issue no. 51 (vol. 3) of *Astonishing X-Men* and subsequently reprinted as the cover for the book *Astonishing X-Men: Northstar* (2012). The book also features the issue of *Alpha Flight* (no. 106, published in 1992) in which Northstar first announces that he is gay.

3. While some might question my identification of heroes like Extraño and Bunker as "Latino" given that they hail from Latin American countries (respectively, Peru and Mexico), when these characters migrate to both the United States and the pages of the comic book they become rendered as such, given how their identities are contoured in particular racial and cultural terms. For example, these heroes—like their US-Latino/a counterparts in the history of Latinos/as in comics—often code-switch between Spanish and English, a strategy that, as Frederick Luis Aldama importantly argues, "force[s] English-only readers to engage with [their] culture on [their] terms." See Aldama's *Your Brain on Latino Comics: From Gus Arriola to Los Bros Hernandez* (Austin: University of Texas Press), 13.

4. I limit my investigation here to gay Latino male superheroes in particular although there are other queer Latina/o figures—such as bisexual Julio Esteban Richter, also known as Marvel Comics' Rictor—one might speak of.

5. My use of "queer" is indebted to Eve Kosofsky Sedgwick, who writes that the term

can refer to "the open mesh of possibilities, gaps, overlaps, dissonances and resonances, lapses and excesses of meaning when the constituent elements of anyone's gender, of anyone's sexuality aren't made (or *can't be* made) to signify monolithically." See her *Tendencies* (Durham: Duke University Press, 1993), 8.

6. Nick Nadel, "Meet Extraño, the Gay Superhero DC Comics Would Rather You Forget." http://thefw.com/extrano-dc-comics. Last accessed 7 Apr. 2014.

7. Readers clearly identified Extraño as gay although he never "officially" declared he was. One need only consider his brief reunification in issue no. 7 with Paco, a man who is clearly a love interest in Gregorio's past. Confessing their HIV status to one another (Paco: "No lo tengo." Gregorio: "Lo tengo"), Paco wonders if their meeting again was fate's way of saying they belonged together. Gregorio responds by declaring that his "fate was sealed when [he] became a New Guardian" (10).

8. Interestingly, the Hemo-Goblin was the creation of a white supremacist organization overseen by Janwillem Kroef.

9. Most critical accounts of Extraño fail to comment on the fact that Gregorio attempted to commit suicide in the pages of *Millennium* no. 3 by jumping off a dock drunk (an act which was clearly in response to the homophobic harassment he received) but was saved by the Flash. While some might say that associating suicide and alcoholism with queers is stereotypical, one might also read this as DC's attempt to deal with serious issues that deeply impact LGBT communities as a result of queer phobia.

10. See http://www.gayleague.com/wordpress/hero-cruz/#sthash.r1Izu4qN.dpuf.

11. See http://www.gayleague.com/wordpress/living-lightning/#sthash.YpBB35yp.dpuf. Last accessed 7 Apr. 2014.

12. See http://www.comicvine.com/bunker/4005-79548. Last accessed 7 Apr. 2014.

13. In their feature on Bunker, *Latina Magazine* notes how Bunker had already been "criticized by some in the LGBT community." http://www.latina.com/lifestyle/news/teen -titans-welcomes-new-gay-latino-superhero. Last accessed 15 May 2014.

14. Superboy not only is represented as an always-provisional member of the Teen Titans but also commands his own title in the New 52 lineup.

15. The title, however, continues with a new series that began in September 2014 and features Bunker, perhaps because of popular demand.

16. See http://alessthanreputablesource.blogspot.com/2013/09/why-i-will-miss-bunker -and-why-titans.html.

17. Sara Ahmed, *On Being Included: Racism and Diversity in Institutional Life* (Durham: Duke University Press, 2012), 164.

18. Jonathan Risner, "'Authentic' Latinas/os and Queer Characters in Mainstream and Alternative Comic," in *Multicultural Comics: From* Zap *to* Blue Beetle (Austin: University of Texas Press, 2010), 39–54.

19. See Frederick Luis Aldama's insightful interview with Velez in *Your Brain on Latino Comics*, 279–291.

PART V

MULTIVERSES, ADMIXTURES, AND MORE

EVERYBODY WANTS TO RULE THE MULTIVERSE: LATINO SPIDER-MEN IN MARVEL'S MEDIA EMPIRE

KATHRYN M. FRANK

ONE OF THE RECURRING themes in discussions of Latina/o characters—particularly superheroes—in mainstream comics (those published by the "Big 2," Marvel and DC) has been the issue of these characters' only appearing in large team ensembles or as supporting characters in a series headlined by a white hero.[1] A few notable Latina/o superheroes have headlined their own titles; these efforts have been few both in number and in issues actually published. The Jaime Reyes incarnation of Blue Beetle saw thirty-six issues from 2006–2009, and then only sixteen issues before cancellation in DC's New 52 relaunch. The second Spider-Girl, Anya Corazón, is featured in twelve issues headlining her own title.[2] As of January 2014, only one ongoing series from DC or Marvel had a Latina/o superhero as the title character.[3] However, second-tier status and/or short shelf lives are not the only trends in mainstream comics affecting Latina/o superheroes. As Frederick Luis Aldama and Christopher González note in the introduction to this volume, "the specific formal features, structures, and devices" of comics are not just aesthetic elements; they also "generate meaning and feeling." In the case of the two Latino Spider-Men presented by Marvel, the structure of the Marvel universe has provided a space for Latino characters to take up famous and beloved roles while simultaneously discouraging readers from seeing these Spider-Men as the "true" Spider-Man.

In this essay, I examine the impact that one particular formal element and industry practice—the multiverse—has had through two case studies of Latino superheroes in Marvel universes. While the multiverse has, on one hand, allowed publishers to experiment with new characters in prominent roles and portray different types of superheroes without sacrificing the audience or continuity of their flagship titles, this structure has also resulted in Latina/o superheroes appearing inconsistently in publication and rarely at all across other comics-derived media. Two Latino Spider-Men have been used by Marvel to fill in the "gaps" between newer readers and Marvel's comics but then have been left to languish in those gaps rather than be promoted through merchandise, film, and television as the "original" Anglo Spider-Man has.

THE MULTIVERSE: FUNCTIONS AS BOTH FORMAL
ELEMENT AND INDUSTRY TESTING GROUND

No definitive history of how the term *multiverse*—a descriptor for the sum total of a publisher's titles across different story continuities—first came into common use in comics has been agreed upon by comics historians; however, what is certain is that its use came about in order to articulate that while a publisher's "original" story line and characters were distinct from "alternative universe" versions, they were still at least tangentially related. These alternate universes involved familiar characters and stories from the "original" story line but did not affect the plot of those stories. For instance, Marvel's *What If . . . ?* series creates alternate universes in which small elements of heroes' backgrounds are changed, which results in major differences in these universes. These alternate universes might see familiar characters change their career paths or might pick up a plot point from the "original" story line and change it to explore how the story might have turned out differently.[4] Today, both DC and Marvel have stories that take place in different universes; stories in Marvel's Ultimate universe in particular remain consistently published, and at large conventions Marvel holds different panels to discuss stories happening in its main title line and in the Ultimate line.

The multiverse continues to provide publishers with a way to experiment with new characters and allow creative teams to change long-standing continuity elements. Nonprimary universes can also have definitive endings or character deaths, such as those seen in Marvel's *2099: Manifest Destiny*, which details what ultimately happens to many of the 2099 universe characters. The introduction of new universes can also serve an important function for the publisher in several ways.[5] Alternate universes can provide creators with more freedom in constructing story lines and creating characters since there are fewer (or no) existing canonical elements to which they must adhere. New universes can also be used as a strategy for drawing in new readers, who can start reading the comics without needing to first familiarize themselves with years of continuity. These functions can be seen clearly in the two cases examined here, as Marvel used the introduction of Latino Spider-Men to respond to trends in the comics industry and increase attention to their products in the face of competition from live-action adaptations.

Marvel has a number of different universes; in publication, the two main universes are the Earth-616 primary continuity and Earth-1610, the Ultimate universe. The 616/primary universe is the one from which most of the stories and characters for film adaptation are drawn; although these film and animated series have their own universe designations, most are inspired by the 616 continuity. Elements of the Ultimate universe, perhaps the second-best-known Marvel line, have found their way onto the big screen—most notably in the form of Samuel L. Jackson's Nick Fury—but the majority of characters are the "original" Earth-616 versions. The designation of 616 as the "primary" continuity gives it something of a prominence over the other universes. Moviegoers or TV viewers who aren't comic readers are more likely to know characters as they appear in this universe.

A TALE OF TWO SPIDER-MEN: THE FORM AND FUNCTION OF MIGUEL O'HARA AND MILES MORALES

Two case studies illustrate how the element of multiple story universes—a feature used both within stories and by the publisher to categorize different titles and characters—has functioned in regard to Latina/o superheroes in recent years: first, the creation of the 2099 universe and publication history of its star, Spider-Man 2099 Miguel O'Hara, and, second, the 2010 "Donald Glover 4 Spiderman" Facebook campaign and subsequent creation of the new Ultimate universe Spider-Man Miles Morales.

Marvel's 2099 universe was created in 1992 and represented an effort to join the "gritty" trend that creator-owned studios like Image had just begun pioneering in the early 1990s, as well as to capitalize on the popularity of 1980s cyberpunk literature and films. In contrast to the primary Marvel universe's fairly realistic New York setting, the 2099 universe presented a potential post-apocalyptic future, where major corporations had taken over every facet of life and left much of the country a burned-out shell. One of the original 2099 titles, Peter David and Rick Leonardi's *Spider-Man 2099*, became the most consistently published 2099 series, and its star, Miguel O'Hara, the most frequently recurring 2099 character. The half-Irish, half-Mexican O'Hara also holds the distinction of being the first Latino to use the Spider-Man identity. Spider-Man 2099 lasted forty-six issues, fourteen of which have been collected into trade paperbacks; O'Hara also appeared in subsequent 2099 titles, as well as in the primary universe Marvel titles *Captain Marvel, Exiles,* and, most recently, *Superior Spider-Man*.

While some elements of O'Hara's story are similar to that of the "original" Spider-Man, Peter Parker, O'Hara is physically marked by his powers in a way that Parker is not, leading to difficulty in concealing his identity. The O'Hara version of Spider-Man also was used as inspiration for the *Spider-Man Unlimited* animated TV series, but the main character was Peter Parker. These similarities and differences between the Latino O'Hara Spider-Man and the white Parker Spider-Man illustrate some of the ways in which the multiverse allows for experimentation but also helps to preserve the status quo in terms of character identity. A sarcastic scientific genius, O'Hara gains his spider powers when he is betrayed by a co-worker and subjected to an experiment that gives him 50% spider DNA.

Although O'Hara has light skin and hair, the visible markers of his spider powers distinguish him from "normal" society and cause difficulties for him that are easily read as metaphoric of racial/ethnic minority status and the ways in which this difference can be both alienating and empowering. O'Hara not only gains spider powers from his accident but is irreparably physically marked as well. His canine teeth elongate into fangs, which he cannot hide, and he has sharp talons protruding from his forearms that he can only sometimes retract. His fangs also give him a noticeable accent, and he has to learn to speak in such a way as to compensate for this problem (see figure 12.1). As Mauricio Espinoza's examination of the "alien-ness" and "other-ness" of Latina/o superheroes (also presented in this collection) contends, this physical deformity is not only a problem that sets O'Hara apart from society but also the source of his abilities. He is able to use his difference in order to challenge corrupt power structures.

Given Marvel's long history of using physical mutation as a metaphor for other identity categories with X-Men, having O'Hara face these issues alone as Spider-Man brought a new dimension to both the character and Marvel's reputation as engaging social issues in subtle, accessible ways. In *Manifest Destiny: 2099*, which depicts the end of the 2099 universe, O'Hara works together with Captain America and Ghost Rider to bring peace and prosperity to the 2099 universe; he is even deemed worthy enough to lift Mjolnir, Thor's hammer, an honor bestowed only on a select few Marvel characters. The idea of a Latino genius and an all-American war hero being able to successfully usher in world peace—at which point the Latino hero governs the world for the next thousand years—lends an unprecedented level of authority and power to O'Hara's character, but this grand and unusual vision is only possible within the confines of a universe totally removed from the "reality" of the primary continuity.

Despite the popularity of *Spider-Man 2099*—O'Hara appeared in more issues of the 2099 universe than any other character and has crossed over into the Earth-616 universe on several occasions—when Marvel created their

12.1. Miguel O'Hara's talons and fangs, from *Spider-Man 2099*.

animated series *Spider-Man Unlimited* in 1999, O'Hara was not the titular web-slinger. Instead, Peter Parker inhabited a costume and a world strikingly similar to O'Hara's,[6] with no mention of O'Hara given and no Latina/o characters present. Risks—like a disfigured Latino Spider-Man—that were possible within universes on the margins like 2099 were not translated into universes with larger audiences, like the television animation universe. Over a decade later, Ultimate Spider-Man Miles Morales would be in a similar position: innovative in terms of background and used to draw in new readers to Marvel's comics, but largely constrained to a second-tier universe.

Prior to the creation of Morales, a particularly large and impassioned controversy broke out over the 2012 live-action film *The Amazing Spider-Man* when comedian and actor Donald Glover jokingly suggested he ought to be considered for the role of Spider-Man. While many fans and industry professionals supported Glover's idea and started a Facebook campaign to get him an audition, others insisted that it would be inappropriate—and even racist— to have Glover, who is black, portray a character who is white in the comics.[7] Despite positive feedback on Glover's potential for the role from Spider-Man creator Stan Lee, the studio that owns the rights to live-action Spider-Man adaptations did not consider Glover and eventually cast a white British actor.[8] Although Stan Lee and Marvel Entertainment were not involved with the film's casting since the rights are owned by Sony, Marvel did capitalize on the controversy by introducing a half-black, half-Latino Spider-Man in their Ultimate Comics line, whose creator has stated he was partially inspired by the image of Glover in a Spider-Man costume.[9,10]

Marvel's responses to the campaign and ensuing controversy demonstrated an awareness of the potential publicity that could come from introducing a non-white Spider-Man character, but also an effort not to dilute their brand cohesion around Spider-Man, which necessarily resulted in less merchandising of non-white Spider-Man characters. Marvel also took advantage of their licensing position in terms of live-action Spider-Man rights to appear more open to diversity than Sony Pictures and paint the comics industry as a whole as progressive-thinking and open-minded.[11] As Adilifu Nama and Maya Haddad argue in their essay on "Blatino" comics characters in this volume, Morales's racial and ethnic background plays only a small role in the character's development; however, Marvel's apparent willingness to acknowledge diverse identities in the face of "big Hollywood" appearing unwilling to consider minorities in leading roles provided Marvel with an opportunity to build publicity for a new Spider-Man.

Stan Lee, one of Spider-Man's original creators, was interviewed for his opinion on the controversy. Although Lee has not had any authority in the company or had any input into Spider-Man stories for some time, his status as the longtime public face of Marvel and co-creator of many of its most famous characters often sees him provide commentary or promotional interviews for Marvel about upcoming projects. Lee's specific role as co-creator of Spider-Man also allowed Marvel to present him as a figure of some authority on what Spider-Man should look like and on who would or would not be an appropriate choice to portray Spider-Man in a live-action adaptation. Lee stopped short of endorsing either Glover or the campaign but did remark that he thought Glover should be allowed to audition for the role.[12] This interview with Lee was promoted by Marvel on popular culture blogs and websites as a "response from Spider-Man's creator," explicitly establishing Lee's authority on the matter.[13]

The fact that Lee's response carried no weight in relation either to the live-action adaptation and its casting or to anything Marvel was doing with the Spider-Man character in their publishing, television, or toy divisions facilitated use of the interview as evidence that Marvel and its creators were open-minded and progressive in regard to their characters without committing them to any particular course of action. It also enabled Marvel to subtly emphasize that Spider-Man was one of the properties for which they did not own the live-action rights and to thus distinguish their "in-house" films from those made by other entities. A prior controversy over the casting of Idris Elba as the Norse-god-inspired character Heimdall in 2011's *Thor* as well as a smaller controversy over casting Michael Clarke Duncan as *Daredevil*'s Kingpin were also rehashed and discussed in concert with the Spider-Man campaign, further emphasizing a link between Marvel, diverse casting, and "listening to fans" and a link between other companies and not caring about fans' input.[14]

Sony's lack of response to the campaign and subsequent casting of white British actor Andrew Garfield as Spider-Man further allowed Marvel to present themselves as a company that listens to fans when it comes to live-action adaptations; by implication, Marvel suggested that other companies holding Marvel licenses do not necessarily care what fans think or want.

In 2011 writer Brian Michael Bendis killed off the character of Peter Parker in his *Ultimate Spider-Man* comic and introduced a new Spider-Man for the Ultimate universe, black and Puerto Rican middle-school student Miles Morales (see figure 12.2). The introduction of the character created a brief storm of publicity for Marvel and their Ultimate line, and Bendis credited part of the inspiration for the character to a picture of Donald Glover dressed as Spider-Man on the show *Community*.[15] While not directly referencing the Glover 4 Spiderman campaign, the promotion of Glover as an inspiration for the character allowed Marvel to implicitly suggest that they had "listened" to fans and

12.2. Miles Morales as Spider-Man in *Ultimate Comics: Spider-Man.*

created a character that appealed to what fans had expressed they wanted. As with most changes in long-running story lines, whether in comics or in other media, an inevitable backlash followed, but Marvel stood by Bendis's decision to kill Parker and debut Morales, again citing the excitement fans had shown at the prospect of a more diverse Spider-Man.[16] Since his debut, Miles Morales has been the only Spider-hero in the Ultimate universe, and even crossed over into the Earth-616 continuity to work with Peter Parker in a special limited series. Although not a genius or eventual world leader like O'Hara, the Morales version of Spider-Man has become quite influential in its own right.

When Miles Morales debuted as Spider-Man in the Ultimate universe, attention was given to the fact that Spider-Man was Latino; Miguel O'Hara and his status as the first Latino Spider-Man were not mentioned in promotional copy for the new *Ultimate Comics: Spider-Man*. A few commentators noted that Morales was not the first Latino Spider-Man, but most did not.[17,18] The inactivity of the 2099 universe and the assumption that the new readers Miles Morales might attract would not remember O'Hara undoubtedly influenced the presentation of the Morales character as being an innovative or daring move by Marvel when they had in fact taken a similar "risk" over a decade earlier. The existence of multiple universes allowed Marvel to present themselves as having taken a risk by killing Peter Parker to debut a non-white Spider-Man, but without disturbing the existence of the "original" Peter Parker (who was alive and well in the pages of *Amazing Spider-Man*),[19] and with the knowledge that a Latino Spider-Man had already been successful.

Despite critical acclaim and solid sales for *Ultimate Comics: Spider-Man* with Miles Morales, this character has so far been mainly confined to print and not promotion through character licensing (as the Peter Parker version of Spider-Man has enjoyed). While Marvel sought to capitalize on the controversy regarding the Glover campaign and Sony's lack of response, Marvel's publishing and television arms both introduced new Ultimate Spider-Man series with Peter Parker in the title role, which compete directly with *Ultimate Comics: Spider-Man* and dilute the brand cohesion for the character. Although Peter Parker is not Spider-Man as of the end of 2013 in any of Marvel's print continuities, his version of Spider-Man continues to dominate merchandise, television animation, and live-action film. To Spider-Man fans or casual viewers of film and television who do not read comics, Spider-Man continues to be a white character.

THE REST OF THE MULTIVERSE: OUTSIDE COMICS

There has been little merchandising for either Latino Spider-Man, and no appearances on television or film. When asked about potential merchandise or appearances outside of comics for Morales at a 2013 convention, Marvel Director of Communications Arune Singh directed fans to the animated *Ultimate Spider-Man* cartoon featuring Peter Parker and remarked that Marvel was looking for avenues to promote Morales but did not mention any specific plans. Instead, he suggested that Marvel "likes making money"—whether this was meant to suggest that fans could expect Morales merchandise or not was not explained.

The lack of branding or merchandising of these Spider-Men of color is consistent with work on Latina/o racial formations in the contemporary era; scholars including Arlene Dávila and Isabel Molina-Guzmán have argued that Latina/o characters (and real individuals) have been used to present visions of minority success (in contrast, these images insinuate, to black American failure)[20] or to add ethnic "flair" to a media text without alienating white audiences.[21,22] It seems to be important for Marvel to be able to say they have a black and/or Latino Spider-Man, but not necessarily to make these characters household names, lest the characters confuse the branding of the original

Spider-Man. As Lisa Nakamura explains, "[I]dentity is more important than the individual," and the existence of these characters is more important than their status in viewers' or readers' minds.[23] Marvel can promote these characters when a controversy over diversity in comics erupts or give them new story lines when their flagship titles stagnate and they need to bring in new readers. These characters' position outside the center of the multiverse[24] allows for innovation and increased representation for Latino superheroes on one level but also provides a built-in constraint that most Latina/o superheroes have yet to transcend.

NOTES

1. Frederick Luis Aldama, *Multicultural Comics: From Zap to Blue Beetle*, Cognitive Approaches to Literature and Culture Series (Austin: University of Texas Press, 2010), 5; Frederick Luis Aldama, *Your Brain on Latino Comics: From Gus Arriola to Los Bros Hernandez*, Cognitive Approaches to Literature and Culture Series (Austin: University of Texas Press, 2009), 31; Frederick L. Aldama, "Spandexed Latinos: Geometric Storytelling in Superhero Comics" (presented at the Latino Comics Expo Los Angeles, Long Beach, CA, August 17, 2013).

2. *Araña*. Corazón was also the titular *Amazing Spider-Girl* for a few issues.

3. *Ultimate Comics: Spider-Man* from Marvel.

4. For instance, Captain America once declined a third-party presidential nomination; *What If Captain America Were Elected President? (What If . . . ?* no. 26, Apr. 1981) sees Cap accept the nomination and eventually win the election.

5. Derek Johnson, "Will the Real Wolverine Please Stand Up?: Marvel's Mutation from Monthlies to Movies," in *Film and Comic Books* (Jackson: University Press of Mississippi, 2007), 285–300.

6. "What If . . . We Got a Spider-Man 2099 Cartoon instead of Spider-Man Unlimited?," accessed 14 Jan. 2014, http://www.comicbookmovie.com/fan_fic/news/?a=68029.

7. Marc Bernardin, "Donald Glover for Spider-Man: The Evolution of a Meme," *io9*, accessed 6 July 2013, http://io9.com/5552684/donald-glover-for-spider+man-the-evolution-of-a-meme.

8. Cyriaque Lamar, "Smilin' Stan Lee Weighs in on Donald Glover for Spider-Man," *io9*, accessed 6 July 2013, http://io9.com/5559655/smilin-stan-lee-weighs-in-on-donald-glover-for-spider+man.

9. Adam Chitwood, "Donald Glover Talks New ULTIMATE SPIDER-MAN | Collider," *Collider.com*, accessed 6 July 2013, http://collider.com/donald-glover-new-spider-man/.

10. "How Donald Glover Finally Secured the Role of Spider-Man," *Robot 6 @ Comic Book Resources*, accessed 24 Dec. 2013, http://robot6.comicbookresources.com/2011/08/how-donald-glover-finally-secured-the-role-of-spider-man/.

11. "Thanks to Donald Glover, the New Ultimate Spider-Man Is a Man of Color," *Gothamist*, accessed 24 Dec. 2013, http://gothamist.com/2011/08/02/thanks_to_donald_glover_the_new_ult.php.

12. Lamar, "Smilin' Stan Lee Weighs in on Donald Glover for Spider-Man."

13. "What Stan Lee Thinks of Donald Glover's 'Spider-Man' Casting Campaign," *Splash*

Page, accessed 24 Dec. 2013, http://splashpage.mtv.com/2010/06/09/stan-lee-donald-glover-spider-man-casting-campaign/.

14. Ibid.

15. Bernardin, "Donald Glover for Spider-Man: The Evolution of a Meme."

16. Ora C. McWilliams, "Who Is Afraid of a Black Spider(-Man)?," *Transformative Works and Cultures* 13.0 (12 Nov. 2012), doi:10.3983/twc.v13i0.455.

17. Bryan Robinson, "Remembering the First—and Forgotten—Latino Spider-Man," Text. Article, *Fox News Latino*, 16 Aug. 2011, http://latino.foxnews.com/latino/lifestyle/2011/08/16/remembering-first-and-forgotten-latino-spider-man/.

18. "A Black Spider-Man? So What? Miguel O'Hara Already Paved the Trail!," *Crimson Monkey*, accessed 14 Jan. 2014, http://www.crimsonmonkey.com/blogs/daveomac/a-black-spider-man-so-what-miguel-o-hara-already-paved-the-trail/.

19. The "original" Parker would be killed in December 2012 but return in April 2013.

20. Although Miles Morales is half-black, his Latino identity also distances him, when convenient, from other black representations, including "stereotypical" black superheroes like Black Panther or Luke Cage.

21. Arlene Dávila, *Latinos, Inc.: The Marketing and Making of a People* (Berkeley: University of California Press, 2001).

22. Isabel Molina-Guzmán, *Dangerous Curves: Latina Bodies in the Media* (New York: New York University Press, 2010).

23. Lisa Nakamura, *Digitizing Race: Visual Cultures of the Internet* (U of Minnesota Press, 2008), 74.

24. One might argue that the current center of the multiverse is Marvel's cinematic universe, which features even fewer Latina/o characters than their primary comics (Earth-616) universe does.

THIRTEEN

MAPPING THE *BLATINO* BADLANDS AND BORDERLANDS OF AMERICAN POP CULTURE

ADILIFU NAMA AND MAYA HADDAD

FOR SCORES OF ACADEMICS, social critics, and philosopher dilettantes, American pop culture is like Felix the Cat's bottomless black magic purse, an unending grab bag that contains innumerable cultural artifacts of all shapes and sizes that amaze as well as underwhelm. Despite such variety and range of significance, a constant theme persists: American pop culture has served as an enduring space where racial pathos, ethnic fears, post-racial fantasies, and political anxieties are engaged and (re)imagined. Take, for example, the frequent romantic pairing of black lead actors with a Latina actress in Holly-wood films, a trend that demonstrates how representation and economics are transparently tied to unstated sociocultural anxieties around race. Ostensibly, a Latina figure assists in making sure not to alienate potential white viewers that might pass on what might be considered a "black" film if both leads are clearly African American. Put another way, having two black leads in a sci-fi, dramatic, or comedic film make it a "black" film. Consequently, in this case, Latinaness is used to undercut the blackness represented by having two black actors as the principal characters and helps to construct a crossover platform for potential audiences. Emblematic of this tendency are Will Smith's pairings with Salma Hayek in *Wild Wild West* (1999), Eva Mendez in *Hitch* (2005), Alice Braga in *I Am Legend* (2007), and Rosario Dawson in *Seven Pounds* (2008), along with Eva Mendez with Denzel Washington in *Training Day* (2001) and to a lesser extent *Out of Time* (2003). These examples demonstrate the vulgar pragmatics of mass marketing and racial demographics taking root when black and Latinoness are combined in American pop culture.

Without question, pop culture industries are guilty of cutting, pasting, and milking race for profit and entertainment, but there are also insurgent moments of cultural production that provide cultural critiques and points of analysis concerning racial taboos and racialized ideology in America not expected when blackness and Latino ethnicity are paired. Most emblematic of this culturally insurgent articulation of the organic and syncretic hybridity of blackness and Latinoness is articulated in the area of music. Take, for example, the racial idiom "Spanish Tinge" used by the seminal jazz pioneer Jelly Roll Morton to describe what set apart his New Orleans version of jazz from other run-of-the-mill Roaring Twenties music associated with the so-called Jazz Age. In addition, the Afro-Cuban collaboration between bebop architect Dizzy Gillespie and Cuban conga player Chano Pozo not only delivered the classic tune *Manteca* but spawned multiple musical Afro-Latino movements: Cubop, Afrobop, Latin Jazz, boogaloo, Latin R & B, and let us not forget Reggaeton.[1] Take your pick. Such racial, cultural, expressive, and creative synergy speaks to the best of what an organic mash-up of blackness and Latinoness can create. This point is also germane to the creation of hip-hop. The music emerged out of the black and brown miasma of the South Bronx, a culture, style, and music that was a response to Lyndon B. Johnson's failed War on Poverty, Richard M. Nixon's benign neglect, Jimmy Carter's failed leadership, and Ronald Reagan's political indifference.[2] In this sense, prospective economic profits along with racial anxieties do not fully account for or define the ideological nexus of Afro-Latino representation across popular culture in America. Take, for instance, the buzz created around a black and Latino teenager named Miles Morales as the new Spider-Man in the *Ultimate Spider-Man* comic book series. Admittedly, Spider-Man is arguably Marvel Comic's most signature character across the Marvel superhero universe and an iconic white superhero in American pop culture, but as a black and Puerto Rican Spider-Man, the superhero is a source of debate concerning increased ethnic diversity and shifts in the popular discourse surrounding race in America.[3] Before, however, delving into a deep discussion about emergent articulations of Blatinoness as a particular fusion of black and Latino identity in the realm of pop culture, the term itself and how it is deployed in this essay compels a preliminary analysis.

"Blatino" is constructed from the literal combination of the words "black" and "Latino." When the term is typed into an Internet search engine, it also appears as a highly sexualized term related to male homosexuality and a particular ethnic–racial niche in gay pornography. Ultimately, history will be the judge as to how the term is canonized. Nevertheless, in this essay "Blatino" is used as a contemporary version of the term "Afro-Latino," with the former constructed to address the intersection (and possibly the privileging) of black racial formation alongside Latino ethnicity. Admittedly, the attempt to free "Blatino" from the prison house of language is problematic. Upon first blush the term appears to uncritically stress blackness as the primary identity rather than Latinoness, but the construction of Blatinoness as applied in this setting functions more as a synergetic proposition than a closed circuit of racial meaning and ethnic experience. In this essay the term "Blatino" is situated and discussed as a critical model of being that offers a potential and example for being. Admittedly the stress on the "black" prefix may not adequately address the miasmic mix of duality that goes with simultaneously being black and Latino. Yet, as a strategic form of black essentialism, the benefits the term offers in analytic insights outweigh the knotty shortcomings of trying to split the difference into neat categories. Consequently, the essentialist impulse circulating in the construction of Blatinoness in this essay views black Latinos and black Americans as calling, knowingly and unknowingly, to African culture, history, and place.

Arguably, the unknowingness is one of disguise, not merely nonrecognition. Unknowing Blatinos, whether or not they feel allegiance to their new world home of black racial formation after generations and centuries separated from the source, still create according to the core of what most likely comes from the coast of a continent histories away but of the now. In the United States, the touchstones of popular black racial formation are found in the blues, jazz, house music, hip-hop, and deep organ-driven gospel sermons that summon backsliders and believers, the dancers, B-boys/girls, the faithful, preachers, and folks getting the spirit, or, as they say, "catchin'" the Holy Ghost. But the same African "blackness" found today and in the music scores of tomorrows hails from ancestral spirits of the past, beginning in the Third World and back, that also include indigenous peoples of the New World. Moreover, history, race, and culture have all collided to create something greater than the sum of the individual parts, a syncretic synergy witnessed in Cuba with the wailing vocals of *Son* sung by the sons and daughters of Taíno forbearers singing stories and righteous requests of the orishas informed by African songs and oral traditions. Africa may be full of modern Africans, but the world is populated with African Americans, Afro-Cubans, and Afro-Brazilians (all of whom are racialized in America as Black). And now there are *Blatinos*, a demographic group added to this socially constructed reality that has many Americans, white and black, wondering, *Why is that black person speaking Spanish?* To this point, this essay examines how the amalgamation of blackness and Latinoness, aka Blatinoness, ensconced in American pop culture is not merely a topic bounded by demographic statistics and limited to a discussion of demographic shifts but often signifies broader racial discourses, social implications, tensions, and progressive possibilities in American society. For example, "Blatinoness" as phrase, representation, and identity crops up with the comic book "Blatinoness" of Miles Morales, a comic book Spiderman that offers a striking racial contrast in meaning against the mainstream whiteness of the Spiderman franchise with Peter Parker.

The white web-slinger made his first appearance in the 1960s in one of the most important comic book stories ever published, *Amazing Fantasy* no. 15.[4] Spider-Man was the alter ego of the quiet and geeky Peter Parker, a high school student who was more successful with science than girls and eventually was bitten by a radioactive spider. The Cold War anxiety of the 1960s around the atomic bomb is clearly present in Spidey's origin narrative.[5] While Marvel didn't help calm any fears with story lines that often used atomic radiation as the causal agent for gaining mutant powers, the radioactive mutation of Peter Parker did unleash a storm of popular products and commodities that have come to define and redefine Spider-Man over several decades. Comic books, bubblegum cards, puzzles, toy action figures, kites, Halloween costumes, animated television shows, and films have presented various versions of Spider-Man for consumer consumption. Alongside the multitude of Spidey products, multiple comic book story lines also arose to meet the reading audience's appetite for more Spider-Man. These imprints offered alternative universes that allowed for more narrative latitude and innovation with the history, direction, and timeline than the original comic superhero. As a result, Spider-Man fans no longer needed to mull over a variety of "what ifs" concerning various events and hallmark scenarios associated with the web-slinger. Instead, an assortment of Spider-Man titles allowed for various incarnations of the superhero.[6] Case in point: in 2000 Marvel launched *Ultimate Marvel*, a comic imprint that reimagined different versions of signature Marvel superheroes like The Fantastic Four, The Avengers, X-Men, and Spider-Man. Just over a decade later the *Ultimate Marvel* had their *Spider-Man* title take a radical turn. Peter Parker would die in the line of superhero duty, and a black and Puerto Rican kid named Miles Morales emerged to replace him.

Not surprisingly, now that Marvel comics is a corporate subsidiary of Disney, the creation of a Blatino Spider-Man easily invites speculation about the timing of and motivations for replacing the white Peter Parker. Is a black and Latino Spider-Man merely a crude attempt to capitalize on the excitement and historic nature of America's having a black president, a boardroom-meeting-inspired publicity stunt to attract Latino consumers because of their growing demographic stature in the United States, or a ploy to create a more masculine product line for a company that has the princess market covered? Regardless of the intrigue surrounding the raison d'être for why Miles Morales was created, it is not as compelling as what the actual figure articulates, symbolizes, and signifies about race, hybrid racial identities, and multiculturalism in America. Miles Morales, however, is not the first "black" Spider-Man.

In 1984, Peter Parker unsuspectingly became the first human host for the "symbiote," alien black goo that bonds with its victim in Marvel's comic universe. As a result, Spider-Man's signature red and blue costume became black (see figure 13.1) along with Spider-Man's powers becoming enhanced.[7] The "black" Spider-Man was a hit along with the symbiote villain Venom as the most popular incarnation of the alien black goo that bonds with different human hosts for Spider-Man to fight. Accordingly, Sam Raimi's *Spider-Man 3* (2007), the third installment of the blockbuster film franchise, brought the black suit and Venom to the big screen. Interestingly, the film uses the symbiote suit to create a "black" alter ego for Peter that displays various stereotypical signifiers of male blackness in contrast to the white geekiness of Peter Parker.[8] However, with the introduction of Miles Morales into the Marvel universe of superheroes, the literal takes the place of the symbolic.

Issue 1 introduces Miles Morales as a young teenager and resident of New York vying for the last remaining spot to gain entrance into a charter school. His name is the last lottery pick. Unlike in the original Spider-Man story, in the Miles Morales story the social politics of race and class kick-start the origin issue and are clearly telegraphed with the *Ultimate* incarnation of America's favorite web-head. Establishing a school charter lottery as the opening setting for Miles Morales's origin narrative does more than foreshadow his uncanny ability to beat the odds, a point fully registered when he is also bitten by a genetically enhanced spider and luckily lives to acquire superpowers like the previous Peter Parker. Having Miles Morales win the charter school lottery also invokes the arduous and contentious struggle that black folk have faced and that continues to crop up today over access to quality education. Although the *Brown vs. Board of Education* (1954) Supreme Court case made racial segregation in the United States unconstitutional, the landmark decision that allowed access to education by black and brown folk was marred by de facto segregation in the form of residential racial patterns. As a result, school busing became the stopgap measure for racially integrating America's schools and the source of a "forced busing" backlash.

Arguably, the most controversial and divisive development concerning access to quality education was the occurrence of violent protests to black integration of the Boston Unified School District by working-class whites during the mid-1970s.[9] Against this historical backdrop, Miles Morales's seemingly innocuous origin narrative sets the stage for a subversive political and racially relevant reading of how education, economics, opportunity, and luck are scarce resources for folks of color. Despite the subversive narrative setup concerning racial disparity and equal access to education in the first issue, given that Miles Morales was the son of an African American man and a Puerto

13.1. Miles Morales as the Blatino Spidey.

13.2. "The Santerians" created by Joe Quesada.

Rican mother, the hype and heated debates generated across the blogosphere and traditional news outlets about the new Spider-Man were overwhelmingly focused on his Blatino racial identity. Yet, for all of his racial novelty as a Blatino Spider-Man, the racial import and meaning of this new racialized figure was amazingly bland. In other words, the biracial construction of Miles Morales has so far only impacted the deep-brown complexion of his skin and the jet-black waviness of his hair. The anticlimactic racial sensibility present in Marvel's *Ultimate Comics All New Spider-Man* is rather interesting given the overdetermined tendencies of superheroes of color to symbolize or articulate a specific and very blunt racial politics.[10]

In stark contrast to the underwhelming Miles Morales Spider-Man is Marvel Comics's *Santerians* (see figure 13.2), a staunch foray into the borderlands of Afro-Latino representation of superheroes. The *Santerians* draw their origin directly from the crosscurrents of Santeria, a religious tradition that merges the West African Yoruba religion with Roman Catholicism; this is the template used to create a superhero team composed of members that embody the various orisha deities of the Santeria religion.[11] In *Daredevil: Father* nos. 1–6 (2005/2009) these Afro-Latino superheroes are first introduced. As Mauricio Espinoza mentions in his essay earlier in this volume, Nestor Rodriguez aka NeRo is the team's leader, whose namesake is Eleggua. The other members are Chango, Ogun, Oshun, and Oya.

Bankrolled by NeRo's financial wealth as an independent hip-hop music tycoon and entertainment brand, the Santerians work to rid New York of rampant crime and catch a serial killer whom the provincial Daredevil appears to overlook. Although Joe Quesada, the former editor-in-chief of Marvel comics, uses a traditional African religion fused with Latino ethnic formation, in this story line the Santerians shade more to ethnically Latino figures, except for the superhero Ogun. He is the character that most demonstrates the intersection of blackness with Latinoness as fundamentally articulated as a particular phenotype. He has the darkest complexion along with a braided, cornrowed, dreadlocked hairstyle often associated with African Americans and Caribbean blacks. Lastly, Ogun possesses superhuman strength literally represented by a giant physique and extreme muscularity, making hyper-masculinity the go-to trope of choice that marks his racial blackness.[12] Ultimately, this type of Afro-Latino representation suffers from too strident a rendering and too literal an interpretation of the syncretic intersection of blackness and Latino identity.[13]

Unfortunately, as groundbreaking as the Santerians are as characters, the entire enterprise feels more like an alternative means to teach a history lesson and make a stilted point concerning the need for diversity in comics. The real-world political and cultural urgency that these characters represent is fully observed with the rapid attempt at pop-cultural canonization of this obscure group of Latino superheroes with the comic book gallery show *Santerians: The Art of Joe Quesada* (2007), at the Franklin H. Williams Caribbean Cultural Center African Diaspora Institute. In addition, the trade paperback version of *Daredevil: Father* (2009) also includes Quesada's schematic notes on the qualities of each deity of Santeria, which read like an educational glossary. The exhibit and the edifying glossary demonstrate the overdetermined cultural politics in play in the drive to make enduring representations of minorities in America when ethnic diversity is at stake even in a comic book, one of America's most disposable pop mediums. In contrast to the fanfare and trepidation surrounding the racial and ethnic pedigree of Miles Morales and *The Santerians* representation of Blatino characters overdetermined by history and the burden of being a "positive" image of diversity in the mainstream comic book universe, there is a relatively unknown and significantly under-advertised comic book called *Vescell* (see figure 13.3) that is covering new territory and providing a style of Blatinoness that approaches the more idealized construction of the category as discussed earlier.

In the postmodern high-tech setting of *Vescell*, people live in a world that has advanced to the point where technology can now transfer a person's mind and soul into a body of that person's choosing. Along with this scientific breakthrough, the supernatural realm also looms large in the everyday world of *Vescell*. Demons and fairies share a world of robots, cyborgs, and para-normal police officers with ESP. Against this genre mash-up, Agent Mauricio "Moo" Barrino traverses a landscape littered with deceptive double-crosses, buxom femmes fatales, violent shoot-outs, raunchy sex, and even raunchier

13.3. Cover art from Issue 1, *Vescell*.

language. Upon first blush the mature themes offered threaten to overwhelm the character study of the lead character, what he symbolizes as a compelling character of color and the sharp social commentary woven throughout the series. A deeper and sustained reading, however, reveals a comic milieu layered with cultural cues that are greater than the sum of its parts. Maybe it is the fact that the creator of the comic, Enrique Carrion, is black and Puerto Rican or that the setting is a sci-fi Neverland of super science and fantasy futurism that mesh together with nearly imperceptible precision that renders any traditional racial stereotype obsolete on arrival. Whereas the *Santerians* drew directly from the Santeria religion to articulate a literal expression of syncretic Afro-Latino culture, Carrion's *Vescell* has Agent Barrino's actions articulate a subtler deployment of Afro-Latino cultural cues. For example, issue no. 1 opens with Barrino holding an impromptu spirit ritual in a hotel room that will channel his deceased girlfriend, Avery, the love of his life, to possess the body of a prostitute he's paying.[14] This is a more complicated and ambitious allusion to the tension between the sacred and the profane than the type represented by Quesada's *Santerians*.

Furthermore, the figure of Barrino foregrounds blackness in a manner that is not wedded to provincial notions of race that make his black and Latino personhood a dueling point of distress for the character. For instance, Barrino is not circumscribed to primarily protecting his community of color from various villains or devoted to cleaning up his neighborhood from the local street gang.[15] These two dilemmas are quite often interchangeably used to situate and signal to the audience the racial expectations of a lead character of color. Certainly, the Santerians suffer from this trope along with a myriad of black superheroes. *Vescell* stands in contrast to this trend by presenting the lead character operating in a totally alternative and futuristic earth world where racial distinction is present but not a source of objection. Issue no. 5 of *Vescell* provides a great example of how race and ethnic distinction are present in the comic without indulging in the type of race neutrality that serves to flatten "blackness" and negate the racial hybridity that Barrino represents. The cover provocatively displays Agent Barrino surrounded by several differently dressed figures that resemble Adolf Hitler, with a blonde woman sharing center stage with Barrino as she smooches his cheek. Like the covers of the Green Lantern and Green Arrow superhero comic books from the 1970s, the front image telegraphs what type of controversy to expect inside.[16]

In the alternative world of *Vescell*, a Nazi super-science experiment saved Adolf Hitler from capture. In the aptly titled double entendre "Hitler's a Bitch," Agent Barrino finds himself trying to save Hazel Braun, a beautiful blonde tycoon who had the mind and soul of Adolf Hitler fused to her when she was a little girl.[17] (See figure 13.4.)

Decades later Barrino stands between the men who wish to transfer Hitler into another body in order to unleash the full fury of Hitler's evil. Hazel Braun confides to Barrino that she has fought to control him but her willpower is diminishing. Despite this dire development, she tells Barrino she enjoys infuriating her unwelcomed parasite by celebrating Hanukkah and making love to black men. Barrino accommodates her. The raw sexual politics of race are clearly on display across several panels in this story line. Adolf Hitler represents white supremacy writ large, and Barrino's response to Hazel Braun's invitation indicates that Barrino identifies as black (at least) in the political sense of the word. Given the context, black identity for Barrino articulates black sexuality as not only an act of political defiance but possibly an act of liberation. Of course, this is a problematic formula which is part of a well-trod debate that surfaced in Richard Wright's novel *Native Son* (1940) with Bigger Thomas, Melvin Van Peebles's black sex performer turned revolutionary in the film *Sweet Sweetback's Baadasssss Song* (1971), and the cresting hyper-masculinity of hip-hop in the 1990s. Nevertheless, Barrino's sexual amenability to Hazel Braun's request signals that black is an identity he embraces in relationship to his Latinoness. Accordingly, this particular issue of *Vescell* offers a potent mix of racial and sexual politics that prompts the reader to recognize that Mauricio Barrino is not merely a character that happens to be black but a figure that dialogues with blackness comfortably and is self-aware of his racial identity. For that reason, a Blatino character that is not rendered as some exotic and by implication nonblack black figure is a significant point of analysis in *Vescell*. In other words, blackness appears to hold a privileged position and is self-consciously deployed in the face of potent expressions of white racism in the comic. To their credit, Enrique Carrion as writer and John Upchurch as illustrator have embraced and integrated "blackness" as a political aspect of a holistic racial identity of the Blatino lead character.

Most importantly, the example above is a symbol for how Blatinoness can work to articulate a political meaning rather than operating solely as a facile representation of difference. If this political sensibility is present, an accurate fusing of Black with Latino as a representation of Blatino identity requires some type of connection to the struggles for racial justice in America and across the globe. Certainly within an American sociocultural context the danger of privileging blackness to such an extent is that it limits or denies the expression of language, meaningful dialogue, and affirmation of Latino ethnicity. Nonetheless, as we go back and forth between blackness, nationalities, and origins, we begin to list over and over again the categories and details that

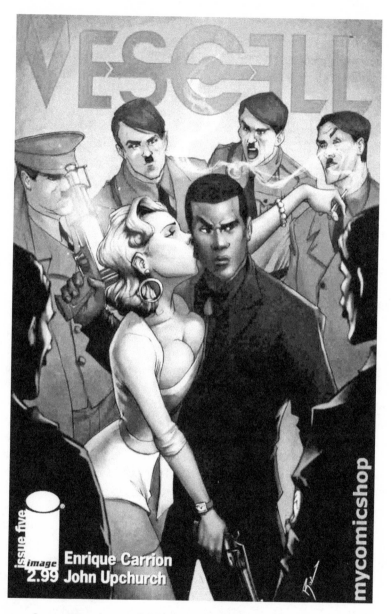

13.4. Cover art from Issue 5, "Hitler's a Bitch," *Vescell*.

in the end reveal the illusion of the concrete border between peoples. Merging experiences curve the identities and delicate association Latinos have with one's own blackness. One may claim Cuban, Belizean, Dominican, or even American with the blurring of lines and complexion categories that continue to push people to either divide or attach, separate or accept their new world reality that they are also "black." This is Blatinoness at its most centered articulation of racial and ethnic identity, a united sense of self along with African Americans, black Caribbean folk, and various Latino populations. From this *idealized* position as a reference point, "blackness" enters into a conversation geared toward mapping the syncretic and fluid boundaries of black racial representation and Latino ethnicity as a result of the Great Migrations stemming from Mississippi, Jamaica, a relative from Haiti, or some scattered attachment to Africa in general.

At its best, an Afro-Latino identity should not disproportionately express values or an identity that is exclusive of the other but provide an opportunity for blackness to become connected to other communities of color across Latin America and vice versa. Arguably, a textbook pop cultural example of such a sensibility is Ricardo "Rico" Tubbs (Philip Michael Thomas), the co-star of the 1980s television show *Miami Vice* (1984–1989). Say what you will about the pastel fashion choices, the no-socks-with-loafers look, five o'clock shadows for twenty-four-hour days, and the constant barrage of stereotypical South American drug lords that spanned the series, *Miami Vice* was also responsible for broadcasting an innovative take on Blatino representation. The backstory for Tubbs's character has his older brother, Rafael Tubbs, a detective for the New York Police Department like himself, murdered by the notorious drug baron Esteban Calderon (Miguel Piñero). Rico chases several leads that take him to Miami and eventually lead to his partnering with Sonny to take down various criminals and drug kingpins over a five-year run that oscillated between being a spectacularly hip and a pathetically mundane cop show.

Although James "Sonny" Crockett (Don Johnson) was the lead character in the television crime drama series, on the whole, Rico Tubbs supplied the hipness quotient of the show about two undercover detectives working in Miami. Admittedly, as the series progressed, not only did Rico Tubbs's screen time significantly diminish, but when he was on screen, he was often a mute bystander. Nevertheless, the first two seasons of the show stand out as a noteworthy representation of a cutting-edge Afro-Latino identity. While the show avoided definitively delving into the racial pedigree and politics of the character, a variety of cultural clues were put in place that clearly telegraphed that Tubbs was black and Latino. On one hand, Ricardo Tubbs and his brother Rafael have Latino-sounding names, and Tubbs speaks fluent Spanish in various episodes, which clearly signal he is not only African American. On the other hand, Tubbs never appears estranged from his blackness, a point suggested by his romantic involvement with African American women and also articulated with his use of a Jamaican/Caribbean patois in several undercover guises. In this sense, Rico Tubbs signifies a multilayered hybridity of race and culture that transcends American borders and the stringent notions of race found in America. Moreover, given that Rico Tubbs emerges in America's collective pop cultural consciousness during the conservative racial politics of the Reagan era, a bilingual black character swaggering to and fro in designer double-breasted suits with grace and style is ideologically striking.

Admittedly, *Miami Vice* would wear out its welcome as a synth-pop music-video crime drama shortly after its tremendous popularity, but the subversive magnitude of Rico Tubbs left an extant racial image, a Blatino character unapologetically secure in being both black and Latino. A similar sensibility registers in *Vescell* with Enrique Carrion's Agent Barrino character, an Afro-futuristic 007 that makes James Bond look like Napoleon Dynamite. This is an important sensibility given the historical record of deeming blackness a social and cultural albatross when linked to Latinoness. Take, for example, the status of blackness in the island country of the Dominican Republic, where an invented category, "indio," is used to recategorize black Dominicans as something other than black and descendants of African people that were enslaved for sugar production and, later, cattle ranching.[18] Unquestionably, African Americans have also engaged in all kinds of racial tomfoolery when it comes to anxieties concerning skin complexion, and this is an issue across Latin America as well. There is Michael Jackson's public transformation and struggle with racial insecurity around his complexion and the width of his nose. (For more on this topic see Ginetta E. B. Candelario's *Black Behind the Ears*.) Unfortunately, Afro-Latinos are not removed from similar public spectacles of racial transmogrification. The retired Dominican-born major league baseball slugger and formerly dark-complexioned Sammy Sosa began making public appearances after his "rejuvenation" treatments with green contact lenses, a conkified hairstyle, and significantly lighter skin. The result was a pale version of Sammy Sosa that stood in stark contrast to the "black" man that had hit more than five hundred homeruns as a professional baseball player.

To what extent and degree Blatinos struggle with their blackness is for sociologists and psychologists to operationalize. But as a cultural signifier, the connection and attachment to their blackness are inescapable for Blatina/o individuals whether or not they accept it. Even if they come from a place more attached to the idea of being "Spanish" and actively reach for their Latina/o roots, they must also reach for their blackness and reject exoticism when the question, "*What are you?*" is asked. Consequently, one must reject the internal impulse or socially acceptable tendency to indulge in imagining an exotic mix of backgrounds and feel a sense of dubious pride by volunteering a long list of ethnic backgrounds that place black/African at the end (if at all) of that list. Rather, a Blatina/o exists in a third space whereby blackness is not denied and one's Latin heritage is not diminished. Ultimately, however, in the political sense of racial formation, America has a habit of reminding the Latina/o person how black she or he is or can become.

The Zoot Suit Riots of the 1940s, urban gentrification, racial tensions in Arizona over undocumented immigration, and the perverse racial punditry of celebrity presidential candidate Donald Trump concerning Mexican immigrants are a few of the political stepping-stones that Latinos have faced and continue to confront that resonate with the type of racial struggles black folk have encountered in the past. Nevertheless, against the current cultural backdrop of America's first black president, the articulation of black racial formation as social protest and unrest has receded into the background as an informed source of identity, aesthetic, or grounds for critiquing white privilege. Apparently, with a black man in the White House, everything is post-racial in America. Yet, brown and Blatino racial formation in America poses new vistas of racial transformation. Scholar and cultural critic Patricia Hill Collins defines the issue of the shifting multiracial character of America most succinctly:

> Latino populations play a pivotal role in reinforcing and challenging long-standing racial meanings. Latino populations have an established history in the United States. What is new is the size of this population and the diversity of groups who now fall under the rubric "Latino." On the one hand, Latino populations may choose to replicate racial triangles *within* the category of Latino, giving benefits to those who are biologically White and discriminating against those who appear to be native or Black. On the other hand, because Latino populations encompass multiple racial categories, such populations can dissolve power dynamics of the foundational racial triangle by embracing the multiracial character of their own population. Moreover, because no fixed boundary exists between Latino and other groups . . . the Latino population has the ability to constitute a new center of American national identity that is deeply enmeshed with other populations.[19]

Whether this transformation fully surfaces as only a symbolic nod toward diversity or a literal incorporation and remapping of this nation's racial Badlands to reflect an expansive pan-racial borderland, popular culture mediums may provide the best clues to the grand guessing game that is race relations in America. The latter sensibility is being asserted, albeit tentatively, in the ethnically overdetermined Santerians, a racially blasé Blatino Spider-Man, the racially self-assured comic book Agent "Moo" Barrino, Blatino baseball players (from the Caribbean in particular) who hold significant stature across America's national pastime (special old-school shout-out to Roberto Clemente), and the scores of black and brown folk that have self-consciously committed to claiming the indeterminate cultural geography of what it means to be both Black and Latino not as existential quandary but as distinctive expressions of the face of the global future, a pan-racial and multicultural America.

NOTES

1. John Storm Roberts, *The Latin Tinge: The Impact of Latin American Music on the United States* (Oxford University Press: 1999), and Miriam Jiménez Román and Juan Flores's *The Afro-Latin@ Reader: History and Culture in the United States* (Duke University Press: 2010).

2. Jeff Chang, *Can't Stop Won't Stop: A History of the Hip Hop Generation.* (New York: St. Martin's Press, 2005).

3. Brian Truitt, "Half-Black, Half-Hispanic Spider-Man Revealed," *USA Today* (2 Aug. 2011), and Michael Cavna, "Miles Morales: Check Out Sara Pichelli Inking the New Ultimate Spider-Man," *The Washington Post* (16 Aug. 2011).

4. Steve Saffel, *Spider-Man the Icon: The Life and Times of a Pop Culture Phenomenon* (Titan Books: 2007).

5. Spencer R. Weart, *Nuclear Fear: A History of Images* (Cambridge, MA: Harvard University Press, 1988).

6. See, in this volume, Kathryn M. Frank's essay "Everybody Wants to Rule the Multiverse: Latino Spider-Men in Marvel's Media Empire" and Isabel Millán's "Anya Sofía (Araña) Corazón: The Inner Webbings and Mexi-Ricanization of Spider-Girl" for in-depth discussions of the comic book industry practice of marginalizing Latina/o characters.

7. *The Amazing Spider-Man*, Marvel, May, no. 252, 1984.

8. *Super Black: American Pop Culture and Black Superheroes* (University of Texas Press: 2011), 144–145.

9. Ronald P. Formisano, *Boston against Busing: Race, Class, and Ethnicity in the 1960s and 1970s* (The University of North Carolina Press: 2003).

10. See *Super Black: American Pop Culture and Black Superheroes* (University of Texas Press: Austin, 2011).

11. See "The Alien Is Here to Stay: Otherness, Anti-Assimilation, and Empowerment in Latino/a Superhero Comics" by Mauricio Espinoza in this volume. See also George Brandon, *Santeria from Africa to the New World: The Dead Sell Memories* (Indiana University Press: 1997).

12. See Jeffery Brown, *Black Superheroes, Milestone Comics, and Their Fans* (University of Mississippi Press: 2000).

13. See George Brandon, *Santeria from Africa to the New World: The Dead Sell Memories* (Indiana University Press: 1997), 158–162, for a rigorous discussion around the syncretic features of Santeria.

14. Enrique Carrion's *Vescell* (Image Comics: Aug., no. 1, 2011).

15. Phillip Lamarr Cunningham, "The Absence of Black Supervillains in Mainstream Comics," *Journal of Graphic Novels and Comics* 1.1 (June 2010): 51–62.

16. *Super Black: American Pop Culture and Black Superheroes* (University of Texas Press: 2011), 9–35.

17. *Vescell* (Image Comics: January, no. 5, 2012).

18. See Ginetta E. B. Candelario's insightful book *Black Behind the Ears: Dominican Racial Identity from Museums to Beauty Shops* (Duke University Press: 2007).

19. See *From Black Power to Hip Hop: Racism, Nationalism, and Feminism* by Patricia Hill Collins (Temple University Press: 2006), 51.

FOURTEEN

THE PARADOX OF MILES MORALES: SOCIAL GATEKEEPING AND THE BROWNING OF AMERICA'S SPIDER-MAN

BRIAN MONTES

Marvel is taking the mantle of their flagship character—one of the most important characters in the hands of a kid who reflects a more accurate portrayal of the diversity of where we are in the world right now. DAVID BETANCOURT (*WASHINGTON POST*)

Oh my God, it's Lou Dobbs' worst nightmare, a Latino that can climb walls. JON STEWART (AUGUST 4, 2011)

ON AUGUST 4, 2011, Jon Stewart, then host of Comedy Central's *The Daily Show*, aired a segment titled "The Dividing of America." In this segment Stewart satirically admonished Lou Dobbs's criticism of Miles Morales (see figure 14.1), Marvel Comics's new Ultimate Spider-Man, for being Latino.[1] "It's Lou Dobbs' worst nightmare," Stewart remarked, "a Latino that can climb walls." While brief and entertaining, the segment shed light on two rather distinct issues: (1) the controversy surrounding the reimagining of Marvel's Ultimate Spider-Man as Afro-Latino and (2) the nativist stance on immigration and the "browning" of the United States of America. Lou Dobbs, an anchor for the CNN network at the time, was denounced by the Southern Poverty Law Center for his affiliation with the anti-immigration group FAIR (Federation for American Immigration Reform). A strong proponent of the mass deportation of undocumented persons, Lou Dobbs included Miles Morales in one of his diatribes against the rapid growth of Latina/o populations in the United States. Sadly, Lou Dobbs was not alone in his sentiment. While many fans of Marvel's *Ultimate Comics Spider-Man* series were optimistic concerning the creative direction in which a new and reimagined Spider-Man could take them, others, like Dobbs, questioned the rationale for Spider-Man's sudden change in race and ethnicity.

Reflecting the paradox of multiculturalism imbued within multiracial and

14.1. Miles is bitten by a radioactive spider, from *Ultimate Comics Spider-Man*.

multiethnic societies, the introduction of Miles Morales as Marvel's new Ultimate Spider-Man not only signifies a progressive shift in attitude by mainstream literary outlets in promoting characters traditionally reserved for niche markets but also reveals the preservation of hegemonic structures that further subordinate historically marginalized groups. In this essay I examine the angst and controversy surrounding the introduction of Miles Morales through the theoretical lens of border crossings and social inspections. Through an analysis of demographic representation and spatial isolation, I argue that even within the multicultural imaginary of Marvel's multiverse, social borders are still maintained in safeguarding a white, Eurocentric spatial privilege. Despite being a rather progressive medium, the superhero genre continues to reflect our nation's unrelenting struggle with race and the politics of multiculturalism (Rifas, "Race and Comix").

MILES MORALES: A SPIDER-MAN FOR THE TWENTY-FIRST CENTURY

Addressing the significance of New York City within the genre of comics, Dennis O'Neil, former editor of *Batman*, once infamously described Gotham as "Manhattan below Fourteenth Street at 3 a.m., November 28 in a cold year" and Metropolis as Manhattan "between Fourteenth and One Hundred and Tenth Street on the brightest, sunniest July day of the year" (Boichel 9). Reflecting upon O'Neil's statement, I contend that the characterization of

New York City within the pages of Marvel Comics is indeed indicative of a divided metropolis. However, rather than focusing simply on the dichotomy of its neighborhoods, I argue, in line with Frederick Luis Aldama (*Multicultural Comics*) and Leonard Rifas ("Race and Comix"), that this division is also predicated on the existence of a constructed racial dichotomy that continues to marginalize and tokenize persons of color.[2] Despite significant efforts made to diversify its imagery and its imaginings of New York City, the city remains, even within the genre of nonwhite superhero comics, a racially white city.

Contrary to popular imaginings in both television and print, however, New York City is not a racially monolithic society. According to data collected in 2013 by the Hispanic Federation, Latinas/os account for one quarter of New York City's population, with the New York City metro area comprising 2.4 million Latinas/os.[3] Puerto Ricans, a group of which Miles Morales is attributed to be a member, have a long and well-established history in New York City. By 1960, more than one million Puerto Ricans had migrated to the United States, with well over six hundred thousand Puerto Ricans living in the city of New York (according to the US Census). Today Puerto Ricans make up the largest Latina/o population in New York City and account for nearly one third (31.2 percent) of New York City's Latina/o population (according to the Hispanic Federation). Representing a large demographic of the New York City population, it would only seem fitting that Latinas/os, and more specifically Puerto Ricans, play a prominent role in the story lines surrounding New York's most beloved crime fighters. Regrettably, they do not.

With the exception of a few notable characters (Angel Espinosa, aka Skin; Antonio "Tony" Stark, aka [Ultimate] Iron Man; Angela del Toro, aka White Tiger; and Añya Sofia Corazon, aka Spider-Girl), Marvel's Latina/o population remains relatively absent from New York's comic lore.[4] This is not to say that Latina/o characters do not play an important role in the genre; they do (see Aldama, *Your Brain on Latino Comics*). As Frederick Luis Aldama and Christopher González note in the introduction to this anthology, "Today, Marvel and DC (including its Vertigo imprint) have a fuller array of fleshed-out, single-issue Latino characters." Most, as Aldama and González also note, are relegated to a secondary or peripheral status, emerging simply for the purpose of establishing a multicultural anecdote. While the absence of a Latina/o demographic is noticeable in several of Marvel's New York–centric series, their most conspicuous absence occurs in Marvel's flagship series, *The Amazing Spider-Man*. Spanning more than five decades, characters such as Peter Parker, Mary Jane Watson, Gwen Stacy, Ben Reilly, Felicia Hardy, Eddie Brock, John Jonah Jameson, Jr., Max Modell, Harry Osborn, Cletus Kassidy, and Dr. Kurt Conners represent a rather homogenous and/or Eurocentric imagining of New York City.

This white spatial imaginary is compounded by the fact that Parker lives in the relatively suburban neighborhood of Forest Hills, Queens. According to 2010 data collected by the Forest Hills Chamber of Commerce, the neighborhood of Forest Hills, Queens, is a relatively prosperous neighborhood that includes one of New York City's most exclusive neighborhoods, Forest Hills Gardens. Miles Morales, on the other hand, resides in an undisclosed Brooklyn neighborhood. Based on 2012 statistics gathered by the U.S. Census Bureau, about 22 percent of families and one quarter (25.1 percent) of the population of Brooklyn live below the poverty line. This is in stark contrast to Forest Hills, Queens, which, with a median household income of $65,000, is well above the Brooklyn average of $42,000 (citydata.com).

According to Jesse Schedeen of IGN.com, the *Ultimate Comics: Spider-Man* series starring Miles Morales is meant to take place in a "more urban, racially diverse, and tense landscape" (n. pag.). Schedeen (n. pag.) further goes on to state that "Miles is simply a character who speaks to a slightly different teen experience, and one not nearly as well represented in superhero comics as Peter's." This urban "teen experience" includes the winning of admission into a charter school (see Nama and Haddad, this volume), interracial children, and the presence of other diverse ethnic/racial characters, including his best friend, Ganke, roommate, Judge, superhero Cloak, and the villains the Prowler, the Taskmaster, and the Scorpion. What you have, according to Axel Alonso (n. pag.), Editor-in-Chief of Marvel Comics, "is a Spider-Man for the 21st century."[5]

Despite the efforts made by Alonzo and others to create a New York City representative of its proper demographics, Latinas/os continue to exist in what Scott McCloud (61) refers to as the "limbo of the gutters": the white space formed by the inner margins of two facing pages or panels. Gutters, according to McCloud, are one of the most important narrative tools in comics. They delineate the boundaries and allow the reader to understand what is happening from one scene to the next. This, McCloud (66) points out, includes seeing what is not there. Excluded from the white spatial imaginary of Marvel Comics, Latinas/os are sentenced to exist within the margins of the panels. That is, while minorities are not actually seen, readers are to believe that they are nonetheless there, residing somewhere in the gutter.[6]

The term *gutter*, however, is also defined by Merriam-Webster's dictionary as "the lowest or most vulgar level or condition of human life." Relegated to the literary imaginations of comic readers, Latinas/os are also placed in the gutters of US society through their attempted exclusion from a real-world white spatial imaginary. This has included, within the past several years, the singing of "God Bless America" by famed Puerto Rican salsa singer Marc Anthony during the 2013 Major League Baseball All-Star Game, the 2010 Tucson Unified School District book ban that included Latina/o literary classics such as *Yo Soy Joaquin/I Am Joaquin* by Rodolfo "Corky" Gonzales, and the proposed textbook changes by the Texas State Board of Education that would seek to downplay topics like civil rights and Latina/o, particularly Mexican-American, history. As demonstrated by the example of Lou Dobbs earlier in this essay, this system of social gatekeeping would also target Miles Morales. Attempting to move beyond the plane of white space known as the gutter, Morales, like many of his real-world counterparts, would also encounter social inspections part and parcel of a larger project of white racial hegemony.[7]

INSPECTIONS AND BORDER CROSSINGS

Following the epic announcement that Miles Morales would become Marvel's new Ultimate Spider-Man, comic enthusiasts, pundits, and Internet bloggers quickly turned to social media outlets in an effort to rationalize Peter Parker's new successor. The commentary was both encouraging and unfriendly. Those who welcomed the change inundated Marvel's editors with praise and approval. In a letter published in the editorial section of issue 24 (2012) of Marvel's *Ultimate Comics: Spider-Man*, Michael Minaya, a Dominican from New York, writes,

> I am an average Dominican teenager from Uptown, New York. I am new when it comes to reading comic books. Ever since the late 90's and early 00's I've watched animated TV shows based on heroes like Spider-Man. I rarely picked up a comic book until I started reading about Miles Morales the new Spider-Man. I couldn't believe it: A hero with the same skin color and a last name almost identical to mine. (n. pag.)

Others, however, branded Miles a media ploy, a liberal attempt to market diversity and garner media attention. One such comment, posted August 14, 2011, on Chicagonewsreport.com, read, "The comic industry is ridiculously liberal and never misses an opportunity to crap all over white culture and world contributions." Another comment posted on the above-mentioned website anonymously read that "political correctness comes at the expense of another [white] race . . . affirmative action, special demands/special concessions and acknowledgments are inherently racist." Partaking in the vitriol against political correctness, another blogger posted on Entertainmentweekly.com that

"minorities always seem to find their way into roles established by white characters (Matrix's Fishburne as Perry White?), but it never seems to work the
opposite way does it?"[8] Glenn Beck, a politically conservative American television and radio host, even made note that Miles Morales looked a lot like
Barack Obama and blamed the Obama administration for wanting to change
what he asserted was American tradition.

By assigning the alleged disadvantages of whites to Miles Morales, these
individuals articulate an investment in whiteness through a discourse of cultural inheritance. References to "special demands" and "PC bullying" become semantic signifiers employed to prevent Anglo cultural corrosion by
reinforcing white supremacy through the inspection and the rejection of non-
white characters. The social inspection of Miles Morales is particularly useful
in the imaginary of New York City, where not only has the white population
become the minority population but cultural and national identities continue
to overlap and blend in a multicultural and multiracial borderland (Anzaldúa).

The "erosion" of the cultural and ideological hegemony of the United
States by the mere presence of a fictitious character like Miles Morales caused
racially conservative segments of our society to perpetuate a fictitious status
quo of privilege that for many people remains till this day "a vested right,
a status, [and] a part of the order of things" (Rosaldo xii). Equating Miles
Morales with affirmative action not only reinforces white hegemony but also
positions the city of New York, at least within the pages of tales of our nation's
superheroes, as a space that should remain inherently white.

Like Arizona's controversial Senate Bill 1070, which serves as the basis
for the social inspection of Arizona's nonwhite population, the policing of
and angst toward Miles Morales function as a form of social gatekeeping that
allows some to be the sole proprietors of tradition through the discriminatory
objectification of others. This form of societal gatekeeping is upheld by the use
of inspections stations "which inspect, monitor, and survey what goes in and
out in the name of class, race, and nation" (Lugo 355), a sociocultural passport
that acknowledges one's social validity.

Ironically, Miles Morales demonstrates no Puerto Rican or Latina/o
cultural markers. Unlike other notable Latina/o characters, such as Araña,
Vibe, and Blue Beetle, we never see Miles speak in Spanish. There is no code
switching. There is no indication that Miles has ever been to Puerto Rico
or that he even knows any other Puerto Rican/Latina/o kids. Brian Michael
Bendis, writer and creator of Miles Morales, barely makes any mention of
Miles's ethnicity. There is no cultural mythology to Miles Morales in the
vein of *El Muerto* (1989) by Javier Hernandez—a character that Mauricio
Espinoza discusses at length in this collection. There is no attempt on the

part of Bendis to use Morales as a token for multiculturalism in the vein of Aña Sofía Corazón, aka Araña. The only marker of Miles's *latinidad* is his last name.⁹ The storytelling of Miles is centered on his experiences not as an Afro-Latino, as is the case with other nonwhite characters, but rather as a young urban kid. Miles, for all intents and purposes, remains culturally unmarked: a sanitized version of multiculturalism that ought to remain palatable to a white, normative America.

In addition, Miles Morales was not the first attempt at Hispanicizing Spider-Man. In 1992, Marvel Comics introduced Miguel O'Hara, a light-skinned biracial variation of Spider-Man, for their 2099 imprint (again see Kathryn M. Frank's essay in this volume). What sets Miles apart from Miguel O'Hara—and this is where Miles's racialization as a *Blatino* (see Adilifu Nama and Maya Haddad in this volume on their use of the term *Blatino*) becomes significantly substantial—whereas Miguel O'Hara was the first attempt at a Latino Spider-Man, Morales was created subsequent to the racial reimagining of Marvel's standard 616 Universe Nick Fury.

Inspired by the actor Samuel L. Jackson, Marvel reimagined Nick Fury for their Ultimate Universe imprint in 2001. Originally a character created as a white male in 1963, Nick Fury was reimagined as an African American male in Marvel's Ultimate Universe. Samuel L. Jackson would later go on to appear as Nick Fury in a number of commercially successful films based on several Marvel properties, including Marvel's *The Avengers*. The result was rather unprecedented. In 2012, as a result of the popularity and iconography of Jackson's Nick Fury in both the films and animated television, Marvel retired the original Nick Fury and replaced him with his son, Nick Fury, Jr., who just so happened to be African American. Marvel, in a surreptitious move that would echo political correctness, literally changed Nick Fury from a white character to a black character in its standard canonical universe.

Unwilling to accept another Nick Fury and blind to the fact that Miles exists in an alternate universe, conservative pundits and comic traditionalists lashed out at Miles Morales and immediately sought to delegitimize him for reasons that are emblematic of our nation's culture wars. Morales became more than another version of Spider-Man. Instead, Morales became a literal rewriting of Spider-Man and had the potential to replace Peter Parker as Spider-Man. As with Parker, a radioactive spider bites Miles. Miles also suffers the death of a loved family member—a death for which he, like Parker, blames himself.

Ill-prepared for the burden of power and responsibility bestowed upon him, Miles, again like Parker, renounces his duties as Spider-Man. It is discernible throughout the narrative of the series that Miles is not some arbitrary "arc" that would see the return of a deceased or vanquished superhero but an actual reimagining of both Parker and Spider-Man, a retelling that features corresponding events, corresponding characters, corresponding images but that stars as its protagonist a young Afro-Latino.

When considered pragmatically, however, the disdain toward Miles becomes moot. Peter Parker's death occurs in Marvel's Ultimate Universe. Simply put, Miles is not a part of Marvel's canon. Rather, Miles's existence is restricted to Marvel's Ultimate Universe, an alternate reality that I argue exists apropos of the United States during the Jim Crow era. This, however, was thought to change. In late 2013, rumors began circulating on the Internet and other social media outlets that Cataclysm, an epic event in the Ultimate Universe timeline, would end the fourteen-year run of Marvel's Ultimate Universe and that Miles, being the sole survivor, would at last cross over into Marvel's standard 616 universe. Many even speculated that Miles Morales would replace Peter Parker as Marvel's Superior Spider-Man.[10] Alas, the reports were untrue. On January 14, 2014, various media outlets reported that Miles Morales would star in two new Ultimate series: in *Miles Morales: Ultimate Spider Man* and as the leader of the *All-New Ultimates*. Despite a short visit to Marvel's standard universe, Morales was once again confined to exist in a parallel universe. Unlike Nick Fury, Spider-Man would not undergo any changes in either his race or his ethnicity.

The ramifications of Miles's exclusion from Marvel's standard universe are telling. Despite its roots in a white spatial imaginary, comics are and have long been notorious for crossing social and metaphysical borders. Characters like Green Arrow and the X-Men are particularly celebrated within the white spatial imaginary of mainstream comics for confronting racial and socioeconomic barriers. It becomes disquieting, then, when one considers the limitations placed upon Miles Morales. Comics, for the uninitiated, are well known for participating in crossover events. During this period, comic book characters often bleed into the pages of other comic books, allowing epic scenarios as well as fantasy team-ups to transpire. The mini-series *Spider-Men* is an example of this. In this six-issue mini-series, Peter Parker is transported to the Ultimate Universe, where he not only deals with the death of his alternate ultimate self but eventually approves of Mile Morales as the new Ultimate Spider-Man. What stands out in this mini-series is the fact that Miles, for reasons that are perhaps essential to the development of his own mythology within Marvel's Ultimate Universe, never crosses over into Marvel's standard universe. It is Parker who crosses into Miles's universe. At the end of the series we see Parker, back in Marvel's standard universe, looking up Miles on the Internet (see figure 14.2). The rest is open for interpretation.

After looking Morales up, Peter's face, along with the aid of a text bubble

14.2. Peter Parker searching for Miles Morales on the Internet.

that reads "Oh my God," suggests that Miles does indeed exist, in some shape or form, in Marvel's 616 universe. Remarkably, however, we don't see Miles. His existence, like most Latinas/os in mainstream comics, is once again relegated to the imagination of the reader. Miles exists exclusively in the gutter.

The separate-but-equal status of Miles and Parker furthers the argument that the social imaginary of Marvel Comics, while more diverse than before, remains structured by a white spatial imaginary. Like contemporary discourses that position Latinas/os as foreigners, aliens, and undeserving inheritors of "special demands," Miles's exclusion further constitutes his illegitimacy. Marvel Comics's Ultimate Universe, while essential to the reimagining of Marvel's standard universe, also serves as a border delineator, one in which Miles is not given permission to pass. Like all social relations, comic book characters also exist within an interpersonal binary "that exists, historically, between subjects in relations of power" (Clifford 15). Even when rumors suggested that Miles would cross over into the 616, we were reassured that Miles would stay in the Ultimate Universe.

Read collectively with borderlands studies (Rosaldo, Anzaldúa) and social border inspections (Lugo, *Reflections on Border Theory*), the pages of Marvel Comics's *New Ultimate Spider-Man* simultaneously function as sites of inclusion and exclusion, where diversity is exhibited but dominance is fortified through the maintenance of a Eurocentric status quo. The use of borderland theories along with a social purview function makes clear Miles Morales's limited access to the social domain through the regulation of inclusion.

Noting that it is common for mainstream comics to ignore borders, and recognizing the fact that Miles Morales remains confined to Marvel's Ultimate Universe, however, creates a stunning realization that despite the efforts by writers and publishers to diversify the genre, these individuals, along with their creations, remain subject to the scrutiny of social border inspections. By utilizing Miles Morales as a case study, I argue, in the vein of Aldama, Nama, and Royal, that Miles Morales is indeed symbolic of the politics of multiculturalism in that he represents the disputed spaces of power, privilege, and national identity. Like Arizona's controversial Senate Bill 1070 or the angst surrounding the singing of the national anthem during the 2013 MLB All-Star Game, the policing of Miles Morales functions as a form of societal gatekeeping which serves to reify the presumed inheritors of this nation. Spider-Man, along with his emblematic costume of red, blue, and some white, is a privilege to be inherited and enjoyed exclusively by whites, and despite being a pioneering figure in the genre, Miles Morales reminds us of the fact that even in the twenty-first century, not all border crossings are possible.[11]

NOTES

1. For more on Morales, please see Kathryn M. Frank and Adilifu Nama and Maya Haddad within this edited volume.

2. Isabel Millán and Kathryn M. Frank document in their respective essays in this volume the strategic yet paradoxical ways in which *latinidad* is marketed to consumers.

3. New York State has the fourth-largest Latina/o population in the United States, representing 6.6 percent of the total Latina/o population in the nation (Hispanic Federation 2013).

4. The Latinization of Tony Stark is only reflected in Marvel's Ultimate Universe. For more on the functionality of the multiverse, please see Kathryn M. Frank's essay in this volume.

5. Noting the demographic shifts in society, the movie industry has also taken the liberty of altering the racial/ethnic background of several notable characters to reflect a more diverse twenty-first century. These include The Kingpin in *Daredevil* (2004), Perry White in *Man of Steel* (2013), Electro in *Amazing Spider-Man 2* (2014), and Johnny Storm in the recent *Fantastic Four* film.

6. The only significant Latina/o character in the fifty-year run of Marvel's *Amazing*

Spider-Man is Michele Gonzales, a stereotypical Latina with a spitfire attitude who also happens to be preoccupied with her looks.

7. Marc Anthony sang "God Bless America" for the MLB 2013 All-Star Game. During his rendition, social media became abuzz with references to Marc Anthony's race and ethnicity. Detractors made note that Marc Anthony, who was incorrectly identified as Mexican and a noncitizen, did not have the right to sing what was an "American song."

8. The notion that only whites are replaced by people of color is not true. Bane, Latin American born and raised, is whitened in the film *The Dark Knight Rises* (2012). Actor Tom Hardy, who plays Bane, reveals to Vulture.com (July 17, 2012) that his accent was inspired by Irish boxer Bartley Gorman.

9. I believe that the use of his maternal surname, Morales, also represents a strategic attempt on behalf of his creators to deracialize Morales and decentralize Morales's racial sensibility as an African American male.

10. In June 2015 it was announced that Miles Morales, following the aftermath of Marvel's *Secret Wars* story line, would finally become part of Marvel's standard canonical universe (Forrest C. Helvie, "Miles Morales Moves to the Marvel Universe in Spider-Man," 22 June 2015, http://marvel.com/news/comics/24751/miles_morales_moves_to_the_marvel_universe_in_spider-man#ixzz3h7QOtas1). Both Miles Morales and Peter Parker would share the mantle of Marvel's Spider-Man.

11. In early February 2015, it was reported that Marvel Studios had acquired the rights to use Spider-Man for upcoming movies ("Sony Pictures Entertainment Brings Marvel Studios into the Amazing World of Spider-Man," 9 Feb. 2015, http://marvel.com/news/movies/24062/sony_pictures_entertainment_brings_marvel_studios_into_the_amazing_world_of_spider-man#ixzz3h7Qxp3NT). It was later reported that Andrew Garfield, the actor who had played Peter Parker in the previous two *Amazing Spider-Man* films would not reprise his role as Spider-Man. This has led to the rumor that Donald Glover, the actor who inspired the creation of Miles Morales and who voices Miles Morales in the cartoon series *Ultimate Spider-Man: Web Warriors*, could star as Miles Morales in any upcoming film produced by Marvel Studios. However, in June 2015 it was announced that actor Tom Holland would be cast as the new Spider-Man. Furthermore it was revealed that same month that Peter Parker and his alter ego, Spider-Man, under a licensing agreement between Sony Pictures Entertainment and Marvel Entertainment, must legally be portrayed as white, straight, and male in any future theatrical interpretation. That is, although Miles Morales had finally been accepted into Marvel's standard canon, he would not be making any theatrical appearances as Marvel's Spider-Man.

Acosta-Belen, Edna, and Carlos E. Santiago. "Merging Borders: The Remapping of America." *Latino Studies Reader: Culture, Economy, and Society.* Ed. Antonia Darder and Rodolfo D. Torres. Malden: Blackwell, 1998. 29–42. Print.

Ahmed, Sara. *On Being Included: Racism and Diversity in Institutional Life.* Durham: Duke UP, 2012. Print.

Alcaraz, Lalo. *La Cucaracha,* Kansas City: Andrew McMeel, 2004.

———. laloalcaraz.com. Web. Visited 15 Dec. 2013.

———. *Migra Mouse. Political Cartoons on Immigration,* New York: RDV Books, 1994. Print.

Aldama, Frederick Luis. "Characters in Comic Books." *Characters in Fictional Worlds: Understanding Imaginary Beings in Literature, Film, and Other Media.* Ed. Jens Eder, Fotis Jannidis, and Ralf Schneider. Berlin: De Gruyter, 2010. 318–328. Print.

———. *Mex-Ciné: Mexican Filmmaking, Production, and Consumption in the 21st Century.* Ann Arbor: U of Michigan P, 2013. Print.

———, ed. *Multicultural Comics: From Zap to Blue Beetle.* Austin: U of Texas P, 2010. Print.

———. *The Routledge Concise History of Latino/a Literature.* New York: Routledge, 2012. Print.

———. *A User's Guide to Postcolonial and Borderland Fiction.* Austin: U of Texas P, 2009. Print.

———. *Your Brain on Latino Comics: From Gus Arriola to Los Bros Hernandez.* Austin: U of Texas P, 2009. Print.

Aldama, Frederick Luis, and Patrick Colm Hogan. *Conversations on Cognitive Cultural Studies: Puzzling Out the Self.* Columbus: The Ohio State UP, 2014. Print. ✓

Alonso, Axel. "Reinventing Today's Heroes." *LatinRapper.com,* 2011. Web. 20 Mar. 2014. http://www.latinrapper.com/axel-alonso-interview.html.

Alonzo, Juan J. *Badmen, Bandits, and Folk Heroes: The Ambivalence of Mexican American Identity in Literature and Film.* Tucson: U of Arizona P, 2009. Print.

The Amazing Spider-Man, Issue 252 (May), Marvel, 1984. Print.

Anonymous. Review of *Chance in Hell. Entertainment Weekly* 974 (18 Jan. 2008): 85. Print.

Anonymous. Review of *Chance in Hell. Publisher's Weekly* 254.35 (2 Sept. 2007): 45. Print.

Anonymous. Review of *Troublemakers. Publisher's Weekly.* 257.1 (Jan. 4, 2010): 36. Print.

Anzaldúa, Gloria. *Borderlands/La Frontera: The New Mestiza.* San Francisco: Aunte Lute Books, 1987. Print.

Aparicio, Frances R. "On Subversive Signifiers: Tropicalizing Language in the United States." *Tropicalizations: Transcultural Representations of Latinidad.* Ed. Frances R. Aparicio and Susana Chávez Silverman. Hanover and London: Dartmouth College, 1997. Print.

Aparicio, Frances, and Susana Chávez-Silverman. *Tropicalizations: Transcultural Representations of Latinidad.* Hanover and London: Dartmouth College, 1997. Print.

Appadurai, Arjun. *Fear of Small Numbers: An Essay on the Geography of Anger.* Durham: Duke UP, 2006. Print.

Avery, Fiona. *Araña, Vol. 1: The Heart of the Spider.* New York: Marvel, 2004–2005. Print.

———. *Araña, Vol. 3: Night of the Hunter.* New York: Marvel, 2006. Print.

————. *Araña, Vol. 2: In the Beginning.* New York: Marvel, 2005. Print.

Barbosa, Liria, and Angelina Villarreal. "Acculturation Levels Play Role in Marketing Strategy." *Marketing News* 42.3 (15 Feb. 2008): 26–28. Print.

Bates, Cary, Joe Staton, and Mark Farmer. *The New Guardians.* Issue 7 (Feb.). New York: DC Comics, 1989. Print.

Bedard, Tony, Ig Guara, J. P. Mayer, and Ruy Jose. *Blue Beetle: Vol. 1: Metamorphosis.* New York: DC Comics, 2012. Print.

Bendis, Brian M., Sara Pichelli, and Justin Ponsor. *Spider-Men.* Issue 6. Marvel. Print.

————. *Ultimate Comics All New Spider-Man.* Issue 24. Marvel. Print.

————. *Ultimate Spider-Man.* Issue 3 (Dec.). 2011. Print.

Berlatsky, Eric. "Lost in the Gutter: Within and between Frames in Narrative and Narrative Theory." *Narrative* 17.2 (2009): 162–187. Print.

"A Black Spider-Man? So What? Miguel O'Hara Already Paved the Trail!" *Crimson Monkey.* Web. 14 Jan. 2014. http://www.crimsonmonkey.com/blogs/daveomac/a-black-spider -man-so-what-miguel-o-hara-already-paved-the-trail/.

Boas, Franz. *The Central Eskimo.* Washington, DC: Bureau of American Ethnology Annual Report, Smithsonian Institution, 1888; Lincoln: U of Nebraska P, 1964. Print.

Boichel, Bill. "Batman: Commodity as Myth." *The Many Lives of the Batman: Critical Approaches to a Superhero and His Media.* Ed. Roberta E. Pearson and William Uricchio. New York: Routledge, 1991. 4–17. Print.

Bolling, Ben. "The U.S. HIV/AIDS Crisis and the Negotiation of Queer Identity in Superhero Comics, or, Is Northstar Still a Fairy?" *Comic Books and American Cultural History.* Ed. Matthew Pustz. New York: Continuum, 2012. 202–220. Print.

Brandon, George. *Santeria from Africa to the New World: The Dead Sell Memories.* Indiana UP, 1997. Print.

Brown, Jeffrey A. *Black Superheroes, Milestone Comics, and Their Fans.* Jackson: UP of Mississippi, 2004. Print.

————. "Panthers and Vixens: Black Superheroines, Sexuality, and Stereotypes in Contemporary Comic Books." *Black Comics: Politics of Race and Representation.* Ed. Sheena C. Howard and Ronald L. Jackson II. New York: Bloomsbury, 2013. 133–149. Print.

Buhle, Paul. "History and Comics." *Reviews in American History* 35.2 (2007): 315–323. Print.

Candelario, Ginetta E. B. *Black Behind the Ears: Dominican Racial Identity from Museums to Beauty Shops.* Durham: Duke UP, 2007. Print.

Cantú, Hector, and Hector Castellanos. *Night of the Bilingual Telemarketers: Baldo Collection No. 2.* Kansas City: Andrews McMeel, 2002. Print.

————. *The Lower You Ride, the Cooler You Are: A Baldo Collection.* Kansas City: Andrews McMeel, 2001. Print.

Carrier, David. *The Aesthetics of Comics.* University Park: Pennsylvania State UP, 2000. Print.

Carrillo, Rosario, and Erin Mackinney. Review of *El Alambrista: The Fence Jumper* by Alfonso Sahugun Casus. *Aztlán: A Journal of Chicano Studies* 34.2 (Fall 2009): 225–229. Print.

Carrion, Enrique. *Vescell.* Issue 1 (Aug.). Image Comics, 2011. Print.

————. *Vescell.* Issue 5 (Jan.). Image Comics, 2012. Print.

Cavna, Michael. "Miles Morales: Check Out Sara Inking the New Ultimate Spider-Man." *The Washington Post* 16 Aug. 2011. Print.

————. "MILES MORALES & ME: Why the new biracial Spider-Man matters." *The Washington Post.* Web. 30 Mar. 2014. http://www.washingtonpost.com/blogs/comic

-riffs/post/miles-morales-and-me-why-the-new-biracial-spider-man-matters/2011/08/04
/gIQABzlGuI_blog.html.

Chang, Jeff. *Can't Stop Won't Stop: A History of the Hip Hop Generation.* New York: St. Martin's Press, 2005. Print.

Clifford, Marcus. "Introduction: Partial Truths." *Writing Culture: The Poetics and Politics of Ethnography.* Ed. James Clifford and George E. Marcus. Berkeley: U of California P., 1986. 1–26. Print.

Corona, Ramón, and Mary Beth McCabe. "Acculturation in Marketing to Latinos in the US." *Journal of Business & Economic Research* 9.9 (Sept. 2011): 67–70. Print.

Critchley, Simon. *On Humour.* London: Routledge, 2002. Print.

Cunningham, Phillip Lamarr. "The Absence of Black Supervillains in Mainstream Comics." *Journal of Graphic Novels and Comics* 1.1 (June 2010): 51–62. Print.

"Dan Slott on Spider-Man 2099's Return, Superior & Breaking Bad Comparisons." Newsarama. Web. 12 Jan. 2014. http://www.newsarama.com/18656-dan-slott-on-spider-man -2099-s-return-superior-breaking-bad-comparisons.html.

Dávila, Arlene. *Latinos, Inc.: The Marketing and Making of a People.* Berkeley: U of California P, 2001. Print.

Davis, Rocío G. "Autographics and the History of the Form: Chronicling Self and Career in Will Eisner's Life, in Pictures and Yoshihiro Tatsumi's A Drifting Life." *Biography* 34.2 (2011): 253–276. Print.

DeConnick, Kelly Sue, and Warren Ellis. *Avengers Assemble,* Issue 21. New York: Marvel, 2013. Print.

———. *Avengers Assemble,* Issue 22. New York: Marvel, 2013. Print.

———. *Avengers Assemble,* Issue 23. New York: Marvel, 2014. Print.

———. *Avengers Assemble,* Issue 24. New York: Marvel, 2014. Print.

———. *Avengers Assemble,* Issue 25. New York: Marvel, 2014. Print.

DeFalco, Tom, Peter Sanderson, Tom Brevoort, Michael Teitelbaum, Daniel Wallace, Andrew Darling, and Matt Forbeck. *The Marvel Encyclopedia.* New York: Marvel, 2010. Print.

Del Rio, Tania. *Spider-Man & Araña: The Hunter Revealed.* New York: Marvel, 2006. Print.

Doležel, Lubomír. *Heterocosmica: Fiction and Possible Worlds.* Baltimore: Johns Hopkins UP, 1998. Print.

Dong, Lan. "Thinly Disguised (Autobio)Graphical Stories." *Shofar* 29.2 (2011): 13–33. Print.

Drucker, Johanna. "Graphic Devices: Narration and Navigation." *Narrative* 16.2 (2008): 121–139. Print.

Duany, Jorge. *The Puerto Rican Nation on the Move: Identities on the Island and in the United States.* Chapel Hill: U of North Carolina P, 2002. Print.

Duncan, Randy, and Mathew J. Smith. *The Power of Comics: History, Form, and Culture.* New York: Continuum Press, 2009. Print.

Emad, Mitra C. "Reading Wonder Woman's Body: Mythologies of Gender and Nation." *The Journal of Popular Culture* 39.6 (2006): 954–984. Print.

Espinosa, Frank. *Rocketo Vol. 1 & 2: Journey to the Hidden Sea.* Berkeley: Image Comics, 2006–2007. Print.

"Exploratory Market of Hispanic Smokers." Mangini v. RJ Reynolds Tobacco Company. Bates no. 507132498/2425. Web. 1 Nov. 2013. http://legacy.library.ucsf.edu/tid/tha72doo.

Fingeroth, Danny. *Disguised as Clark Kent: Jews, Comics, and the Creation of the Superhero.* New York: Continuum, 2007. Print.

Fitz, Timothy. "Miles Morales, Black Hispanic Spider-Man Stirs Racial Controversy." *Chicago News Report*. Web. 30 Mar. 2014. http://www.chicagonewsreport.com/2011/08/miles
-morales-black-hispanic-spider-man.html.

Flagg, Gordon. "Review of *Chance in Hell*." *Booklist* 104.1 (1 Sept. 2007): 68. Print.

———. "Review of *Speak of the Devil*." *Booklist* 105.6 (15 Nov. 2008): 26. Print.

———. "Review of *Troublemakers*." *Booklist* 106.8 (15 Dec. 2009): 25. Print.

Forest Hills Chamber of Commerce. Web. 30 Mar. 2014. http://foresthillschamber.org/en
/demographics/?PHPSESSID=a062e73aa10c3184eb8a3ede43dd6255.

Formisano, Ronald P. *Boston against Busing: Race, Class, and Ethnicity in the 1960s and 1970s*. Durham: U of North Carolina P, 2003. Print.

Foster, David William. "Latino Comics: Javier Hernandez's El Muerto as an Allegory of Chicano Identity." *Latinos and Narrative Media: Participation and Portrayal*. Ed. Frederick Luis Aldama. New York: Palgrave Macmillan, 2013. 225–240. Print.

Foucault, Michel. *The History of Sexuality. Vol. 1. An Introduction*. Trans. Robert Hurley. New York: Pantheon Books, 1978. Print.

Franich, Darren. "The New Spider-Man Will Be a Half-Black Half-Hispanic Teenager." *Entertainment Weekly*. Web. 30 Mar. 2014. http://popwatch.ew.com/2011/08/02/spider
-man-new-ultimate-black-hispanic.

Gabilliet, Jean-Paul. *Of Comics and Men: A Cultural History of American Comic Books*. Trans. Bart Beaty and Nick Nguyen. Jackson: UP of Mississippi, 2010. Print.

Gay League. Web. http://www.gayleague.com/wordpress/hero-cruz/#sthash.r1Izu4qN
.dpuf.

Gayles, Jonathan. White Scripts and Black Supermen: Black Masculinities in Comic Books. 1080/24p 16:9. California Newsreel, 2010. Film.

Giffen, Keith, John Rogers, and Cully Hamner. *Blue Beetle: Shellshocked*. New York: DC Comics, 2006. Print.

Glaser, Jennifer. "Picturing the Transnational in Palomar: Gilbert Hernandez and the Comics of the Borderlands." *ImageTexT: Interdisciplinary Comics Studies* 7.1, 2013. http://
www.english.ufl.edu/imagetext/archives/v7_1/glaser/gocomics.com.

Gonzales, Juan. *Harvest of Empire: A History of Latinos in America*. New York: Penguin Books, 2011. Print.

González, Christopher. "Turf, Tags, and Territory: Spatiality in Jaime Hernandez's 'Vida Loca: The Death of Speedy Ortiz.'" *ImageTexT: Interdisciplinary Comics Studies* 7.1, 2013. Web. http://www.english.ufl.edu/imagetext/archives/v7_1/gonzalez/.

Gray, Herman. *Watching Race: Television and the Struggle for "Blackness"*. Minneapolis: U of Minnesota P, 1995. Print.

Groensteen, Thierry. *The System of Comics*. Jackson, MI: UP of Mississippi, 2009. Print.

Hamilton, Patrick. "Lost in Translation: Jessica Abel's La Perdida, the Bildungsroman, and 'That "Mexican" Feel.'" *Multicultural Comics: From Zap to Blue Beetle*. Ed. Frederick Luis Aldama. Austin: U of Texas P, 2010. 120–131. Print.

Harvey, Robert C. "The Aesthetics of the Comic Strip." *Journal of Popular Culture* 12 (1979): 641–652. Print.

Hatfield, Charles. *Alternative Comics: An Emerging Literature*. Jackson, MI: UP of Mississippi, 2005. 68–107. Print.

Hayman, Greg, and John Henry Pratt. "What Are Comics?" *Aesthetics: A Reader in Philosophy and the Arts*. Ed. David Goldblatt and Lee B. Brown. Upper Saddle River: Pearson, 2005. 419–424. Print.

Herman, David. *Story Logic: Problems and Possibilities of Narrative*. Lincoln, NE: U of Nebraska P, 2002. Print.

Hernandez, Gilbert. *Chance in Hell*. Seattle: Fantagraphics Books, 2007. Print.

———. *Heartbreak Soup: A Love and Rockets Book*. Seattle: Fantagraphics Books, 2007. Print.

———. *Maria M*. Seattle: Fantagraphics Books, 2014. Print.

———. *Speak of the Devil*, Milwaukie: Dark Horse Comics, 2008. Print.

———. *Troublemakers*. Seattle: Fantagraphics Books, 2009. Print.

Hernandez, Jaime. "Camp Vicki." *Perla La Loca: A Love and Rockets Book*. Seattle: Fantagraphics Books, 2007. 144–159. Print.

———. "In the Valley of the Polar Bears." *The Girl from H.O.P.P.E.R.S: A Love and Rockets Book*. Seattle: Fantagraphics Books, 2007. 165–194. Print.

———. "Locas 8:01 A.M." *The Girl from H.O.P.P.E.R.S: A Love and Rockets Book*. Seattle: Fantagraphics Books, 2007. 50–65. Print.

———. "Mechanics." *Maggie the Mechanic: A Love and Rockets Book*. Seattle: Fantagraphics Books, 2007. 30–70. Print.

———. "The Navas of Hazel Court." *Perla La Loca: A Love and Rockets Book*. Seattle: Fantagraphics Books, 2007. 164–166. Print.

———. *Maggie the Mechanic: A Love and Rockets Book*. Seattle: Fantagraphics Books, 2007. Print.

———. *Whoa Nellie!* Seattle: Fantagraphics Books, 2000. Print.

Hernandez, Javier. *Destroy All Mexicans! Javzilla: The Official Site of Javier Hernandez*. Web. 22 Nov. 2013. http://www.javzilla.com.

———. *El Muerto: Dead and Confused*. Whittier: Los Comex, 2008. Print.

———. *El Muerto: The Aztec Zombie*. Whittier: Los Comex, 2002. Print.

———. *Weapon Tex-Mex vs. El Muerto*. Whittier: Los Comex, 2011. Print.

Hernandez, Javier, and Mort Todd. *Mark of Mictlantecuhtli*. Whittier: Los Comex, 2007. Print.

Hernandez, Mario. "Mission Statements." In *The Comic Book Guide to the Mission: A Cartoon Tour through San Francisco's Mission*. Ed. Lauren Davis. San Francisco: Skoda Man Press, 2010. 53–56. Print.

Hetrick, Nicholas. "Chronology, Country, and Consciousness in Wilfred Santiago's *In My Darkest Hour*." *Multicultural Comics: From Zap to Blue Beetle*. Ed. Frederick Luis Aldama. Austin: U of Texas P, 2010. 189–201. Print.

Hignite, Todd. *The Art of Jaime Hernandez: The Secrets of Life and Death*. New York: Abrams Comicarts, 2009. Print.

Hill Collins, Patricia. *From Black Power to Hip Hop: Racism, Nationalism, and Feminism*. Philadelphia: Temple UP, 2006. Print.

Hispanic Federation. "Nueva York and Beyond: The Latino Communities of the Tri-State Region." Web. 30 Mar. 2014. http://www.hispanicfederation.org/images/pdf/hf_nueva yorkandbeyond_small.pdf.

Horrigan, John. *America Unwired*. Pew Research Center. Wireless Internet Use—Pew Internet & American Life Project. Web. 1 Nov. 2013. http://pewresearch.org/pubs/1287 /wireless-internet-use-mobile-access.

Howe, Sean. *Marvel Comics: The Untold Story*. New York: HarperCollins, 2012. Print.

Hudson, Laura. "Drudge Report Thinks New Spider-Man 'Could Be Gay,' Glenn Beck (and Colbert) Protest Diversity." *Comics Alliance*. Web. 30 Mar. 2014. http://comicsalliance .com/drudge-report-thinks-new-spider-man-could-be-gay-glenn-beck-a/.

Huntington, Chris. "A Superhero Who Looks Like My Son." *The New York Times*. Web. 30 Mar. 2014. http://parenting.blogs.nytimes.com/2013/06/13/a-super-hero-who-looks -like-my-son/?_php=true&_type=blogs&_r=0.

Jhally, Sut, and Justin Lewis. *Enlightened Racism: The Cosby Show, Audiences, and the Myth of the American Dream*. Boulder: Westview Press, 1992. Print.

Jiménez Román, Miriam, and Juan Flores. *The Afro-Latin@ Reader: History and Culture in the United States*. Durham: Duke UP, 2010. Print.

Johnson, Derek. "Franchise Histories: Marvel, X-Men, and the Negotiated Process of Expansion." *Convergence Media History*. Ed. Janet Staiger and Sabine Hake. London: Routledge, 2009. 285–300. Print.

———. *Media Franchising: Creative License and Collaboration in the Culture Industries*. New York: NYU Press, 2013. http://books.google.com/books?hl=en&lr=&id=dEBsiqOO D9QC&oi=fnd&pg=PT6&dq=%22might+be+assumed+to+be+%E2%80%9Cbigge st+media,%E2%80%9D+embodying+the+wide%22+%22CBS,+Sony,+and+Time+ Warner+controlled+most+film,+television,%22+%22hegemony+over+one-third+of +the+market,+while+three+dominant%22+&ots=UMF47kOwfU&sig=kfZgFPdnyo xGWXofxtqG7OvkL6Q.

———. "Will the Real Wolverine Please Stand Up?: Marvel's Mutation from Monthlies to Movies." *Film and Comic Books*. Ed. Ian Gordon, Mark Jancovich, and Matthew P. McAllister. Jackson, MI: UP of Mississippi, 2007. 285–300. Print.

Johnson-Woods, Toni, ed. *Manga: An Anthology of Global and Cultural Perspectives*. New York: Continuum, 2010. Print.

Jones, Yasmin M. Previous Hispanic Research. 16 Dec. 1987. Mangini v. RJ Reynolds Tobacco Company. Bates no. 507129143/9151. Web. 1 Nov. 2013. http://legacy.library.ucsf .edu/tid/eqz62doo.

Kelly, Joe, Fred Van Lente, Phil Jimenez, and J. M. Dematteis. *The Amazing Spider-Man*. Issue 611. New York: Marvel, 2009. Print.

———. *The Amazing Spider-Man: Grim Hunt*. New York: Marvel, 2010. Print.

Korzenny, Felipe, and Betty Ann Korzenny. "The Composition of the Hispanic/Latino Market." *Hispanic Marketing: Connecting with the New Latino Consumer*. New York: Routledge, 2011. 39–79. Print.

Kunka, Andrew J. "Intertextuality and the Historic Graphic Narrative: Kyle Baker's Nat Turner and the Styron Controversy." *College Literature* 38.3 (2011): 168–193. Print.

L'Hoeste, Héctor Fernández, and Juan Poblete, eds. *Redrawing the Nation: National Identity in Latin/o American Comics*. New York: Palgrave Macmillan, 2009. 1–16. Print.

Laó-Montes, Agustín, and Arlene Dávila. *Mambo Montage: The Latinization of New York*. New York: Columbia UP, 2001. Print.

Laroche Michel, Chankon Kim, Michael Hui, and Marc A. Tomiuk. "Test of a Non-Linear Relationship between Linguistic Acculturation and Ethnic Identification." *Journal of Cross Cultural Psychology* 29.3 (1998): 418–433. Print.

Levi, Heather. *The World of Lucha Libre: Secrets, Revelations and Mexican National Identity*. American Encounters/Global Interactions ser. Ed. Gilbert M. Joseph and Emily S. Rosenburg. Durham: Duke UP, 2008. Print.

Liesse, Julie. "The Latino Identity Project: Understanding a Market." *Advertising Age* 78.8 (19 Feb. 2007): A5–A8. Print.

Liu, Marjorie, and Mike Perkins. *Astonishing X-Men*. Vol. 3, issue 51 (Aug.). New York: Marvel, 2012. Print.

————. *Astonishing X-Men: Northstar*. New York: Marvel, 2012. Print.

Lobdell, Scott. *Alpha Flight*. Issue 106 (Mar.). New York: Marvel, 1992. Print.

Lockpez, Inverna, and Dean Haspel. *Cuba: My Revolution*. New York: Vertigo, 2010. Print.

Lugo, Alejandro. "Reflections on Border Theory, Culture, and the Nation." *Border Theory: The Limits of Cultural Politics*. Ed. Scott Michaelsen and David E. Johnson. Minneapolis: U of Minnesota P., 1997. 43–67. Print.

————. "Theorizing Border Inspections." *Cultural Dynamics: Dilemmas at the Border* 12.3 (2002): 332–352. Print.

Maaddi, Rob, and Susan Nuaddi Darraj. *Roberto Clemente*. New York: Chelsea House, 2009. Print.

Machete. Dir. Robert Rodriguez. 20th Century Fox, 2010. Film.

MacNicol, Glynnis. "Jon Stewart on Why New, Biracial Spiderman Is Lou Dobbs' Worst Nightmare: 'A Latino That Can Climb Walls!'" *Business Insider*. Web. 30 Mar. 2014. http://www.businessinsider.com/jon-stewart-spiderman-lou-dobbs-2011-8.

Maraniss, David. *Clemente: The Passion and the Grace of Baseball's Last Hero*. New York: Simon and Schuster, 2006. Print.

————. "Roberto Clemente." *American Experience*. Directed by Bernardo Ruiz. PBS. Aired 21 Apr. 2008. Transcript. http://www.pbs.org/wgbh/americanexperience/films/clemente/.

McCloud, Scott. *Understanding Comics: The Invisible Art*. New York: Kitchen Sink Press, 1993. Print.

McDonald, Kelly. "Relating, Not Translating: Why and How to Market to U.S. Latinos." *Illinois Banker* 1.3 (Mar. 2006): 12–13. Print.

McHale, Brian. "Beyond Story and Discourse: Narrative Time in Postmodern and Non-mimetic Fiction." *Narrative Dynamics: Essays on Time, Plot, Closure, and Frames*. Ed. Brian Richardson. Columbus, OH: The Ohio State UP, 2002. 47–63. Print.

McKeever, Sean. *Young Allies*. New York: Marvel, 2010–2011. Print.

Merino, Ana. "The Bros. Hernandez: A Latin Presence in Alternative U.S. Comics." *Redrawing the Nation: National Identity in Latin/o American Comics*. Ed. Héctor L'Hoeste Fernández and Juan Poblete. New York: Palgrave Macmillan, 2009. 251–269. Print.

Meskin, Aaron. "Defining Comics?" *The Journal of Aesthetics & Art Criticism* 65.4 (2007): 369–379. Print.

Mittell, Jason. *Genre and Television: From Cop Shows to Cartoons in American Culture*. New York: Routledge, 2004. Print.

Molesworth, Jesse. "Comics as Remediation: Gilbert Hernandez's Human Diastrophism." *ImageTexT: Interdisciplinary Comics Studies* 7.1 (2013). Web. http://www.english.ufl.edu/imagetext/archives/v7_1/molesworth/.

Molina, Laura. *The Jaguar*. Arcadia: Insurgent Comix, 1996. Print.

Molina-Guzmán, Isabel. *Dangerous Curves: Latina Bodies in the Media*. New York: New York UP, 2010. Print.

Montijo, Rhode. *Pablo's Inferno*. Oakland: ABISMO, 2004. Print.

Morreall, John, ed. *The Philosophy of Laughter and Humor*, Albany: State U of New York P, 1987. Print.

Murray, Christopher. *Champions of the Oppressed? Superhero Comics, Popular Culture, and Propaganda in America during World War II*. Cresskill: Hampton Press, 2011. Print.

Nadel, Nick. "Meet Extrano, the Gay Superhero DC Comics Would Rather You Forget." Web. Last accessed 7 Apr. 2014. http://thefw.com/extrano-dc-comics.

Nama, Adilifu. "Staking Out a Blatino Borderlands." *Latinos and Narrative Media: Participation and Portrayal.* Ed. Frederick Luis Aldama. New York: Palgrave Macmillan, 2013. 131–142. Print.

———. *Super Black: American Pop Culture and Black Superheroes.* Austin: U of Texas P, 2011. Print.

Navarro, Rafael. *Sonambulo: Sleep of the Just, A Complete Case.* La Habra: 9th Circle Studios, 2001. Print.

Negrón-Muntaner, Frances. *Boricua Pop: Puerto Ricans and the Latinization of American Culture.* New York: New York UP, 2004. Print.

Neill, F. Vance. "Gilbert Hernandez as a Rhetor." *ImageTexT: Interdisciplinary Comics Studies* 7.1 (2013). Web. http://www.english.ufl.edu/imagetext/archives/v7_1/neill/.

Ogden, David C. "Roberto Clemente: From Ignominy to Icon." *Reconstructing Fame: Sports, Race and Evolving Reputations.* Ed. David C. Ogden and Joel Nathan Rosen. Jackson, MI: UP of Mississippi, 2008. 16–28. Print.

Omi, Michael, and Howard Winant. *Racial Formation in the United States: From the 1960s to the 1980s.* New York: Routledge, 1986. Print.

Otheguy, Ricardo, and Ana Celia Zentella. *Spanish in New York: Language Contact, Dialectal Leveling, and Structural Continuity.* New York: Oxford UP, 2012. Print.

Palmer-Mehta, Valerie, and Kellie Hay. "A Superhero for Gays? Gay Masculinity and Green Lantern." *The Journal of American Culture* 28.4 (2005): 390–404. Print.

Palumbo, Frederick A., and Ira Teich. "Marketing Segmentation Based on the Level of Acculturation." *Marketing Intelligence and Planning.* ABI/INFORM Global 22.4 (2004): 472. Print.

Peaslee, Robert Moses, and Robert G. Weiner, eds. *Web-Spinning Heroics: Critical Essays on the History and Meaning of Spider-Man.* Jefferson, NC: McFarland & Company, 2012. Print.

Penaz, Mary Louise. "Drawing History: Interpretation in the Illustrated Version of the 9/11 Commission Report and Art Spiegelman's In the Shadow of No Towers as Historical Biography." *a/b: Auto/Biography Studies* 24.1 (2009): 93–112. Print.

Phelan, James. *Living to Tell about It: A Rhetoric and Ethics of Character Narration.* Ithaca: Cornell UP, 2005. Print.

Pieraccini, Cristina, Leonardo Hernandez, and Douglass Alligood. "The Growing Hispanic Market." *International Journal of Integrated Marketing Communications* 2.1 (Spring 2010): 29–39. Print.

Pizzino, Christopher. "Autoclastic Icons: Bloodletting and Burning in Gilbert Hernandez's Palomar." *ImageTexT: Interdisciplinary Comics Studies* 7.1 (2013). http://www.english.ufl .edu/imagetext/archives/v7_1/pizzino/.

Poblete, Juan. "Americanism/o: Intercultural Border Zones in Post–social Times." *Keywords in Caribbean and Latin American Thought.* Ed. Yolanda Martínez-San Miguel, Ben Sifuentes Jáuregui, and Marisa Belausteguigoitia. New York: Palgrave, 2015, pp. 45–59.

———. "U.S. Latino Studies in a Global Context: Social Imagination and the Production of In/visibility." *Work and Days* 47/48 24.1–2 (2006): 243–265. Print.

Pratt, Henry John. "Narrative in Comics." *The Journal of Aesthetics & Art Criticism* 67.1 (2009): 107–117. Print.

Quesada, Joe. *Daredevil: Father.* New York: Marvel, 2006. Print.

Rabkin, Eric. "Reading Time in Graphic Narrative." *Teaching the Graphic Novel.* Ed.

Stephen E. Tabachnick. New York, NY: Modern Language Association, 2009. 36–43. Print.

Ramírez Berg, Charles. *Latino Images in Film: Stereotypes, Subversion, and Resistance*. Austin: U of Texas P, 2002. Print.

Reed, Brian. *Ms. Marvel: Monster Smash*. New York: Marvel, 2007–2008. Print.

Regalado, Samuel O. "Roberto Clemente: Images, Identity, and Legacy." *Sports and the Racial Divide: African American and Latino Experience in an Era of Change*. Ed. Kenneth L. Shropshire. Jackson, MI: UP of Mississippi, 2008. 166–177. Print.

Renteria, Robert, with Corey Michael Blake, and Shane Clester. *Mi Barrio*. Palo Alto: Smarter Comics, 2011. Print.

Richardson, Brian. "Introduction: Narrative Temporality." *Narrative Dynamics: Essays on Time, Plot, Closure, and Frames*. Ed. Brian Richardson. Columbus: The Ohio State UP, 2002. 9–14. Print.

Rifas, Leonard. "Globalizing Comic Books from Below: How Manga Came to America." *International Journal of Comic Art* 6.2 (2004): 138–171. Print.

———. "Race and Comix." *Multicultural Comics: From Zap to Blue Beetle*. Ed. Frederick Luis Aldama. Austin: U of Texas P, 2010. 27–38.

Risner, Jonathan. "'Authentic' Latinas/os and Queer Characters in Alternative and Mainstream Comics." *Multicultural Comics: From Zap to Blue Beetle*. Ed. Frederick Luis Aldama. Austin: U of Texas P, 2010. 39–54. Print.

Rivera, Jules. *Misfortune High: Book 1*. Los Angeles: 2013. Print.

"Roberto Clemente Sports City." Web. http://64.78.33.77/rcsc21/index_en.cfm.

Roberts, John Storm. *The Latin Tinge: The Impact of Latin American Music on the United States*. Oxford: Oxford UP, 1999. Print.

Robinson, Bryan. "Remembering the First—and Forgotten—Latino Spider-Man." Fox News Latino. Web. 16 Aug. 2011. http://latino.foxnews.com/latino/lifestyle/2011/08/16/remembering-first-and-forgotten-latino-spider-man/.

Rodríguez, América. *Making Latino News: Race, Language, Class*. London: Sage, 1999. Print.

Rodriguez, Erik. *Hispanic Batman*. Vol. 1. New York: Royal Flush Magazine, 2010. Print.

Rodríguez, Juana María. *Queer Latinidad: Identity Practices, Discursive Spaces*. New York: New York UP, 2003. Print.

Rodriguez, Ralph. *Brown Gumshoes: Detective Fiction and the Search for Chicana/o Identity*. Austin: U of Texas P, 2005. Print.

Rogers, John, and Rafael Albuquerque. *Blue Beetle: End Game*. New York: DC Comics, 2008. Print.

Rogers, John, Keith Giffen, Cully Hamner, and Rafael Albuquerque. *Blue Beetle: Road Trip*. New York: DC Comics, 2007. Print.

Rosaldo, Renato. *Culture and Truth: The Remaking of Social Analysis*. Boston: Beacon Press, 1993. Print.

Royal, Derek Parker. "Drawing Attention: Comics as a Means of Approaching U.S. Cultural Diversity." In *Teaching Comics and Graphic Narratives: Essays on Theory, Strategy and Practice*. Jefferson, NC: McFarland & Company, 2012. Print.

———. "Foreword; or Reading within the Gutter." *Multicultural Comics: From Zap to Blue Beetle*. Ed. Frederick Luis Aldama. Austin: U of Texas P, 2010. ix–xi. Print.

———. "Introduction: Coloring America: Multi-Ethnic Engagements with Graphic Narrative." *MELUS* 32.3 (2007): 7–22. Print.

———. "Palomar and Beyond: An Interview with Gilbert Hernandez." *MELUS* 32.3 (2007): 221–246. Print.

———. "Review of Recent Books from Gilbert Hernandez." In *ImageText: Interdisciplinary Comics Studies*. 7.1 (2013). Web. http://www.english.ufl.edu/imagetext/archives/v7_1/introduction/introduction.shtml/.

Royal, Derek Parker, and Christopher González, ed. "The Worlds of the Hernandez Brothers: A Special Issue of *ImageTexT.*" *ImageText: Interdisciplinary Comics Studies*. 7.1 (2013). Web. http://www.english.ufl.edu/imagetext/archives/v7_1/

Saffel, Steve. *Spider-Man the Icon: The Life and Times of a Pop Culture Phenomenon*. London: Titan Books, 2007. Print.

Saldívar, Ramón. *Chicano Narrative: The Dialectics of Difference*. Madison: U of Wisconsin P, 1990. Print.

Santa Ana, Otto. *Brown Tide Rising: Metaphors of Latinos in Contemporary American Public Discourse*. Austin: U of Texas P, 2002. Print.

Santiago, Wilfred. *In My Darkest Hour*. Seattle: Fantagraphics Books, 2004. Print.

———. *Michael Jordan: Bull on Parade*. Seattle: Fantagraphics Books, 2014. Print.

———. *21: The Story of Roberto Clemente*. Seattle: Fantagraphics Books, 2011. Print.

Schedeen. Jesse. "Ultimate Comics: Spider-Man #1 Review: Peter Parker Is Gone, but the Ultimate Universe Still Needs a Spider-Man." IGN.com, 2011. Web. 30 Mar. 2014. http://www.ign.com/articles/2011/09/14/ultimate-comics-spider-man-1-review.

Schoell, William. *The Silver Age of Comics*. Duncan: BearManor Media, 2010. Print.

Schow, David J. "Introduction: ¡Qué La Canción! Or Dream of the Masked Man." *Sonambulo: Sleep of the Just, A Complete Case*. By Rafael Navarro. La Habra: 9th Circle Studios, 2001. 7–8. Print.

Sedgwick, Eve Kosofsky. *Epistemology of the Closet*. Berkeley: U of California P, 1990. Print.

———. *Tendencies*. Durham, NC: Duke UP, 1993. Print.

Seven, John. "History, Identity and Baseball: Wilfred Santiago Tells 'The Story of Roberto Clemente,'" *Publishers Weekly*, Feb. 22, 2011. http://www.publishersweekly.com/pw/by-topic/booknews/comics/article/46232-history-identity-and-baseball-wilfred-santiago-tells-the-story-of-roberto-clemente.html.

Slott, Dan. Interview. Web. Last accessed 7 Apr. 2014. http://www.gayleague.com/wordpress/living-lightning/#sthash.YpBB35yp.dpuf.

Smith, Elizabeth A., and Ruth E. Malone. "The Outing of Philip Morris: Advertising Tobacco to Gay Men." *American Journal of Public Health* 93.6 (2003): 988–993. Print.

Smith, Matthew. "The Tyranny of the Melting Pot Metaphor: Wonder Woman as the Americanized Immigrant." *Comics and Ideology*. Ed. Matthew McAllister, Edward Sewell, and Ian Gordon. New York: Peter Lang, 2001. 129–150. Print.

Spanish USA, 1984 Summary. RJ Reynolds Tobacco Company. Bates no. 504616837/6839. Web. 1 Nov. 2013. http: legacy.library.ucsf.edu/tid/wnf65doo.

Stavans, Ilan, and Lalo Alcaraz. *Latino U.S.A.: A Cartoon History*. New York: Basic Books, 2000. Print.

Stavans, Ilan, and Steve Sheinkin. *Rabbi Harvey Meets Ilan Stavans*, 2012. Web. 14 Dec. 2013. http://jbooks.com/common/uploads/ilan_stavans/.

Stewart, Jon. "Culture War Update—The Dividening of America—Lou Dobbs vs. Biracial Spider-Man." The Daily Show with Jon Stewart. Web. 30 Mar. 2014. http://thedailyshow.cc.com/videos/5yugto/culture-war-update-the-dividening-of-america-lou-dobbs-vs-biracial-spider-man.

Tellez, Edward E., and Vilma Ortiz. *Generations of Exclusion. Mexican Americans, Assimilation, and Race*. New York: Russell Sage Foundation, 2008. Print.

Tobin, Paul. *Avengers Academy: Giant-Size*. New York: Marvel, 2010. Print.

———. *Spidergirl: El corazón de la araña*. Trans. Santiago García. Modena: Panini Comics, 2011. Print.

———. *Spider-Girl: Family Values*. New York: Marvel, 2011. Print.

Tobin, Paul, Pepe Larraz, and Andres Mossa. *Spider Island Spider-Girl*. Issue 1. New York: Marvel, 2011. Print.

Truitt, Brian. "Half-Black, Half-Hispanic Spider-Man Revealed." *USA Today* Web. 2 Aug. 2011. http://usatoday30.usatoday.com/life/comics/2011-08-01-black-spider-man_n.htm.

Trushell, John M. "American Dreams of Mutants: The X-Men—'Pulp' Fiction, Science Fiction, and Superheroes." *The Journal of Popular Culture* 38.1 (2004): 149–168. Print.

US Census Bureau. "Kings County, New York—Selected Social Characteristics in the United States: 2009." Web. 30 Mar. 2014. http://factfinder2.census.gov/legacy/aff_sunset .html?_bm=y&-geo_id=05000US36047&-qr_name=ACS_2009_1YR_G00_DP2& -context=adp&-ds_name=&-tree_id=309&-_lang=en&-redoLog=false&-format=.

———. "Race and Hispanic or Latino Origin." Web. 30 Mar. 2014. http://factfinder2.census .gov/faces/tableservices/jsf/pages/productview.xhtml?pid=DEC_10_SF1_QTP3.

———. "2010 Census shows America's diversity." Web. 1 Nov. 2013. http://www.census .gov/newsroom/releases/archives/2010_census/cb11-cn125.html.

Warhol, Robyn. "The Space Between: A Narrative Approach to Alison Bechdel's *Fun Home*." *College Literature* 38.3 (2011): 1–20. Print.

Washington, Harriet A. "Burning Love: Big Tobacco Takes Aim at LGBT Youths." *American Journal of Public Health* 92.7 (2002): 1086–1095. Print.

Weart, Spencer R. *Nuclear Fear: A History of Images*. Cambridge, MA: Harvard UP, 1988. Print.

"What If . . . We Got a Spider-Man 2099 Cartoon instead of Spider-Man Unlimited?" Web. 14 Jan. 2014. http://www.comicbookmovie.com/fan_fic/news/?a=68029.

Whitlock, Gillian, and Anna Poletti. "Self-regarding Art." *Biography* 31.1 (2008): v–xxiii. Print.

Wright, Bradford W. *Comic Book Nation: The Transformation of Youth Culture in America*. Baltimore: Johns Hopkins UP, 2011. Print.

CONTRIBUTOR NOTES

Frederick Luis Aldama is Arts & Humanities Distinguished Professor of English and University Distinguished Scholar at The Ohio State University, where he is also founder and director of the mentor center, LASER. He is the author and editor of over twenty-one books. He coedits the series Cognitive Approaches to Literature and Culture, Global Latin/o Studies, and World Comics and Graphic Nonfiction. He also edits several additional book series, including the Latino Pop Culture and Latino American Profiles.

Mauricio Espinoza received his PhD from the Department of Spanish & Portuguese at The Ohio State University. His research and teaching focus is on Latino and Latin American literatures and culture. He has published numerous articles on Latino popular culture, including on Latino comics.

Kathryn M. (Katie) Frank received her PhD in Communication Studies at the University of Michigan, Ann Arbor. She is broadly interested in the intersections of race/ethnicity, gender, and sexuality and representations of these topics in visual and popular media—especially in comic books, graphic novels, and the online fandom and media industry spaces in which these texts are discussed, promoted, and contested. Her current work explores adaptations of comics and animated series to live-action film and television and how media industries negotiate the adaptation process.

Ellen M. Gil-Gómez is Professor of Chicano/a Literature at Cal State University San Bernadino. She is author of numerous articles and books, including *Performing La Mestiza: Textual Representations of Lesbians of Color and the Negotiations of Identity* (2000).

Christopher González is Assistant Professor of English at Texas A&M University–Commerce, where he teaches twentieth- and twenty-first-century literatures of the United States. He has published articles on authors such as Edward P. Jones and Philip Roth, the comics artist Jaime Hernandez, and filmmakers Alex Rivera and Robert Rodriguez. He is managing editor of *Philip Roth Studies* and editor of a special issue of *POST SCRIPT: Essays in Film and the Humanities* that focuses on the films of Robert Rodriguez. He is author of *Reading Junot Díaz* (2016) and coauthor with Frederick Luis Aldama of *Latinos in the End Zone: The Brown Color Line in the NFL* (2013). He has a forthcoming volume on the works of Gilbert Hernandez.

Maya Haddad is a dancer, writer, and documentarian, born and raised in Southern California, who explores the topics of culture, art, and global identity in her work. Her craft has taken her to Cuba, Brazil, and the Middle East. She continues to travel, examining and articulating the depths of human systems and expression worldwide.

Patrick L. Hamilton is an Associate Professor of English at Misericordia University in Dallas, Pennsylvania. He specializes in Chicano/a and US multiethnic literature as well as race and ethnicity in comics and popular culture. In addition to his book *Of Space and Mind: Cognitive Mappings of Contemporary Chicano/a Fiction* (2011) he has published several articles, including on Jessica Abel's *La Perdida* and the comic and TV series *The Walking Dead*. He is completing a coauthored book manuscript titled "All-New, All-Different?: A Graphic History of Race and the American Superhero."

Héctor Fernández L'Hoeste is Professor of Modern and Classical Languages at Georgia State, where he is also director of the Center for Latin American and Latino/a Studies. His publications include *Narrativas de representación urbana* (1998); *Rockin' Las Americas* (2004); *Redrawing The Nation* (2009), coedited with Juan Poblete; and *Cumbia!* (2013). His articles have appeared in numerous journals, including *International Journal of Comic Art*. He is coeditor with Robert McKee Irwin and Juan Poblete of *Sports and Nationalism in Latin/o America* (2015). He has a forthcoming volume on the works of Lalo Alcaraz.

Isabel Millán is Assistant Professor in the Department of American Ethnic Studies at Kansas State University. She was the recipient of the Carlos E. Castañeda Postdoctoral Fellowship at the Center for Mexican American Studies, University of Texas at Austin. She is currently completing a book on Latino children's literature, television, short films, and comics.

Brian Montes is Assistant Professor in Latin American and Latina/o Studies at John Jay College, City University of New York. His research, teaching, and writing are grounded in US Latino/a studies, Latin American Studies, and Maya studies, with particular interest placed on the lived experience of race and ethnicity within Latin American and Latina/o ethnic groups. His current project examines the memory, through discourse and performance, of Yucatán's Caste War from the perspective of the native indigenous Maya within the municipality of Felipe Carrillo Puerto in Quintana Roo, Mexico.

Adilifu Nama is Professor and Chair of the Department of African American Studies at Loyola Marymount University. He is the author of the American Book Award–winning *Super Black: American Pop Culture and Black Superheroes* (2011), *Black Space: Imagining Race in Science Fiction Film* (2008), and *Race on the QT: Blackness and the Films of Quentin Tarantino* (2015). His work explores how popular culture via film, comics, Afro-futurism, and music is a provocative site for examining the cultural politics of race in America.

Juan Poblete is Professor in the Literature Department at the University of California, Santa Cruz. He is the author of numerous articles and several co-edited volumes, including *Sports and Nationalism in Latin/o America* (2015) and *Redrawing The Nation: National Identity in Latin/o American Comics* (2009).

Richard T. Rodríguez is Associate Professor at the University of Illinois at Urbana–Champaign, where he also served as Chair of the Department of Latina/Latino Studies. He is the author of numerous articles and the award-winning book *Next of Kin: The Family in Chicano/a Cultural Politics* (2009).

Ilan Stavans is Lewis-Sebring Professor in Latin American and Latino Culture at Amherst College. He has published dozens of books, including *El Illuminado: A Graphic Novel* (2012) with Steve Sheinkin; *¡Muy Pop! Conversations on Latino Popular Culture* (2013), co-authored with Frederick Luis Aldama; and *A Most Imperfect Union: A Contrarian History of the United States* with cartoonist Lalo Alcaraz (2014).

Page numbers in italics indicate figures.